THE
EARLY AMERICAN PRESS,
1690–1783

THE
EARLY AMERICAN PRESS,
1690–1783

Wm. David Sloan
and
Julie Hedgepeth Williams

THE HISTORY OF AMERICAN JOURNALISM,
NUMBER 1

James D. Startt and Wm. David Sloan,
Series Editors

GREENWOOD PRESS
Westport, Connecticut • London

Library of Congress Cataloging-in-Publication Data

Sloan, W. David (William David).
   The early American press, 1690–1783 / Wm. David Sloan and Julie
Hedgepeth Williams.
      p. cm.—(The History of American journalism, ISSN 1074–4193 ; no. 1)
    Includes bibliographical references and index.
    ISBN 0–313–27525–4 (alk. paper)
    1. Press—United States—History—18th century. I. Williams,
Julie Hedgepeth. II. Title. III. Series.
PN4855.H57   1994
[PN4861]
071'.3 s—dc20
[071'.3'09033]   94–4777

British Library Cataloguing in Publication Data is available.

Library of Congress Catalog Card Number: 94–4777
ISBN: 0–313–27525–4
ISSN: 1074–4193

First published in 1994

Greenwood Press, 88 Post Road West, Westport, CT 06881
An imprint of Greenwood Publishing Group, Inc.

Printed in the United States of America

The paper used in this book complies with the
Permanent Paper Standard issued by the National
Information Standards Organization (Z39.48–1984).

10 9 8 7 6 5 4 3 2

Contents

Series Foreword

Since the renowned historian Allan Nevins issued his call for an improved journalism history in 1959, the field has experienced remarkable growth in terms of both quantity and quality. It can now be said with confidence that journalism history is a vital and vitalizing field full of scholarly activity and promise.

The new scholarship has widened the field's horizons and extended its depth. Today, especially with new bibliographic technologies at their disposal, journalism historians are able to explore literature pertinent to their studies to a greater extent than was previously possible. This expansion of literary sources has occurred in conjunction with other advances in the use of source materials. Today's historians incorporate primary and original records into their work more than was common when Nevins issued his call, and they also utilize sources produced by the electronic media. As the source foundation for journalism history has grown, so its content has undergone a substantive expansion. Previously neglected or minimized subjects in the field now receive fairer and more concerted treatment. Contemporary journalism history, moreover, reflects more consciousness of culture than that written a generation ago.

Growth, however, has created problems. Abundance of sources, proliferation and diversity of writing, and the stimulation of new discoveries and interpretations combine to make scholarship in the field a formidable task. A broad study covering journalism history from its beginnings to the present, one combining the rich primary materials now available and the older and newer literature in the field, is needed. *The History of American Journalism* series is designed to address this need. Each volume will be written by an author or authors who are recognized scholars in the field. Each is intended to provide a coherent perspective on a major period, to facilitate further research in the field, and to engage general readers interested in the subject. A strong narrative and interpretive element will be found in each volume, and each contains a bibliographical essay pointing readers to the most pertinent research sources and secondary literature.

The present volume, the first in the series, begins with the earliest printing in the American colonies and takes the story through the Revolutionary War. As subsequent volumes will do, it focuses on the nature of journalism during the years surveyed, chronicles noteworthy figures, examines the relationship of journalism to society, and provides explanations for the main directions that journalism was taking. The remaining five volumes will complete *The History of American Journalism* in chronological order and are scheduled to appear over the next five years.

Preface

When one first thinks of America's earliest printing, one is tempted to imagine that it was simplistic and that Americans' thinking about it was unsophisticated. In our imagination we can see colonial newspapers as small, crude affairs run by proprietors with mechanical ideas. With their exploratory efforts to discover what newspapers properly should be doing, the proprietors laid the timorous groundwork for some of the developments in American journalism that would follow. Then in our mind's eye we see the colonial period quickly giving way to the brief era of the Revolution, populated by publishers who give little thought to anything other than the great political issues of the age. That period fades, and the American press dissolves into an ephemeral fifty-year period of partisanship, which soon surrenders to the superior journalism of the penny press.

Despite the simplification and telescopic view that the passage of time brings to us of a later age, early American printing was in truth animated by remarkable vitality and sophistication. The life of every newspaper and every printer was marked by individual ideas and individual struggles. No monolithic story can describe any of them. Each, indeed, is worthy of its own story. In the following pages, despite the authors' efforts to approach each on its own terms, we have only hinted at the fullness of the story. Yet we hope that the surface picture we present suggests the complexities that lie beneath it. Not only was the early American press complex, but the thinking of early Americans about the role and operation of the press was quite sophisticated, even when compared with that of later generations. Printers and colonists dealt with a number of sensitive and complicated questions involving the press, and their discussions exhibited mature thought on a medium that was in its infancy. We hope that some of that complexity is made apparent in the story told in this book.

We have attempted to address the most important questions that confront histo-rians: Why did newspapers first appear? What purpose did newspaper operators see for themselves? What role did ideas about the practice of journalism play in the colonial press? What role did the press play in influencing public opinion? Un-derlying our approach, however, have been two questions of paramount impor-tance: What was the essential nature of the early American press? and, What factors accounted for that character? In attempting to discover the answers, we hope we are able to share with readers some of the spirit and vigor that excited the times.

THE
EARLY AMERICAN PRESS,
1690–1783

1

The Boston Press, 1690–1735

Massachusetts in 1690 was on the verge of anarchy. The royal government had been overthrown, and the governor thrown into jail. Under his policies, taxes had become onerous, and now taxpayers revolted. "This people are now so very poor," declared an official, "that many profess they have not corn for their families, and those to whom wages are due, cry, that if they have them not, they and their families must starve."[1] Indians, who had renewed hostilities two years earlier, destroyed frontier communities. "Sundry plantations easterly, in the province of Maine," the official reported, "are utterly ruined and depopulated." A provisional government, hoping to impress the new English king, had mounted a military expedition against the Indians and their French allies in Canada, but the expedition was going badly. Its revenue depleted, the government was unable to pay soldiers, and they refused to perform their duties. Amid this chaos, the colonies' agents were in London attempting to negotiate a new charter, and factions had sprung up over the question of what form a new government should take. Compounding the problem, rumors spread and publications appeared that were critical of the authorities.

The provisional governing council found itself helpless to control the situation. Officials proposed a variety of remedies, ranging from warning people not to make false reports to asking the British crown to take over the government. Benjamin Harris, a confident and bold Bostonian experienced in London journalism, decided a newspaper was needed and conferred with a few knowledgeable townspeople. He was especially concerned that the newspaper carry nothing but accurate reports. Meeting the young Puritan cleric Cotton Mather on the street, he obtained from him suggestions on how to prepare a detailed account of the military expedition into Canada.

Despite Harris's good intentions, the governing council suppressed the paper almost immediately after publication. Thus this first American newspaper, entitled

Publick Occurrences, Both Forreign and Domestick, lasted but one issue, prohibited for a variety of reasons.

The brief episode of *Publick Occurrences* was the upshot of the strong religious and political influences that had been at work in English life for the past century and in Massachusetts since the founding of the colony. The political chaos that confronted the colony in 1690 was instrumental in both the newspaper's founding and its suppression. Playing active roles in its brief life and death were some of the most important personalities in the colonies. They included, among others, Increase Mather's son Cotton, a supporter of the newspaper; and the Mathers' adversary, council member Elisha Cooke. The key player, however, was Benjamin Harris. Although Harris was influenced greatly by strong religious motivations, the newspaper's suppression was not, as some historians have implied, the handiwork of Massachusetts's Puritan clergy. On the contrary, the government's action was motivated in part by efforts of an energetic faction opposed to the leading clergyman, Increase Mather. Nor was it a simple matter of a defiant journalist being silenced as he tried to strike a blow for freedom of the press.[2]

Harris was a man of deeply held beliefs and determined action, and his experiences in the fierce British political battles of the 1670s and 1680s had prepared him particularly well for his career in America. Born in London, Harris[3] was an ardent Anabaptist in religion and Whig in politics. He set up as a printer and bookseller in London in 1673 and immediately rose to prominence with publication of the tract *War with the Devil* by the bold Anabaptist preacher and anti-Catholic Benjamin Keach. He soon became the leading printer and publicist for the Anabaptist cause. Even more than most Anabaptists, he was embroiled in politics. Although based fundamentally on religious tenets, Anabaptism became involved in the political arena because of its radical beliefs in the authority of the individual (rather than church leaders) in spiritual matters and the total separation of church and state.[4] In these matters of faith, Anabaptists found themselves not only in opposition to Roman Catholicism but to the Church of England as well. Harris was bold in presenting these dissident views—"a brisk Assertor of English Liberties," a fellow publisher called him.[5] In politics, he supported the Earl of Shaftesbury and the Whig parliament in their opposition to King Charles II, and he was ardent in advocating the efforts of the parliament to exclude the Duke of York (James II), Charles's Catholic brother, from succession to the throne.[6]

Because of his vigorous and visible support of the Whig and dissident Protestant side,[7] the Tory/Anglican authorities made Harris a continuing target for prosecution. Between 1680 and 1683 they proceeded against him three times and imprisoned him twice.[8] Despite the legal difficulties, he continued to sell books and pamphlets on the superiority of Protestantism to Catholicism and on English liberties. However, with the defeat in 1685 of the Duke of Monmouth, whose rights to the throne Harris had advocated, he fled England, probably with the purpose of escaping retribution for his support of the rebellion and publication of a book entitled *English Liberties*.[9]

Harris sailed first to Holland in 1685 and then to the Puritan refuge of Boston in Massachusetts colony in the fall of 1686. Boston was the North American colonies' largest city, home to 5,000 inhabitants, and one of only two towns with its own printing trade.[10] In Boston, Harris entered printing and bookselling, his familiar occupations. He soon had a prosperous business going, issuing in December 1686 the first of a series of annual almanacs.[11] Part of his motivation was simply to make a living. There was, however, more behind his work than mere occupation, for much of it was distinctive for its emphasis on political and dissident Protestant works.

Because of his publishing experience and his capacity for supporting the Whig/Protestant cause, Harris was able to gain the confidence of others and to exercise a visible public role. Through his publishing activities, soon after arriving in Boston he became acquainted with the activist Puritan leadership and helped advocate their political goal of autonomy for Massachusetts. He was on speaking terms with Cotton Mather, the Puritan cleric, for whom he printed several volumes. Mather also assisted him in compiling material for publications.[12]

Harris's escape from the authority of the British crown was, however, shortlived. In 1684 Charles II had revoked the Massachusetts charter, and in 1686 James II appointed the staunch Anglican and Tory Sir Edmund Andros as governor of the colony. Andros arrived in Boston in December 1686, bringing with him a communication from the king that "[w]e do here will and require and command that . . . all persons . . . especially [those] as shall be conformable to the rites of the Church of England be particularly countenanced and encouraged."[13] The new governor immediately demanded that Anglicans be allowed the use of the Old South Church building, but the Puritan ministers would agree only to permit the use of the Town House. Andros would not willingly submit to this affront to his faith, and in March, on Good Friday, of the following year commanded that the South Church be opened. On Easter Sunday, the Anglicans took the building for their service and did not vacate it for the church's Puritan congregation until after 2 P.M.[14] Finally, the two sides reached an understanding by which the Puritans offered one of their churches for use of Anglican services on Sunday afternoons. Throughout Andros's brief administration, Harris supported the Puritan side and acted as a public opponent of Andros.

Andros's power to oppress Puritan Massachusetts lasted only briefly. James II was overthrown in 1688 in the Glorious Revolution, and Andros's downfall followed shortly thereafter.[15] Soon after James was dethroned, Harris made clear the intensity of the opposition of Massachusetts to his rule in the broadside entitled "The Plain Case Stated of Old." It was an attack in verse on James for his Catholicism and for policies that Harris believed brought misery to the colonies. The tone of the broadside is evident from the beginning. It read:

> The wretched . . . James, with Papal Benediction
> and Popish principles assum'd the Throne . . .
> Under his umbridge did the Birds of Night
> Sing their damn'd notes, and sang them with delight.

James and his appointed officials, the broadside claimed, had tried to impose Catholicism on the British empire. James's administration had been equally as harsh in the colonies, imposing severe taxes and trying to take the land of earlier settlers, treating them not "as free-born English, but as poor French slaves." They also had perverted the judicial system and abolished "Freedom of Discourse"— "We were made," as Harris phrased it, "Offenders for a Word." The broadside concluded with an appeal to King William to "set us free/From arbitrary Power and Slavery."[16]

Harris backed the local rebellion that forced Andros from office.[17] Colonists seized Andros and confined him and several other officials to jail. Increase Mather and other dissenting clergy were suspected of being the main instigators of the revolt.[18] Revolting against a crown-appointed governor raised great possible danger, and Harris was one of few supporters of the rebellion not afraid of letting his stance be known. While most, such as the "council of safety" that assumed formal control of the political situation, took steps to protect themselves, he published a pamphlet favorably detailing the revolution.[19] He then supported Increase Mather in the debate over his attempts to negotiate a new charter for Massachusetts. His ties with Increase and Cotton Mather and support of the elder Mather's charter negotiations later provided one of the motives behind the suppression of *Publick Occurrences*.

Following the overthrow of Andros, the colony began to sink into a period of anarchy. The council that had been elected in 1686 reassumed office, but it was ineffectual in bringing order to the situation. Under this interim government and while Massachusetts was waiting for a new charter, internal order began to disintegrate.

It was in this political situation that on September 25, 1690, Harris published the first issue of what he intended to be a periodic newspaper, naming it *Publick Occurrences, Both Forreign and Domestick*. It contained four pages measuring 7½ inches by 11½ inches, with one page left blank. He had several reasons for publishing the newspaper. One was simply that he had experience at publishing newspapers. He had been among England's most energetic journalists, and *Publick Occurrences* offered an opportunity both to pursue the trade he knew so well and to expand his Boston printing and publishing business. His primary purpose, though, was to provide a medium that the public could rely on for accurate information amidst chaotic conditions. He also intended to use the paper to speak out on issues.

The internal disorder that Massachusetts was facing was of utmost concern to Harris. Political stability in the colony was breaking down, factions had arisen, and the chaos fed a variety of rumors, many of them false. Harris hoped that *Publick Occurrences* could serve as an antidote. In his statement of purpose at the head of the first column on page one, he went to considerable lengths to emphasize his concern that reports be accurate. He would take, he explained to readers, "*what pains he can to obtain a* Faithful Relation *of all such things; and will particularly make himself beholden to such Persons in* Boston *whom he knows to have been for their own use the diligent Observers of such matters.*" Furthermore, he declared, he would make a point of exposing falsehoods. He hoped that *Publick Occurrences* might serve as a cure for the "Spirit of Lying, *which prevails among us.*" To that end, he promised that *"nothing shall be entered, but what we have reason to believe is true, repairing to the best fountains for our Information. And when there appears any* material mistake *in any thing that is collected, it shall be corrected in the next.*" He would attempt, he promised, to expose in print anyone found guilty of maliciously providing false information for publication in the paper.[20]

As for providing news, Harris stated that the purpose of *Publick Occurrences* was to furnish "the Countrey . . . once a month (or if any Glut of Occurrences happen, oftener) with an Account of such considerable things as have arrived unto our Notice," so that "Memorable Occurrents of Divine Providence may not be neglected or forgotten, as they too often are." In carrying out that plan, Harris, the experienced journalist, filled the pages of the newspaper with domestic reports of such items as Christianized Indians planning a "day of Thanksgiving to God for his Mercy in supplying their extream and pinching Necessities," the abduction of two children by Indians, a recently widowed man hanging himself, the status of a smallpox epidemic which was then on the decline in Boston, and the damages caused by a local fire. He devoted the greatest amount of space to the expedition of a Massachusetts militia against the French and their Indian allies in Canada. It was this last report which was to raise the opposition of the colonial governing council.

Despite Harris's evident efforts to assure that the reports he included were accurate, the governing authorities moved to suppress the newspaper almost immediately upon publication. Some reacted negatively as soon as they saw it,[21] and only four days after *Publick Occurrences* appeared the governing council issued an order forbidding Harris to continue publication.[22]

In suppressing *Publick Occurrences*, the council was acting within what it considered to be its legitimate authority. After the Licensing Act had expired, in May 1680 Charles II—now intent on suppressing the Whig opposition and dissident Protestants—accepted his judges' recommendation that "his Majesty may, by law, prohibit the printing and publishing of all News-Books and Pamphlets of News whatsoever, not licensed by His Majesty's Authority, as manifestly tending to the breach of the Peace, and disturbance of the Kingdom."[23] By 1682 licensing was back in force in England, and it continued until allowed to lapse in 1695. After James II ascended to the throne in 1685, it became the established policy of the British crown to order colonial governors to exercise control over the printing press. Thus, when Andros assumed the governorship of Massachusetts in 1686, he received the same instructions that were given to all colonial governors. They ordered:

[F]orasmuch as great inconveniences may arise by the liberty of printing within our said province, you are to provide by all necessary orders that no person KEEP any press for printing, NOR that any book, pamphlet, or other matters whatsoever be PRINTED without your especial leave and license first obtained.[24]

Accordingly, the following month Andros informed his council that it was the king's express command "that the printing Presses in the Towns of Boston and Cambridge in New England should be effectuall taken care of." The council then passed an order "that no Papers, Bookes, Pamphlets &c should be printed in New England untill Licensed according to Law."[25] With the overthrow of the Andros government in April 1689, the policy remained in effect. It was under that authority that the council ordered *Publick Occurrences* shut down. Although the council had assumed authority as a direct result of the revolt against Andros, members were not revolutionary in their philosophy. Still believing in adherence to propriety, they attempted to act as if the provisional council were the legally constituted government. Rather than creating new laws, they simply adopted those that already were in effect, such as the instructions that the British crown had issued to colonial authorities. Included was the legal authority of colonial governments to control the printing press.

The reasons for the suppression of *Publick Occurrences* were complex. The council did not spell out its reasons exactly, but its order made clear that it was pressed to action on two accounts. Some members feared free publishing and its possible consequences, and some objected to parts of the newspaper's contents. The council's fears about published reports loomed large. The chaotic political situation in the colony was especially critical. The problems that the provisional government faced were broad-ranging and already so deeply rooted that the council was beginning to despair of solving them. Indian raids were destroying the colony's settlements in Maine, and internal order had broken down. The council was unable to deal effectively with either situation. Many people rejected the authority of the government and the courts, some refused to pay their taxes, and soldiers, unpaid, balked at performing their duties.[26] In these deteriorating circumstances, the council was especially sensitive to criticism, particularly any made in public print. In 1689 Governor Simon Bradstreet tried to blame the problems on false reports spread by Andros's supporters,[27] and the following month the House of Representatives issued a warning to anyone who might print or publish anything "tending to the disturbance of the peace & subversion of the govermt."[28]

Even though the council clearly had the authority to suppress *Publick Occurrences*, whether it would have done so if some of its members had not objected to the contents is unknown. The suppression order made a point of stating the reason for the council action—thus hinting that the council was spurred to act by reasons other than the mere fact of unlicensed printing. The council stated that it was concerned about "Reflections of a very high nature" and about "doubtful and uncertain Reports" contained in the newspaper, but it did not specify what those particular items were. An explanation was provided, however, by one of the council members, Judge Samuel Sewall. On September 25, he wrote in his diary: "A printed sheet entituled publick Occurrences comes out, which gives much distaste because not Licensed; and because of the passage referring to the French King and the Maquas [Mohawks]."[29]

The Mohawk passage may have aggravated the council because it clearly criticized the government, and it appears that the reference to Louis XIV was offensive because it contained a rumor about incest. Both passages were contained in Harris's report of the expedition into Canada. One of Harris's criticisms in the Mohawk affair was that the colony in depending on the Mohawks was placing too much trust in an unreliable ally. He reported that the Mohawks had failed to perform the tasks in the expedition that they had promised, and he complained that "we have too much confided" in them. The authorities may, however, have found particularly offensive a passage referring to the Mohawks' barbarous treatment of French prisoners. Harris declared that "if Almighty God will have Canada to be subdu'd without the assistance of those miserable Savages . . . we shall be glad, that there will be no Sacrifice offered up to the Devil." The devout councilmen probably would have found no charge more repugnant than that they might be in league with the Devil. That this passage was the offending one is suggested in a letter that Cotton Mather wrote about the suppression of *Publick Occurrences*. "[T]here is not a Word said Of the *Maqua's*," he declared to his uncle, "but what wee ought to say *To* them, or else wee bring Guilt upon oursel[ve]s."[30] Mather's reference would appear to be to the Mohawks' treatment of prisioners rather than to their unreliability.

The offending statement about Louis XIV probably was one reporting a rumor that he had had sexual relations with his daughter-in-law. Harris's references to Louis were limited to a two-sentence passage. It read, "[Louis] is in much trouble (and fear) not only with us but also with his Son, who has revolted against him lately, and has great reason if reports be true, that the *Father used to lie with the Sons Wife*. He has got all the *Hugonots*, and all the dissatisfied Papists, with the great force of the D.[Duke] of *Lorraign*, and are now against him, resolving to depose him of his life and Kingdom."[31] In reporting Louis's son revolting and the king committing incest with his daughter-in-law, Harris simply repeated an unconfirmed rumor. Although the council membership was Puritan and anti-Catholic, it was made up of men more moderate than Harris, and they apparently felt he had gone too far in printing a rumor about such a matter as incest. As with the passage on the Mohawks, Cotton Mather also criticized the council for condemning Harris for this passage. "As for the French Tyrant," he wrote, "nothing is mention'd of him but as a remote report, and yett wee had the thing in Print long ago." With England and France at war, Mather reasoned, it was ludicrous for the council to punish Harris out of fear that the *Publick Occurrences* report might offend Louis.[32]

Along with the public reasons that the council gave for suppressing *Publick Occurrences*, there was a third that grew out of the maneuvering in Massachusetts's political system. It is clear from Mather's criticism of the council that *Publick Occurrences* was not suppressed because the Puritan clergy objected to the paper. The council membership, rather than being under the clergy's control, represented a diversity of interests and of political and religious views. Mather did not support the council's action. Rather, he claimed that some of its members had used the

Publick Occurrences issue to attack him by implying that he was responsible for the newspaper's publication. The first record of Mather's response to the council was left by Judge Sewall in his diary. On October 1, he recorded: "Print of the Governour and Council comes out shewing their disallowance of the Public Occurrences." The following day, he added a subsequent note: "Mr. Mather writes a very sharp Letter about it."[33]

A copy of the Mather letter to which Sewall referred has not been found, but two weeks later he wrote another letter to his uncle John Cotton that made clear his belief that some council members were trying to use the issue to damage him. Among other points, the letter reveals some secondary items of particular interest. It states, for example, that Harris in producing the newspaper did not act alone but that "three or four . . . Ingenious men" provided assistance. It shows that Harris and Mather were acquainted well enough that Harris relied on Mather for advice in producing some of the contents. It also reveals that Mather, who first reacted negatively to the passages on the Mohawks and Louis's incest, had come to appreciate the newspaper, praising it as "a very Noble, useful, & Laudable Design."[34]

More importantly, however, the letter provides evidence of sharp differences existing between some of the councilors and Mather. Although only twenty-seven, Mather already was one of the most prominent Puritan clergymen and thus was becoming a frequent target of opponents. Mather declared:

The Late sheet of *Public Occurrences*, has been the Occasion of much Discourse, it seems, about the Countrey; & some that might as well have been spared. People had & have a Notion, that I was the Author of it; but as it happened well, the Publisher had not one Line of it from mee, only as accidentally meeting him in the high-way, on his Request, I show'd him how to contract & express the report of the expedition at *Casco* & the East. However, the Government, knowing that *my name* was tossed about it, & knowing nevertheless that there was but *one* Publisher, who pick't up here & there what hee inserted, they emitted a very severe Proclamation against the poor Pamphlett, the first Line whereof thunders against *Some*, that had published that scandalous Thing.—This Accident gave a mighty Assistance to the Calumnies of the People against poor *mee*, who have deserved soe very Ill of the countrey. . . . [T]hey that had a mind to make *mee* odious, have attained their End, with as much Injustice as could well have been used; & a few such Tricks will render mee uncapable of serving either God or Man in N. *England*.

Judging from Mather's terminology, which refers not to a few councilors but to "the government," he believed his opponents held a strong hand in the council. Furthermore, it would appear that the differences were not superficial but deeply antagonistic. While he believed council members were trying to make him "odious," he declared that they instead "might do well to endeavour themselves to do something that may render them worthy to bee accounted *Serviceable*, before they discourage such Honest men, as those [responsible for *Publick Occurrences*]."

Mather did not specify why certain councilors were opposed to him, but evidence points to the dispute involving Increase Mather's efforts to negotiate a new charter for the colony. Although a number of the councilors, most of whom were judges, were close friends of the Mather family,[35] others formed an opposing faction that believed staunchly that the old charter should be restored. The negotiations that Increase Mather, Elisha Cooke, and two other agents were conducting in England for a new charter formed the burning issue in Massachusetts in 1690.[36] Cooke, the most politically active member of the council, was a vocal advocate of keeping the old charter in unaltered form; and when he found Mather and the other agents prepared to agree to a new charter, he refused to continue to work with them. The new charter altered or eliminated several items from the old one. Cooke blamed Mather for what he considered to be a number of shortcomings of the new charter, and he was joined by a considerable body of sympathizers.[37] Indicating how deep his opposition to Mather ran, later he was at the forefront of efforts to remove Mather from the presidency of Harvard College.[38]

Although Cooke was in England at the time of the *Publick Occurrences* controversy, he had several adherents serving on the council. The faction included at least William Johnson, John Smith, and Peter Tilton, all zealous defenders of the old charter.[39] It is also likely that the Mathers could number among their opponents the governor, Simon Bradstreet, and councilor John Pynchon. When Increase Mather submitted his list of council nominees after Massachusetts was granted its new charter, his list *did not* include Cooke, Johnson, Pynchon, Smith, Tilton, Humphrey Davy, or Daniel Gookin.[40] That it was Cooke and his supporters who Cotton Mather believed were trying to make him "odious" is suggested by his comments on the new council nominated by his father. Cotton recorded happily that he no longer would be "made a Sacrifice to wicked *Rulers*."[41]

Although Governor Bradstreet was not one of Cooke's lieutenants, he also had reasons to oppose the Mathers. Eighty-seven years old at the time of the *Publick Occurrences* controversy, he was a prominent figure in Massachusetts affairs. He had held appointed or elected offices since his arrival in the colony in 1630. Although originally he had been on good terms with the leading Puritan clergy, differences arose over negotiations in the 1670s concerning Massachusetts's original charter. The charter, of which the clergy were energetic advocates, assured Massachusetts more autonomy than any other colony enjoyed. With Charles II attempting to annul it, Massachusetts dispatched Bradstreet and John Norton to England to negotiate. Charles confirmed the charter, but he placed such demands on the colonists that they claimed Bradstreet and Norton had been too weak and had made concessions for personal gain. Bradstreet argued that the colonists could not successfully resist Charles's efforts and therefore should submit. After being elected governor of the colony in 1679, he was so conciliatory toward England and supportive of its actions in Massachusetts affairs that he gained the favor of Tories. As the struggle over the charter intensified in the early 1680s, he found himself increasingly at odds with the Puritan supporters of the old charter; and in 1684 he was declared an enemy of the colony, although he continued to hold office as governor until James II abolished the old charter and established the Dominion of New England. After James was overthrown and Andros removed from office in 1689, Bradstreet temporarily resumed the governorship and was serving in that position at the time of the *Publick Occurrences* controversy. Nevertheless, despite Bradstreet's growing differences with Increase Mather over the years, the latter nominated the old statesman for the council membership under the new charter.[42]

John Pynchon, the other councilman who can be identified as a Mather opponent, was a prosperous merchant and judge in Springfield. Born in England in 1626, he moved with his family to Massachusetts in 1630. He was on close terms with Dudley and Andros, the two governors appointed by the British crown after the revocation of the Massachusetts charter in 1686. Both appointed him to their councils, and Andros commissioned him a colonel in the military.[43]

Whatever their personal allegiances, the council members were men of diverse views; and each one likely had his own particular reasons for voting for or against suppressing *Publick Occurrences*. No such thing as unanimity or perfect harmony existed. The cause of the demise of *Publick Occurrences* was not, it is clear, opposition from the Puritan clergy, but a combination of factors working in the political environment. The *Publick Occurrences* episode offers evidence that religious commitment was a strong ingredient in the mix. Contrary to general assumptions, however, Puritanism was on the side of America's first newspaper as it opposed royal authority. The Puritans had comparatively little interest in restricting or suppressing newspaper expression.

After the suppression of *Publick Occurrences*, Harris's fortunes did not appear to have been adversely affected by the controversy. Instead, he became Boston's most successful publisher.[44] Of most interest in its relation to the history of American journalism was a pamphlet he published in 1692 containing four pages of news,[45] against which the government took no action. He also continued to be on good terms with the Puritan leadership. With the appointment of William Phips, the commander of the Canadian expedition whom Harris had lauded in *Publick Occurrences*, as Massachusetts's governor, Harris was named the colony's official printer in December 1692.[46] Phips, a member of Cotton Mather's North Church, had been named governor upon nomination by Increase Mather.

Following his return to England in 1695, Harris published at least three newspapers,[47] remaining active not only in journalism, but in Whig politics and religious controversies also. He stated his intent as to oppose what he claimed were the lies of Catholicism and to "write nothing but truth and certainty, and if I thereby disoblige my old implacable adversaries . . . I doubt not but to please and divert my old Protestant friends, whose zeal for their freedoms of the land of their nativity in the worst of times I shall have a justr value for."[48] He continued a thorn to Tory authorities, who in 1695 arrested him "for printing false news" and again in 1711 for printing the *Protestant Postboy*, which they charged as being a "Scandalous and Seditious Libell."[49] (See Table 1.1.)

Following the suppression of *Publick Occurrences*, it was fourteen years before anyone attempted to publish another colonial newspaper. (See Table 1.1.) Like the first, the second also had Boston as its home. Indeed, one of the most evident features of America's earliest journalism was the prominent role of that city. Not only were the first three newspapers printed there; but of the fifteen American news-

Table 1.1
Chronological List of Boston Newspapers, 1690–1735

1690	*Publick Occurrences*
1704–1719	*Boston News-Letter*
1719–1721	*Boston News-Letter*
	Boston Gazette
1721–1726	*Boston News-Letter*
	Boston Gazette
	Boston *New-England Courant*
1726–1727	*Boston News-Letter*
	Boston Gazette
1727–1731	*Boston News-Letter*
	Boston Gazette
	New-England Weekly Journal
1731–1734	*Boston News-Letter*
	Boston Gazette
	New-England Weekly Journal
	Weekly Rehearsal
1734–1735	*Boston News-Letter*
	Boston Gazette
	New-England Weekly Journal
	Weekly Rehearsal
	Boston Post-Boy
1735–	*Boston News-Letter*
	Boston Gazette
	New-England Weekly Journal
	Weekly Rehearsal
	Boston Post-Boy
	Boston Evening Post

papers published in the period ending in 1735, eight—slightly more than half of the total—were in Boston. (See Table 1.2.) Why was it so prolific?

The easiest answer is population.[50] Boston was the colonies' largest town in the second half of the seventeenth century, with approximately 5,500 inhabitants in 1690, and retained that status until Philadelphia overtook it in the 1750s.[51] Population offered a number of advantages for newspaper publication, including a body of potential readers, cosmopolitanism, businesses needing to advertise, systems such as shipping and postal services for the reception of information, printing establishments and booksellers, and potential writers. By 1700 Boston was shedding

Table 1.2
Boston Newspapers, 1690–1735

Publick Occurrences, Sept. 25, 1690
    Founder: Benjamin Harris, bookseller
    Printer: Richard Pierce

Boston News-Letter, April 24, 1704–Feb. 22, 1776
    Titles: *Boston News-Letter,* April 24, 1704–Dec. 29, 1726; *Boston Weekly News-Letter,*
    Jan. 5, 1727–Aug. 25, 1757; *Boston News-Letter,* Sept. 1, 1757–March 18, 1762;
    Boston News-Letter. And New-England Chronicle, March 25, 1762–March 31, 1763;
    Massachusetts Gazette. And Boston News-Letter, April 7, 1763–Oct. 31, 1765; *Massa-*
    chusetts Gazette, Nov. 7, 1765–May 15, 1766; *Massachusetts Gazette. And Boston*
    News-Letter, May 22, 1766–May 19, 1768; *Boston Weekly News-Letter,* May 26,
    1768–Sept. 21, 1769; *Massachusetts Gazette. And Boston News-Letter,* Sept. 28,
    1769–Feb. 22, 1776.
    Founder: John Campbell, postmaster (April 24, 1704–January 1722)
    Proprietors:
        *Bartholomew Green (January 1722–Dec. 28, 1732)
        *John Draper (Jan. 4, 1733–Nov. 29, 1762)
        *Richard Draper (Nov. 29, 1762–June 5, 1774)
        *Margaret Draper with John Boyle and then John Howe (June 5, 1774–Feb. 22,
        1776)

Boston Gazette, Dec. 21, 1719–Dec. 25, 1780
    Titles: *Boston Gazette,* Dec. 21, 1719–Oct. 12, 1741; *Boston Gazette, or, New England*
    Weekly Journal, Oct. 20, 1741; *Boston Gazette, or, Weekly Journal,* Oct. 27, 1741–Dec.
    26, 1752; *Boston Gazette, or, New England Weekly Advertiser,* Jan. 3, 1753–April 1,
    1755; *Boston Gazette, or [and], Country Journal,* April 7, 1755–Dec. 25, 1780.
    Founder: William Brooker, postmaster (Dec. 21, 1719–Sept. 19, 1720)
    Proprietors:
        **Philip Musgrave (Sept. 26, 1720–May 17, 1725)
        **Thomas Lewis (July 19, 1725–April 18, 1726)
        **Henry Marshall (April 25, 1726–Oct. 2, 1732)
        **John Boydell (Nov. 20, 1732–Dec. 10, 1739)
        Boydell's heirs (Dec. 17, 1739–Oct. 12, 1741)
        *Samuel Kneeland and Timothy Green (Oct. 19, 1741–Dec. 26, 1752)
        *Samuel Kneeland (Jan. 3, 1753–April 1, 1755)
        *Benjamin Edes and John Gill (April 7, 1755–April 17, 1775)
        *Benjamin Edes (June 5, 1775–April 5, 1779)
        *Benjamin Edes, Benjamin Edes, Jr., and Peter Edes (April 12, 1779–Dec. 25, 1780)

New-England Courant, Aug. 7, 1721–June 4, 1726
    Founders: John Checkley, Anglican High-Churchman; and William Douglass, physi-
    cian
    *Proprietor: James Franklin

New-England Weekly Journal, March 20, 1727–Oct. 13, 1741
    Merged with *Boston Gazette,* Oct. 20, 1741.

Table 1.2   (continued)

Founders: Thomas Prince, Puritan clergyman; and Samuel Kneeland, printer
*Proprietors: Samuel Kneeland and Timothy Green

Weekly Rehearsal, Sept. 27, 1731–Aug. 11, 1735
Founder: Jeremy Gridley, lawyer
Proprietors:
    Jeremy Gridley (Sept. 27, 1731–March 26, 1733)
    *Thomas Fleet (April 2, 1733–Aug. 11, 1735)

Boston Post-Boy, October (or November) 1734–April 17, 1775
    Titles: *Boston Weekly Post-Boy*, October 1734–June 4, 1750; *Boston Post-Boy*, June 11,
    1750–Dec. 23, 1754; *Boston Weekly Advertiser*, Aug. 22, 1757–Dec. 25, 1758; *Green
    & Russell's Boston Post-Boy & Advertiser*, Jan. 1, 1759–May 23, 1763; *Boston Post-
    Boy & Advertiser*, May 30, 1763–Sept. 25, 1769; *Massachusetts Gazette and Boston
    Post-Boy and Advertiser*, Oct. 2, 1769–April 17, 1775.
    Founder: Ellis Huske, postmaster
    Proprietors:
        **Ellis Huske (1734–Dec. 23, 1754 [?])
        *John Green and Joseph Russell (Aug. 22, 1757–April 19, 1773)
        *Nathaniel Mills and John Hicks (April 26, 1773–April 19, 1775)

Boston Evening Post, Aug. 18, 1735–April 24, 1775
    Founder: Thomas Fleet, printer
    Proprietors:
        *Thomas Fleet (Aug. 18, 1735–July 17, 1758)
        *Thomas Fleet, Jr. and John Fleet (July 24, 1758–April 24, 1775)

---

*These proprietors were also printers.
**These proprietors were also postmasters.

its wilderness image and becoming a small model of London. Population alone, however, did not guarantee that a newspaper would appear. New York City, for example, attained a population of 5,000 around the year 1710, but it did not have its first newspaper until 1725 when its population was more than 8,000. Its second newspaper appeared only in 1733, by which time its population had grown to approximately 9,400.

Along with population, the publication of newspapers was related to other particular circumstances. Of special importance were political situations—ones that either provided a supportive climate or were so controversial as to provoke publishers into action. Furthermore, the role of the individual publisher should not be overlooked. The recent emphasis among journalism historians on enviromental factors has diminished the importance attached to individuals, but the life history of each early colonial newspaper makes clear that it was started because a particular publisher found himself in a particular situation. It is doubtful, for example, that Boston would have had a newspaper in 1690 if Benjamin Harris, the experienced London publisher, had not moved to the colonial town, or that the *New-England Courant* would have appeared in 1721 if the zealous Anglican John Checkley had not made Boston his home. Would a newspaper have started up in New York City in 1733 unless particular political leaders had wanted a publication to advocate their cause?

But why did Boston provide such opportunities so much more frequently than other towns? One reason lies in the fact that it was the leading town in the most Puritan colony in North America. As such it had developed a vigorous intellectual environment. No other colony presented a climate that encouraged freedom of inquiry to the extent that Massachusetts did or was so favorable to freedom in printing. Puritans, as compared to their opponents in England and their counterparts in other colonies, had created an intellectual environment that encouraged inquisitiveness and free expression.[52] It was from their interest in inquiry and knowledge that the Puritans established Harvard College in 1638 and required parents to send their children to schools.[53] Similarly, the first printing presses in the colonies were imported into Massachusetts; and they did a voluminous business, mainly in producing religious tracts but also in publishing political, scientific, and other material. In the English-speaking world, by 1700 Boston was second only to London as a center for book publishing and selling.[54] By 1719, when the first colonial newspaper outside Massachusetts appeared, Boston was home to five presses.

The Puritans' intellectual outlook grew directly out of their theology. In migrating to America, Puritans were especially eager to remove themselves as far as possible from Anglicanism, thus gaining the ability to take ecclesiastical and spiritual authority from the central church heirarchy, to emphasize the freedom of the individual believer, and to place church matters in the hands of the local autonomous congregation.[55] Because they emphasized the individual, rather than the established church, as having the authority to interpret God's word, they declared that the individual must be free to inquire and that diversity of views had to be tolerated.

The foregoing is not intended to argue that Puritans were ubiquitously tolerant or that they were unwavering libertarians.[56] At times they objected, as other groups did, to opposition printing; and they did not have the same toleration for views, such as Anglicanism and Catholicism, extremely different from their own that they had for disagreements among themselves. For their age, however, they were at the forefront in arguing for the right of the individual to inquire into ideas and to express them freely;[57] and one does not find in Puritan Massachusetts the severity of punishment for offensive printing as elsewhere. When Benjamin Harris, for example, offended the colony's governing council, he was not fined or imprisoned, as he had been in England, but was simply told to desist from publishing.[58]

However, with the revocation of the colony's charter in 1685, the British monarchy, in effect, expropriated everything that the Puritans had built. The intellectual climate that Puritans had created was altered. The monarchy assumed the authority to appoint the colony's governor; the authority to regulate the press was placed in his hands; and the new charter which was issued in 1691 continued that policy. With the exception of William Phips and William Stoughton, whose administrations covered the period from 1692 to 1697, the appointed governors were Anglicans in religion and Tories in politics. The strongest efforts at repression in Massachusetts, where Anglicans never made up more than one-fifth of the population, came when royal Anglican authorities held control of the government. Actions to prosecute for publishing offenses increased. Increase Mather, for example, was being hunted by the government of Edmund Andros when he escaped to England to serve as Massachusetts's agent in 1688, and his son Cotton faced a variety of legal proceedings for his writings.

The government philosophy of restriction collided, however, with the tradition of expression which the Puritans had established. Authorities never were completely successful at preventing critical publications. Pamphlets abounded, written by both Puritans and their Anglican opponents. The idea that one should be free to publish spilled over into politics. Thus, Massachusetts, which had the most dynamic political situation in the colonies, had spawned a vibrant printing atmosphere by the early 1700s.

Throughout the history of colonial Massachusetts, religion played a key, perhaps even the central, role. The same thing is true for its early newspapers. One of the most distinctive features was an ongoing struggle between Puritans and Anglicans, centering on the issue of the freedom of the individual believer and the local congregation versus the authority of the church. In that debate, Puritans' efforts were aimed at establishing local autonomy, while the Church of England aimed its energies at exerting its control. Anglicans argued that authority rested ultimately with the British monarch, exercised through the crown-appointed Archbishop of Canterbury. Massachusetts Puritans had managed to keep their religious freedom by aggressively opposing the efforts of the Church of England and the English monarchy to establish Episcopacy in the colony. The Puritans' efforts had the effect of helping to assure both political and religious independence in Massachusetts. In defending their religious freedom, it is true, Puritans did attack Anglicanism energetically, but still they permitted the Anglicans and members of other minority churches to practice their faith. Anglicans' efforts, on the other hand, were aimed at officially establishing the Church of England and displacing Puritanism.

Puritans originally had held hope that the Church of England could be cleansed; but with the ascension of Charles I to the throne of England, they began to migrate to the New World when their cause appeared to be dead in the Old. In the British authorities' minds, however, residence in the colonies did not free one from the authority of the Church of England. Charles and the Anglican monarchs who followed him were as religiously zealous as their Puritan adversaries, and they were energetic in promoting the Church in their colonies. Some colonies, such as Virginia, were set up originally with Anglicanism established as the official church; but the efforts of the Church to establish its authority over the colonies outside its control began in earnest with the appointment of William Laud as Archbishop of

Canterbury in 1633. He worked energetically to quell dissent at home and impose conformity abroad, not shrinking from official sanction, fines, imprisonment, and physical punishment of nonconformers. To prevent the continued increase of separatism in the colonies, he issued orders in February 1633 that all ships bound for the colonies "cause the Prayers contayned in the Booke of Common Prayers established in the Church of England, to be sayde dayly at the usuall howers for morning and Evening Prayers, and that they cause all persons aboard theise said Shippes to be present at the same."[59] He recognized that dissenting ministers provided a foundation for the separatist movement; and in 1634, therefore, the Star Chamber prohibited the escape from England "of persons ill-affected to the religion established in the Church of England, . . . of ministers who are inconformable to the ceremonies and discipline of the Church" and ordered "all that had already gone forth . . . forthwith to be remanded back."[60] That same year, Laud received a commission from the king ordering that—since ministers "take liberty to nourish their factions and schismatical humours, to the hindrance of the good conformity and unity of the Church"—"no clergyman [be suffered] to transport himself without a testimonial from the Archbishop of Canterbury and the Bishop of London."[61] Likewise, Charles issued a commission to change the government of New England and transfer it to Laud and "two or three" bishops of his choosing, with power to establish "the clergy government for the cure of souls, tithes, to appoint magistrates, levy fines, inflict penalties, and send home the refractory to England."[62] As a means of setting up Anglicanism in New England, Laud next made plans to send a bishop there with enforcement from a military force,[63] but the outbreak of civil war in England forced him to abandon the plan.

In those colonies where Anglicanism was established, it worked toward conformity in both religion and politics and toward a joining of the two. In New Hampshire, for example, Governor Cranfield wrote to England to propose "that it will be absolutely necessary to admit no person into any place of trust, but such as will take the sacrament and are conformable to the rites of the Church of England." Opposing clergy and views had to be quieted. "I utterly despair," Cranfield added, "of any true duty and obedience paid to his Majesty until their college be suppressed and their ministers silenced."[64]

Owing largely to popular opposition and to the ministers' talents, Puritans successfully resisted the intrusions of Anglicanism throughout most of the seventeenth century. Massachusetts, and particularly the town of Boston, remained safe from Anglican threats until the colony was made a royal province and on May 16, 1686, a ship brought Joseph Dudley to be president of Massachusetts, New Hampshire, and Maine. Arriving on the same passage was the Reverend Robert Ratcliffe to conduct Episcopal services in Boston—the equivalent, Puritans believed, of worshipping Baal. Expressing the Puritans' common abhorrence of Anglicanism, Cotton Mather wrote in his diary in November of that year: "The Common-Prayer-Worship [is] being sett up in this Country. I would procure and assist the Publication of a Discourse written by my Father, that shall enlighten the *rising Generation*, in the *Unlawfulness* of that Worship, and antidote them against Apostasy from the Principles of our First Settlement."[65] The Puritan leaders refused the Anglican churchmen's request that one of the local church buildings be made available for Anglican services. The issue was soon forced with the arrival of Edmund Andros as royal governor of New England and his order that a Puritan church be turned over for Anglican use.

Shortly thereafter, the Anglicans began construction of their own building, King's Chapel, "the Church of England as by law established." Inspired by that success, Edmund Randolph, one of the royal commissioners and a devout Anglican, proposed to King James that the costs of supporting the church and its minister be paid by the Puritan congregations.[66] It was as if being allowed to exist conferred on Anglicans special status. The Puritans unremittingly opposed that attitude.[67]

With the founding of King's Chapel, its members at once became energetic in the attempts to establish Anglicanism in Massachusetts. Their view was that the colonies were possessions of Britain and were therefore subject to that government in all matters civil and religious. Since the Anglican Church was the official church of England, it was therefore automatically the established church in England's colonies. The King's Chapel members were at the forefront of efforts to tie church matters to political ones and thus gain success. One of their goals was to secure a governor who was an adherent of the Church of England and therefore would assist in the establishment efforts of the church. As one of the first official acts of King's Chapel, its minister, the Reverend Samuel Myles, and the church wardens petitioned the crown, who "has bin graciously pleased to have particular regard to the religion of the Church of England," to appoint a new colonial governor and council so that the Church might "grow up and flourish, and bring fruites of religion and loyalty, to the honour of Almighty God, and the promotion and increase of Your Majesty."[68] Their hopes were satisfied with the appointment of Joseph Dudley, the Puritans' old nemesis, as governor.

Dudley was the son of Thomas, one of the most respected of the first generation of Massachusetts settlers. The younger Dudley, however, had been suspect ever since his mission as colonial agent to England in 1682.[69] Having placed his own interests above those of the colonists, he returned to tell them that they must submit to the monarchy. In 1685 James II named him president of New England in the interim before Andros assumed the position. Under Andros, he served as chief justice of the superior court and acted as overseer of the press. Along with Andros he was imprisoned by Bostonians during the 1689 rebellion. Appointed governor of Massachusetts in 1702, he adhered uncompromisingly to a doctrine of submission to royal prerogative and, having converted to the Anglican church, episcopal authority. His duty of enforcing unpopular British laws combined with the enmities created during his first administration made him the most disliked man in Massachusetts. He was, Cotton Mather declared, a "wretch."[70]

It was under Dudley that Boston acquired its first continuing newspaper, published by the Anglican John Campbell. He began the paper, the *Boston News-Letter*, without any conception of its being a true newspaper or of exercising any publishing independence. Producing a quasi-official report in the form of a newspaper was, Campbell believed, one of the responsibilities required by his position as postmaster. He thus looked on himself not as an energetic editor but as an official conduit of information and on the newspaper as a formal, chronological record of news items. Tied so plainly to the unpopular Dudley administration, he never gained the confidence of the populace, and he found that his life as a publisher was an ongoing, tiresome struggle for mere existence.

Campbell had emigrated from Scotland to the colonies in the 1690s, became acquainted with some of Boston's most prominent figures, joined King's Chapel, and was appointed a constable in 1699.[71] In 1702, upon the death of his brother, Duncan, he was named to replace him as Massachusetts's postmaster.[72] The postal system had been set up in 1692 under a royal grant that gave it a monopoly on "any letters or Pacquets which shall be brought into . . . or shipped from" any colony from Virginia northward.[73] That monopoly, along with the privilege that each colonial postmaster enjoyed to send mail without charge, made the position of postmaster ideal for obtaining information and for mailing letters and printed material.

As part of his job, Campbell had the official task of writing letters of important information to the main office.[74] As postmaster in an important commercial center and seaport town, he was in a position to obtain news conveniently from incoming letters, newspapers, and ship crews. He circulated his handwritten "public news-letters" to postal officials, merchants, and other affluent colonists. The reports were chiefly about commerce, shipping, and governmental activities. Many subscribers shared them with nonsubscribers, and some letters ended up posted in taverns and other public places for anyone who wished to learn about the news.

With an increasing number of clients, Campbell found that producing the letters by hand required too much time. The increased numbers also convinced him that a sizable potential market of readers probably existed for the letters. So he decided to begin printing the letters and making them available for purchase by the general public. Producing a public newsletter would require, he calculated, little more work than he was already doing. His franking privilege would help keep costs down. Furthermore, he expected that a newspaper could attract income through advertising. He worked out an arrangement with Nicholas Boone, a bookseller, to serve as the advertising solicitor.[75] He then contracted with Bartholomew Green to set one of the handwritten letters in type and print copies. Printing allowed Campbell to produce as many copies as he wanted at a much faster speed and more economical rate than he could ever imagine writing them with his quill.

Thus on April 24, 1704, began the *Boston News-Letter*. This, the colonies' first continuous newspaper, was a half sheet of paper, about 8 inches by 12 inches, made up with two columns on each of its two pages. A machine-printed version of Campbell's handwritten newsletters, it did not use headlines and varied the type only slightly, thus presenting a monotone page, on which the news items were arranged without any graphic order or emphasis. Subsequent issues followed the same rigid page makeup with clocklike regularity. Foreign news was printed on the front page and part of the second and third pages, followed by colonial news, and finally local news on the last page.

The *News-Letter* served as a semi-official report summarizing items of news for reader convenience. Many Bostonians came to rely on it for their own information and used it as a means of keeping friends in other towns supplied with news of Boston happenings.[76] It supplied readers with extracts of news of England and Europe, commercial-shipping news, news of the seaboard colonies and the West Indies, governmental items, local Boston news, and occasionally sermons and philosophical discourses.

The foreign news items, culled from English newspapers, were mostly political in nature. British government activities occupied the front page. Also reprinted were reports about the court intrigues and gossip, wars, and peace treaties. The *London Flying Post* and *London Gazette* were used most frequently as sources of news. To obtain the foreign news, Campbell would watch ships sailing up the harbor until they docked. Then he would run to the docks, hasten aboard to greet the captain, and secure the London papers.[77]

Campbell's domestic news covered the seaport settlements with which Boston had business and other contacts, from Nova Scotia to Charleston, South Carolina. Most of the news was about the arrival and departure of ships, and other maritime happenings. He received his domestic news through the colonial post. Because transportation was slow and the post ran only weekly out of Boston, the reports almost always were at least a fortnight old; when winter snows hampered travel, they were older.[78] Nevertheless, the trade news was important to shippers, officials, farmers who had products and goods to ship or merchandise to buy, and businessmen who owned the ships or had investments in them. Adding excitement and drama to the *News-Letter*'s pages were accounts of fights with pirates and French privateers who infested the waters of the Atlantic and about warfare against the Indians who prowled outside the settlements. Functioning as a journal of public affairs, the *News-Letter* reported on the activities of colonial government and the assembly. It also laconically summarized such occurrences as deaths, disease, fire, and floods. It carried, however, little local news of Boston and the immediate neighborhood. The stories that it did publish formed a weekly chronicle of Boston events: disease, natural deaths, executions of pirates, religious news, official court news, and political news. Of the political news, the governor's activities always made front page stories—an exception to Campbell's practice of relegating local news to the back.

Historians frequently have suggested that colonial newspapers downplayed local news on the assumption that local residents already knew what had happened in town. News of Governor Dudley's street fight with two farmers, for example, already would have been much talked about in taverns and probably superceded by other more recent topics by the time it appeared in Campbell's weekly medium. With the *News-Letter*, however, as with most other colonial newspapers, one finds that some local news was printed. What the *News-Letter* did not print was local news that involved Dudley and his supporters unfavorably. Campbell thus appears to have had partisan motives for news decisions. As for other colonial newspapers, decisions about running news of local events appear to have been based normally on the proprietors' judgment about what would be of interest to local readers, thus accounting for a mix of foreign, domestic, and local news.

Campbell was so conscientious in providing a complete chronicle of news as to be inflexible. He cherished the foreign news so much that he would not throw away any part, however old it might be. He tried to carry all items as a "thread of occurrence," running a brief summary of the important events and then publishing serially all the items he had on hand. Ever attentive to foreign happenings, incoming boats, and local events, he attempted to include as much in each issue as space allowed, but the weekly space simply could not hold all he wished to relay. The result was that, as time passed, the *News-Letter* lagged farther and farther behind. The news items were so stale, a year old in some instances, that Cotton Mather called them "antiquities."[79]

Criticized for the *News-Letter*'s mundaneness, Campbell stated his editorial policy as having "always been to give no offence, not meddling with things out of his Province."[80] It was this spirit that prompted him to shy away from controversial political and social issues. He published the newspaper with permission from the Dudley administration, with each issue prominently displaying the line "Printed by Authority."[81] Producing the newspaper was, he believed, a responsibility of his position, and he thought of his own function as that of the government's provider of information. He never thought of being an independent, imaginative editor whose role was to scrutinize government action or analyze issues or indulge in controversy. On only one occasion was he reprimanded for offending authorities, and he willingly apologized.[82] As a friend of Dudley and many of his associates,[83] it was natural that he sided with government positions.

Most of the important issues facing Bostonians centered on contentious differences between Dudley and the townspeople. Campbell, however, had no wish to give attention to the dissensions in the *News-Letter*. As a result, he failed to cover many of the major events that were shaping Boston and that were of greatest interest to its citizens. This deficiency was especially noticeable in political events. In the early 1700s, Massachusetts confronted a variety of critical issues, ranging from the ongoing and acrimonious controversies between Anglicans and Puritans to frontier defenses, the issuance of paper currency, taxation, the imbalance of trade with Great Britain, the dispute over a private banking system, a struggle for more autonomy from royal power, and a fight between the mercantile class and the old charter party. The *News-Letter* kept clear of these controversies. It also turned a blind eye on questionable and controversial activities of Dudley and his friends, including such actions as Dudley's high-handed political tactics with opponents; his acrimonious efforts to have his salary increased; a brawl that he had with two farmers on a Boston street; a mob's attack on the grain warehouses of Andrew Belcher, a merchant friend of Campbell; the open flaunting of an adulterous affair by Dudley's mercantile associate, Arthur Lawson, which enraged Bostonians; and a trial in which Lawson and other merchants were convicted of selling English supplies to enemy troops in Canada and in which charges were made that Dudley himself was involved. While pamphleteers argued over these episodes incessantly, the pages of the *News-Letter* could have led a reader to believe they never happened.

For its news treatment and other reasons, the *News-Letter* struggled. Although receiving occasional government subsidies, Campbell faced hard times almost perpetually. The number of subscriptions remained small, and advertising volume never provided substantial income. With a circulation of fewer than 300 copies, Campbell frequently called upon the public and officials for support. Subscribers seemed to have been habitually tardy, sometimes by more than a year, in paying their bills, and Campbell repeatedly had to publish pleas for payment.[84] Most of his calls went unrequited.

Part of the problem was that some Bostonians simply found Campbell's writing graceless and the paper dull. Cotton Mather, although a reader, ridiculed it as "our paltry news-letter."[85] More damaging, however, was the knowledge that the *News-Letter* was the official record for the unpopular and, some thought, immoral Dudley regime. Mather's statements to acquaintances that the "filthy and foolish" *News-Letter* provided only "a thin sort of diet" were so harsh as to appear motivated by more than the paper's dullness.[86] Most of the Puritan citizenry and Dudley's other political opponents held the *News-Letter* in low regard. The Puritan leadership seemed, at best, to accord the paper scornful toleration as a mouthpiece of the royal government, about which they could do little but ridicule. Opponents such as Cotton and Increase Mather produced pamphlets attacking the Dudley administration and its Anglican supporters. Ministers preached on the necessity for public officials to follow Biblical standards in the conduct of local affairs. In spite of commercialism and other changes taking place in Boston society, Puritan traditions still were strong enough to provoke public anger against Dudley's vanity, government corruption, the British monarchy's efforts to expand its control over the colony, and the exertions of Boston's small Anglican minority to gain favored status.

Still, Campbell persevered. He displayed a tenacious determination to carry out his arduous publishing duties despite the continuing problems. Revenues were barely enough to pay costs, and Campbell gave his "Labour for nothing."[87] Committed to fulfilling what he considered to be a public obligation, he worked conscientiously at the paper "(according to the Talent of my capacity and Education; . . .) in giving a true and genuine account of all Matters of Fact, both Foreign and Domestick, as comes any way Attested."[88] He made periodic pleas to the public for support, while promising that he would continue even if the small number of subscribers did not increase.[89] The *News-Letter*, troublesome and never prosperous, provided no more than a small source of income, and an individual less dedicated to his duties than Campbell might have stopped publication on any number of occasions.

The situation, difficult as it was, grew worse in 1718. Campbell was replaced with another postmaster, William Brooker. Campbell's philosophy about operating the *News-Letter* as if it were an official journal led his successor to assume that the newspaper was a part of the postmaster's position. Campbell, however, refused to give the paper to Brooker, and the two quarrelled. Campbell continued publishing the *News-Letter* himself. However, he no longer was allowed to use the mail for sending the paper to subscribers.[90] Some subscribers were no longer able to obtain the *News-Letter*, and the government was deprived of its journal. Brooker thereupon decided to start another newspaper, publishing the first issue of the *Boston Gazette* on December 21, 1719. When, in September of the following year, another postmaster was appointed to replace him, Brooker surrendered the newspaper to him. The *Gazette* became the organ of the postmaster and, it was assumed, of the colonial governor as well. When Brooker's successor, Philip Musgrave, was replaced in 1726, he likewise gave the paper to his successor. Thus the newspaper continued through a succession of five postmasters.[91]

Newspapering had become a part of Campbell's life. Faced with competition from the *Gazette*, however, he began to change his approach. Whereas formerly he had moaned to readers about the paper's difficulties, he now told them that the subscription list was long, and he invited them to compare the quality of his newspaper to that of its competitor.[92] He began to insert his personality more, and along with the short summary news items he had always carried he now began including occasional essays and observations.[93]

The change occurred as soon as Brooker began publishing the *Gazette*. Piqued that Campbell had kept the *News-Letter*, Brooker printed an article stating that Campbell had been fired from the postmaster's job.[94] That charge led to an exchange of personal insults between the two,[95] and it was not long before they were taking sides on public issues. Generally, the *Gazette* under Brooker and Musgrave favored the interests of Governor Samuel Shute,[96] while the *News-Letter* took the side of the assembly.

Neither newspaper could be accused, however, of being a tool exclusively for one side. Political issues were intricate, and both papers frequently published material from contending sides. Some material was paid for as "advertisements" by the authors, whereas some was published as straight news matter. Cotton Mather's attitude toward the *News-Letter* had moderated, for example, and he wrote a number of pieces for it.[97] In 1722 he began publishing a nine-part series on "The State of Religion," which among other things criticized Anglicanism—despite Campbell's Anglican membership. Because of that criticism and remarks the essay made about the British monarchy, the government proceeded against Mather as a "publisher of dangerous libels."[98] On the other hand, in the acrimonious public debate over smallpox inoculation in 1721–1722, it was the *Gazette* which served as the primary outlet for Mather and his supporters.

Contentions between the royal governor and the elected representatives came to a head in 1720, and the dispute dealt the death blow to the governor's licensing of the press. Royal governors never had been fully able to control publishing in Massachusetts, as the lively pamphleteering scene had shown; but, even after licensing had expired in England in 1695, they still officially retained the authority given by the crown to oversee printing and prohibit obnoxious publishing. In November 1719 Governor Shute delivered an address in which he blamed the colony for failing to manage forests as required for the construction of masts on naval ships.[99] The House of Representatives responded that the problem lay not with the colony but with the forest surveyor, who was appointed by the crown.[100] Shute then asked the House not to include that passage in its printed proceedings. The House refused, declaring that since the governor's criticism had been printed, it was appropriate that the response should be also. Shute replied that if the passage were not omitted, he would use his power as licenser of the press to prevent its publication. His instruction to Bartholomew Green, the official government printer, was sufficient to dissuade him from doing the work, but House members from Boston contracted with Nicholas Boone to proceed with the printing. Upon asking his council what action he should take, Shute discovered that council members were divided.[101] The governor and the representatives continued at loggerheads over a variety of issues, the main one being the respective authority that belonged to each, during the remainder of Shute's stormy term of office. When in March of 1721 Shute proposed a law to give him through legislation the authority to license printing, the House replied that licensing would raise "innumerable inconveniences and danger" for the colony and that punishment *after* publication would be preferable.[102] When Shute's council then approved a bill for preventing and punishing libels, the House refused to pass it. The entire disagreement between the governor and the House was aired in the pages of the *Gazette* and *News-Letter*[103] and in an array of pamphlets.

Because of their moderation, neither the *News-Letter*[104] nor the *Gazette* could satisfy the combative High Church faction in King's Chapel, and it was the dissatisfaction of that small group which provided the motive for a third newspaper, the *New-England Courant*. The *Courant* brought the differences between radical Anglicanism and Boston Puritanism to a head. Ever since the founding of King's Chapel, its members had hoped that Anglicanism would be established as the official church in Massachusetts. Thus, one finds continual contention between the Boston Anglicans and their Puritan neighbors' efforts to restrain them. Since Anglicans were greatly outnumbered and their presumptions and practices held in contempt by most of the populace, they had found it necessary to act with a degree of prudence. When John Checkley burst onto the scene, however, they gained a zealous spokesman who did not shrink from controversy but relished it. Seeking a forum from which he could attack Puritanism, in 1721 he decided upon the tack of founding the *Courant*.

Checkley was Boston's leading voice for the most extreme positions of the High Church party in the Anglican Church. That faction believed that the Anglican Church was the only legitimate church and that there was no salvation outside of it. Staunchly Tory in politics, the High Churchers tended to tie religion to state. Checkley himself still held to the view that kings ruled by divine right and subjects must be passively obedient—although that notion had been outdated in England since the Glorious Revolution. While other Boston Anglicans shared Checkley's dogma that no church other than the Anglican was legitimate, they were circumspect in making their beliefs known. Checkley, in contrast, declared them fiercely.

Checkley began the polemics in 1719 when he published a tract by the zealous Anglican Charles Leslie, with the implication that Puritans were as misguided in their religious faith as were deists. In that and other tracts published over the next few years, Checkley declared that ecclesiastical authority rested in bishops; that Puritans were "Carnal Libertines" and Christianity's enemies; that "the Church of England, and NO OTHER, is established" in New England; that sacraments, ordinances, and baptisms administered by dissenting clergy, specifically Boston's Puritan clergy, were a "Sacrilege, and Rebellion against Christ" and that any Puritan parent having a child baptized by the Puritan clergy was "guilty of the blood of [the] child."[105]

Checkley's arguments were so strident that they created dissension in his own church and animosity from without. While some Anglicans wished he would desist, a High Church faction coalesced around him. Although small in number, its aggressive members dominated the affairs of King's Chapel for awhile.[106] It was this faction that served as the original group of writers for the *New-England Courant*. By 1721, as Checkley's attacks intensified, the contention between that faction and Puritan leaders had taken on the nature of a personal feud between Checkley and Cotton Mather. Possessing the best mind and most articulate pen in the colonies, Mather had been especially vigilant in opposing Anglican maneuvers. He therefore became the prime target for the High Churchers.

The unpopularity of their theological views with the general populace had prevented the Anglican advocates from making much headway in their efforts to advance the Church of England. A medical plague that entered Boston in 1721, however, gave the High Church faction an opportunity to attack Mather and his fellow Puritan clergymen in a way that, on the surface, seemed unrelated to Anglicanism. Although members of the faction used religious arguments for part of their assault, their arguments were not framed in Anglican theology, and for the most part they never rose above personalized invective; their intent, though, was to persecute Mather and the Puritan clergy in order to destroy their popularity. It was all part of a strategy to establish the Anglican Church on the ruins of Puritanism. Having failed to carry the theological argument in their earlier encounters, they now resorted to vilification based on the Puritan clergymen's unpopular advocacy of inoculation for smallpox.

In the early 1700s in Europe and America, more deaths resulted from smallpox than from any other cause. The mortality and the loathsome nature of the disease made it the most dreaded. Boston itself had experienced six outbreaks before 1721.[107] In April 1721, smallpox again entered Boston. By June it was out of control. Hundreds of Boston's residents fled the town, and of those who remained virtually every household experienced the contagion. By September the number of deaths was so great that the selectmen limited the length of time that funeral bells could toll. By the time it had receded the following year, 6,000 of Boston's 10,500 residents had contracted the disease, and more than 800 had died.

Soon after authorities learned of the presence of smallpox, Mather—who had learned of the experimental method of inoculation from reading accounts in the journal *Philosophical Transactions* and from his African slave—proposed to Boston's physicians that they attempt the procedure. Only one of the ten physicians, Dr. Zabdiel Boylston, a neighbor of Mather, agreed to try the procedure.

The other physicians, along with the public, responded ferociously. Injecting a disease into a healthy person seemed to most laymen, and to most physicians also, not only a ludicrous strategy but hazardous as well. Mather, however, had not foreseen how intense the public reaction would be; and he had not expected that his Anglican adversaries would take advantage of his goodwill to unleash a withering and prolonged attack on him. This being the first attempt at immunology in the English-speaking world, word quickly spread around the little town of Boston, already hysterical because of the pervasive danger of smallpox, that Boylston was deliberately spreading the disease. The populace was furious at both Boylston and Mather.[108] The public case against inoculation was led by the physicians,[109] with William Douglass at the forefront, and it gained government support through the selectmen. Whether the opponents and the proponents divided along religious lines is unclear,[110] but it is notable that none of the seven most visible advocates of inoculation was Anglican.[111] A number of the prominent opponents, including Douglass, were members of King's Chapel.

It was Douglass's sense of superiority to Boston's other physicians that led him to attack Boylston publicly, thus starting the newspaper war over inoculation. In a letter to the *Boston News-Letter*, signed with the pseudonym "W. Philanthropos," Douglass called Dr. Boylston a "Cutter for the Stone," a "quack," "Ignorant," and "unfit" and challenged his professional competence in administering inoculations. He argued that using inoculation was theologically wrong, for it attempted to place the cure of a disease in man's ability rather than leaving it in God's providence.[112] The proponents of inoculation responded to the attack with a letter of their own to the *Boston Gazette*. Written mostly by Benjamin Colman, Boylston's pastor, but signed by inoculation's other five clerical supporters, the letter defended Boylston as a skilled and tender physician, criticized Douglass's conceit, called for more charity than Douglass's letter exhibited, and refuted his religious argument against inoculation.[113] Throughout the following months of the controversy, the High Churchers frequently repeated the argument that inoculation violated man's requirement to depend on God,[114] thus paradoxically requiring the faithful clergy to defend medical science from theological attacks.

Conditions were ripe for the Anglican opposition to found a newspaper. The *New-England Courant* began publication on August 7. The key figure was Checkley, who was supported by a group of affluent Anglicans, all members of the High Church party in King's Chapel, including Douglass. Checkley originated the idea and approached Douglass about it. After they had laid the plans, they arranged with James Franklin to print it and recruited their fellow High Churchmen into the enterprise.[115]

The lead article on page one of the two pages was an essay Checkley wrote introducing himself as the "Author" of the paper and lampooning the Puritan clergy for their advocacy of inoculation. The remainder of the front page was filled with an essay by Douglass arguing against inoculation, which included personal attacks on Dr. Boylston and the clergy, "Six Gentlemen of Piety and Learning, profoundly ignorant of the Matter."[116] The focus on anti-inoculation was made clear in the August 21 issue, in which Checkley wrote that the "chief design of the *New-England Courant* is to oppose the doubtful and dangerous practice of inoculating the small pox."

Douglass's motive in starting the *Courant* was, likewise, to oppose inoculation and attack Mather. He opposed inoculation for a variety of reasons, ranging from his belief that it was an unsound medical procedure and interfered with God's providential working in human affairs to the fact that he was irritated at Mather for having used information about inoculation from copies of *Philosophical Transactions* borrowed from Douglass. The latter therefore believed he had a proprietary right to the work.[117] Furthermore, he was angry at Mather for presuming to offer advice in the field of medicine, Douglass's domain.[118]

The underlying implication of the *Courant*'s content was that the Puritan clergy could not be trusted.[119] With the clergy's stature eroded, a void might be created which the Anglican church could fill. In his writings in the *Courant*, Checkley avoided his normal strident Anglican theology and instead emphasized ridicule of the Puritan leaders, apparently hoping to diminish their standing with the public. Abrasive in his style, he upset even the Anglicans when in the third issue of the *Courant* he called the Reverend Thomas Walter, Cotton Mather's nephew, an "obscene and fuddling Merry-Andrew" and accused him of drunkenness and debauchery.[120]

Dr. Douglass, Checkley's main partner in the *Courant* venture, although a member of the High Church group, was not as zealous in his advocacy of Anglicanism as was Checkley. He was drawn into the operation mainly because of his personal animosity toward Mather and Dr. Boylston. His articles in the *Courant* dealt in medical and legal objections to inoculation and in ridicule and attacks on proponents.[121] By early 1722, after the success of inoculation had been demonstrated, he was slowly coming around to accepting the procedure, although he wrote that "For my own Part, till after a few Years, I shall pass no positive Judgement of this bold Practice."[122] He harbored a dislike for both Boylston and Mather for the remainder of his life and demeaned their efforts even after inoculation had become a standard practice.

Along with Douglass and Checkley, the other main figures in the founding of the *Courant* were two physicians in King's Chapel, George Steward and John Gibbins, both members of the High Church party and close associates of Checkley.[123] These two wrote all essays in the first three issues of the *Courant* not authored by Douglass or Checkley. Steward's contribution to the *Courant*, although using strong language, dealt less in personal attack than that of the other *Courant* writers. He criticized inoculation on the grounds that reports from Turkey indicated unfavorable reactions to the procedure; that inoculation, while it might benefit some people, resulted in some deaths; and that Boylston inoculated in a way that resulted in the inoculees' spreading the disease to other people. He charged Boylston and the Puritan clergy of violating the Sixth Commandment against murder.[124] Gibbins's writing, on the other hand, dealt solely in personal attacks. His major contribution was an attack in the third issue on Cotton Mather's nephew, Thomas Walter. He repeated a rumor that Walter drank excessively, although he claimed in different parts of his essay that the drink was rum, wine, cider, and dram.[125] Having converted from Congregationalism to Anglicanism, Gibbins exhibited the marks of someone who simply wanted to attack the ministers of his former faith and had no goal of helping advance any useful discussion.

Following Gibbins's and Checkley's two-pronged attack on Walter, uneasiness about the direction the *Courant* was taking intensified. The pastors of King's Chapel were disturbed. Checkley, they thought, had gone overboard. The rector, perhaps with the support of the church's other members who produced the *Courant*, directed him to desist from such writings and "reprove[d]" Franklin for printing them.[126] Thereafter, Checkley dropped his association with the paper, refusing even to subscribe to it.[127]

In order to continue publishing the newspaper, King's Chapel's assistant rector, the Reverend Henry Harris, took over writing duties for the issue of August 28. More moderate than the High Churchmen, he showed more civility than Checkley. Still, his essay, which filled most of the non-news space in the paper, argued that it was a religious duty and a requirement of the Sixth Commandment that inoculators avoid spreading smallpox deliberately.[128]

After the *Courant*'s fourth issue, the newspaper passed out of the hands of its original operators. Without Checkley's leadership, the High Churchmen Steward and Gibbins apparently had no burning desire to continue with the paper. Douglass was more interested in his medical practice than in producing a newspaper each week; and the Reverend Mr. Harris's Anglican passion was not hot enough to induce him to continue the project. Steward, Douglass, and Harris would write other articles, but no longer were they involved in operating the paper. With the fifth issue, that duty passed into the hands of printer James Franklin, and the responsibility for providing the content was taken up by a "Mr. Gardner."[129]

Despite the change in management, the *Courant*'s content did not change significantly. Members of King's Chapel continued to have a dominant hand in writing its content.[130] Although claiming to be neutral on inoculation and "promis[ing] that nothing for the future shall be inserted, anyways reflecting on the Clergy . . . and nothing but what is innocently Diverting,"[131] the newspaper still opposed inoculation,[132] fought Puritanism, attacked opponents with ridicule, used theological grounds as a basis for much of the attack, and attempted satire. The opposition clergy continued to believe that the *Courant*'s "main intention . . . [was] to Vilify and abuse the best Men we have, and especially the principal Ministers of Religion in the Country,"[133] with Cotton Mather believing the purpose was to "lessen and blacken the Ministers of the Town, and render their Ministry ineffectual."[134]

That the *Courant* should continue a strong Anglican tenor under James Franklin is not surprising. A devout Christian, he was a member of King's

Chapel.[135] Nevertheless, he was not in the social or intellectual circle of the High Churchers who ran the *Courant*. Having gained his printing knowledge through an apprenticeship, he was not as well educated as they. Young (twenty-five years old in 1721) and struggling in his printing business, neither did he possess their social standing. His younger brother, Benjamin—admittedly biased because of the treatment he received as James's apprentice—described him as demeaning, envious, passionate, and hot-headed.[136] While his writing in the *Courant* was sometimes passable in style and substance, it was not scintillating, and it was prone to be petty and capricious, often revealing him sulking over criticism he received from people he had first attacked. The clearest personality that emerges is that of an immature, rash young man unable to handle the criticism and pressure that his own actions provoked.

The *Courant*'s targets responded in several ways. Friends of the Puritan clergymen and Dr. Boylston defended them. The most devastating charge they made was that the *Courant*'s writers were the equivalent of the sacriligious and infamous Hell-Fire Club of England,[137] and the *Courant*'s writers went to great lengths to refute the charge.[138] Although the pro-inoculators sometimes used rash language, in general they were more restrained than the *Courant* writers. Since the key public issue in the controversy was inoculation, they argued for the efficacy of the practice, relying more on medical knowledge and facts. They produced a number of pamphlets and newspaper articles attempting to show the evidence in support of inoculation. In the long run, their argument worked because of the demonstrated success of the practice. Especially effective was their use of mortality figures. Dr. Boylston reported that he had inoculated 242 patients, of whom six died.[139] The fatality rate for inoculees was 2.5 percent, whereas among people who contracted the disease naturally, the rate was 14.8 percent.

Another ingredient in the pro-inoculators' ultimate victory was their demonstrated concern for those who contracted smallpox. At the height of the epidemic, when scores were dying weekly and the *Courant* was running satire on women's fashions, the clergy were visiting the sick, providing the poor with firewood for the winter, trying their best to comfort them and their families, and in their visits facing the possibility of contracting a disease themselves.[140]

With the end of the smallpox epidemic, the *New-England Courant* lost the public issue that had provided the immediate cause for its founding. Although the public did not immediately change its views on inoculation, Mather and Boylston soon were to be widely recognized for their achievements, the first in preventive medicine in the English-speaking world. By contrast, the *Courant*'s opposition to the practice made its writers look credulous and reactionary. Thereafter, it resorted to petty personal attacks on Cotton Mather and other Puritan clergy. Its original High Church group no longer wrote for the paper, but theological differences with Puritanism continued to provide material for its group of newer contributors. Although promising readers to be bright and entertaining, it continued to publish for only four years after the smallpox epidemic ended, outlived by both the *Boston Gazette* and the *Boston News-Letter*.

The main reason for the *Courant*'s quick death was the unpopularity of Anglicanism in Boston. Even though for a time the inoculation hysteria had led to outrage against the Puritan clergy, Puritanism remained the faith of the vast majority of the populace. The continuing arguments of Anglicanism's most belligerent advocates, that no other church had any validity, annoyed rather than persuaded. Because of that narrow view, combined with the Anglican Church's ties to the British monarchy, Anglicanism made itself repugnant to most Massachusetts inhabitants.[141] Although the *Courant* stayed away from arguing the unpopular dogma of Anglican preeminence, it did take positions that Anglican authorities held. One, for example, was the large amount of space it devoted in late 1722 to the defection to Anglicanism of the Congregational administrators of Yale College. In a town as overwhelmingly Puritan as Boston was, the *Courant*'s position was far from popular.

The *Courant* also suffered when its methods were contrasted with those of its opponents. The *Courant*'s writers and its critics described the paper in many ways, but one word they did not use was "moderation." With an avowed purpose of "expos[ing] the Vices and Follies" of people with whom it disagreed, the paper was unlikely to set an example of propriety. The objects of its darts, on the other hand, while sometimes responding in kind, tried to resist meanness and pettiness. Cotton Mather, as the most obvious example of their temperate approach, left in his diary frequent reminders to himself to "Exercise . . . a forgiving Spirit."[142] In the passion of the smallpox epidemic, some newspaper readers may have welcomed the *Courant*'s language, but in calmer times they recognized the superior value of the opponents' moderation.

Likewise, the genuine concern that Mather and other pro-inoculators showed for those suffering with smallpox spotlighted the *Courant*'s writers' egocentric and querulous nature. While the *Courant* published lampoons, the clergy were working with the sick and the poor.[143] The due regard Bostonians had for Mather's benevolence was attested to best, in terms of the *Courant*, when Benjamin Franklin near the end of his life told Mather's son, "I have always set a greater value on the character of a *doer of good*, than on any other kind of reputation; and if I have been, as you seem to think, a useful citizen, the public owes the advantage of it to that book [Mather's *Bonifacius*]."[144]

With his benevolence Mather combined the best mind in colonial America. The *Courant*'s aspersions, made during the inoculation controversy, that he was naive and ill-informed did not hold up in calmer times. His was the first colonial work to gain wide recognition in Europe. Upon his death in 1728, he was eulogized as the most learned mind and the most prolific writer the colonies had produced.

A large share of the blame for the death of the *Courant* can be placed, however, directly on the paper's operators. There is no reason to assume that Bostonians in the 1720s liked scurrility or awkward style any more than readers do today. The entire tenor of the *Courant* was off-key for it to be a popular or respected newspaper.[145] In the *Courant*'s early issues, essays and news items each occupied about half of its space (sometimes two pages and sometimes four per issue). The essays either attacked opponents, especially the Puritan clergy, or commented on contemporary behavior, such as male-female relationships. Some attacks were simply heavy-handed and direct, while others attempted to use satire for their ridicule.[146] Most of the essays come across as sarcastic, gratuitously insulting, unsophisticated in style, dull, and devoid of wit. In addressing issues, they tended to ignore facts and concentrate on minor points that opponents raised. Over time the essays decreased in number and finally disappeared, leaving the *Courant* as a compilation, like its competitors, of brief news items.

The characteristic that finally doomed the *Courant* was perhaps its own pretentiousness and hypocrisy, the exact features it condemned in the Puritan clergy. It opposed inoculation because the clergy favored it. Rather than consider the arguments for and against the practice out of a concern for saving lives from smallpox, it was more eager to attack. While hundreds of Boston residents were dying, it went on with its satire, its abusiveness, and its self-centeredness. Then, as the final paradox, it decried the clergy's sanctimony in berating other people's sins.

Benjamin Franklin provided evidence that the general public was getting annoyed with the *Courant* when it was less than a year and a half old. After the government ordered James to stop printing the newspaper because of his criticism of officials' slowness in pursuing pirates, he substituted Benjamin's name as printer beginning in the issue of February 4, 1723. Benjamin's salutatory address began: "Long has the press groaned in bringing forth an hateful brood of pamphlets, malicious scribbles and billingsgate-ribaldry." He described the new operator as having morals that were "clearly Christian" and as a "man of good temper, courteous Deportment, sound judgment, a mortal Hater of Nonsense, Foppery, Formality, and Endless Ceremony."

Benjamin Franklin, who wrote the youthful series of "Silence Dogood" letters for the *Courant*, remained with the paper only a short time until he seized the opportunity to escape his apprenticeship and fled Boston. The *Courant* from then on went downhill. No records exist of its circulation figures, but its advertising diminished. After the inoculation controversy ended, its share of advertising shrank to one-fifth of the total published in all three Boston newspapers.[147] No financial records of the *Courant* are available, but it does not appear from the advertising figures that James Franklin was doing well. He published the *Courant*'s final issue on June 25, 1726, and thereafter moved to Rhode Island.

Most of Boston's populace probably was happy to see the *Courant* go, but during its short life the newspaper left a mark on the town's journalism. The *News-Letter* and the *Gazette* had emphasized news, but the *Courant* devoted its space mainly to essays. Shortly after the *Courant*'s demise, Boston gave birth to a new newspaper, the *New-England Weekly Journal*, whose intentions were literary. It was, however, better at playing the role than the *Courant* had been, and neither was it guilty of the *Courant*'s excessive violations of moderation and tact. The newspaper enjoyed a considerably longer and more successful life, employing literary essays better than the *Courant* had and publishing works on science and history for the edification of colonial readers.

The printer Samuel Kneeland, a pious member of the Old South Church, and his pastor, the Reverend Thomas Prince, most likely conceived of the enterprise.[148] Prince then recruited his friend Mather Byles, nephew of Cotton Mather. Although only twenty years of age, Byles was already the colonies' best-known poet, and he agreed to join the newspaper as chief writer. The first issue of the *Weekly Journal*, published March 20, 1727, announced that several of the "most knowing and ingenious Gentlemen" in the colony had agreed to contribute material. They had "the happiness of a liberal Education," and some had improved their talents "by Travels into distant Countries."[149] The *Weekly Journal*'s group of writers was more respectable than the *Courant*'s club had been and came from the best traditions that the colony had to offer.

One of the men was the Reverend Prince, who was considered "the most learned scholar, with the exception of Cotton Mather, in New England."[150] During his entire ministerial career, he was a leading advocate of Puritanism in New England and a forceful opponent of Anglicans' continuing efforts to win a favored place for their church. His interests included history, geography, medicine, and science. He had been one of the advocates of inoculation during Boston's smallpox epidemic of 1721–1722, and he carried on his own experiments in medicine. His extensive collection of historical works and the latest books on science were later to become the nucleus for the Boston Public Library. He was at the forefront of marrying religious faith to natural science. He refuted the deistic belief that God stood distant from His creation, while he argued that the Holy Scriptures were "but very brief Abridgments of large Histories."[151] His special concerns dealt with cosmology, disease, natural disasters, and the role of the clergy as scientists. Along with his scientific endeavors, he was a prolific author of works on colonial and European history,[152] and he frequently published articles on geography in the *Weekly Journal*.

Admirers claimed that Mather Byles, who had turned twenty only one week before the newspaper appeared, was America's Alexander Pope.[153] His father having died shortly after Mather's first birthday, he came under the care and tutelage of his uncle Cotton Mather, who freely shared his encyclopedic knowledge. Byles became friends with Benjamin Franklin, another young visitor to the Mather study. At the age of fourteen he was ready for college, and his uncle enrolled him at Harvard, where he prepared for the ministry. While he was still a student, several of his poems, modeled after the extremely popular work of Pope, were published in London. By the time he graduated at the age of eighteen he had gained a reputation as the colonies' best poet and essayist.[154] His prose was noted for its use of pun.

Byles and Prince, assisted by Judge Samuel Danforth, a Harvard graduate whose interests were law, medicine, and science, provided original essays for the *Weekly Journal* for its first full year of operation.[155] Under their guidance, it devoted a substantial portion of its space to poetry, literary essays, and scholarly discussions of such subjects as geology, astronomy, and natural curiosities, mixed with short news items. It was characterized more by wit than diatribe, as the *New-England Courant* had been; and its purpose was information and entertainment rather than public controversy. Polemical discussion was not absent from its columns, as demonstrated in its first issue by a satire on Elisha Cooke and his "Brahmin Club." Generally, however, its tenor mirrored Byles's later description of an ideal clergyman, possessing "universal Knowledge . . . understand[ing of] the Controversies of the Polemical Systems . . . Good Taste for Writing," while being "truly Learned, without Pedantry; and truly Eloquent, without Stiffness and Affectation."[156] Over the years, the *Weekly Journal* took up a growing proportion of its space with news and other material reprinted from English newspapers and magazines. That approach made it successful enough to continue publishing until 1741, when Kneeland and his cousin Timothy Green purchased the Boston *Gazette* and merged the two papers.[157]

The *Weekly Journal*'s success encouraged Jeremy Gridley to found a paper based on the *Journal*'s formula, the *Weekly Rehearsal*, in 1731. Gridley was an assistant director of Boston's South Grammar School who had graduated from Harvard and had literary aspirations. Aimed at the "learned and polite," the *Rehearsal* was even more ambitious than the *Weekly Journal*. Before its first year was out, however, it had ceased publishing original essays and had become a journal of news. Gridley first hired John Draper[158] as his printer and then Thomas Fleet. The latter assumed proprietorship[159] on April 2, 1733, and changed the *Weekly Journal* from a literary journal to a news publication. In 1735, the enterprising Fleet discontinued using the name *Weekly Rehearsal* and began publication of a newspaper under the name of the *Boston Evening Post* the following week.

A native of England, Fleet was a moderate member of the Anglican King's Chapel and printed for authors of diverse views. Nevertheless, he was the printer of several of the most contentious religious tracts published in Boston. They included, among others, several works by the controversialist Checkley, tracts opposed to the evangelist George Whitefield, and a tract that originated the "Mayhew Controversy" in 1763 which centered on the argument that the Church of England should be the state-established church in the colonies.[160] In the *Weekly Rehearsal* and the *Evening Post*, Fleet published frequent criticisms of the non-Anglican clergy.[161]

Fleet's approach to printing with an ideological motive typified early newpaper publishing in Boston. By the time that he had entered the newspaper field, however, south of Boston in the colony of Pennsylvania, printers were taking a much more pragmatic approach. There, in the metropolis of Philadelphia, Andrew Bradford and Benjamin Franklin, the former *Courant* apprentice, were concentrating on the practical concerns of building their printing businesses. Whereas Boston publishing strove after lofty ideals, Philadelphia's printers were more interested in pursuing earthly gains.

NOTES

1. Dep. Gov. Thomas Danforth to Sir Henry Ashurst, April 1, 1690, quoted in Thomas Hutchinson (1711–1780), *The History of the Colony and Province of Massachusetts-Bay*, 2 vols. (Cambridge, Mass.: Harvard University Press, 1936), 1:337 n.

2. Since no study has concentrated on the suppression of *Publick Occurrences*, the most familiar assumptions about the action come mainly from general survey histories. George Henry Payne, for example, characterized Harris as a bold advocate of "humanity and progress" who opposed the "authorities" and "was an exceptional figure in the fight for a free press." Cotton Mather, Payne declared, "cried out against" *Publick Occurrences*. (*History of Journalism in the United States* [New York: D. Appleton & Company, 1920], 21, 22, 12, 30.) Frank Luther Mott described Harris as a publisher who "presumptuously . . . defied the . . . government" in a colony that was a "Puritan theocracy." (*American Journalism* [New York: Macmillan, 1941], 9, 18.) More recently Edwin and Michael Emery have described Harris as a "troublemaker" with "progressive views" and declared that "the Puritan clergy was scandalized" by the contents of *Publick Occurrences*. They equate the clergy with the "licensers" of the press. (*The Press and America*, 5th ed. [Englewood Cliffs, N.J.: Prentice-Hall, 1984], 28, 29, 30.) Sidney Kobre, in *The Development of the Colonial Newspaper* (Pittsburgh: Colonial Press, 1944), wrote that the "ruling governmental officials and the Puritan clergy did not like the tone" of the contents of *Publick Occurrences* (p. 16). Victor Hugo Paltsits has shown, however, that Cotton Mather, one of the most prominent Puritan clergymen, supported Harris's efforts. ("New Light on 'Publick Occurrences': America's First Newspaper," *American Antiquarian Society* [April 1949]: 75–88.) The best recent effort to deal with the *Publick Occurrences* episode is provided by Charles E. Clark's "The Newspapers of Provincial America" (*Proceedings of the American Antiquarian Society* 100 [1990]: 367–89). Although touching on a number of relevant factors, the article is unable to develop them fully owing to the breadth of the topics included in the study.

3. Harris is the subject of a number of brief, mainly encyclopedic biographies. They generally tend to be critical of him because of his strong anti-Catholic views. The fullest accounts of his life can be found in George Emery Littlefield, *Early Boston Booksellers, 1642–1711* (New York, 1900; reprint ed., New York: Burt Franklin, 1969), 147–93; Paul L. Ford, "Introduction" in Ford, ed., *The New England Primer . . .* (New York: Dodd, Mead, 1897); James Runcieman Sutherland, *The Restoration Newspaper and Its Development* (Cambridge, England: Cambridge University Press, 1986); and the Tory historian J. G. Muddiman's critical "Benjamin Harris, the First American Journalist," *Notes and Queries*, 20 August 1932, 129–33; 27 August 1932, 147–50; 3 September 1932, 166–70; 24 September 1932, 223; 15 October 1932, 273–74. Most biographies have concentrated mainly on Harris's English, rather than American, career. Most textbooks on American journalism history make passing references to him as the publisher of *Publick Occurrences*.

4. Anabaptism was a complicated movement with a variety of adherents who held to various beliefs. Most of them, however, had a combination of both social and religious concerns. On the nature of Anabaptism, see Thomas M. Lindsay, *A History of the Reformation* (New York: Charles Scribner's Sons, 1917), 430–45; and George Huntston Williams, ed., *Spiritual and Anabaptist Writers: Documents Illustrative of the Radical Reformation* (Philadelphia: Westminster Press, 1957), 19–27. In his Anabaptism, Benjamin Harris was violently anti-Catholic and gave particular emphasis to the role of faith in political affairs, where he was a staunch Whig and advocate of parliamentary rule.

5. John Dunton, *The Life and Errors of John Dunton* (London: printed for S. Malthus, 1705; reprint ed., New York: Garland Publishing, 1974), 293. In a letter to George Larkin, Dunton added that Harris's works, including the *Book of English Liberties* and the *Protestant Tutor*, had met strong opposition. The latter, Dunton declared, was "not at all relished by the Popish party, because it is the design of that little book to bring up children in an aversion to Popery." (Dunton to Larkin, 25 March 1686, *Letters from New England* [1687],

quoted in Littlefield, *Early Boston Booksellers*, 148.) Harris spoke of himself as being "vigorous" in arguing for his side. (*Intelligence Domestick and Foreign* [London], 14 May 1695.)

6. At the height of the struggle between Charles and the Whigs, Harris, at Shaftesbury's urging, in July 1679 began publication of the first Whig newspaper, *Domestick Intelligence*. The best discussion of the Whig-Tory newspaper battle is provided in Sutherland, *The Restoration Newspaper and Its Development*.

7. "Dissident Protestant" is a term that refers to Protestant churches opposed to the Church of England. Harris supported the Earl of Shaftesbury and the Whig parliament in their opposition to King Charles II, who, Protestants feared, had secretly converted to Catholicism. Harris helped to publicize Titus Oates's exposure of the so-called Popish Plot, a plan in which, Oates claimed, Roman Catholics planned to murder the king, set London afire, and massacre its inhabitants. Harris's accounts of the prosecutions and punishments of the alleged plotters may be found in the *Domestick Intelligence*, 7, 14, 17, and 22 July and 31 December 1679. He also printed broadsides, ballads, and tracts. Although Harris favored the punishments, including some executions, his treatment of them generally was more judicious than that of other newspaper supporters. Luttrell, however, noted that Harris's paper "gave great offense in many things to those in authority." (Narcissus Luttrell, *Narcissus Luttrell's Popish Plot Catalogues* [Oxford: Luttrell Society, 1956], 20.) Harris was ardent in advocating the efforts of the Whig parliament to exclude the Duke of York (James II), Charles's Catholic brother, from succession to the throne. (*Domestick Intelligence*, 3 February 1680; 4 and 7 January and 12 April 1681.) He also supported the rebellion of Charles's son, the Protestant Duke of Monmouth, aimed at obtaining the throne for himself. Accounts by Harris favorable of Monmouth may be found in the *Domestick Intelligence*, 17 July and 2 December 1679; 17 February 1680; and 7 January 1681. Harris was especially concerned with the disagreements between Parliament and the king over the Whigs' attempts to assure a Protestant succession. For accounts of the succession debate, see the *Domestick Intelligence*, 9 December 1679; 6, 9, and 16 January 1680; 11 and 29 January, 1 and 25 February, and 15 April 1681.

8. In 1680 it was discovered that he had been responsible for reprinting a tract entitled "An Appeal from the Country to the City," which supported the Whig parliament in its attempts to "redress the grievances of the subject[s]" of the king and advocated Monmouth's claims to the throne. (The original tract carried the title "An Appeal from the Country to the City, for the preservation of His Majesty's person, liberty, property and the Protestant religion. Salus populi suprema lex. Laopolis, London. Printed in the year 1679.") Within a few days, he was tried on a charge of "maliciously and designedly . . . scandaliz[ing] the King and Government." (*A Compleat Collection of State Trials* [London, 1719], 2:476.) This prosecution began while Harris was under indictment for publishing a report of formal legal charges against Chief Justice William Scroggs. (*Protestant [Domestick] Intelligence*, 20 January 1680.) The jury first found Harris guilty only of selling the pamphlet, but then, bullied by Scroggs, convicted him of all charges. The court sentenced him to be pilloried in public for one hour, fined £500, remanded to prison until he paid the fine, and bound to good behavior for three years. (This account of the trial is taken from the Tory London *Gazette*, 5–9 February 1680. Other references to Harris's indictment, trial, and punishment are included in Nathaniel Thompson's Tory *Domestick Intelligence*, 27 January and 7 February 1680; W. H. Hart, *Index Expurgatorius Anglicanus* [London, 1872], 206–8; *A Compleat Collection of State Trials*, 2:476–78; Narcissus Luttrell, *A Brief Historical Relation of State Affairs*, 2 vols. [Oxford, 1857], 1:34–36; and Dunton, *Life and Errors*, 294.) As Har-

ris stood in the pillory, according to a Whig writer, the public remained steadfast in its support of him, threatening anyone who might insult him. (Mary Anne Everett Greene, ed., *Calendar of State Papers, Domestic Series, of the Reign of Charles II, 1660–1685* [London: Longman, 1860], 1679–1680:397. For similar accounts of the support by his friends, see Luttrell, *Brief Historical Relation of State Affairs*, 1:34; and *A Compleat Collection of State Trials*, 2:560.) When the Whig parliament reconvened in October 1680, it had Harris released from prison, and he started up his newspaper again in December. The courts again prosecuted him in April 1681 for publication of the *Protestant Petition*, ordered him to cease publishing, jailed him for a year and a half, and ordered him to post security for his good behavior in the future. While Harris was facing these legal troubles, one of his foes printed a broadside claiming that his wife had been unfaithful. ("The Protestant CUCK-OLD: A New Ballad. Being a full and perfect Relation how B. H. the Protestant-News forger, caught his beloved Wife Ruth in ill Circumstances. To the Tune of Packingtons Pound; Or Timothy Dash the Scriveners Apprentice" [London: printed for Francis Smith, 1681].) Beginning in 1682, Charles, who had effectively taken authority from Parliament and who was now assisted by new Tory sheriffs, began a crackdown on opposition publishers. (*Moderate Intelligencer* [London], 23 October 1682.) In the summer of 1683, the government proceeded against Harris again for his publishing activities, but he managed to elude arrest. (Henry Muddiman [the leading Tory publisher], newsletter, 7 August 1683, quoted in J. G. Muddiman, "Benjamin Harris, the First American Journalist," 150.)

9. After returning to England in 1695, Harris gave this explanation of his reasons for leaving: "[U]pon all occasions I vigorously asserted the Laws and Liberties of England against the bold and open violators of both; which procured me so many and inveterate enemies that, to save my life and family from ruin, I was compell'd to be an exile from my native country" (*Intelligence Domestick and Foreign*, 14 May 1695). John Dunton gave this explanation: "Old England is now so uneasie a Place for honest Men, that those that can will seek out for another Countrey: And this I suppose is the Case of Mr. Benjamin Harris and the two Mr. Hows. . . . Mr. Ben Harris, you know, has been a noted Publick Man in England, and I think the Book of English Liberties that you [George Larkin] Printed, was done for him and Mr. How. No wonder then that in this Reign they meet with Enemies." (Dunton to Larkin, 25 March 1686, *Letters from New England* [1687], quoted in Littlefield, *Early Boston Booksellers*, 144.)

10. The other was Cambridge. George Emery Littlefield provides a chronology of colonial printing in *The Early Massachusetts Press 1678–1711* (1907; reprint, New York: Burt Franklin, 1969). For a useful overview of the printing-publishing environment in the colonies and in Boston in particular, see Charles A. Clark, "Boston and the Nurturing of Newspapers: Dimensions of the Cradle, 1690–1741," *New England Quarterly* 64 (1991): 243–71; and Clark, "The Newspapers of Provincial America."

11. The first edition carried the imprint "An Almanack for the Year of Our Lord MDCLXXXVII. By John Tulley. Boston. Printed by S. Green for Benjamin Harris: and are to be Sold at his Shop, by the Town Pump near the Change. 1687."

12. Mather's contribution to *Publick Occurrences* is discussed later. He also is believed to have provided material for Harris's most famous publication, *The New England Primer*.

13. Massachusetts Historical Society, *Collections* 3: 7, 148. This directive resembled the standard one that was later given to most colonial governors: "You shall take especial care that God Almighty BE devoutly and duly served THROUGHOUT your GOVERNMENT, the Book of Common Prayer as by law established read each Sunday and holy day, and the Blessed Sacrament administered ACCORDING to the rites of the Church of England." ["Pro-

tection and Encouragement of Established Churches"], *Royal Instructions to British Colonial Governors 1670–1776*, Leonard Woods Labaree, ed., 2 vols. (New York: D. Appleton-Century, 1935), 2:482.

14. The diarist Sewall recorded, " 'Twas a sad sight to see how full the street was with people gazing and moving to and fro, because they had not entrance into the house." (29 March 1687, *The Diary of Samuel Sewall, 1674–1729*, ed. M. Halsey Thomas [New York: Farrar, Straus & Giroux, 1973], 136.)

15. For details on the rebellion see David S. Lovejoy, *The Glorious Revolution in America* (New York: Harper & Row, 1972), particularly Chapter 13.

16. "The Plain Case Stated of Old—but Especially of New England. . . . Boston, Printed for and Sold by Benjamin Harris . . . 1688."

17. Harris shortly afterwards published a pamphlet favorably detailing the revolution: "An Account of the Late Revolutions in New-England by A.B." Boston: 1689. Reprinted in *The Andros Tracts: Being a Collection of Pamphlets and Official Papers . . .* , 6 vols. (Boston: Prince Society, 1868–1874), 6:189–201.

18. Edward Randolph to Boards of Trade, 5 September 1689, *Calendar of State Papers, Colonial Series. America and West Indies* (London), 13:#407.

19. "An Account of the Late Revolutions in New-England by A.B.," 189–201.

20. This and the following quotations are taken from *Publick Occurrences*.

21. Samuel Sewall, a member of the council, recorded on 25 September objections to the newspaper. *The Diary of Samuel Sewall*, 267.

22. It read: *"Whereas Some have lately presumed to Print and Disperse a Pamphlet, Entituled,* Publick Occurrences, Both Forreign and Domestick: Boston, Thursday, *Septemb. 25th,* 1690. *Without the least Privity or Countenance of Authority.*

"The Governour and Council having had the perusal of the said Pamphlet, and finding that therein is contained Reflections of a very high nature: As also sundry doubtful and uncertain Reports, do hereby manifest and declare their high Resentment and Disallowance of said Pamphlet, and Order that the same be Suppressed and called in; strickly [*sic*] forbidding any person or persons for the future to Set forth any thing in Print without License first obtained from those that are or shall be appointed by the Government to grant the same.

"By Order of the Governour & Council.

"Isaac Addington, Secr.

"Boston, September 29th. 1690"

This order is included in the *Early American Imprints* series issued by the American Antiquarian Society. It is reprinted in a number of secondary sources.

23. London *Gazette*, 6 May 1680. For the king's proclamation of the new policy, see the *Gazette* of 20 May. (The *Gazette* was the officially sanctioned government newspaper.)

24. ["Licensing of Printing Presses and Printing"], *Royal Instructions to British Colonial Governors 1670–1776*, 2:495. For similar instructions to the governor of New York, see *Documents Relating to the Colonial History of New York*, 3:548. See also Clyde Augustus Duniway, *The Development of Freedom of the Press in Massachusetts* (New York: Longmans, Green, & Co., 1906), 64–65.

25. *Council Records*, 2:111, quoted in Duniway, ibid., 65–66.

26. See William Pencak, *War, Politics, & Revolution in Provincial Massachusetts* (Boston: Northeastern University Press, 1981), 16–18, for a fuller discussion of the chaotic situation.

27. Bradstreet to Lords of Trade (London), 26 October 1689, *Calendar of State Papers, Colonial*, #513.

28. *Andros Tracts*, xxxv, 77–78.

29. 25 September 1690, *The Diary of Samuel Sewall*, 267. Similarly, the Reverend Cotton Mather wrote three weeks later that there were people who "Disliked the two Passages of the *Maqua's* and the monster *Louis* [XIV]." (Mather to John Cotton, 17 October 1690, Kenneth Silverman, comp., *Selected Letters of Cotton Mather* [Baton Rouge: Louisiana State University Press, 1971], 27.) See also Paltsits, "New Light on 'Publick Occurrences'," 88. Although not a member of the governing council, Mather was well acquainted with a number of the members and might easily have received his information from one of them.

30. Mather to John Cotton, 17 October 1690, in Silverman, *Selected Letters of Cotton Mather*, 27.

31. The events to which this passage referred occurred within the context of the War of the League of Augsburg against France. In 1688 France had invaded the Palatinate. Holland; the German states of Bavaria, Saxony, and the Palitinate; England; Spain; and other European states allied themselves against France. To help finance the war, the Catholic Louis XIV expropriated the property of French Protestants, who then rebelled against this and other repression which Louis had imposed on them. Some exiled Huguenots joined the forces fighting France. The tardiness of the news available to colonists is apparent from the fact that the Duke of Lorraine had died April 18, five months before *Publick Occurrences* carried this report of his military activities.

32. Mather to John Cotton, 17 October 1690, in Silverman, *Selected Letters of Cotton Mather*, 27–28. Mather's describing the offending statement as "a Remote Report" suggests that it was, indeed, the incest charge that bothered the council.

33. 2 October 1690, *The Diary of Samuel Sewall*, 268.

34. Mather to John Cotton, 17 October 1690, in Paltsits, "New Light on 'Publick Occurrences'," 87–88.

35. Along with Bradstreet and the Cooke supporters, the council included Samuel Appleton, Humphrey Davy, Daniel Gookin, John Hawthorne, Elisha Hutchinson, Robert Pike, John Richards, James Russell, Nathaniel Saltonstall, Samuel Sewall, and William Stoughton (William H. Whitmore, *The Massachusetts Civil List for the Colonial and Provincial Periods, 1630–1774* [1870; reprint ed., Baltimore: Genealogical Publishing Co., 1969], 26). This council membership was the one elected in 1686, which, after the overthrow of the Andros government, temporarily reassumed office until a new charter could be issued for Massachusetts. Several were members of Cotton Mather's North Church. (*Diary of Cotton Mather, 1681–1708*, 29 April 1692.) Among the membership, close friends of the Mathers included Hutchinson, Richards (Cotton Mather's father-in-law), Sewall, and possibly Appleton, Gookin, Hawthorne, Pike, Russell, Saltonstall, and Stoughton. Samuel Nowell, one of the councilors elected in 1686 and a close friend of Increase Mather, had died in 1688 while staying in England as a Massachusetts agent with Mather.

36. The complex nature of the political alignments involved with the charter issues is discussed in Pencak, *War, Politics, & Revolution in Provincial Massachusetts*, 13–22. See also Michael G. Hall, *The Last American Puritan: The Life of Increase Mather, 1639–1723* (Middletown, Conn.: Wesleyan University Press, 1988), Chapter 7 and especially pp. 224–54.

37. For accounts of Cooke's stance, see Hall, ibid., 250–53; Kenneth Ballard Murdock, *Increase Mather: The Foremost American Puritan* (Cambridge, Mass.: Harvard University Press, 1925), 246ff, 333–34; and Gerard B. Warden, *Boston, 1689–1776* (Boston: Little, Brown, 1970), 39–57. The latter provides a highly favorable treatment of Cooke.

38. *Calendar of State Papers, America and West Indies*, Vol. 14: 23 March 1693.

39. See Hutchinson, *The History of . . . Massachusetts-Bay*, 1:414; John Gorham Palfrey, *History of New England* (Boston: Little, Brown, 1858–1890), iv, 86; and Richard R. Johnson, *Adjustment to Empire: The New England Colonies, 1675–1715* (New Brunswick, N.J.: Rutgers University Press, 1981), 229–30.

40. Hutchinson, ibid., 11. See also Murdock, *Increase Mather*, 249–53. Of this group, only Gookin can be identified as a possible friend of the Mathers.

41. *Diary of Cotton Mather,* 29 April 1692.

42. Pertinent details on Bradstreet's career are contained in *Calendar of State Papers, Colonial, 1681–1685*, 1445, 1589; *Massachusetts Records*, 4, pt. I: 37; and *Clarendon State Papers* (Bodleian Library, Oxford), 10–12.

43. *The Pynchon Papers, Vol. I: Letters of John Pynchon, 1654–1700*, ed. Carl Bridenbaugh (Boston: Colonial Society of Massachusetts, 1982), xv–xxi and passim. See also *Diary of Samuel Sewall*, 138.

44. In 1691 Harris formed a printing partnership with John Allen, nephew of the pastor of Boston's First Church, and that firm became the most prolific in the town. After two years, the Harris-Allen partnership dissolved. In 1693 Harris bought the lone printing press in Boston and became Boston's largest printer of books and continued as its leading bookseller, with his shop and coffeehouse serving as a favorite spot for ministers and other prominent Bostonians. Harris's most enduring fame rested, however, with *The New England Primer*. Using an approach similar to Harris's earlier *Protestant Tutor*, the *Primer* employed moral and religious lessons to teach generations of American children to read. Although there has been some disagreement as to the authorship of the *Primer*, persuasive evidence that Harris deserves the credit is provided in Ford, ed., *The New England Primer*. Also, see Littlefield, *Early Boston Booksellers*, 154–59.

45. "Monthly Observations and Predictions for this present year." Boston, 1692.

46. Phips's declaration naming Harris public printer is quoted in *An Historical Digest of the Provincial Press*, compiled and edited under the direction of Lyman Horace Weeks and Edwin M. Bacon (Boston: Society for Americana, 1911), 26.

47. Harris was one of a growing group of publishers who began newspapers with the expiration of the Licensing Act in 1695. See Raymond Asbury, "The Renewal of the Licensing Act in 1693 and its Lapse in 1695," *The Library* 33 (1978): 296–322. The punishment for what one published, however, remained severe.

48. *Intelligence Domestick and Foreign*, 14 May 1695. His contemporary publisher, John Dunton, stated that on his return from the colonies he "continued Ben. Harris still" and praised him in these words: "his Conversation is general (but never Impertinent) and his Wit pliable to all Inventions. But yet his VANITY (if he has any) gives no *Alloy* to his Wit, and is no more than might justly Spring from conscious Vertue; and I do him but Justice in this part of his Character, for in once travelling with him from *Bury Fair*, I found him to be the most Ingenious and Inocent, [sic] Companion, that I had ever met with." (Dunton, *Life and Errors*, 294.)

49. Luttrell, 11 July 1695, *A Brief Historical Relation of State Affairs*, 3:495; *Calendar of State Papers, Domestic Series,* Entry Book 77.

50. The fullest argument for the population thesis is made by the sociologist-historian Sidney Kobre in *The Development of the Colonial Newspaper*, 10–13.

51. Colonial population figures are not always precise. The most detailed source, however, is Evarts B. Greene and Virginia D. Harrington, *American Population Before the Federal Census of 1790* (New York: Columbia University Press, 1932).

52. For a forceful essay arguing this point, see Clifford K. Shipton, "The Locus of Authority in Colonial Massachusetts," 136–48 in George A. Bilias, *Law and Authority in Colo-*

nial America: Selected Essays (Barre, Mass.: Barre Publishers, 1965). Also, see Chapter 3 of this book.

53. Increase Mather wrote, for example, "Believe not those that would perswade you that Schools of Learning, Colleges, &c. are Antichristianism, or late Popish Inventions. . . . Books are Talents in God's service. They are a weariness to the flesh, but a testimony to be produced." (Mather, *Some Important Truths*, 1674.) Norwood Marion Cole ("The Origin and Development of Town-School Education in Colonial Massachusetts, 1635–1775," Ed.D. diss., University of Washington, 1957) concluded that Puritan leaders believed that education was "essential . . . for good citizenship and world accomplishment."

54. See Kenneth B. Murdock, *Literature and Theology in Colonial New England* (Cambridge, Mass.: Harvard University Press, 1949) for an elaboration of the publishing and writing activities of the Puritans.

55. The Congregational churches that the Puritans set up were marked, according to religion historian John Winthrop Platner, by six main structural features: "[1] the independence of the local congregation, [2] its constitution under a covenant, [3] the absence of an episcopate, [4] the conception of the ministry as exercising delegated powers of a purely spiritual nature, [5] reliance upon the sole authority of Scripture, and [6] the separation of church and state." Platner, "The Congregationalists," in *The Religious History of New England* (Cambridge, Mass.: Harvard University Press, 1917), 7.

56. Duniway, whose *The Development of Freedom of the Press in Massachusetts* is the most detailed study on the subject, takes the view that Puritans were intolerant. One is tempted to conclude, however, that he neglects the statements Puritans made supportive of freedom and exaggerates those that can be read as suppressive.

57. Cotton Mather, for example, wrote, "No man may be Persecuted, because he is Conscienciously not of the same Religious Opinion, with those that are uppermost." (*Theopolis Americana* [Boston, 1692], 29.)

58. Walter Franklin Terris found that Puritans never inflicted punishment that exceeded that allowed by the common law. Terris, "The Right to Speak: Massachusetts, 1628–1685" (Ph.D. diss., Northwestern University, 1962).

59. *New England Historical and Genealogical Register* 8:137.

60. Ibid., 135. Ministers, a contemporary Anglican wrote, because of their increasing numbers "began to carry a face of danger. For how unsafe must it be thought both to Church and State, to suffer such a Constant Recepticle of discontented, dangerous, and schismatical Persons, to grow up so fast." (*Cyprianus Anglicus*, 347, quoted in Arthur Lyon Cross, *The Anglican Episcopate and the American Colonies* [Cambridge, Mass.: Harvard University Press, 1924], 21.)

61. Rushworth, *Historical Collections,* quoted in Cross, *The Anglican Episcopate and the American Colonies*, 21.

62. Punishment could include "imprisonments or other restraints, or . . . loss of life or members, according as the quality of the offence shall require." Hutchinson, *The History of the Colony and Province of Massachusetts-Bay*, 1:503.

63. *Cyprianus Anglicus* 347, quoted in Cross, *The Anglican Episcopate and the American Colonies*, 21.

64. Quoted in George Hodges, "The Episcopalians," in *The Religious History of New England*, 213.

65. *Diary of Cotton Mather*, 11 November 1686.

66. "I humbly represent to your Grace," he wrote, "that the three meeting houses [Puritan churches] in Boston might pay twenty shillings a week a piece, out of their contribu-

tions, towards defraying our Church charges." (Hutchinson, *Collections*, 549, quoted in Cobb, *The Rise of Religious Liberty in America*, 231.)

67. In Randolph's earlier proposal to the Puritans themselves, they had rebuffed him. "They tell us," he explained to the king, "those that hire him [the Anglican minister] must maintain him, as they maintain their own minister, by contributions." Hutchinson, *Collections*, 549, ibid.

68. "The humble Address of Your Majesty's most loyal and dutiful Subjects of the Church of England in Boston ... ," quoted in Henry Wilder Foote, *Annals of King's Chapel*, 2 vols. (Boston: Little, Brown, & Co., 1896), 1:102.

69. The fullest study of Dudley is Everett Kimball's sympathetic *The Public Life of Joseph Dudley* (New York: Longmans, Green, & Co., 1911).

70. *Diary of Cotton Mather*, 16 June 1702.

71. For church membership, see Foote, *Annals of King's Chapel*, 1:173. Samuel Sewall recorded in his diary for 19 December 1699 that Campbell was one of seventeen guests at a dinner in Sewall's home attended by, among others, Gov. Richard Coote, Earl of Bellomont. Campbell's appointment as constable is recorded in Robert Francis Seybolt, *The Town Officials of Colonial Boston 1634–1775* (Cambridge, Mass.: Harvard University Press, 1939), 97.

72. Massachusetts Historical Society, *Collections*, 3d series, 7:55–58, 60, 65.

73. The grant was given to Thomas Neale, a favorite of the royal court. He never visited the colonies and appointed the Scotchman Andrew Hamilton his deputy to administer the system. The grant is reprinted in Harry Myron Konweiser, *Colonial and Revolutionary Posts; A History of the American Postal Systems* (Richmond, Va.: Dietz Printing Co., 1931), 16–17. See also Wesley Everett Rich, *The History of the United States Post Office to the Year 1829* (Cambridge, Mass.: Harvard University Press, 1924), 12ff.

74. Littlefield, *Early Boston Booksellers*, 134.

75. The initial issue of the *News-Letter* carried this notice: "[A]ll Persons who have any Houses, Lands, Tenements, Farmes, Ships, Vessels, Goods, Wares, or Merchandizers, &c. to be sold or Lett: or Servants Runaway: or Goods Stoll or Lost may have the same Inserted at a Reasonable Rate; from Twelve Pence to Five Shillings, and not to exceed: Who may agree with Nicholas Boone for the same at his shop next door to Major Davis's." 17–24 April 1704. Boone's association with the newspaper lasted four weeks.

76. Samuel Sewall, the Boston judge, may have been typical. Frequently in his diary he made references to the content of the *News-Letter* and his having sent the paper to acquaintances. See *Diary of Samuel Sewall*, 12 June 1704; 19 September 1706; 3 April, 30 September 1708; 6 December 1714; 4 June, 15 October 1716; 18 March 1717; 11 March, 10 June 1718; 14 April, 7 November 1720; 18 November 1721; 19 March 1722. See also Silverman, *Selected Letters of Cotton Mather*, 86, 219.

77. *News-Letter*, 5 November, 2 December 1706; 23–30 April 1711; 3–10 August 1719. For a detailed discussion of transatlantic travel and its impact on news, see Ian K. Steele, *The English Atlantic 1675–1740: An Exploration of Communication and Community* (New York: Oxford University Press, 1986).

78. The *News-Letter* of 5 February 1705 contained this description of the road conditions: "The East post came in Saturday ... who says there is no Travailing with horses, especially beyond Newbury, but with snow-shoes, which our people do much use now that never did before. The West post likewise says't is very bad Travailing."

79. Cotton Mather, 15 October 1716, in Silverman, *Selected Letters of Cotton Mather*, 219.

80. *News-Letter,* 14 August 1721.

81. The paper continued to carry that legend during the administrations of Gov. Elizeus Burges (1715–1716) and Samuel Shute (1716–1728) until 11 July 1720 after Campbell was replaced as postmaster in 1719.

82. The *News-Letter* of 29 October 1705 had accused Quakers of misrepresenting conditions in Massachusetts. Campbell promised to the Council of Trade and Plantations in London that in the future he would "carefully forbear reflecting upon those people, who I observe are very well and easily treated by the Government here, and for ought I know are peaceable in their places." Campbell to Wm. Popple, Council of Trade and Plantations, *Calendar of State Papers, Colonial,* Vol. 23 (1706–1708), #510.

83. Some evidence of relationships can be gathered from pallbearer services. Campbell served at the funerals of Roger Lawson, John Foy, John Frizell, and Sarah Williams. At Campbell's funeral, the pallbearers were Samuel Sewall, Nathaniel Byfield, Andrew Belcher, Daniel Oliver, Judge John Menzies, and Capt. Steel (John or Thomas). *Diary of Samuel Sewall,* 13 April 1709; 25 November 1716; 15 April 1723; 7 March 1727; 4 March 1728. All except Sewall and Oliver were members of King's Chapel, and several were prominent Dudley allies.

84. In 1708, on the fourth anniversary of the newspaper's publication, Campbell published this dun: "This being the last day of the fourth Quarter of this Letter of Intelligence: All persons in Town and Country, who have not already paid for this fourth Year, are hereby desired now to pay or send it in." See issue of 10 August 1719 for a lengthy recitation of Campbell's troubles.

85. Cotton Mather, 2 May 1706, in Silverman, *Selected Letters of Cotton Mather,* 77.

86. Mather to Stephen Sewall, 13 December 1707, and Mather to Stephen Sewall (?), 30 January 1706, in Silverman, *Selected Letters of Cotton Mather,* 70 and 76.

87. *News-Letter,* 10 August 1719.

88. *News-Letter,* 14 August 1721.

89. The fourth-anniversary issue of the *News-Letter* carried this vow: "[T]hough there has not as yet a competent number appeared to take it annually so as to enable the Undertaker to carry it on effectually; yet he is still willing to proceed with it, if those Gentlemen that have this last year lent their helping hand to support it, continue still of the same mind another year, in hopes that those who have hitherto been backward to promote such a Publick Good will at last set in with it." *News-Letter,* 24 April 1708.

90. It is unclear whether Brooker simply refused to allow Campbell to use the mail, or whether Campbell could not afford to pay postage fees from the newspaper's income when his franking privilege ended with his postmastership. In the Boston *Gazette* of 21 December 1719, Brooker stated that some subscribers to the *News-Letter* "have been prevented from having their newspaper sent them by the post, ever since Mr. Campbell was removed from being postmaster."

91. Brooker (1719–1720), Musgrave (1720–1726), Thomas Lewis (1726–1727), Henry Marshall (1727–1732), and John Boydell (1732–1734). Boydell retained the paper after leaving the postmastership. Upon his death, the *Gazette* became the property of his heirs. They operated it until 1741, when they sold it to the printers Samuel Kneeland and Bartholomew Green. When Boydell decided to keep the *Gazette,* his successor as postmaster, Ellis Huske, began the *Post-Boy* (1734).

92. *News-Letter,* 26 December 1720.

93. His lampoon of the *New-England Courant* on 28 August 1721, for example, turned the *Courant*'s criticism that Campbell was dull.

94. *Gazette*, 21 December 1719; 11 and 25 January 1720.

95. In the *News-Letter* of 4 January 1720, Campbell implied that Brooker was a drunkard, and in the following issue of the *Gazette* (11 January) Brooker said that he had been kind in reporting that Campbell had been "removed" from the postmastership rather than "turned out." Almost nothing of a personal nature is known about Brooker. The diarist Samuel Sewall recorded in October 1720 that a Boston resident named Brooker "was a little before sent to prison for Debt." (*Diary of Samuel Sewall*, 24 October 1720.) His nomination for the postmastership apparently was turned down by the London office.

96. Elizeus Burges replaced Joseph Dudley as governor in 1715 but served only one year. Shute succeeded him and served until the end of 1728, although he was *in absentia* in England after 1722.

97. See *Diary of Cotton Mather*, 7 July, 18 August, 17 November 1721.

98. Mather to Lt. Gov. William Dummer, *Diary of Cotton Mather*, 1 April 1724.

99. The speech is reprinted in *News-Letter*, 9 November 1719.

100. *General Court Records*, 10:417, quoted in Duniway, *The Development of Freedom of the Press in Massachusetts*, 87.

101. *Sewall Papers*, 3: 238–39, quoted in Duniway, ibid., 88.

102. Quoted in Hutchinson, *The History of the Colony and Province of Massachusetts-Bay*, 185–86. In illustrating the types of material that should be punished, the House referred to a pamphlet entitled *News from Robinson Crusoe's Island* (Boston, 1720) written by Cotton Mather, which criticized Elisha Cooke, Increase Mather's old adversary and now a leader of the anti-Shute faction in the House. Cotton Mather was concerned that the House's wrangling to assert its power might endanger Massachusetts's charter.

103. The episodes involving the governor and the House are recounted in detail in Hutchinson, ibid., 163–218, and Duniway, *The Development of Freedom of the Press in Massachusetts*, 79–96.

104. After eighteen years of publishing the paper, Campbell finally sold it to Bartholomew Green in January 1722. Campbell was appointed a justice of the peace the following year (Whitmore, *Massachusetts Civil List*, 127) and died in 1724. (Samuel Sewall recorded that "Monday night, March 4th. Mr. John Campbell dies, who writ the first News-Letter. Was inter'd Saturday March 9th." *Diary of Samuel Sewall*, 1060.) Green, a pious Congregationalist, tried to make the newspaper impartial and temperate. (The 7 March 1723 issue of the *News-Letter* contained a detailed statement of his editorial philosophy.) Green published the paper until his death on 28 December 1732, altering the title to the *Weekly News-Letter* with the first issue of January 1727. He also abandoned Campbell's philosophy of publishing a "Thread of occurrences" no matter how old the news and began to publish weekly the latest intelligence he could procure. Under Green's successors, the *News-Letter* became a supporter of the royal authorities and a straightforward, innocuous journal. It was one of the longest-lived newspapers in colonial America, spanning seventy-two years. On 4 January 1733, John Draper, Green's son-in-law, took over as publisher. Under him, the *News-Letter* kept its strongly Christian tone, colonial news and advertising increased, and letters from readers were added. On his death in 1762, the paper was transferred to his son, Richard. He renamed it the *Massachusetts Gazette*. On his death in 1774, his widow, Margaret Draper, assumed control and, in partnership with John Boyle and then John Howe, continued publication until 1776, when, with the evacuation of British troops from Boston, the newspaper finally ceased.

105. "The Religion of Jesus Christ the only True Religion; or, A Short and Easie METHOD with the DEISTS, Wherein the Certainty Of The Christian Religion Is demon-

strated by Infallible Proof from FOUR RULES, which are Incompatible to any Imposture that ever yet has been, or that can possibly be . . . ," Boston: printed by Thomas Fleet, 1719; "Choice Dialogues Between A Godly Minister and an Honest Country Man Concerning Election and Predestination," Boston, 1720; "Modest Proof of the Order & Government Settled by Christ and his Apostles in the Church," Boston, 1723; "A Defence of . . . A Modest Proof," Boston, 1724; "A DISCOURSE Shewing Who is a true Pastor of the Church of Christ," and "The Speech of Mr. John Checkley upon his Tryal at Boston, in New England, for publishing the Short and Easy Method with the Deists, etc.," London, 1730. Clergy who had not been ordained by proper bishopic authority, Checkley declared, acted as a "vile Prostitution" of the true priesthood of Christ. They "outdid the wickedness of [the Jews] in persecuting" the apostles. "[E]very Tag, Rag, and Long-tail call themselves [Christ's] Ambassadors . . . by a call from the People! Good God!—Good God!—How has the Priesthood been vilify'd of late!" Appendix to Charles Leslie, "A Short and Easie Method," 8th ed. (Boston and London, 1723).

106. Dr. William Douglass to Cadwallader Colden, 13 February 1728 and 18 March 1728, in Massachusetts Historical Society, *Collections* 4, 2:179 and 182.

107. The epidemic of 1677–1678 took the lives of 700 residents, 12 percent of the town's population.

108. "The Destroyer," Mather recorded in his diary for 16 July, "being enraged at the Proposal of any Thing, that may rescue the Lives of our poor People from him, has taken a strange Possession of the People on this Occasion. They rave, they rail, they blaspheme; they talk not only like Ideots but also like Franticks, And not only the Physician who began the Experiment, but I also am an Object of their Fury; their furious Obloquies and Invectives." (*Diary of Cotton Mather*, 16 July 1721.) There is no record of exactly what proportion of the population was opposed to his effort; but only about 240 of Boston's 10,500 residents received inoculation, and the strength of the opposition suggests that it was a substantial majority.

109. Mather wrote that "our unhappy physicians . . . poisoned and bewitched our people with a blind rage." Mather to Hans Sloane, 10 March 1722, in Silverman, *Selected Letters of Cotton Mather*, 347. He wrote in 1724 that the physicians played "the part of butchers or tools for the destroyer to our perishing people, and with envious and horrid insinuations infuriated the world against [Boylston]." Mather to Dr. James Jurin, 15 December 1724, in Silverman, *Selected Letters of Cotton Mather*, 402.

110. Later, after the epidemic had abated, Cotton Mather wrote Dr. James Jurin of the Royal Society of London that the opposition had been contrived by a "political or ecclesiastical" party whose main purpose was to discredit the Puritan clergy. "It is with the utmost indignation," he wrote, "that some have sometimes beheld the practise made a mere party business, and a Jacobite, or High-flying party, counting themselves bound in duty to their party to decry it, or perhaps the party disaffected unto such and such persons of public station and merit, under the obligations of a party to decline it." 21 May 1723, in Silverman, *Selected Letters of Cotton Mather*, 361.

111. Dr. Boylston was a member of Brattle Street Church, and the others were all clergymen in dissenting Protestant churches. Along with Increase and Cotton Mather, they were Benjamin Colman and his associate pastor William Cooper of Brattle Street Church, Thomas Prince of Old South Church, and John Webb of New North Church.

112. *Boston News-Letter*, 24 July 1721. Although most media historians have argued that it was the *New-England Courant* which opened the "crusade" against inoculation, an examination of the already existing newspapers and pamphlets makes it obvious that an ac-

rimonious public debate was already being waged before the *Courant* appeared. For an elaboration of this point, see C. Edward Wilson, "The Boston Inoculation Controversy: A Revisionist Interpretation," *Journalism History* 7: 1 (1980): 16–19, 40. It also is clear from entries in Cotton Mather's diary that acrimony existed several weeks before the *Courant* began publication. The *Courant's* writers merely jumped on the bandwagon.

113. Boston *Gazette*, 31 July 1721.

114. See, for example, William Cooper, *A Letter to a Friend in the Country, Attempting a Solution to the Scruples & Objections of a Conscientious or Religious Nature, Commonly Made against the New Way of Receiving the Small-Pox* (Boston, 1721).

115. It quickly became clear in the small town of Boston, where such things were easy to discover, who the operators were. Two weeks following the appearance of the *Courant*, a letter published in the *News-Letter* lamented that "what likewise troubles us is, That it goes Currant [*sic*] among the People, that the Practitioners of Physick in Boston, who exert themselves in discovering the Evil of Inoculation and its Tendencies (several of whom we know to be Gentlemen by Birth, Learning, Education, Probity and good Manners that abhors any ill Action) are said, esteem'd and reputed to be the Authors of that Flagicious and wicked paper." *Boston News-Letter*, 21 August 1721. Checkley referred to himself as author of the newspaper. Judging from printing arrangements for pamphlets and other publications of the time, the arrangement provided either for Checkley to pay Franklin for the printing or for Franklin to print the *Courant* at his own expense and retain whatever income he could derive through copy sales and advertising. Considering that Franklin continued to print the newspaper after Checkley's departure, it appears likely that the second arrangement was the one he and Checkley entered into. Wm. David Sloan, "The New-England Courant: Voice of Anglicanism," provides more information on the operations of the newspaper. (*American Journalism* 7 [1991]: 108–41.) The fullest research into who founded the *Courant* has been done by Carolyn Garrett Cline ("The Hell-Fire Club: A Study of the Men Who Founded the New England Courant and the Inoculation Dispute They Fathered." Master's thesis, Indiana University, 1976). She concluded that Checkley and Douglass deserve the credit.

116. *New-England Courant*, 7 August 1721. The authorship of articles in the first forty-three issues of the *Courant* is indicated in Benjamin Franklin's marked files.

117. Douglass, "Inoculation of the Small-Pox as practised in Boston . . . ," Boston, 1722; Douglass, *Boston News-Letter*, 17 July 1721; Douglass to Cadwallader Colden, 20 February 1722, Massachusetts Historical Society, *Collections*, 4th series, 2:164. Benjamin Colman, pastor of Brattle Street Church, later claimed that some physicians opposed inoculation "because it would have saved the Town Thousands of pounds that is now in their pockets." Douglass himself, explaining to a colleague in the medical field why he had not had time to record his medical observations, wrote that he found it "more natural to begin by reducing my smallpox accounts into bills and notes for the improvment of my purse." Quoted in Kenneth Silverman, *The Life and Times of Cotton Mather* (New York: Harper & Row, 1984), 345.

118. In a letter to a medical colleague in England, he referred contemptuously to "a certain credulous Preacher of this place called Mather . . . [who] preached up Inoculation." (Douglass to Dr. Alexander Stuart, 24 September 1721, Royal Society, quoted in Otho T. Beall, Jr. and Richard H. Shryock, *Cotton Mather: First Significant Figure in American Medicine* [Baltimore: Johns Hopkins Press, 1954], 112.)

119. The *Courant*, wrote a grandson of Increase Mather, was "written on purpose to destroy the Religion of the Country." (*Boston Gazette*, 8 January 1722. This letter frequently

has been attributed to fifteen-year-old Mather Byles, but it more likely was written by his older cousin Samuel Mather.)

120. *New-England Courant*, 21 August 1721.

121. Douglass wrote anti-inoculation articles in the 7, 14, and 21 August 1721 and four other issues of the *Courant* beginning in January of 1722.

122. *New-England Courant*, 22 January 1722.

123. The Reverend Thomas Harward to Bishop of London, 19 July 1731, in Foote, *Annals of King's Chapel*, 414.

124. *New-England Courant*, 14 August and 11 December 1721.

125. *New-England Courant*, 21 August 1721.

126. James Franklin, recounting the episode, in *New-England Courant*, 27 November 1721.

127. *New-England Courant*, 15 January 1722. Checkley's Puritan opponents, however, continued to believe for some time that he directed the *Courant*, as shown by a letter from Mather Byles, a grandson of Increase Mather, published in the 8 January 1722 issue of the *Boston Gazette*. Checkley, although no longer writing for the *Courant*, increased his other activities aimed at promoting the Anglican cause and, as one of his critics declared, "with an uncharitable and bitter Zeal contend[ed] for the Episcopal Pre-eminence" (Edward Wigglesworth, *Sober Remarks on a Book late reprinted at Boston, Entituled "A Modest Proof of the Order and Government settled by Christ and his Apostles in the Church"* [Boston, 1724]). Almost incessantly contentious, he provoked his opponents inside and outside the Anglican church.

128. *New-England Courant*, 28 August 1721.

129. J. A. Leo Lemay identified him as "Nathaniel Gardner" but provided no explanation of how he arrived at that conclusion. See Lemay, "Franklin and the Autobiography," in *Eighteenth-Century Studies: A Journal of Literature and the Arts* 1, no. 2 (1967): 193. Because of the assumption that "Mr. Gardner" was a man several years older than Benjamin Franklin, Lemay apparently had in mind a Nathaniel Gardner who was born in 1681. He apparently died at an early age, however, for his parents, John and Susanna, had another son born in 1692 and named that son "Nathaniel." (*A Report of the Record Commissioners Containing Boston Births, Baptisms, Marriages, and Deaths, 1630–1699* [Boston: Rockwell & Churchill, 1883].) The latter would have been twenty-nine years old in 1721, which probably would not have led Benjamin Franklin to refer to him as "Mr." when he did not use that form of address for the other *Courant* writers. Since, with a minor exception, the other *Courant* writers were Anglicans, it seems reasonable to guess that "Mr. Gardner" also was a member of King's Chapel, perhaps John Gardiner, Esq., or the Reverend James Gardiner, both of whom may have had the educational background to compose written material for the *Courant* and who died in 1738 and 1739, respectively, suggesting that in 1721 they may have been old enough to inspire Benjamin Franklin to call them "Mr."

130. All but three of the paper's contributors can be identified as Anglicans. Of the ten writers who, along with the original High Church group, contributed to the paper between the fourth and forty-third issues, six can be identified as members of King's Chapel, one can be identified as an Anglican and therefore a probable member of King's Chapel, one ("Mr. Gardner") cannot be identified, and one writer perhaps was not an Anglican, although he was a friend of the Reverend Henry Harris. The other writer was sixteen-year-old Benjamin Franklin, whose first "Silence Dogood" essay was printed in the issue of 2 April 1722. Since he was an apprentice in James's shop, religious motives may have been irrelevant to

his desire to write for the *Courant*. Eliminating his articles and those by Gardner, one can calculate that about nine-tenths of the remainder were written by people who can be identified as members of King's Chapel. Along with Gardner and James and Benjamin Franklin, the writers were the following: Matthew Adams, a member of King's Chapel; Thomas Fleet, the printer for King's Chapel and member of the church; Thomas Lane, a member of and generous contributor to King's Chapel; John Williams, a member of King's Chapel and proprietor of a "tobacco-cellar"; John Eyre, a member of King's Chapel whose parents had been members of the Old South Church; John Valentine, a leading lawyer in Boston and a warden at King's Chapel; and Capt. Christopher Taylor, whose church membership is unknown but who owned the rental housing where Harris lived.

131. *New-England Courant*, 4 September 1721.

132. Of all items, approximately fifty in number, related to inoculation that the *Courant* published by the end of 1721, only one, a report from London, was slightly favorable toward the practice.

133. *Boston Gazette*, 15 January 1722. The author probably was Mather Byles, nephew of Cotton Mather.

134. *Diary of Cotton Mather*, 9 December 1721. Typical of the religious ridicule was James Franklin's "Essay against Hypocrites" in the issue of 14 January 1723. The only notable change in the *Courant*'s content after the fourth issue was more occasional publication of essays on public and private manners. A favorite topic was relationships between spouses. The *Courant* also published a considerable number of attacks on Philip Musgrave, who in 1720 had taken the printing contract for the *Boston Gazette* from James Franklin and given it to Samuel Kneeland.

135. When challenged for the *Courant*'s attacks on the Puritan clergy, he responded that he was confident of his own salvation. "I expect and Hope to appear before God," he declared, "with safety in the Righteousness of Christ." (*New-England Courant*, 29 January 1722.) In responding to a charge that he used the *Courant* to "Banter and Abuse the Ministers of God," he asserted that "*My own pastors* are as faithful to their Flock as [Cotton Mather] can be to his" (italics added for emphasis). (*New-England Courant*, 27 November 1721.) King's Chapel records contain this account of funds donated for improvements: "A List of the Well disposed Gentlemen and other Persons that Contributed their assistance for the Building a Gallery, a New Pulpit, and adorning the Kings Chappel in Boston, and the Paving before it in the Year 1718." The list includes "J: Franklyn," who along with "Capt. Richd. Quick" made a contribution of £10. (King's Chapel records, reprinted in Foote, *Annals of King's Chapel*, 265.)

136. Benjamin Franklin, *Autobiography* (New York: Modern Library, 1944), 24–25.

137. *Boston News-Letter*, 21 August 1721.

138. There is no evidence to suggest, as some historians have stated, that the *Courant* writers accepted the name as a badge of pride. To the contrary, the *Courant*'s response indicates that the charge was unsettling to them. See, for example, *New-England Courant*, 28 August 1721 and 15 January 1722.

139. Zabdiel Boylston, *Historical Account*, 50, in John B. Blake, "The Inoculation Controversy in Boston: 1721–1722," *New England Quarterly* 25, no. 4 (1952): 496–97.

140. For examples, see *Diary of Cotton Mather*, 26 and 29 September; 7, 8, 14, 15, and 16 October 1721.

141. Of the eleven Boston churches in 1721, seven were Congregational and one was Anglican. The other three were Anabaptist, Quaker, and Huguenot. Material relating to the comparative popularity of Anglicanism and Puritanism can be found in such works as John

Frederick Woolverton, *Colonial Anglicanism in North America* (Detroit: Wayne State University Press, 1984).

142. Although the main target of the town's anger and the *Courant's* sarcasm, Mather was cautious about using intemperate language. When he succumbed to the human desire to retort publicly, he usually chided himself. Even as the *Courant's* contumely was most vicious at the height of the smallpox epidemic, he wrote, "I must beware, that I don't harbour or admitt, any Tendency towards the least Wish of Evil, unto such as may have displeased me. . . . I must beware, that upon the Provocations . . . my Speeches be not intemperate and unadvised, or any Ebullitions of Impatience; and Trespasses upon the Rules of Meekness and Wisdome. I must beware, that I don't spread any false Reports." (*Diary of Cotton Mather*, 3 December 1721. For similar statements during the same period, see diary entries of 29 October, 3 and 12 November, 3, 17, and 24 December 1721; and 14 and 17 January 1722.)

143. Writing of Dr. Boylston almost three years after the epidemic, Mather observed that "When the rest of our doctors . . . with horrid insinuations infuriated the world against him, this worthy man had the courage and conscience to enter upon the practise [of inoculation]; and . . . he alone, with the blessing of Heaven, saved the lives of I think several hundreds. . . . With an admirable patience he slighted the allatrations of a self-destroying people, and the satisfaction of having done good unto mankind made him a noble compensation for all the trouble he met withal." Mather to Dr. James Jurin, 15 December 1724, in Silverman, *Selected Letters of Cotton Mather*, 402. In a similar tone, he wrote the same correspondent: "[W]e that cry with a loud voice to them, *Do yourselves no harm*, and show them how to keep themselves from the paths of the destroyer, are conscious of nothing but of a pity for mankind under the rebukes of God . . . a desire to have our neighbors *do well*, and a solicitude for a better state of the world. And all the obloquies and outrages we suffer for our charity, we shall entertain as persecutions for a good cause, which will not want its recompenses." Mather to Jurin, 21 May 1723, in Silverman, *Selected Letters of Cotton Mather*, 367.

144. Quoted in Ronald W. Clark, *Benjamin Franklin: A Biography* (New York: Random House, 1983), 19.

145. In his autobiography, Benjamin Franklin recalled that the High Church group of writers for the *Courant* said their compositions were received with "approbation" (p. 23). Several considerations related to their reports make it virtually impossible to verify or refute their accuracy. It may be that during the inoculation controversy a considerable number of members of the public agreed with the *Courant's* approach, or that the *Courant's* writers repeated comments from selected readers. On the other hand, it also is possible that Cotton Mather's later comment was true that anti-inoculators were of such disreputable character that some people came to support inoculation because "they were ashamed of their [anti-inoculaton] company." Mather to Dr. James Jurin, 21 May 1723, in Silverman, *Selected Letters of Cotton Mather*, 362.

146. John Eyre's essay from 23 October 1721, criticizing Cotton Mather for dealing with medical matters, provides an example: "Doubtless, a Clergyman . . . when he shall degenerate from his own Calling, and fall into the Intriegues of State and Time-Serving, he becomes a Devil; and from a Star in the Firma-Ment [*sic*] of Heaven, he becomes a sooty Coal in the blackest Hell, and receiveth the greatest damnation."

147. During the inoculation controversy, from August 1721 through May 1722, it averaged 7.9 column inches of advertising per issue. That gave it 30 percent of the advertising published in Boston's three newspapers. The *Gazette* averaged 10.4 column inches for 40

percent of the total, and the *News-Letter* 7.8 inches for 30 percent. After the May 1722 issue, the *Courant*'s advertising shrank to an average of 3.8 inches per issue and 21 percent of the total. While all three newspapers published ads for pamphlets and other items they printed and sold, such house-ads accounted for a larger amount of space in the *Courant* than in either the *Gazette* or the *News-Letter*.

148. Kneeland had served as printer of the *Boston Gazette* from 1720 to 1727. When Henry Marshall became postmaster in 1727, he replaced Kneeland with another printer, Bartholomew Green, Jr., the son of the printer of the *News-Letter*. Kneeland had become a prolific publisher of books, tracts, pamphlets, and broadsides, making him one of Boston's most successful printers. Most of his publishing was of religious material, with Cotton Mather his most frequent author. Although he printed for Anglican authors also, the works that he published for himself were devoutly Puritan. With the *Weekly Journal*, Kneeland became the first Boston printer to originate a newspaper. Three months later, he took on his cousin Timothy Green (son of the printer Bartholomew Green) as his printing partner, and thereafter they served as co-publishers of the paper. Green apparently was the partner mainly responsible for the publication, while Kneeland devoted his attention to operating a bookstore.

149. *Weekly Journal*, 20 March 1727.

150. The Reverend Charles Chauncy, quoted in "Thomas Prince," *National Cyclopaedia of American Biography*, 7:144. See similar remarks in Massachusetts Historical Society, *Collections*, 1st series, 10:164.

151. Thomas Prince, *Christ Abolishing Death* (Boston, 1736), 7. For a discussion of Prince's approach, see Theodore Hornberger, "The 'Science' of Thomas Prince," *New England Quarterly* 9 (1936): 26–43. For a broader account of Prince's career, see Clifford Shipton, ed., *Sibley's Harvard Graduates* (Boston: Massachusetts Historical Society, 1937), 5:341–68; John Edward Van de Wetering, "Thomas Prince: Puritan Polemicist," Ph.D. diss., University of Washington, 1959; and Maxine Schorr Van de Wetering, "The New England Clergy and the Development of Scientific Professionalism," Ph.D. diss., University of Washington, 1970.

152. His most ambitious historical work was the *Chronological History of New-England*, 2 vols. (Boston, 1736–1755), and he was co-founder with his son of *Christian History*, the colonies' first religious periodical.

153. For Byles, the fullest biographies are Arthur Wentworth Hamilton Eaton, *The Famous Mather Byles: The Noted Boston Tory Preacher, Poet, and Wit, 1707–1788* (Boston: W. A. Butterfield, 1914) and "Mather Byles" in Shipton, *Sibley's Harvard Graduates*, 7:464–93.

154. He still enjoys a stature surpassed only by Anne Bradstreet and Edward Taylor among poets that Puritan America produced. Of the three, only Byles was born in the American colonies. His collected works included *Poems on Several Occasions* (1744) and *A Collection of Poems by Several Hands* (1745).

155. Biographical details on Danforth are provided in "Samuel Danforth" in Shipton, *Sibley's Harvard Graduates*, 6:80–86.

156. Mather Byles, *The Man of God* (New London, 1758). The most detailed discussion of the *Weekly Journal*'s literary tone is found in Elizabeth Christine Cook, *Literary Influences in Colonial Newspapers 1704–1750* (New York: Columbia University Press, 1912), 31–56.

157. The merged paper continued until 1752.

158. Draper was the son-in-law of Bartholomew Green and on 4 January 1733, assumed proprietorship of the *Boston News-Letter* upon Green's death.

159. Gridley soon began practicing law and became one of New England's most promi-nent attorneys. In the 1740s he was connected with the literary *American Magazine*. For bi-ographical material, see "Jeremiah Gridley" in Shipton, *Sibley's Harvard Graduates*, 7:518–30.

160. Fleet was the printer, for example, of Checkley's reprints of Charles Leslie's ". . . A Short and Easie METHOD with the Deists . . ." (1719) and "A Choice Dialogue . . ." (1719); Checkley's "A Defense of a Book . . . Entituled a Modest Proof of the Order" (1724); "A Vin-dication of the Practice of the Antient [*sic*] *Christians*, As well as the *Church of England*, and other *Reformed* Churches, in the Observation of Christmas Day . . ." (1731, by the Anglican missionary in Marblehead); Edward Wigglesworth's anti-Whitefield tract, "Some Distin-guishing Characters of the Extraordinary and Ordinary Ministers of the Church of Christ" (1754); and Anglican missionary East Apthorp's "Considerations on the Institution and Con-duct of the Society for the Propagation of the Gospel in Foreign Parts . . ." (1763). Fleet also served as the printer for King's Chapel. (King's Chapel ledger notes for 1748, reprinted in Foote, *Annals of King's Chapel*, 102.)

161. Paradoxically, he also was one of the most vociferous of printers in claiming that he was impartial and always willing to print both sides of an issue. See Chapter 2 of this book.

2

=====

The Philadelphia Press, 1719–1735

While serving an apprenticeship in England under Andrew Sowle, William Bradford not only learned the trade of printing. He also adopted the Quaker faith of his master. Then he married his daughter. Through Sowle, he was introduced to George Fox, the founder of Quakerism, and William Penn, a Quaker leader and the founder of Pennsylvania. When the Society of Friends began searching for a printer for the North American colony, Bradford moved there in 1685 with his press, a letter from Fox commending him as a "civil [and] . . . sober young man," and the personal endorsement of Penn.[1] In 1685 he produced the first printed item in Pennsylvania, an almanac, *Kalendarium Pennsilvaniense, or, American Messenger*. In a preface to readers, Bradford wrote, "Hereby understand that after great Charge and Trouble, I have brought that great Art and Mystery of Printing into this part of America believing it may be of great service to you in several respects, hoping to find Encouragement, not only in this Almanack, but what else I shall enter upon for the use and service of the Inhabitants of these Parts."[2]

Bradford soon prospered by printing books for the Friends, almanacs, and other tracts. Dissatisfied, however, with restraints that the governing council attempted to place on him, in 1689 he threatened to leave the colony and return to England. Thereupon the Quaker Quarterly Meeting asked him to reconsider and agreed to pay him an annual salary of £40 and to buy at least 200 copies of any book that he "printed by the advice of Friends."[3]

William Bradford was a practical man bent on practical ends. He could be quick and forceful, though, in arguing a controversial point, and his livelihood sometimes suffered as a consequence. Despite his brushes with controversy, practicality was the distinguishing characteristic of early Philadelphia journalism. It ran in the Bradford family, which had a long career in printing. Likewise, Pennsylvania's most notable printer, Benjamin Franklin, was remarkable for his ability to get on in the world. He and the Bradfords held to definite ideas, to be sure, in politics and religion, those two arenas of great import in eighteenth-century America. They were usually careful, however, not to let politics or religion endanger their printing business.

One of the rare occasions that William Bradford allowed his sentiments to over-rule his business judgment was in the controversy created in the 1690s by George Keith's attacks on Quaker dogma. An itinerant Quaker preacher, Keith believed that the Quaker emphasis on an "inner Light" in spiritual matters was not strong enough to maintain the faith in the wilderness conditions of America. As a solu-tion, he proposed requiring a confession of faith from individuals seeking to be-come Quakers, the election of deacons and elders, more order and discipline in church meetings, and a greater reliance on the Bible and less on the inner light. Or-thodox Quakers brought a charge of heresy against Keith, thinking it would silence him. Instead, it fired the controversy.

Only nominally Quaker, Bradford readily came to Keith's aid when approached to print several trenchant and scurrilous tracts that the radical reformer had writ-ten. Although an adherent to Keith's views, Bradford had printed for the opposing side also, but he balked when the opposition attempted to dissuade him from pub-lishing further for Keith. In September 1692 Quaker officials arrested him and confiscated his printing equipment. The formal charge was that he had published seditious material that Keith had written.[4] Confined in jail, Bradford asked the Quaker court for a speedy trial. At the hearing to consider his request, the court also charged that he had published material without indicating the name of the printer, as the judges claimed was required by law.[5] They postponed his trial, how-ever, until the next session of court, six months later, in March 1693.

At the trial, Bradford argued that the jury should be allowed to determine not only the facts but the law also—that is, not simply that the material had been pub-lished but that it was indeed illegal. This contention predated the same argument made famous by the trial of John Peter Zenger in New York more than forty years later. As to whether the publication violated the law, Bradford argued that it was "not Seditious, but wholly relating to a Religious Difference." The Quaker judges were divided on the role of the jury. David Lloyd, who was later to become the leader of the popular party in Pennsylvania politics, countered Bradford's interpre-tation, arguing that the jury was not to "meddle with" the question of whether the material was seditious, but had only to decide whether Bradford had printed it, and that "the Bench is to judge whether it is a Seditious Paper." In his formal charge to the jury, however, Judge Samuel Jennings, speaking on behalf of the court, indi-cated that it was up to the jury, not the judges, to determine whether the publication was seditious. Jennings instructed the jury to decide on three points: whether the publication had "a tendency to the weakening of the hands of the Magistrates, and encouragement of Wickedness," whether it tended "to the Disturbance of the Peace," and whether Bradford had printed it "without putting his Name to it."[6]

The jury split on a verdict, with the nine Quaker members voting for conviction and the three non-Quakers for acquittal on the basis of inadequate evidence.[7] Bradford then requested that he be discharged from prison and his printing equipment returned, but the court denied both requests and bound him over for retrial. Nevertheless, he was released and, on appeal to the governor's council, succeeded in getting his equipment returned to him in April 1693.[8]

Almost immediately, he decided to leave Pennsylvania after the Society of Friends ordered that in the future he would be required to get prior approval before printing anything.[9] He moved to New York, which had been attempting to secure an official government printer, and received the appointment. Along with Keith, he converted to Anglicanism and continued to print anti-Quaker tracts for distribution in Pennsylvania.

In his New York establishment, Bradford took on his son, Andrew, as an apprentice to learn the trade of printing. By 1709 the two were in partnership, and soon Andrew began looking for a location to set up business on his own. He approached the colony of Rhode Island, and its assembly offered him the position of official printer.[10] However, William interposed, and Andrew continued to work with him.

Pennsylvania, in the meantime, had been without an accomplished printer since William Bradford's departure. The Quakers had imported a press from England and arranged with Reinier Jansen to manage it. Having immigrated to the colony in 1698, Jansen, a lace-maker, had no experience in printing. Following his death in late 1705, his son, Joseph Reyniers, carried on the printing business for a short time, and then Jacob Taylor took charge of the press.[11]

William Bradford still owned large tracts of land and had business interests in Pennsylvania.[12] At his encouragement, in 1712 Andrew returned there, certain that the colony, although still Quaker, offered him opportunities in the printing trade and in other fields. The Quakers had purchased their own press in hopes of attracting a printer, and Andrew worked out an arrangement to set up shop in the upper floor of the Quaker schoolhouse where the press was located, paying the Meeting £10 annually for the use of the room, the press, and its materials. He printed his first work—a book containing the laws of the colony—for £100, with the paper being provided by the colony. He never purchased his own press, continuing, instead, to rent the Quakers' equipment even after moving to another location.[13]

With a studious eye on his business, he prospered at printing and in other affairs. In 1717 he was made a freeman of the colony. Alongside his printing establishment, he opened a store in which he sold stationery and a variety of items such as tea, chocolate, and other imports. He was not a prolific printer, but he managed to run a sound business, branching out to the other middle colonies for work. In 1719 he began publication of Philadelphia's first newspaper, the *American Weekly Mercury*. He ventured into other profitable enterprises as well. Like his father, he speculated in land, leasing and later purchasing two large city lots. In 1724, he moved to Second Street to a house owned by Richard Hill, a prominent Quaker with whom Bradford had frequently had business dealings. Now, as he neared forty years of age, his importance in local business affairs, the church, and government quickly rose. In 1726 he joined with several other local businessmen in starting the Durham Iron Company. That same year he was appointed to the vestry of the local Anglican congregation, Christ Church. The following year he was elected to the city council, and in 1728 was appointed postmaster. By the 1730s his printing business was hardly more than a sideline, with most of his income coming from the iron company, the shop, the *Mercury*, and land speculation.

As with the rest of his printing, Bradford started the *American Weekly Mercury* mainly as a business venture. His decision to start the newspaper may have resulted simply from the fact that his store and printing shop became a center of unofficial inquiry where lost and found articles could be claimed or deposited, where information about runaway slaves was sought, and where other queries about purchasing slaves, land, and houses were made. Such inquiries formed the majority of advertisements placed in the *Mercury*.

Bradford began the paper as a partnership with John Copson, publishing the first issue December 22, 1719. Copson bowed out in 1721 to sell insurance. In 1720, Bradford's father, William, became associated with the *Mercury* and remained as a partner until he began his own newspaper, the *New York Gazette*, in 1725.

In the first issue of the *Mercury*, Bradford declared that the paper would "contain an Impartial account of Transactions, in the Several States of Europe, America, etc." and asked readers to "encourage so useful an undertaking" by ordering subscriptions.[14] Two months later he published his next statement of purpose, and it emphasized the promotion of trade through the publication of advertising.[15]

Bradford's approach to the *Mercury* reflected his own character; he was a businessman who for the most part kept his political and religious sentiments in the background. His main motivation was to operate a financially successful enterprise. In the *Mercury*, therefore, there was little of the burning idealism and ideology found in the newspapers of Boston. Although he was a prominent Anglican and a supporter of the proprietary party in government affairs, as a businessman he willingly printed material for Quakers and the popular party. Although partisan, he generally avoided controversy. Responding in 1734 to some irreverent remarks in Benjamin Franklin's competing *Pennsylvania Gazette*, Bradford avowed that his own motive was to publish material that had "a tendency to raise and refine human kind; to remove it as far as possible from the unthinking brute; to moderate and subdue men's unruly appetites; to remind them of the dignity of their nature; to awaken and improve their superior faculties and direct them to their noblest objects."[16] On those rare occasions when he did offend the government, the offensive material usually had been written by other people, and the government accepted that explanation as mitigating Bradford's culpability.

Bradford's main objective in the content of the *Mercury* was not to offer opinion or literary fare but to provide news. For the most part, the news was European, especially English. Except for official government news or especially sensational occurrences, the *Mercury*, like the typical colonial newspaper, overlooked local events, on the assumption that local readers would already have heard about them by word of mouth before the paper was published. It chose, instead, to emphasize news that was unknown to most local readers—news to which the publisher had special access through correspondence and other newspapers. In selecting foreign news to publish, Bradford catered to the mercantile class and concentrated on wars, financial activities, international politics, religion, and British domestic affairs. English events appealed especially to Bradford and his American readers because of their strong ties to the mother country and because of their common language.

The *Mercury*'s coverage of intercolonial events and issues, as compared with the thoroughness of its foreign news, was uneven and fragmentary. Domestic news seemed to be published with little attempt to provide a coherent or cohesive narrative. Yet with time, the space devoted to such news steadily increased. Both the internal development of the colonies and the increase in the number of newspapers contributed to this heightened interest in domestic news. Colonial growth meant more news was occurring, and the proliferation of newspapers resulted in more published accounts upon which other journals could draw.

As sources of news, the *Mercury* relied primarily on other newspapers, on letters, and on word of mouth. Bradford subscribed to a variety of English and colonial newspapers and drew upon them frequently.[17] During the first few years of publication, the *Mercury* drew mainly on foreign newspapers; but in the 1730s— probably as a result of the increased number of American newspapers in existence—it made increasing use of domestic journals. He could also depend on many local residents to share with him the contents of private letters that they received containing news of events in other locales. Like any other person, he also occasionally picked up pieces of information through conversations with acquaintances and individuals who visited his office.

Whatever the source of news might be, it presented difficulties for the *Mercury*, as it did as well for other colonial newspapers. The main problem was unpredictable delays in the delivery of newspapers and correspondence. Boston, the colonial metropolis closest to England along the shipping lanes, welcomed, on average, eleven news-bearing ships a month. The more southerly the port, however, the fewer ships docked there. New York City, for example, the next major city south of Boston, averaged only four ships per month,[18] while passages to Philadelphia averaged only two.[19] During the good weather months of March through November, the number of passages increased, but from December through February they were often cut to one or none per month. With the passage of time, however, and the continuing growth of the colonies, the number of ships steadily increased, regularity of passage became more predictable, and publication of foreign news fluctuated less.

Intercolonial news traveled overland through the post. Nevertheless, like the transatlantic shipping, it, too, faced frequent interruptions and delays. The dependability of the post was critical for the *Mercury* not only for domestic news, but for foreign news as well, since many of the foreign newspapers that Bradford relied on were shipped to Boston or New York and then sent by mail to Philadelphia.

The postal service that linked the three towns after 1693 worked efficiently, but problems commonly occurred during bad winter weather, sometimes to the extent of delaying publication of the *Mercury*. Bradford frequently apologized to readers, usually explaining that the cause of the tardy publication was the failure or slowness of the mail to arrive.[20]

Because of the transportation system, nonlocal news normally was several weeks old when published. Although news from New York reached Philadelphia within a week, accounts from Boston took ten to twenty days. News from South Carolina normally took close to two months. Foreign news appeared in the *Mercury* not less than two months after it occurred, and often much later. News from the European continent, for example, might require a month before being published in an English newspaper, and three more months might pass before that newspaper account reached Philadelphia. Delays of six months were not rare.[21] Because of the time needed for an English ship to cross the Atlantic to Maryland and Virginia, newspapers in the those colonies normally published news at least twelve weeks after it occurred.

Colonial readers were not, however, impatient with the slowness of news. A lapse of four weeks between a European occurrence and its publication was accepted as normal. Speeds for postriders on good roads could average six miles per hour, while carrier wagons averaged three. Contemporaries greeted with astonishment feats that reduced the time of overland travel between cities to a matter of days. When in 1745, for example, an English horsemen, upon a wager, rode a 213-mile course in less than 12½ hours, thus averaging seventeen miles per hour, an amazed observer recorded: "This is deservedly reckon'd the greatest performance of its kind ever known. Several thousand Pounds were laid on this affair; and the roads for many miles lined with people to see him pass."[22]

Other than news, during the first decade of publication, the *Mercury* carried little else. Literary content was virtually nonexistent. It was not until publication of the *Busy-Body* essays in 1728 that any continuing effort was made to include such material. Afterwards, however, essays on a variety of topics and locally written poetry occupied a substantial amount of space.

Because of its strong news content, the *Mercury* circulated widely; and as other newspapers were started in other colonies, it served as an often-quoted source of domestic material for them. In starting the paper, Bradford apparently assumed that he was producing a journal not for Philadelphia alone but for Pennsylvania and the other middle colonies. He arranged with vendors in other towns to distribute the *Mercury*, and it circulated as far north as Rhode Island and Massachusetts and south into Virginia. Bradford's appointment as postmaster in 1728 assisted the intercolonial character of the paper, giving him greater access to information sent through the mail and allowing him to send the *Mercury* through the post free of charge.[23]

Typographically, it was clean, and its printing quality good. Its pages measured approximately 7½ inches by 12 inches, divided into two columns, a conventional design for colonial newspapers. In its early years it normally included only two pages, but a larger size of four pages was not uncommon. In 1728 the four-page size became the standard, and in 1734 the *Mercury* often printed six pages. Obtaining paper from the Rittenhouse mill in Philadelphia, which William Bradford had assisted in starting,[24] the *Mercury* printed on a higher quality stock than most newspapers; and it was prosperous enough to allow Bradford to replace worn type with new. It also stood out from other colonial newspapers with its comparatively generous use of woodcut illustrations.

Bradford stayed away from controversial topics and generally avoided political issues until the 1730s. For the most part, he avoided offending authorities, despite the fact that as a devout Anglican he had fundamental doctrinal differences with the dominant Quakers. While maintaining a low ideological profile, he nevertheless let his sympathies affect some decisions. In religious matters, he opposed Catholicism and deism; and in politics, he backed the proprietary party. Composed principally of merchants and large landowners, that faction supported the Penn family and its authority in the affairs of Pennsylvania.

On two occasions, the governor's council ordered him to appear for printing material it found reprehensible. In 1721, his print shop issued an anonymous pamphlet criticizing Pennsylvania's troubled economic situation.[25] He compounded the crime by printing in the *Mercury* a statement expressing the hope that the colonial assembly might find a remedy "to revive the dying Credit of this Province, and restore us to our former happy Circumstances."[26] The writers proposed issuing paper money, a solution favored by the popular party.

Upon questioning by the council, Bradford "declared that He knew nothing of the printing or publishing the said Pamphlet." Reprimanded for the paragraph in the *Mercury*, he explained that "it was inserted by his Journey-Man, who composed the said Paper, without his Knowledge, and that He was very sorry for it, and for which he humbly submitted himself and ask'd Pardon of the Govr. and the Board."[27] Since the proprietary party opposed paper money, it is likely that Bradford also held that view; and his excuse of ignorance of the publications appears credible.

Bradford encountered the anger of the council again in 1729 for publication of another contribution written by someone else. In it, Number 31 of the *Busy-Body* essays, the writer,[28] calling himself "Brutus, or Cassius, or both," advised readers to "exert our Selves for Liberty and don't Tamely sit by and allow any Part of it to be wrested from us by any Man, or Combination of Men whatsoever."[29] The essay being published on the eve of an election hotly contested between the proprietary and popular parties, the council reacted to it as an attack on the government cloaked in the guise of a general comment on liberty. Two days after publication, the council concluded that the essay was seditious and ordered that Bradford be arrested. Upon questioning him, the council decided that he, "without considering or knowing its Tendency, printed it as he did other Papers in his Mercury." His "ignorance therefore, gave some Abatement to the prosecution." Nevertheless, "he was . . . committed, & then Bound over to the Court."[30]

Despite the impending prosecution, the next issue of the *Mercury* carried a follow-up essay on a similar theme, preceded by the caveat that the essay had been written prior to the council action. The writer of the introduction assured readers that the essay was not intended to reflect on the council action.[31] In publishing the second essay, Bradford took probably the brashest step of his entire newspaper career; but there is no record that the council initiated any proceeding against him for it, or that he was ever prosecuted for the first essay.

Bradford published many other contributions that contained opinions, but he was ordinarily on safe ground. In 1723 when James Franklin of Boston, printer of the *New-England Courant*, had his own troubles with authorities, Bradford printed an outspoken attack, evidently written by a *Courant* contributor, on the Massachusetts Assembly.[32] Even though the Pennsylvania council had forbidden him to publish criticism of other colonial governments, he was not reprimanded. Quaker officials in Pennsylvania had no particular desire to protect Puritan authorities in Massachusetts. The episode would be barely worth noticing except for the fact that a number of writers have cited it as evidence of one printer, Bradford, supporting the endangered press freedom of another. The argument implies that printers shared a common commitment to press freedom and that Puritan theocrats were some of its severest enemies. The stronger tie between Bradford and Franklin, however, was their common Anglican faith. Bradford's opposition to Puritanism was his reason for printing the diatribe.

Of more substance was the *Mercury*'s prolonged feud with Andrew Hamilton, the Philadelphia politician and lawyer who was to gain international fame with his defense in the Zenger trial in 1735. The dispute saw print first in 1733, when writers in the *Mercury* opposed Hamilton's bid for election to the Pennsylvania assembly. The origins of the dispute are uncertain, but partisanship played the most apparent role. Hamilton had been appointed attorney general by Governor William Keith in 1717 and, continually gaining political power, was elected to the assembly in 1727. There he opposed Keith, who had become a leading voice of the popular party, and became a political crony of the new governor, Patrick Gordon, and of James Logan, the most prominent member of the proprietary party. Gordon and Hamilton split in 1732, however, beginning with quarrels between their children. The following year, Gordon blamed Hamilton for the assembly's opposition to his reappointment as governor. He determined to get him defeated in the elections that year.[33]

Pamphlets and the columns of the *Mercury* served as the outlets for attacks on Hamilton. Most were written by his opponents in the proprietary party. They carried on the attack mostly in personal terms, claiming that Hamilton, a deist, was irreligious; that the circumstances of his birth and even his name were uncertain; that he had gained his wealth by cheating widows and orphans; that he had managed the colony's financial affairs to his own advantage; that he was profane and abusive; that he gained political advantage only by bullying; and that he was a tyrannical despot. Given Bradford's character, he may have considered each of those arguments a strong reason to oppose Hamilton. The fact that Hamilton had been a member of the council and served as its attorney general when the council reprimanded Bradford in 1721 added a personal reason for Bradford to dislike him. The feud with Hamilton continued for several years, and Bradford questioned the sincerity of Hamilton's devotion to liberty on numerous occasions. Years later, when Hamilton

was gaining fame for his role in the Zenger trial, Bradford and his contributors reminded readers that Hamilton had helped suppress the *Mercury*'s freedom, and they
pointed to the 1721 council action as evidence of Hamilton's hypocrisy.[34]

Aligned with Hamilton against Bradford and the proprietary interests was
Philadelphia's other newspaper publisher, the young Benjamin Franklin. Having
escaped his Boston apprenticeship to his tyrannical brother James,[35] he had gone
first to New York City and then was directed by the printer William Bradford to
Philadelphia, where it was thought he might find work with William's son Andrew.
Upon arriving in Philadelphia in October 1723, Franklin found, however, that Andrew had no position to offer. The latter suggested that Franklin inquire of another
of Philadelphia's printers, Samuel Keimer, recently immigrated from England.

Keimer, born in 1688, had been reared by devout parents of the dissident Presbyterian faith. His mother had impressed on him the great importance of morality,
proper conduct, truth, and justice. Dissatisfied with his early training, however, he
later joined the millenarian sect known as the French Prophets. After being imprisoned for debt to one of its most prominent leaders, he quit the group, later deserted his wife, and sailed to Philadelphia, arriving in February 1722.[36] Franklin
observed him to be eccentric in his ideas, slovenly in appearance, and incompetent
at printing, although a scholar possessed of the ability to compose verse at the
typecase without a need to write it and revise it on paper.[37] With him, the young
journeyman found employment.

Eventually, Keimer and Franklin quarrelled and separated, and the latter claimed
that Keimer came up with the idea of starting a newspaper to compete with Bradford's *Mercury* by stealing it from Franklin.[38] In October 1728 Keimer issued a
prospectus for the newspaper, to be entitled *The Pennsylvania Gazette, or the Universal Instructor*.[39] There had been bad feelings between him and Andrew Bradford ever since a dispute over printing Quaker material in 1725. Before setting out
his blueprint for the paper, Keimer opened the prospectus with a criticism of Bradford on the grounds that the *Mercury* "has been so wretchedly perform'd, that it has
been not only a Reproach to the Province, but such a Scandal to the very Name of
Printing, that it may, for its unparallel'd Blunders and Incorrectness, be truly stiled
Nonsense in Folio, instead of a Serviceable News-Paper."

The design of the *Universal Instructor* was influenced greatly by Keimer's religious and epistemological views. In religious matters, his life goal was to marry
spiritual emotional fulfillment with the discovery of intellectual truth about God
and the universe He had created. That vision was apparent in the prospectus.
Keimer promised that the newspaper would contain "the Theory of all Arts, both
Liberal and Mechanical, and the several Sciences both humane and divine, with
the Figures, Kinds, Properties . . . of Things natural and artificial [etc.]." The
means by which he planned to present such diverse knowledge was the reprinting,
in alphabetical order, of the contents of Ephraim Chambers's recently published
Cyclopaedia: or an Universal Dictionary of Arts and Sciences. The intended—and
pretentious—result was to be "the most compleat Body of History and Philosophy
ever yet published since the Creation."

True to Keimer's promise, the *Universal Instructor's* first issue of December 24, 1728, began with a discourse on the letter *a*. It filled one and a half of the four pages. The remainder of the columns contained news items taken from English newspapers, an address from the New Jersey assembly congratulating John Montgomery on his accession to the governorship of that colony and New York, and three advertisements for printed tracts and merchandise that Keimer had available for sale. Later issues added literary material, including the serialization of Daniel Defoe's *Religious Courtship*.

Despite Keimer's lofty intentions, the *Universal Instructor* never gained great popularity. In his largest claims for the newspaper, Keimer stated that its circulation was only 250, and Benjamin Franklin asserted that it was even less, a meager 90. The latter, still hoping to publish a newspaper of his own, wrote a series of *Busy-Body* essays for Bradford's competing *Mercury* with the intent of damaging Keimer.[40] In light of the lack of public support of Keimer's enterprise, they were probably unnecessary. Keimer was experiencing financial difficulties, and his imprisonment for debt briefly interrupted publication of the *Universal Instructor.* Franklin by now had journeyed to England, returned with letters of credit from friends to purchase equipment and supplies, and started his own business. He and his partner, Hugh Meredith, offered to buy the paper for a small sum, and on September 25, 1729, Keimer published his final issue. Its featured encyclopedic reprint was on "Air." Keimer soon moved to Barbados, where in 1731 he founded the island's first newspaper, the *Barbados Gazette*. He continued it for seven years and then died in 1742.[41]

Upon taking over Keimer's newspaper, Franklin shortened its name by dropping *Universal Instructor* and, in an effort to make its contents more popular, threw out the encyclopedia entries. He set to work to increase its readership and place it on sound financial footing.

The popularity of the *Gazette* was helped immensely by Franklin's talent for expository writing. As a youth, he had access to books by Bunyan, Defoe, Cotton Mather, Locke, and others and had read widely in the philosophical works of the age. He set out to imitate the style of the most popular prose writers, especially preferring Joseph Addison's *Spectator* essays, and through disciplined practice developed a style that was notable for clarity, precision, brevity, wit, and smoothness of phrasing. His method was to read a *Spectator* essay, lay it aside for a few days, and then attempt to write the essay in its original style. After comparing the two versions, he would rework his own to make it conform to the original.[42] His essential philosophy about writing style was that form should be suited to purpose, that is, that style is best when effective for attaining the writer's goal.[43] His effort to improve his style had met with early success when his older brother James decided to publish Ben's "Silence Dogood" letters in the *Courant*, not knowing their authorship. The letters showed considerable polish as the work of a sixteen-year-old, but many other essays published in colonial newspapers were of equal or better quality, and it is doubtful the "Dogood" letters would be much noticed today were it not for the later fame that their author achieved.

Like most other newspapers of the colonial period, the *Gazette* was oriented mainly toward news and advertising. Franklin emphasized news taken from English and other colonial newspapers and gathered other items from such sources as Atlantic ship captains, correspondence, and colonial travelers through Philadelphia. In makeup, likewise, the *Gazette* resembled other papers. It ranged in size from two to four pages, with page one devoted to foreign news, page two to local and intercolonial news and contributed essays and letters, and pages three and four to such items as advertisements and mercantile and shipping news.

While oriented toward news and advertising, the *Gazette* did not avoid issues altogether. Franklin supported the popular, antiproprietary party in Pennsylvania politics and soon became one of its leaders. Having been reared in a dissident Protestant family whose father was a tradesman, and trained in a trade himself, it perhaps was only natural that Benjamin Franklin should join the antiproprietary side. Although he deserted his family's strong Puritan beliefs, his background had accustomed him to the role of opposition to authority.

Pennsylvania's Charter of Privileges of 1701 had laid the basis for the political power struggle that was to occur over the next several decades. Supporters of the Penn family, led by James Logan, William Penn's loyal advisor, believed the ultimate authority rested with the colony's proprietors. Those who believed the power rested with the Assembly formed the popular party, led by the pugnacious lawyer David Lloyd. The two parties constituted not well-developed political organizations in the modern sense, but groups of friends who shared common ideologies or political interests. They often coalesced around a particularly important or effective individual. When Lloyd died in 1731, Franklin succeeded him as leader of the popular party in the Assembly. The most prominent members of the proprietary party tended to be individuals who had been appointed to offices by the Penns. Because of property requirements and the inconvenience of attending polling places, only a small part of the citizenry cast votes in elections. Thus, small groups of individuals usually held office year after year, and public support of their views swayed back and forth from issue to issue. The major issues revolved around military defense, the amount of representation in the Assembly for settlers in the western counties, and the property and political rights of the proprietors. The paramount issue during most of the colonial era, however, was whether the proprietary interests or the popular Assembly should control power.

During the term of Franklin's service in the Assembly, the body faced several major issues, and he often played the central role in their resolution. With the *Pennsylvania Gazette* under his direction, he was able to use its columns to promote his views. A persuasive writer with a printing press at his disposal, he also found it easy to produce his arguments in pamphlet form, where they could get a hearing before the public. One of the earliest issues that he faced was the issuance of paper currency. In the 1720s Pennsylvania was importing so many goods that it faced the prospect of running out of gold and silver to pay for them. With the colony facing an economic depression, the Assembly passed laws providing for the printing of paper money. In 1729 the British Board of Trade, hoping to control inflation, asked that no more be issued. Thereupon Franklin printed an argument for paper currency, a pamphlet entitled *Modest Enquiry into the Nature and Necessity of a Paper Currency*. It was instrumental in helping persuade the Assembly to approve another issue, and Franklin obtained the lucrative contract to print £30,000.

On the issue of providing military defense for the colony, Franklin likewise exerted a key influence. Because of the Quaker aversion to war and because of the contentions between the Assembly and the governor, who was appointed by the Penn family, difficulties frequently arose over funding military activities. The Assembly refused most requests from the governor and the British crown for support of a militia, or the Assembly contrived such legal and procedural restrictions that raising and funding a militia were virtually impossible. The problem grew especially difficult in the 1730s, and it was not until Franklin proposed a solution in 1747 that it was finally resolved. His plan involved setting up a public lottery, with £3,000 of the revenue to be spent on defense and organizing militia associations. The Assembly voted £4,000 for "the purchase of bread, beef, pork, flour, wheat, or other grains"; but it made no reference to the acquisition of munitions. The ingenious Franklin suggested to the governor, however, that "other grains" meant gunpowder; and the governor heartily accepted his interpretation.[44] The lottery was so successful that subsequent ones were held and associations proliferated. Most of the officers elected in the associations were popular leaders, and it quickly became apparent that Franklin had created not only an army for Pennsylvania but an organization that could be used as a political machine.

Throughout his printing and public career in Pennsylvania, Franklin harbored a continuing antipathy for the colony's proprietors. The Penn family felt the same about him. Consequently, political relations between them continually boiled. Franklin expressed open contempt of the Penns' character and challenged their motives.[45] They were, he argued, enemies of popular liberty. For their part, the proprietors claimed that he was a liar who would use any means, no matter how unsavory, to achieve his personal goals. "There will never be any prospect of ease and happiness," wrote John Penn, while serving as governor of the colony, "while that villain [Franklin] has the liberty of spreading about the poison of that inveterate malice and ill nature which is deeply implanted in his own black heart."[46]

Franklin and the Penns especially disagreed on the role of the proprietors and of the general public in the affairs of the colony. As contentions between the proprietors and the popular party intensified with time, Franklin gained an increasingly important position in the strife because of his ability to appeal to the public. The Penns believed that authority should rest in the governor and other appointed officials, while Franklin argued that ultimately political power resided in the governed. "Mr. Franklin's doctrine," wrote Thomas Penn, "that obedience to governors is no more due them than protection to the people, is not fit to be in the heads of the unthinking multitude. He is a dangerous man, and I should be glad if he inhabited any other country, as I believe him of a very uneasy spirit." Despite the proprietors' mistrust of Franklin, however, they approached him cautiously because of his popularity. "[A]s he is a sort of tribune of the people," Thomas Penn explained, "he must be treated with regard."[47]

Franklin's popularity was due in no small part to his writing and printing. The *Pennsylvania Gazette* provided a ready outlet for his views, and *Poor Richard's Almanac*, which he first published in 1732, made him familiar in homes throughout the colonies. Immediately after Franklin began publishing the *Pennsylvania Gazette*, a contentious rivalry developed between him and Andrew Bradford, who for years had held a virtual monopoly in the Philadelphia newspaper field. The rivalry was both professional and political. One must assume that much of Franklin's criticism of Bradford's *Mercury* as "a paltry thing, wretchedly manag'd, and no way entertaining; and yet was profitable"[48] must have resulted from their personal differences as much as from the real quality of the *Mercury*. The two fought over such matters as government printing, and in politics Bradford loyally supported the proprietary side while Franklin worked with the popular party.

Being named postmaster in 1737 enhanced Franklin's opportunities to improve the *Gazette* and hinder Bradford's *Mercury*. Although the postmaster salary was small, the position improved his abilities to carry on correspondence and increased the number of subscribers and advertisements.[49] It also gave him a competitive advantage over his rival Andrew Bradford. At first Franklin allowed Bradford to continue using the mail system on the latter's promise to pay past-due accounts. In 1740, however, when the two fought bitterly over who had first planned to publish a magazine, Franklin forbade Bradford use of the mails for distributing the *American Mercury*.[50]

In his approach to his printing business, as in his philosophy of life, Franklin emphasized industry and virtue, but the purpose behind his industry was financial success, and the motivation behind his virtue was utilitarian. It was a virtue stripped of the spiritual motive, as had moved such clerical lights as Cotton Mather, and it was based in social and business prudence rather than in benevolence simply for the sake of doing good. It was mainly monetary rather than moral. He did not repudiate his Puritan heritage but instead tried to accommodate it to Enlightenment values and philosophies. Throughout his printing and public careers, Franklin maintained a desire to raise himself and improve life for other people. He depended primarily on practical virtue and science to achieve those goals.

Franklin possessed a natural capacity for making friends and a promoter's instinct for advertising himself and his business. From the beginning of his printing career in Philadelphia, he took steps to impress his fellow townspeople with his industry and frugality. Later, in his autobiography, he explained how he "took care not only to be in reality industrious and frugal, but to avoid all appearance to the contrary." He described in detail the methods that he used:

I dressed plainly; I was seen at no place of idle diversion; I never went out fishing or shooting; a book indeed sometimes debauched me from my work, but that was seldom, snug, and gave no scandal; and to show that I was not above my business, I sometimes brought home the paper I purchased at the stores through the streets on a wheelbarrow. Thus, being esteemed an industrious, thriving young man and paying duly for what I bought, the merchants who imported stationery solicited my custom; others proposed supplying me with books, and I went on swimmingly.[51]

While much of Franklin's efforts were devoted to improving his own situation, many of his activities also helped others. Despite the time-consuming task of running a newspaper and a printing business, he still participated energetically in other pursuits. Most were utilitarian in nature. Aside from the practical, Franklin showed little interest in the arts or poetry, and his religious ideas exhibited a shallow deism. He wrote that Mather's *Essays To Do Good* gave him "a turn of thinking that had an influence on some of the principal future events of my life,"[52] but even the list of thirteen virtues that he developed for his own "moral perfection" had a decidedly pragmatic goal. Yet his desire to improve made him a leader in many activities that benefited his community. In 1727, while still working for Keimer, he formed the Junto, a club that discussed scientific, political, moral, and other subjects and that in 1743 became the American Philosophical Society. He was instrumental in the founding of a circulating library, a city fire company and police force, and an educational academy that was the origin of the University of Pennsylvania. In 1742 he invented a freestanding fireplace, the "Franklin stove," and allowed it to be copied by others free of patent fees. "[A]s we enjoy great advantages from the inventions of others," he explained, "we should be glad of an opportunity to serve others by any invention of our own; and this we should do freely and generously."[53] In 1746 he began his experiments with electricity, leading to the invention of the lightning rod. As a result of those experiments, he gained international eminence as a man of science.

Although few Americans have done so much of practical benefit for their fellow citizens, Franklin left the impression that in his dealings with others, though they may have been genuine, he was not completely committed. He rarely revealed himself fully, and he communicated his thoughts and motives only partially, showing but a veneer. Despite his agility in public affairs and in his dealings with other people, he gave the appearance of having been somewhat casual about them, often devising his actions based upon what was useful for the moment. It was as if he were an aloof spectator who looked at life as a game and at himself as one of the players. Rarely in his writings did he reveal his deepest feelings. Rather, he usually wrote in a style or a form to mask himself, as in the "Silence Dogood" letters, and even his *Autobiography* presents only a calculated portrait. Part of the reason for his seeming lack of full commitment was his wide-ranging curiosity over a multitude of subjects, and part perhaps was the inevitable sense of superiority that this creative genius and facile social creature felt toward the minor players around him.

As most colonial printers did, Franklin, at the same time that he was pushing the interests of the popular party in Pennsylvania politics, loudly proclaimed his neutrality. His essential argument was that he could not rightly be criticized for what he printed because it was the nature of his job to print whatever was presented to him. Thus, he and other printers argued, they were not to blame for the content of the items they published. The fact, however, that few colonial newspaper printers gave equal treatment to both sides in arguments, and that most weighted their publications heavily to one side or the other, suggests that their defense of neutrality was a facade. It was a calculated position used to shield them from attacks of bias while publishing with obvious bias.[54]

The concept of newspaper neutrality had its origins in the use of the printing press merely as a mechanical device. The printer was thought of, and thought of himself, as simply the operator of the machine rather than as an independent thinker whose function was to originate and present his own views. Groups such as the Puritan and Quaker churches hired printers to operate the groups' presses, or groups and individuals contracted with independent printers to reproduce material for them. The printer acted essentially as a craftsman operating a business. His function was to serve other people who provided the written content of the publications that the printer reproduced. When a town had competing factions but only one printer, he usually printed equally for both sides. That was true even when the printer was biased toward one of the sides, since the printer looked on any publication as a means of obtaining income. When two printers served a town, each of the competing factions normally gave most of its business to the printer who shared its views. Thus, each printer tended to do the bulk of the printing for one of the factions, although he was willing to print material from anyone. Such a tradition in the printing business easily carried over to the printing of newspapers. Thus there developed in the colonial newspaper field the general concept that newspapers should print material from a variety of points of view. It was obvious, however, that most newspapers took sides. When criticized, editors then found it convenient to argue that they were not biased but had printed offending material because newspapers were expected to print opposing views.

The best known argument for this policy was Franklin's "Apology for Printers," published in 1731 in the *Gazette*. Printers, explained Franklin, "are educated in the Belief that, when Men differ in Opinion, both Sides ought equally to have the Advantage of being heard by the Publick. . . . Being thus continually employ'd in serving all Parties, Printers naturally acquire a vast Unconcernedness as to the right or wrong Opinions contain'd in what they print; regarding it only as a Matter of their daily labour."[55] One can imagine Franklin winking as he wrote the last sentence. Although it exhibited his studied casualness and his sense of superiority to ordinary people, whose opinions did not matter because they were neither right nor wrong, Franklin was not one to remain disinterested in issues. He had, in fact, written his printers' "apology" in response to "being frequently censur'd and condemn'd by different Persons for printing things which they say ought not to be printed."[56]

The "Apology for Printers" demonstrated Franklin's dexterity in appealing for the support of subscribers and advertisers; but the *Pennsylvania Gazette*, while providing a stable income for him, did not provide a lucrative income, and he continued to look for means to gain wealth, hoping to achieve his goal of retiring young so that he could devote himself to pursuits other than business. In 1729 he and Hugh Meredith, his printing partner, were named Pennsylvania's public printers, and in 1732 they were appointed to similar positions for Delaware, Maryland, and New Jersey. Neither those jobs nor the others he was doing, however, allowed Franklin to escape the daily routine of running a business to make a living. He struck upon the right idea, though, with publication of an almanac, *Poor Richard's.* Almanacs were one of the most popular types of reading material in the colonies, and Franklin recognized their potential for providing a dependable income on a yearly basis. *Poor Richard's* was an immediate success, the first three editions selling out in three months. Ultimately reaching annual sales of 10,000 over a period of twenty-five years, the almanac contributed greatly to Franklin's wealth.

Poor Richard's contained the usual almanac material dealing with weather, cures for ailments, and other matters, but it was also an ideal vehicle for the publication of Franklin's homespun wisdom on self-discipline, industry, prudence, moderation, and other virtues and his ideas on politics. In it, using the pen name "Richard Saunders," he taught his poorer, laboring countrymen how to improve their lives through practicality and industry. His lessons reflected the Puritan virtues of his upbringing, but stripped of the Puritan spiritual motivations. Unlike his forebears, he believed the primary value of religion was its social usefulness, and he held the utilitarian view that what was good was what worked. Although he borrowed many of Richard's aphorisms from other writers, he transformed them into his own style of proverbial wisdom. As a result, they were widely repeated both in the colonies and in Europe. Through the popular almanac, Franklin served as the colonial schoolmaster for the young country. Many of the sayings that he coined for the almanac—"God helps those who help themselves" and "Never leave that till tomorrow which you can do to-day," for example—have since entered into American popular thinking.

Gaining a wide reputation, Franklin embarked on a second venture, a network of newspaper publishing, that eventually gave him a stable and continuing source of income. The first link in the network was forged with Thomas Whitmarsh. With the Assembly of South Carolina looking for a printer to set up in the colony, Franklin arranged in 1731 to furnish Whitmarsh with printing equipment, share the cost of materials, and receive a share of the profits. The partnership having succeeded, Franklin was, he wrote, "encourag'd to engage in others, and to promote several of my Workmen, who had behaved well, by establishing them with Printing-Houses in different Colonies."[57] He began by selecting former apprentices and journeymen who had impressed him with their skill and character and then made them printing partners.

Under the working arrangement, Franklin provided the printing equipment and shared the cost of materials, in return for which he received one-third of the profits. The agreement bound the printers to Franklin and discouraged them from developing a business on their own. The partners also served as distributors of *Poor Richard's Almanac.* At the end of six years, the printers had the option of continuing the partnership or purchasing the printing equipment from Franklin. As deputy postmaster general for the colonies, Franklin also was in a position to award local postmasterships to his partners. Along with providing additional income to the partners, the arrangement also aided the publishing network. It meant that the partners were the first to receive newspapers and information from afar, and it allowed them to send and receive newspapers and correspondence through the mails free of charge. The network grew to be the largest in the colonies, including two dozen members and stretching from New England to the West Indies island of Antigua.[58] It offered a variety of benefits to Franklin, including connections, influence, and prestige; but the paramount advantage was a substantial and dependable income.

Having now established for himself a comfortable living, in 1748 Franklin, at the age of forty-two, formally retired from his printing career and devoted his time to the other pursuits that were so attractive to him. Upon his retirement from printing, he maintained a financial interest in his business through a partnership with his foreman, David Hall. The latter was given the responsibility of running the printing business, which had an annual income of about £2,000, thus relieving Franklin of any cares for the office and paying him £1,000 annually. As his part of the deal, Franklin agreed to continue editing the *Gazette* and *Poor Richard's Almanac*. The combined incomes from that arrangement and from the offices that he held with the post office and in the Pennsylvania assembly amounted to £2,000, approximately twice the income of a colonial governor. "I flattered myself," Franklin later wrote, "that, by the sufficient tho' modest fortune I had acquir'd, I had secured leisure during the rest of my life for philosophical studies and amusements."[59]

Science, invention, politics, and diplomacy all appealed to him. Having succeeded financially in his own career, he directed his efforts toward activities that would aid his own self-improvement and assist others in improving their lives. He continued to serve as clerk of the Pennsylvania Assembly, until 1751, when he was elected its speaker, and as postmaster of Philadelphia (1737–1753). Under his guidance, the Philadelphia office became the center for the entire colonial postal system, and in 1753 he and William Hunter of the *Virginia Gazette* were named deputy postmasters general of the colonies. In that position, Franklin attempted to improve the mail service as a means of communication for the colonies and instituted favorable rates for printed matter, which included newspapers. He held the post until 1774, when he was dismissed because of a political controversy involving relations between Massachusetts and Great Britain. In 1754 he represented Pennsylvania at the Albany Congress to consider a common defense against the French and Indians. In preparing for that meeting, he wrote his now-famous essay on the need for the American colonies to join in a common defense, accompanied by his illustration of a divided glass snake with the injunction to "Join, or Die!"[60] For many years, beginning in 1757, he served as a colonial representative in England.

By the time Franklin retired from printing in 1748, journalism had spread and newspapers had been started in most of the other colonies. Franklin's own commitment to quality in printing, writing, and newspaper publishing, along with his support of the partners in his network, had played a major part in that expansion. Earlier, however, in the colony of New York, there had occurred an event that was to become a rallying point for the growing spirit of the rights of American colonists. The trial of John Peter Zenger, in which the printer was acquitted of a charge of seditious libel, served not only as a victory for the popular faction in New York politics. It also provided a dramatic statement on what was meant by the concept of "freedom of the press," and it afterwards became a *cause célèbre* for printers and colonial militants to appeal to whenever they wished to make a point about their rights.

NOTES

1. The endorsements of Fox and Penn are included in the Records of the Philadelphia Monthly Meeting, 4 11th month 1685 (January 1686) and may be found in Frank Willing Leach, *The North American* (8 September 1907): xiv, and in John William Wallace, *An Address Delivered at the Celebration . . . of the Two Hundredth Birth Day of Mr. William Bradford . . .* (Albany, N.Y.: J. Munsell), 23. Of Penn's support, Bradford said, "It was by Governor Penn's encouragement I came to the Province, and by his license I print." Quoted in John Thomson Faris, *The Romance of Forgotten Men* (New York: Harper, 1928), 41. Some historians, following Isaiah Thomas's *The History of Printing in America* (ed. Marcus A. McCorison [1810; reprint, New York: Weathervane Books, 1970], 340–41), state that Bradford arrived in Pennsylvania in 1682 with William Penn on the ship *Welcome*. Relying primarily on the introductory nature of Fox's letter, authorities on the *Welcome* passenger list conclude, however, that Bradford was not on board the ship. See George E. McCracken, *The Welcome Claimants Proved, Disproved And Doubtful* (Baltimore: Genealogical Publishing Company, 1970), 51–53; and Walter Lee Sheppard, Jr., ed., *Passengers and Ships Prior to 1684* (Baltimore: Genealogical Publishing Company, 1970), 7–9.

2. William Bradford, *Kalendarium Pennsilvaniense, or, American Messenger* (Philadelphia, 1685).

3. Minutes of the Meeting of Friends, quoted in Faris, *The Romance of Forgotten Men*, 42.

4. The specific publication that was at issue was Keith's broadside *An Appeal from the Twenty-eight Judges to the Spirit of Truth . . .* (Philadelphia, 1692).

5. A detailed account of the charges, the hearing, and the trial is included in the pamphlet *New England's Spirit of Persecution Transmitted to Pennsylvania* (Philadelphia, 1693), which appears to have been the work of Bradford, Keith, and two of Keith's followers. The pamphlet was reprinted in the same year in London under the title *The Tryals of Peter Boss, George Keith, Thomas Budd, and William Bradford, QUAKERS, For several Great Misdemeanors. . . . .*

6. Ibid.

7. A popular anecdote about the trial says that a sympathetic juror dislodged from the frame the type that Bradford had set for the offending publication, thus destroying the evidence and allowing Bradford to go free. In reality, the prosecution did exhibit a frame to the jurors as evidence, but Bradford simply argued that there was no proof that the frame was his. See *New England's Spirit of Persecution Transmitted to Pennsylvania.*

8. State of Pennsylvania, *Minutes of the Provincial Council of Pennsylvania . . .* (Philadelphia: Jo. Severns & Co., 1852), 1:366–67.

9. Quoted in Faris, *The Romance of Forgotten Men*, 43.

10. *Records of the Colony of Rhode Island and Providence Planations, in New England*, ed. John Russell Bartlett (Providence, 1856–1865), 4:65.

11. These brief details on the Jansen family are taken from "Raynier Jansen," *Appleton Cyclopedia of American Biography*, and "Reinier Jansen," *Dictionary of American Biography*. Details about printing in Pennsylvania from the time of William Bradford's departure to Andrew Bradford's arrival in 1712 are contained in John William Wallace, "Early Printing in Philadelphia. The Friends Press—Interregnum of the Bradfords," *Pennsylvania Magazine of History and Biography* 4 (1880): 432–44.

12. Andrew Sowle, Bradford's maternal grandfather, was a "first purchaser" of land in the province, the holder of a thousand acres in Upper Dublin Township, County of Philadelphia. He left the land to his wife, Jane, and daughter Tacy Sowle Raylton. The daughter later deeded this land to her two colonial nephews, and Andrew purchased his brother's share for £160. Also, as early as 1689, William Bradford had invested in land along the river front.

13. See, for example, records of the *General Meeting of the People, call'd Quakers*, June 1732, reprinted in Wallace, "Early Printing in Philadelphia," 442n. Shortly before Bradford's death in 1742, the Meeting attempted to retrieve the press from Bradford, declaring to him "that as he hath Kept it so long in use, its expected he should pay Rent for it." The Quakers were unable to obtain the press until eight months after Bradford had died.

14. *Mercury*, 22 December 1719.

15. *Mercury*, 16 February 1720. The statement read: "The Design of this Paper, being to Promote Trade it is hoped, that it will be Incouraged by the Merchants of this City, by Acquainting Us with the true price Current of the Several Good's inserted in it, which we presume may be Serviceable to All concern'd in Commerce, Especially to them, that have any of those Good's to Sell, who will find a quicker Sale, by Our Informing those persons that want them where they may be Supplied: We likewise Desire those Gentlemen that receive any Authentick Account of News from Europe, or other places, which may be proper for this paper, that they well please to favour Us with a Copy."

16. *Mercury*, 15 August 1734.

17. Anna J. De Armond's *Andrew Bradford: Colonial Journalist* (Newark, Del.: University of Delaware Press, 1949) lists 49 foreign newspapers from which the *Mercury* took material (pp. 53–55). They included mostly English journals, but a substantial number were from Scotland and Ireland. The *Mercury* got little material directly from continental newspapers. Despite that fact, since the British papers included many accounts taken from other newspapers on the continent, the *Mercury* was able to keep up with European news through them.

18. For detailed calculations on shipping, see Ian K. Steele, *The English Atlantic 1675–1740: An Exploration of Communication and Community* (New York: Oxford University Press, 1986). For figures on Boston and New York, see especially Tables 4.4 (p. 295) and 4.9 (p. 299). The averages are for the years 1711–1739.

19. The figure for Philadelphia is for 1721, as calculated by De Armond, *Andrew Bradford* (p. 58), from reports in the *Mercury*. With time, the number of ships increased, so that in 1731, for example, ships docked at Philadelphia on the average of approximately thirteen per month.

20. In the issue of 23 November 1722, for example, Bradford explained to readers, "Our Delay of this Paper hath been occasioned by the New-York Post coming in so late, who

waited for the Eastern Post, but in vain." See De Armond, *Andrew Bradford*, 59, for other similar instances.

21. See De Armond, *Andrew Bradford*, 61–62, for examples of such delays.

22. *The Torrington Diaries*, ed. C. B. Andrews, 4 vols. (London, 1934), 3:39–40. For a recounting of other such feats and a discussion of concepts of timeliness and speed in the early eighteenth century, see Steele, *The English Atlantic*, 5ff.

23. In his *Autobiography* (New York: Modern Library, 1944), Benjamin Franklin, publisher of the *Pennsylvania Gazette*, said that Bradford was given the job of postmaster because it was thought that the *Mercury* was a superior newspaper for both news and advertising. The postmastership worked to Bradford's advantage in more than one way, according to Franklin, for Bradford prevented Franklin from using the mails to distribute his *Gazette*.

24. The earliest account of this, the first colonial paper mill, is Horatio Gates Jones, "Historical Sketch of the Rittenhouse Paper-Mill; the First Erected in America, A.D., 1690," paper read before the Historical Society of Pennsylvania, May 11, 1863; reprinted in *Pennsylvania Magazine of History and Biography* 20 (1896): 315–33.

25. Authored by Francis Rawle, the leading propagandist for paper money, the pamphlet was entitled *Some Remedies Proposed, for the Restoring the sunk Credit of the Province of Pennsylvania; with Some Remarks of its Trade. Humbly offer'd to the Consideration of the Worthy Representatives in the General Assembly of this Province, By a Lover of this Country* (Philadelphia, 1721). Paper money was favored by the popular party, the majority of the Assembly, and probably by most colonists other than merchants. The paper money debate is discussed in Roy N. Lokken's biography of the popular party leader, *David Lloyd: Colonial Lawmaker* (Seattle: University of Washington Press, 1959), 208–13.

26. *Mercury*, 2 January 1722.

27. *Minutes of the Provincial Council of Pennsylvania*, 1 February 1721, 3:145. See also minutes of 19 January 1721.

28. Benjamin Franklin wrote the first few essays in the *Busy-Body* series, but the majority, including #31, were most probably penned by Joseph Breintnall. Most of the essays were on topics of general interest.

29. *Mercury*, 18 September 1729.

30. *Minutes of the Provincial Council of Pennsylvania*, 20 September 1729, 3:369–70.

31. *Mercury*, 25 September 1729.

32. *Mercury*, 26 February 1723.

33. The best account of the controversy, as it related to the *Mercury*, is told in Chapter 4, "Politics in Philadelphia and the Bradford-Hamilton Controversy," in De Armond, *Andrew Bradford*. An informative supplementary study is provided in Katherine D. Carter, "Isaac Norris II's Attack on Andrew Hamilton," *Pennsylvania Magazine of History and Biography* 104 (1980): 139–61.

34. See, for example, the *Mercury*, 12 March, 11, 18, and 25 April 1734; 4 December 1735; 17 February 1736; 13 April and 25 May 1738.

35. Benjamin Franklin had signed indentures at the age of twelve to serve until he was twenty. When he ran away, he was sixteen, thus having served only half of the term of his apprenticeship.

36. The best source of material on Keimer's life is his autobiography, *A Brand pluck'd from the Burning: Exemplify'd in the Unparallel'd Case of Samuel Keimer* (London: printed by W. Boreham, 1718). Also of value are two other publications that Keimer published during the same period: *A Search After Religion, Among the many Modern Pretenders to it....*

To which is added An Address and Petition to King Jesus. . . . By Samuel Keimer, *a Listed Soldier Under Him. . . .* (London: Printed for the Author . . . 1718); and *The Platonick Courtship A Poem. . . .* (London: 1718.) The best biographical treatments are Stephen Bloore, "Samuel Keimer," *Pennsylvania Magazine of History and Biography* 44 (1920): 255–87; and C. Lennart Carlson, "Samuel Keimer: A Study in the Transit of English Culture to Colonial Pennsylvania," *Pennsylvania Magazine of History and Biography* 61 (1937): 357–86. The best known study among journalism historians, but also the most inadequate, is Chester E. Jorgenson's generally erroneous "A Brand Flung at Colonial Orthodoxy: Samuel Keimer's 'Universal Instructor in All Arts and Sciences,' " *Journalism Quarterly* 12 (1935): 272–77.

37. Franklin, *Autobiography*, 22ff.

38. Ibid., 49–50.

39. When the newspaper appeared, it bore the title *The Universal Instructor in all Arts and Sciences; and Pennsylvania Gazette.*

40. Franklin, *Autobiography*, 50.

41. Although most accounts indicate the year of his death as 1738, records in the Barbados Registration Office state that it was 1742. See Carlson, "Samuel Keimer," 386n.

42. Franklin recounts his method in his *Autobiography*, 19–20.

43. Benjamin Franklin, *The Writings of Benjamin Franklin*, 9 vols. (New York: Macmillan, 1905–1907), 1:37.

44. The quoted material is cited in Wayland Fuller Dunaway, *A History of Pennsylvania* (New York: Prentice-Hall, 1935), 109.

45. Following a conversation with Thomas Penn, for example, Franklin recorded that he "conceived at that moment a more cordial and thorough contempt for him than I ever before felt for any man living, a contempt I cannot express in words." *Shippen Papers*, 111, quoted in William Robert Shepherd, *History of Proprietary Government in Pennsylvania* (New York: Columbia University, 1896), 85n.

46. John Penn to Thomas Penn, 5 May 1764, quoted in Shepherd, ibid.

47. Thomas Penn to Peters, 9 June 1748, quoted in Shepherd, ibid., 222n.

48. Franklin, *Autobiography*, 70. See also the "Busy-Body" essays which Franklin wrote for the *Mercury* as part of his efforts in 1729 to embarass Keimer and the *Universal Instructor.* Although published in the *Mercury*, the essays described Bradford's newspaper as "frequently very Dull." *American Mercury*, 4 February 1729.

49. Franklin, *Autobiography*, 98.

50. Both Franklin and Bradford made an attempt at publishing magazines in 1741, but the efforts were short-lived. See Chapter 4 of this book for an account.

51. Franklin, *Autobiography*, 75.

52. Ibid., 16.

53. Franklin, *Autobiography*, 132.

54. Some historians have argued that colonial publishers really were impartial, primarily to avoid offending customers or government, from which they received their financial support. See, for example, Stephen Botein, "'Meer Mechanics' and an Open Press: The Business and Political Strategies of Colonial American Printers," *Perspectives in American History* 9 (1975): 127–225; Mary Ann Yodelis, "Who Paid the Piper? Publishing Economics in Boston, 1763–1775," *Journalism Monographs* 38 (1975); and Lawrence C. Wroth, *The Colonial Printer* (New York: Grolier Club, 1931).

55. *Pennsylvania Gazette*, 10 June 1731.

56. Ibid.

57. Franklin, *Autobiography*, 123.

58. The most comprehensive discussion of the arrangement can be found in Ralph Frasca, "Benjamin Franklin's Printing Network," *American Journalism* 5 (1988): 145–58.

59. *Writings*, 1: 373–74.

60. *Pennsylvania Gazette*, 9 May 1754.

3

Freedom of the Press, 1638-1735

It was a day of triumph for Andrew Hamilton.

He had come from Philadelphia to defy the governor of New York in court, and he had won. He had gotten no pay for his efforts, and he was quite sick by now. But his client, newspaperman John Peter Zenger, was free after months of imprisonment—and today, September 29, 1735, the mayor and aldermen of New York were presenting Hamilton with a ceremonial document giving him honorary citizenship in the city. The officials had commissioned the making of a special gold box to hold the certificate for the presentation. The glowing box was inscribed with Latin sayings about virtue and liberty, and it weighed a full five and a half ounces.[1]

It was perhaps an unusual award for winning a lawsuit, but Hamilton was pleased to see that Mayor Paul Richards and the aldermen recognized that the Zenger case had meaning in more places than just New York. The document lauded:

We therefore, under a grateful Sense of the remarkable Service done to the Inhabitants of this City and Colony, by *Andrew Hamilton,* Esq; . . . by his learned and generous Defence of the Rights of Mankind and the Liberty of the Press, in the Case of *John-Peter Zenger* . . . do by these Presents, bear to the said Andrew Hamilton, Esq; the public Thanks of the Freemen of this Corporation for that signal Service.[2]

Hamilton had successfully argued before a jury that the truth was a defense against the charge of libel; a true report about a public official, no matter how scandalous, could not be libelous.[3] History, in time, would come to agree with the city of New York on the brilliance of Hamilton's argument. His defense of Zenger would eventually be seen as the colonial period's landmark case in the struggle to define freedom of the press.

Hamilton's defense of free expression, bold though it was, did not spring from a vacuum. From the very start of printing in English North America, people had been sculpting their ideas of what free expression meant. By 1690, the founders of the Anglo-American press, the Massachusetts Puritans, had actually stated that the truth was a cure for libel. Their statement was the culmination of a half-century struggle to define free expression. From the moment the first printed item was peeled off of the first Massachusetts press, colonists had wrestled with the concept of freedom of the press.

The first printed item in English America had debuted in March of 1638.[4] That broadside, "The Oath of a Free-man," printed by Stephen Day, explained the rights and duties of citizens in the Puritan haven of Massachusetts. For the New England Puritans who were busy constructing their "city on a hill" for all the world to see,[5] the Oath was a reminder of the ideal relationship between a man and his government.

With the printing of the "Oath," Americans had to begin looking thoughtfully at free expression. Mechanically, they could now publish literary works without relying on presses an ocean away in England. That fact, in turn, plunged them deeply into the struggle to define free expression. As the printing industry unfolded from Day's first broadside in 1638, the Massachusetts Puritans who first sponsored the American printing industry came to believe that they had a right—in fact, a *duty*—to discuss ideas openly, providing those discussions did not blatantly defy God.

As he pressed his type into the rough rag paper to create "The Oath of a Free-man," Day unwittingly set forth the argument to come over freedom of expression. Freemen took the oath upon becoming voting members of Massachusetts Bay colony. The oath-taker promised that he would be true and faithful to the government of Massachusetts. The freeman also vowed to "truly endeavour to maintain and preserve all the liberties and priviledges thereof, submitting my self to the wholesome Lawes and Orders made and established by the same. And further, that *I* will not plot or practice any evill against it." The oath went on:

Moreover, *I* doe solemnly bind my self in the sight of God, that when *I* shal be called to give my voyce touching any such matter of this State, in which Freemen are to deal, *I* will give my vote and suffrage as *I* shall judge in mine own conscience may best conduce and tend to the publike weal of the body, without respect of persons, or favour of any man.[6]

Obviously, Massachusetts expected and even encouraged its freemen to give their opinions as they saw fit. The colony counted on those opinions to help build the public good. Massachusetts Bay also valued liberty of conscience and an accompanying liberty of expression, at least in political affairs. Clearly, the oath offered a liberal policy toward free expression. Yet, the oath maintained that a man must never do evil against the government. That set up a predicament for freemen who ever wanted to disagree with the government.

In 1638, however, disagreement with the government paled in comparison to disagreement with God. Puritans were far more concerned with God than with mere politics. Since they were the dominant group in Massachusetts Bay colony, the Puritans saw to it that the colony's laws required proper reverence to God in spoken and printed words. According to the 1647 laws of Massachusetts, no Christian could interrupt a preacher in church or falsely charge a minister with "any errour which he hath not taught in the open face of the Church." The law warned that any Christian who dared reproach a preacher or in any other way made "Gods wayes contemptible and ridiculous" faced the wrath of the General Court. First-time offenders would be chastised by a magistrate and bound to their good behavior. If caught a second time, the guilty party had to pay a £5 fine or suffer public humiliation. To be humiliated, the offender would stand on a stool four feet high with a paper affixed to his breast announcing he was "AN OPEN AND OBSTINATE CONTEMNER OF GODS HOLY ORDINANCE." Such an embarrassing punishment, the laws reasoned, would assure that "others may fear and be ashamed of breaking into the like wickedness."[7]

None of the offenses as spelled out in the law specifically mentioned speech or writing, but obviously a person would have to use some form of communication in order to be caught breaking the laws. A person who kept ungodlike thoughts to himself would only be discovered by God, not man—but man could and did restrict unholy speech and writing.

To underline that distinction between public speech and private thoughts, the same set of laws spoke to Jesuits, Indians, and Anabaptists, who were not to display their religions publicly. The restrictions were for the colony's survival. The General Court announced gravely:

THIS *Court taking into consideration the great wars, combustions and divisions which are this day in Europe: . . . the same are observed to be raysed and fomented chiefly by the secret underminings, and solicitations of those of the Jesuiticall Order.*

Jesuits' ability to speak freely in Massachusetts was therefore restricted.[8] Likewise, Indians could not "at any time *powaw*, or performe outward worship to their false gods: or to the devil in any part of our jurisdiction." Disobedient Indians had to pay £5.[9] Anabaptists were also forbidden to display their religion openly. They could not publicly condemn infant baptism or try to persuade people to their point of view.[10] Clearly, Massachusetts defenders of the faith were worried about the communication of heretical beliefs to the flock. Indians, Anabaptists, and Jesuits could presumably conduct private worship, but the open attempt to convert anyone was a grave sin.

The lawbook was not, however, a sour list of "thou shalt nots." It also offered some bold protections for free expression. Every man, whether an inhabitant of Massachusetts or a "Forreiner," whether free or bond, had the right to go to any public court, council, or town meeting. He could either speak his mind or present his views in writing. He could make a motion, complaint, or petition. If he wished, he could just seek information, or he could move any lawful question.[11]

Every legal restriction on free expression in the 1647 laws tied somehow into religion. Men had broad freedom in political expression, but no one had the freedom to condemn God. In the "city on a hill," it was only natural that God come first in the writing of the human law. In that spirit, the General Court had defeated a 1646 petition that called for general toleration of non-Puritan religions. The court had cited the petitioners for seditious proposals.[12] Magistrates in 1649, however, turned down a request that sought licensing of the press in order to eliminate any inconvenience to the commonwealth.[13] Political inconvenience was not a strong enough reason to restrict free expression. That policy would not always be consistent across time, but the Puritans would steadfastly think twice before allowing politics to burden expression. For example, at one point the General Court felt it should excuse an author who opposed the method of electing council members, because his intentions were not evil. However, the court finally made the author acknowledge his mistake.[14] Another publication criticizing the form of the government made the error of attacking the Christianity of both king and Parliament. The General Court censored it without a second thought. The court, however, did not seem disturbed by the writer's speculations on governmental structure.[15]

In general, Puritans felt that printing was a mighty tool for discussion. Religious heresy was the outer boundary of free speech. Within that limit, however, Massachusettsans were permitted to argue about religious topics. Every view deserved a hearing, as long as it was not so deviant as to be sinful or heretical. In fact, the Puritans had an extremely liberal outlook about freedom of discussion. The General Court stated that outlook in its preface to a tract entitled "Propositions Concerning the Subjects of Baptism and Consociation of Churches." The court had read over the pamphlet, which detailed the controversial findings of a church synod in 1662. Commenting on the controversy, the court said emphatically that it would be folly for anyone to tolerate damnable heresies. However, the court was persuaded that various factions could and should publish all nonheretical opinions in disputes. The court said:

[T]o bear one with another in lesser differences, about matters of a more difficult and controversial nature, and more remote from the Foundation, and wherein the godly-wise are not like-minded, is a Duty necessary to the peace and welfare of Religion.

The court added hastily that it did not doubt the truth of the synod's decision.[16] Rather, the court recognized that discussion of baptism by someone other than the synod might offer a new light that would be valuable. After all, as the pamphlet so eloquently put it, free discussion of religion was an actual *duty*.

That call by the court for public discussion in print was not an anomaly. Instead it was a theme. The extreme freedom that the Puritan philosophy allowed was demonstrated in a debate in 1663 over a Congregational policy of church membership. The synod had adopted a proposal that the church baptize children of godly adults who had not attained fully covenanted church membership. The hardline minority complained that the move watered down church principles. John Davenport, a member of the minority, wished to make an appeal to the general populace and wrote a sixty-four-page essay arguing his views. The printing press, however, was under the proprietorship of the church leaders, exactly those individuals whom Davenport had opposed. Thus, the only way he could get the essay printed was by approval of those people whom the essay criticized—but approve it they did.[17] The pamphlet, "Another Essay for the Investigation of Truth," called for toleration of printed opinions, even those out of the mainstream. Especially interesting was the essay's "Apologetical Preface to the Reader," which stated that it was imperative for the opposing side to be heard. People must be concerned with finding the truth, the preface writer declared, and in order to do so readers had to be made aware of both sides of an issue. Even in the early Christian church, the preface said pointedly, the apostles themselves disagreed with one another. Noting that the dissenters were few in number, the preface asked, "Is *Truth bound up to Number?*" The writer added:

Variety of Judgements may stand with Unity of Affections. He that judgeth a Cause before he hath heard both parties speaking, although he should judge rightly, is not a righteous Judge. *[Thus] We are willing that the World should see what is here presented.*

All facets of the matter needed to be debated, the writer said, because any censorship by either side might unintentionally cause the truth to be withheld from mankind. The preface insisted that anything might be put before the public for discussion as long as it did not damage peace and the oneness of affection for God. Indeed, the writer said, he expected to receive an eternal reward for assisting in the publication.[18]

"Another Essay for the Investigation of Truth" was a sterling call for free expression as an obligation of mankind. This view was expansive even as measured by modern libertarian philosophy. Elsewhere in seventeenth-century England and North America, arguments for publishing freedom were made almost exclusively for one side only, and nowhere else was a truly libertarian philosophy being put into practice.

Even though they allowed its publication, "Another Essay" bothered the elders of the church. They sat quietly, however, willing to let the other side have its say— for awhile, anyway. They did not squash "Another Essay," nor did they chastise the pamphlet as blasphemy or heresy. Finally, however, they printed a rejoinder, lumping "Another Essay" together with a tract called "Antisynodalia" for comment. John Allin, writing for the elders, said:

When the Antisynodalia *of our Brethren came to our hands, and* Another Essay *of the same nature was here Published, some godly and wise Christians advised the* Elders *to let them pass in silence; conceiving that they would not so take with the People, as to hinder the Practice of* the Doctrine of the Synod: *and that a Reply would occasion farther Disputes and Contests. But, upon serious consideration of the matter by divers* Elders *met to that End, the* Reasons *on the other side did preponderate.*

Allin added that silence would be sinful, for many followers were inquiring about the ideas on baptism expressed in the pamphlets. Likewise, an existing ordinance said that people should consult the Assembly of Elders in disputes, but the practice was not well-established. The elders felt obliged to set a precedent for such behavior by getting into the fray. They also worried that silence on the tract would encourage the Anabaptists.[19] Clearly, the elders who responded to "Another Essay" and "Antisynodalia" had a sense of toleration of other opinions. To them, printing was a fair tool of debate, as opposed to authoritarian ranting and raving that would only cause louder dissent and deeper stubbornness.

A healthy printed debate on the baptism question continued, with the Reverend Jonathan Mitchel publishing a tract in favor of the synod. "How loth we are to enter the Lists of publick Debate with the *Brethren*," he moaned, "and such Brethren as we love and honour in the Lord, with whom we are Exiles in the same Wilderness for the same Truth."[20] Mitchel's outlook and tone were gentle. Dissenters, he felt, deserved respect, even if he disagreed with them. To Puritans such as Mitchel and the elders in 1664, freedom of expression meant a gentlemanly debate.

That attitude of toleration on the part of church elders extended to other realms. Even government-appointed licensers of the press tried to be broad-minded. The General Court had finally passed an ordinance for licensing to prevent "irregular-itjes & abuse . . . by the printing presse" in 1662,[21] an act that mirrored the fact that licensing was in place in England.[22] Reflecting a liberal philosophy, Massachusetts licensers approved the printing of Thomas à Kempis's *The Imitation of Christ* in 1667, in spite of the title's clear indication that the work offered an earthly imita-tion of the Savior, and despite the fact that Kempis had been a Catholic priest. Ul-timately, it was the court that howled angrily against both *The Imitation of Christ* and the licensers. Kempis, the court scoffed, was "a Popish minister." The court ruled that the work "contayned some things that are lease safe to be infused amongst the people of this place," and ordered that the press licensers look over the work more carefully.[23]

With the court enforcing licensing practices, licensers felt obliged to let every reader in the colony know exactly what was acceptable for print and what was not. Approving "A Narrative of the Trouble with the Indians" by William Hubbard in 1677, the licensers explained:

The worthy *Author* of this *Narrative* (of whose Fidelity we are well assured) by his great pains, and industry in collecting and compiling the several Occurrences of this *Indian Warre*, from the Relations of such as were present in the particular Actions, hath faithfully, and truly performed the same, as far as best information agreeing could be obtained, which is therefore judged meet for publick view.[24]

The licensers valued truth and accuracy in printed matter. Proving it did have teeth, the licensing board did check Hubbard's reports to ascertain their correct-ness. As far as the licensers were concerned, their job was quality assurance. Li-censing was not a matter of personal favor or arbitrary whim, but almost an editorial function of assuring that a mistaken or lying piece of writing did not find its way into print.

Although the licensing board made it look as if any reputable work would be approved, authors found the licensing process distasteful. Hubbard, for one, was afraid colonial governors would censor "A Narrative of the Troubles with the Indians." He was desperate to have the pamphlet published. He would try anything, even begging and flattery. He implored the governors of Massachusetts, Plymouth, and Connecticut to allow him to print the "Narrative." He praised the governors' faithfulness and courage in managing their power and asked them to let the "Narrative" "pass into publick view under the umbrage of your Protection." He assured them everything in the piece was accurate, and he was confident the pamphlet would "meet with a ready Welcome, and suitable entertainment in every honest mind." In an eloquent statement for the responsibility of free expression, Hubbard added that he had taken "great care . . . to give all and every one, any way concerned in the subject of the discourse, their just due, and nothing more or less."[25]

Although Hubbard showed that grovelling may have had something to do with acceptance of a work for public printing, he also illustrated the prevailing thought in 1677 about what type of pieces should make it into print. As the licensing process indicated, a literary work had to be truthful and accurate, and as Hubbard pleaded, a news report should also show all sides of the story.

Licensing was accepted in part because Puritans were quite aware that the press wielded a tremendous influence. They occasionally made that point in their writings. In a pamphlet entitled "A Publick Tryal of the Quakers in Barmudas," for example, the Puritan Reverend Samson Bond bragged that he had tried and defeated the Quakers in the press. The "tryal" was actually a discussion between Bond and Quakers in Bermuda. The impatient and rude Quakers, Bond said, were "found *Guilty*, they are here *Sentenced*, and brought forth unto the deserved *Execution* of the *Presse*." The so-called trial did not involve a real judge and jury, although the sheriff and some justices of the peace were on hand to declare that Bond had bested the Quakers in the argument. No actual execution took place, but Bond saw to it that the losing Quakers dramatically suffered execution by the printed word.[26] He knew that the pathetic nature of the Quaker arguments could be spread from remote Bermuda to New England with ink and paper and type. Thus, Bond made plain that the concept of free expression included the right to unearth and humiliate any wrongdoing, especially in the realm of religion.

That attitude was indicative of an advance in Puritan toleration. In 1659, Massachusetts had executed two Quakers for persistent proselytizing in the colony.[27] By 1682, Puritans had come to realize that the press had poison in its ink, available to clever and daring authors—and they allowed that poisonous ink to flow as an alternative to actual executions. It was part of the privilege of having a press. Thanks to their thought on freedom of expression, the Puritans were growing more tolerant.

But things started going wrong in Puritan Massachusetts. In 1683, the English crown revoked the colony's charter. After that, the Anglican governor, Sir Edmond Andros, failed to have the laws printed. Without a charter or laws to guide them, citizens were in legal limbo. Resentment grew. After five years of pressure, the

time was ripe for an opposition political press. Religious dissenters had been tolerated for years. Now, religious leaders called for dissent against the government.

The Puritan spiritual leader Increase Mather led the way. He complained bitterly
in a 1688 pamphlet that "the people are at a great loss to *know what* is *Law and
what not*."[28] As far as Mather was concerned, printing and distribution of certain
information such as the law was a basic necessity. Massachusetts residents had
long since come to rely on the printing press for the smooth conduct of their everyday affairs. Andros, however, had come to Massachusetts with royal instructions
to watch over the press and allow only prints that he approved.[29] In Mather's eyes,
Andros had carried out his instructions in the wrong spirit, with far too many restrictions. The press was meant to help the people. It was not a means of keeping
people in the dark.

Mather did not stop there. Andros, he charged, had tried to clamp down on free
speech by prohibiting town meetings except for once a year, when people wanted
to meet once a week. "But it is easie to penetrate into the Design of this Law,"
Mather scoffed, "which was (no Question) to keep them in *every Town* from complaining to *England*, of the Oppression they are under."[30]

In his 1688 "Memorial of the Dissenters," Mather brought serious allegations
against the governor of the Puritan colony. Andros did not allow Massachusettsans
to worship as they pleased. "As to matters of religion, [the inhabitants] are inhib-
ited the free exercise thereof, for they are not allowed to set dayes for prayer or
Thanksgiving," Mather reported. Andros had actually "told them that hee should
then send souldiers to guard them and their meeting-houses too. The worship of
the Church of England has been forced into several of their [Puritan] meeting-
houses."[31] Such actions were outrageous in the "city on a hill." While religion was
the boundary that free expression could not cross in Massachusetts, citizens were
now using free expression in order to demand free religion.

Ultimately a group of colonists took up arms against the governor. After the
Glorious Revolution in England had deposed James II, fifteen Massachusetts leaders published a broadside addressed to Andros, advising the governor to surrender
for his own good. If he did not conform, the petitioners warned, the people might
take the governmental fortifications by storm.[32]

The opposition prints provoked a stern reaction from Andros. Late in 1689, his
administration issued an order against seditious publications. It growled:

WHEREAS many papers have beene lately printed and dispersed tending to the disturbance
of the peace and subversion of the government of this theire Majesties Colonie. . . .

   It is therefore ordered that if any person or persons within this Collony be found guilty of
any such like Misdemeanour of printing, publishing or concealing any such like papers or
discourses, or not timely discover such things to Authority, . . . they shall be accounted enemies to their Majesties present Government and be proceeded against as such with utter-
most severity.[33]

The government's threat notwithstanding, dissenters imprisoned Andros.[34]

The opposition to Andros, combined with the growing diversity of the population, helped pry open the attitude toward religious opposition in Massachusetts. By 1690, even prints attacking the Puritan church were more tolerated. One of those attacks resulted in the statement of a cure for libel that would echo in Hamilton's defense of Zenger.

A Boston Anglican had written that most New England Puritans were lax about attending church and were really not interested in being Puritans. Such words might have brought on the wrath of the council in years past, but by now, Massachusetts thinkers were accustomed to using the public press to fight their wars. Mather lashed back in a piece that was "printed with Allowance." It was officially sanctioned, although clearly licensers who would allow the opposition piece to get through had long since toned down control over free expression.[35] Mather's "Vindication of New England" said bluntly that the opposition print was garbage, "a Libell (A *Lie* because False, and a *Bell* because *Loud*), this whole Paper being One Loud *Lie* (sounding from *America* to *Europe*)." Mather argued that the libelous material simply was not true, and he offered his opinion that the truth, as explained in his work, would cure the evil work done by libel.[36]

Thus, by 1690, legal penalties for libel may have been on the books, but a new concept had been stated: the most obvious antidote for libel was the truth.

Two years later, that idea reappeared in Philadelphia. William Bradford shaped it into a slightly different form when Quaker officials hauled him into court for printing tracts by a radical church faction that offended the mainline Quaker majority in Pennsylvania.[37] The Quaker-dominated court deemed the publications seditious and instructed the jury that it was to find simply whether Bradford had printed the offensive works. Bradford, however, insisted that the jury was also to find whether the pieces were truly seditious. He argued that they were religious and were open to interpretation; thus, they could not really undermine the Quaker-based government.[38]

With that plea, Bradford expanded the notion that truth was a remedy for libel. He insisted that any subject whose truth could not be determined, by definition could *not* be untrue. In other words, Bradford built his defense on the notion that truth protected him in his printing. If truth was unknowable, then he was safe, for who could prove that truth had been violated in the publication?

Before his plea could be judged, Bradford was freed, but his argument found its way into literature. Bradford, who was later Zenger's boss, printed his own story of the trial for public distribution.[39] Thus, Zenger perhaps knew the story of Bradford's stand against the Quaker majority. Zenger's lawyer Hamilton, a Philadelphian himself, may have been familiar with Bradford's plea through his study of law.

Clearly, Mather's argument that truth cures libel was made in a religious argument, quite a different context from Hamilton's attempt to free the imprisoned Zenger. Likewise, Bradford's plea that nothing could violate an unknowable truth was not the same as Hamilton's later defense of Zenger. Even if Hamilton had never read Mather's tract on libel or studied Bradford's argument, however, the logical idea that truth was an antidote to libel was certainly in the air in the colonies. Back home in England, thinkers had also been tangling with notions of free expression. In 1644, a few years after the first Massachusetts print appeared, John Milton questioned press control. In 1712, England introduced a Stamp Act to tax paper goods, and Englishmen vigorously debated the impact of the tax on the press. Before John Peter Zenger entered the printing business, Daniel Defoe, the English essayist, wrestled with the idea of press freedom. Englishman John Locke's ideas on the nature of human rights gained influence in the colonies. A number of English works circulating in America reinforced the growing interest in free expression. Zenger and Hamilton would expand on that foundation.

Zenger's 1735 trial was not a swaggering attempt to establish press freedom. Instead it came about as the result of a longstanding political feud among various factions in New York. One faction used the Bradford press as its voice. The other side adopted Zenger's press, and that got him into trouble.

The factions had been battling for prestige and power in New York politics for years. When Governor William Cosby arrived to take his post in 1732, he inherited the deep, festering factional struggle and became a part of it himself. That was just one more problem in his lengthy list of woes, which included the fact that many people thought of him as mad or at least stupid. He also was deeply in debt due to excess spending and gambling. Knowing this, a cagey factional leader and councilman named James Alexander apparently surmised that Cosby would align himself with the rival faction under Adolph Philipse and James DeLancey, for that group controlled the colony's assembly and thereby had a tight rein on the governor's purse strings.

Alexander preferred for Cosby to stay in London as long as possible, because Alexander himself was embroiled in a lawsuit with the Duke of Chandos over property in the Oblong, a prized piece of unsettled land on the Connecticut border. The representative for the Duke of Chandos in the colonies, Francis Harison, was a former ally of Alexander but had shifted sides when the opposition gained power. Fearing that the new governor would not protect his interests in the Oblong, Alexander wrote to Cosby in England and offered him a note for £1,500, to be repaid from the £4,000 in office funds that awaited him on his arrival in New York. True to Alexander's prediction, Cosby accepted the note and stayed on in London, using the £1,500 to pay off his debts.

When the governor arrived in New York, Alexander greeted him by handing him a bill for the loan and demanded immediate payment. Naturally enough, Cosby took an instant dislike to Alexander. The wily governor decided to avoid paying off most of the note by tricking Alexander.

Mrs. Alexander ran a shop in town; so Cosby bought ladies' items for his wife at the store. He paid the bill there when Mrs. Alexander was out, and then presented the supposed receipt to her husband at the council meeting for his signature. Alexander made the mistake of not reading the paper. He signed it and then was angered to realize he had actually signed a document that forgave Cosby the remaining debt on the note.[40]

After that incident, the governor at first seemed to be blessed with peace among the factions, which caused Alexander to comment that "Our Party Differences seemed over and every thing Seem'd to promise an easier Admin. that any Govr. had ever met with in this place."[41] But the political peace proved short-lived as Cosby's greed—or desperation to pay his debts—encouraged the governor to request that Rip Van Dam, president of the governor's council, return half the salary he had received during his thirteen months as interim governor. As president of the council during Cosby's stay in England, Van Dam had received the governor's salary.[42] Van Dam refused, and Cosby filed a suit in an attempt to recover the money. A prominent Dutch merchant, Van Dam was about seventy years old and had served on the council more than twenty-five years. A fellow council member, Cadwallader Colden, remarked, "This Demand was thought to be an Act of mere Power, and gave general Disgust."[43]

The only member of the governor's council to oppose Van Dam on the matter was James DeLancey of the pro-Cosby group. The ambitious DeLancey could now portray himself as the defender of what was rightfully the governor's while at the same time pitting Cosby against Van Dam, the highest-ranking officeholder in the opposing faction. New York Chief Justice Lewis Morris observed that DeLancey wanted to see Van Dam suspended from the council because DeLancey was scheming "to be at the head of the government."[44]

DeLancey, already powerful, had reasons to expect that he might rise even further in New York politics. That year he was the second justice and Frederick Philipse third justice on the New York Supreme Court. In a case going before the Supreme Court, Cosby could count on the support of DeLancey and Philipse, now firmly a part of the pro-Cosby faction. The odds, however, were against Cosby in a common law court, where a jury would likely rule in favor of Van Dam. Thus, Cosby requested that the Supreme Court act as a Court of Exchequer in his lawsuit against Van Dam. On March 15, 1733, Cosby's case against Van Dam came before the court.[45]

Chief Justice Morris ruled that the governor could not create a Court of Equity without the consent of the Assembly. He also "called into question the legality of the existing court of chancery, which also rested upon nothing more than an ordinance of a governor and council."[46] Justice DeLancey upheld the Supreme Court's equity jurisdiction, but Philipse chose to delay ruling on the issue until the next term. Morris attempted to meet with Cosby and discuss his opinion, but Cosby refused to see him because Morris had treated him with "slight, rudeness, and impertinence" ever since the governor had arrived.[47] The personal miffs and ugly behavior of the factional warfare were coming home to roost.

Later, Cosby requested a copy of the chief justice's opinion. Morris responded by having it printed and published, thus challenging Cosby before the public. The publication of the opinion backed Cosby into a corner, and in a show of power, he suspended Morris from the Supreme Court in April 1733.[48]

Morris may have lost his position as chief justice, but his followers won at the polls in the next election. Cosby had become unpopular.[49] With most of the Cosby faction's power eroded in the government, the opposition party, led by Morris and Alexander, now sought to expose Cosby to the public.[50] They turned to the press and thus dragged John Peter Zenger into the ugly, ongoing battle.

Zenger had not yet begun publishing his newspaper, however. New York had one newspaper at the time, the *New-York Gazette*. Its proprietor was William Bradford, the former Pennsylvania printer who had taken a stand for press freedom in 1692. After his argument with the Quakers, Bradford had become the government printer to New York in 1693. Over the years, the government contract had been good to William Bradford. He published the laws of the colony, the acts of the assembly, and pronouncements of the governor and council. When he was almost seventy years old in 1725, he opened his *New-York Gazette*.[51]

Once a brash young man who had defied the power structure in Pennsylvania, Bradford became a wily old fellow bent on seeing the Philadelphia press firmly in Bradford family hands once again. Young Benjamin Franklin appeared in New York in 1723 and asked old Bradford for a job. He had none, but his son Andrew, now a printer in Philadelphia, perhaps did. William Bradford sent Franklin there. To Franklin's surprise, when he arrived in Pennsylvania, old man Bradford greeted him at Andrew Bradford's shop. William Bradford had travelled by horseback to visit his son, making better time than Franklin had made by sea. Andrew Bradford told Franklin that he did not have a job after all, but young Bradford fed the job-hunter some breakfast, and then William Bradford took Franklin to Andrew's rival, a new printer named Samuel Keimer.[52]

Franklin was shocked when the old New Yorker tried to pull the wool over Keimer's eyes. "Neighbour," Bradford said pleasantly to Keimer, "I have brought to see you a young Man of your Business, perhaps you may want such a One." Keimer let Franklin show his skill with a composing stick and promised to hire him in the near future. Then old Mr. Bradford pumped Keimer for all his secrets, which undoubtedly would be of use to young Andrew. Franklin recalled:

And taking old Bradford whom he had never seen before, to be one of the Towns People that had a Good Will for him, [Keimer] enter'd into a Conversation on his present Undertaking & Prospects; while Bradford not discovering that he was the other Printer's Father, on Keimer's Saying he expected soon to get the greatest Part of the business into his own Hands, drew him on by artful Questions and starting little Doubts, to explain all his Views, what Interest he rely'd on, & in what manner he intended to proceed.[53]

The shocked Franklin took in the whole conversation and "saw immediately that one of them was a crafty old Sophister, and the other a mere Novice." Franklin later told Keimer who the old man was, and Keimer was stunned.[54]

Bradford, who was so sly on behalf of his son, was otherwise known as a generous and industrious man. He built what was probably the first paper mill in New Jersey, and he was generally thought of as a sober, hard worker who took pity on the poor and needy.[55]

Perhaps most important of all, Bradford had learned from his Quaker experience so many years ago that he was in the employ of his bosses. At his advanced age in 1734, he had no desire to anger his employers and lose his livelihood again, as he had done when he crossed the Quakers who had hired him in Pennsylvania. In fact, Bradford had a desperate need to please his governmental employers in order to retain his job. His second wife and the ready-made family she had brought with her had been nothing but a financial drain to him.[56]

Bradford's former apprentice, John Peter Zenger, had less to lose.[57] Without government contracts, Zenger did not have a lot of business for his press. With Bradford tightly in the grasp of the pro-Cosby faction, the anti-Cosby group approached the struggling young printer. They wanted him to start a newspaper to tout their views. Apparently Van Dam was behind the effort to finance Zenger in publishing the new paper.[58] Thus, on November 5, 1733, Zenger printed the first copy of *The New-York Weekly Journal*. The main contributor to the paper was James Alexander, but Lewis Morris and Cadwallader Colden also wrote articles.[59]

With such correspondents, the *Journal* quickly won a reputation as a spicy political paper, aimed against the governor and his cronies. In its seventh issue, the *Journal* criticized the governor as stupid and out-and-out dangerous after he allegedly allowed a French ship, the *Le Cæsar*, to gather military intelligence about New York. According to the *Journal*, the *Le Cæsar* claimed to be taking on provisions for hungry people in the French Canadian settlements at Cape Breton, when in reality it was opening the way for a French attack on New York. The *Journal* also howled vehemently against Bradford's *Gazette* as a tool of the governor in obscuring the French ship's true mission. The *Journal's* tirade, perhaps written by Alexander, began:

Mr. Zenger: . . .

In all publick Papers great Regard is to be had to Truth, but your No. V. *Article* New-York, Dec. 3d., *where it is said,* That the Inhabitants of Cape Brittoun were distitute [*sic*] of Provisions, and that to supply the Want of them the Sloop *Le Cæsar* was sent hither, *did not meet with intire Credit, because it was supposed to be taken from the* New-York Gazette, N. 422. *which, if I am rightly informed, is a Paper known to be under the Direction of the Government, in which the Printer of it is not suffered to insert any Thing but what his Superiors approve of, under the Penalty of losing 50L.* per annum *Salary, and the Title of* The King's Printer for the Province of New-York.[60]

Since Bradford was under the control of the pro-governor faction, Zenger found no affection in his heart for the old man who had taught him the printing trade.

The Zenger newspaper did not stop with vague allegations of governmental cheating in the case of the *Le Cæsar*. Instead, the writer of the piece dredged up several affidavits testifying to a governmental faux pas and subsequent cover-up regarding the *Le Cæsar*. According to a mariner named William Ligget, who had recently been in Cape Breton, there was no scarcity of supplies in the Cape Breton/Louisburg area. John Gardner, another sailor, agreed, and pointed out that the

French who controlled Louisburg were up to some underhanded military operations there. Gardner said the French narrowly missed imprisoning him for viewing
fortifications around Louisburg. The two sailors' affidavits were seconded by an
anonymous gentleman, who also swore in the *Journal* that the French were planning something dangerous.[61]

To underscore the importance of the three accusations, Zenger printed a list of
questions that stressed the points hinted at in the affidavits. The questions pointed
out that the French in Canada around Cape Breton had apparently had a fine har-
vest and were certainly not hungry. Thus, they must have sent the *Le Cæsar* to
New York for other than humanitarian purposes. The *Journal* accused the devious
French of tampering with channel markers outside of New York Harbor and taking
soundings of the nautical approach to the city. It also claimed that the French had
viewed the fortifications around New York. "[A]ny Man of the least Penetration"
could see what the French had in mind, the newspaper scoffed, clearly fingering
governmental officials for being so stupid as to fall for the *Le Cæsar's* trick. The
governor surely was able to discern what the French were up to, the article sneered.
He should have seized the *Le Cæsar's* papers and prevented the Frenchmen from
doing their evil deeds. In fact, the *Journal* said, the governor should be severely
punished for his pitiful lack of backbone against the enemy. The author of the
piece did not mince words about what needed to be done. He called for immediate
defense of New York and for the Assembly to come together to combat the French
menace.[62]

If Cosby and his faction were irritated about the attack in the *Journal*, they did
not make any formal complaint just yet. Their silence may have encouraged the
opposition. Instead of simmering down after that one incident, the anti-Cosby
group plunged forward, using Zenger's *Journal* to deride the governor on other political issues.

The Cosbyites eventually complained, and governmental rumblings about articles in the *Journal* became a sore point with the Zenger paper. Zenger reprinted
some of "Cato's Letters," written in the 1720s by English authors John Trenchard
and Thomas Gordon, which stated radical libertarian philosophies about freedom
of speech. In the February 18, 1734, issue of the *Journal*, Cato declared that the security of property and freedom of speech were sacred privileges that went hand in
hand. Cato said:

Without Freedom of Thought, there can be no such thing as Wisdom; and no such Thing as
publick Liberty, without Freedom of Speech: Which is the Right of every Man, as far as by
it he does not hurt and controul the Right of another; and this is the only Check which it
ought to suffer, the only Bounds which it ought to know.

This sacred Privilege is so essential to free Governments, that the security of Property;
and the Freedom of Speech, always go together; and in those wretched Countries where a
Man cannot call his Tongue his own, he can scarce call any Thing else his own. Whoever
would overthrow the Liberty of the Nation, must begin by subduing the Freeness of Speech;
a Thing terrible to publick Traytors.[63]

It was true, Cato went on, that men should speak well of their governors, but only while the governors behaved. Rulers who were involved in public mischief needed to be exposed, and that could only happen when speech was not bridled. "Only the wicked Governors of Men dread what is said of them," Cato said.[64]

Without actually naming Cosby, the Cato piece certainly hinted at the wickedness of the local government. Other attacks were more blatant. One writer, calling himself NO COURTIER, said of Cosby, "We see Mens Deeds destroyed, Judges arbitrarily displaced, new Courts erected without the consent of the Legislature, by which it seems to me Tryals by Juries are taken away when a Governour pleases."[65]

Zenger irritated the governor a great deal by running a serialized modern fairy tale, purportedly set in New Jersey. The governor in the piece was portrayed as an evil power-grabber, who denied both king and constitution.[66] In a phrase heavily salted with double meaning, a character in the tale wished that New York's judges, lawyers, and chief justice had been present to hear the discussion about New Jersey's crooked governor.[67] The comment could be taken two ways. Either the writer of the fable wished the good officials of New York could have been there to steer New Jersey safely through its troubled waters, or the New Yorkers could have been there to acknowledge the New Jersey woes as something of a metaphor for governmental oppression in New York.

Cosby and his council took the comment to mean the latter. They were angry at the tale. They felt it was a critique of them. It was the next issue of the *New-York Weekly Journal*, however, that provoked the Cosbyites into action. The newspaper contained a letter written by citizens of Goshen Precinct to Colonel Vincent Mathews, their representative in the Assembly. They thanked him for his actions and expressed their surprise at the attempts of an unnamed faction to introduce "arbitrary Power" into New York. Judges in this faction, they accused, had tried to take over, when judges really did not have that power. Then the Goshen residents made an insolent suggestion about governors who courted one faction over another. "Governours often smile one Day and frown the next," they commented, "nay, they may make a Sacrifice of those that have lost all other's friendship by courting theirs; and at best they are here to day and gone to morrow."[68]

This time the pro-Cosby faction had had enough. Harison, a faithful Cosby follower, appeared on Zenger's doorstep and swore he would beat the printer with his cane when next they met in the street. The swashbuckling Zenger, a little afraid but also perhaps making a sweeping gesture, starting carrying a sword about town.[69]

Next, Chief Justice DeLancey called in a grand jury and charged it to return indictments against Zenger for seditious libel. The grand jury refused to act. The pro-Cosby faction did not give up; instead, it sought to have the *Journal* condemned in the Assembly. The Assembly, however, declined to cooperate. Finally, the governor's council, dominated by Cosbyites, declared four issues of Zenger's *Journal* libelous and ordered the papers burned by the common hangman on November 5.[70] The issues included the early one about the *Le Cæsar*, two containing the fable from New Jersey, and the number containing the letter from the Goshen residents.[71] The mayor's court, being aligned with the anti-Cosby faction, refused to carry out the order. Thus, the papers were "executed" by order of the governor, with his crony the sheriff letting his servant set fire to the offensive *Journals*.[72]

Shortly thereafter, *Journal* subscribers missed their paper. On November 25, Zenger explained what happened. The governor had issued a warrant for his arrest, and he had been rudely dragged off to the magistrate on a Sunday. Harison had also signed the warrant, perhaps seeing it as a firmer solution than beating Zenger with a cane. Zenger complained that he was put into jail and not allowed to see or speak to anyone, nor was he allowed to write from his cell. His request for *habeas corpus* was denied, "and therefore," he told his readers, "I have had since that time, the Liberty of Speaking through the Hole of the Door, to my Wife and Servants."[73]

Zenger became a martyr to his readers, who ate up such doleful laments as "From my Prison," published in the December 23 *Journal*. Zenger wrote:

> Oh cruelty unknown before,
> To any barbarous savage shore.
> Much more when Men so much profess,
> Humanity and Godliness.[74]

Meanwhile, Bradford was delighting in Zenger's misery. His old apprentice had gotten his due at last for stabbing at the wrong faction. Bradford's *Gazette* made wicked fun of Zenger. Writers found Zenger's sword ridiculous and laughably newsworthy. Aside from that, a letter in Bradford's newspaper said that Zenger's address to his readers sounded "*like the Language of the . . . Poppet-Show Man.*" On a more serious note, the writer accused Zenger of publishing factional writings for the purposes of "*setting the Province in Flames, raising of Sedition and Tumults, &c.*"[75]

Zenger was distressed that Bradford's press and the governmental faction had turned him into a laughingstock. He retorted that he would have readily printed all sides of any story, had anyone from the pro-Cosby group bothered to supply him with information. Defending himself in regard to his sword, Zenger said Harison was responsible. After the threatened beating, the side arm would come in handy, for "Against such Assaults my Sword not only could but would have protected me."[76]

Months passed before Zenger went to trial. The court demanded excessive bail of £600. Zenger swore, speaking of himself in the third person, "that, his debts being paid, he was not worth forty pounds, the tools of his trade and his wearing apparel excepted." Clearly £40 would not cover the bail. The court devised a method of payment for him, but Zenger said:

[K]nowing this sum to be ten times the amount of what indemnity he could give to any person to whom he might apply to be his bondsman, [he] declined to ask that favor of his friends, and submitted to further confinement.[77]

His influential contributors probably could have afforded the bail, but leaving Zenger in jail was to their advantage. He became more of a martyr and public figure. Those qualities helped sell newspapers and increased the interest in his case. He ran the newspaper from his jail cell, apparently communicating instructions for the *Journal* to his wife and staff.[78]

The Van Dam faction was ready to help Zenger. James Alexander and William Smith had defended Van Dam against Cosby's attempt to get the Van Dam salary, and they would defend Zenger, too. They used their defense as a propaganda weapon against Cosby. Still smarting from the governor's suspension of Morris, Alexander and Smith offered exceptions to the commissions of James DeLancey and Frederick Philipse as judges, thus questioning the judges' authority to officiate in the case. The judges considered the question on April 15, 1735, and then declared that they would not hear exceptions in court until two days later. On April 18, however, DeLancey disbarred Alexander and Smith.[79]

After the dismissal of Alexander and Smith, the court assigned John Chambers to defend Zenger, and the lawyer helped prevent the sheriff from packing the jury list with Cosby supporters. When the trial began, however, the defense made its surprise move to bring in Andrew Hamilton. In the Philadelphia statesman, the defense possessed a persuasive advocate unscarred by New York's ongoing factional warfare.

On August 4, 1735, Zenger stood trial for printing and publishing seditious libels against Governor Cosby. After such a lengthy jail stay, Zenger had become something of a folk hero. His supporters packed the courtroom, but Cosby had packed the two seats that presumably counted most—those belonging to Supreme Court Justices DeLancey and Philipse. With such pro-Cosby men sitting on the bench, things looked bleak for Zenger.

Attorney General Richard Bradley built his case against the printer upon the assumption that all he needed to prove was Zenger's role in printing the libelous material. The jury's duty, according to the prosecutor and judges, was to affirm that Zenger was guilty of printing the materials and no more. English common law placed the decision as to whether the material was libelous or not in the hands of the judges, whose loyalty to the governor assured a conviction.

However, Zenger's new attorney Andrew Hamilton, a wily fifty-nine-year-old politician, daringly admitted that Zenger had printed and published the material. The prosecution was shocked. Then Hamilton revealed his plan. "Libels are not to be published," he argued to the court, "but every writing disagreeable to a magistrate is not by his construction to be wrought up into a libel against the government." He added that he thought it was the place of a jury, and not of a judge, to determine whether printed material was libelous.[80]

Although DeLancey insisted that only a judge could rule whether a piece was libelous, Hamilton dramatically addressed the jury and vowed that the charges made in the Zenger newspaper against the government were true. "You are citizens of New York. You are really what the law assumes you to be, honest and lawful men," he told the jury, "and according to my brief, the facts which we offer to prove were not committed in a corner. They are notoriously known to be true. Therefore in your justice lies our safety." Hamilton warned the jurors against the dangers of power and tyranny while praising the virtues of liberty, freedom of the press, and truth. Indeed, he said, the question before the court dealt not with a small or private concern, with the cause of a poor printer, nor with New York alone. Known in Philadelphia for his blustering style of arguing, he then thundered:

No! [This case] may in its consequence affect every free man that lives under a British government on the main of America. It is the best cause. It is the cause of liberty; and I make no doubt but your upright conduct this day will not only entitle you to the love and esteem of your fellow citizens; but every man who prefers freedom to a life of slavery will bless and honor you as men who have baffled the attempt of tyranny and by an impartial and uncorrupt verdict, have laid a noble foundation for securing to ourselves, our posterity, and our neighbors that to which nature and the laws of our country have given us a right—the liberty—both of exposing and opposing arbitrary power (in these parts of the world, at least) by speaking and writing the truth.[81]

The jury withdrew and soon returned with a verdict of not guilty. The crowded gallery of Zengerites responded to the verdict with "three loud Huzzas & scarcely one person except the officers of the Court were observ'd not to join in this noisy exclamation."[82] Zenger returned to jail for one more night before being released the next morning. His supporters, meanwhile, celebrated that very night by honoring Hamilton at the Black Horse Tavern.[83]

The Zenger trial, in time, came to be seen as the landmark case for freedom of the press in the American colonies. It gradually took its place in history as a bold stroke against oppression.

In reality, the case was more of a bold stroke from one faction against another in colonial New York, rather than a brave statement for principles of journalism. Likewise, Increase Mather's 1690 opinion that truth would be the cure for libel sprang from a factional argument between Anglicans and Puritans. William Bradford's 1692 argument that he had not violated the truth and thus had not libelled anyone was the result of a factional argument between various parties of the Quakers.

The fact that Bradford made a switch from his 1692 antigovernmental stance to stodgy support of the ruling party in the time of Zenger was typical of colonial free press ideas. The formulation of colonial press theory was not based on the dawning of some noble, eternal idea about freedom of expression. Rather, notions of free press were shaped by events and by rivalries. Mather vehemently wanted to defend religious doctrine. Bradford's original arguments on free press stemmed from his work for a radical faction. Zenger was under the control of the anti-Cosby faction. That faction just happened to secure a brilliant lawyer, who in turn just happened to argue before the right jury, thus helping create the landmark decision for a free press. The factional warfare was the driving force in the incident. Andrew Hamilton's specific argument was almost an unexpected occurrence.

None of the men who first claimed that truth was a defense against libel particularly started out to prove that point. The argument just seemed logical to them in their attempt to boost their various factions. While it certainly would be folly to deny the farsighted brilliance of Mather, young Bradford, and Hamilton in reasoning that truth was a basis for free speech, it would also be folly to ignore the fact that their logic in each case was presented in an attempt to defend one party over another.

From 1638 to 1735, concepts of press freedom took shape in the prevailing winds of custom, factionalism, need, and logic. Press freedom was not considered a God-given right, or even a constitutional one—but perhaps due to the foundations laid by Anglican-Puritan controversies, squabbles among the Quakers, and bitter rivalries in New York politics, the right to speak the truth in print ultimately became a reality in American law.

As the concept of a free press began to take root in American thought, other ideas, plans, and dreams were starting to take shape. For the next thirty years, the American press would pioneer into new geographical areas, test fresh ideas, and establish itself in colonial life. The concepts of press freedom that had developed out of America's early experiences provided the foundation on which those later newspapers would build.

NOTES

1. City of New York's Common Council to Andrew Hamilton, 29 September 1735, quoted in Isaiah Thomas, *The History of Printing in America*, ed. Marcus A. McCorison (1810; reprint New York: Weathervane Books, 1970), 489–90.

2. Ibid., 489.

3. James Alexander, *A Brief Narrative of the Case and Tryal of John Peter Zenger* (1736).

4. Charles Evans's bibliography of American prints is an excellent guide to locating most of the early prints mentioned in this section. See Charles Evans, *American Bibliography*, 1:1639–1729 (Chicago: Blakeley Press, 1903). According to Evans, no original copies of the first print survive. Thus, the exact date of publication is unknown, but Evans is sure that the work was printed in March of either 1638 or 1639. See Evans entry #1. Extant prints to which Evans refers are preserved on Readex Microprint in Clifford K. Shipton, ed., *Early American Imprints, 1639–1800* (Worcester, Mass.: American Antiquarian Society).

5. Puritan leader John Winthrop adopted the "city on a hill" phrase from Matthew 5:14 in a lay sermon he delivered aboard the ship *Arabella* while it was still at sea in 1630. See John Winthrop, "A Model of Christian Charity," in *The Puritans in America*, ed. Alan Heimert and Andrew Delbanco (Cambridge, Mass.: Harvard University Press, 1985), 91.

6. Massachusetts Bay Colony, "The Oath of a Free-man" (Cambridge: printed by Stephen Day, 1638 or 1639).

7. Massachusetts Bay Colony, *The Book of the General Lauues and Libertyes concerning the Inhabitants of Massachusetts* (Cambridge: 1648), 19–20. Due to the colonial habit of writing paragraphs upon paragraphs of information into titles, titles of most early works mentioned in this chapter have been shortened to their primary title.

8. Ibid., 26.

9. Ibid., 29.

10. Ibid., 1–2.

11. Ibid., 35.

12. Clyde Augustus Duniway, *The Development of Freedom of the Press in Massachusetts* (New York: Longmans, Green, & Co., 1906), 31.

13. General Court action, May 1649, in *Massachusetts Archives* (manuscripts in the office of the Secretary of the Commonwealth), 44:11. Quoted in Duniway, ibid., 25.

14. General Court action, May 1642, *Massachusetts Records*, 2: 5, 20, 21. Cited in Duniway, ibid., 29.

15. General Court action, 22 May 1661, *Massachusetts Records*, 4, pt. 2: 5–6. Quoted in Duniway, ibid., 38–39.

16. Synod of Elders and Messengers of Churches in Massachusetts Colony, "Propositions Concerning the Subject of Baptism and Consociation of Churches" (Cambridge: printed by Samuel Green for Hezekiah Usher, 1662), preface.

17. The first press which the Puritans did not control did not arrive for several more years. Duniway, *The Development of Freedom of the Press in Massachusetts*, gives the time line on pp. 42 and 47.

18. John Davenport, "Another Essay for the Investigation of Truth" (Cambridge: printed by Samuel Green and Marmaduke Johnson, 1663), preface. The preface read, "But especially, being perswaded that the Honour of God, and of his Truth, require this as a duty at our hands, We durst not hinder what is here maintained from coming into light, lest we should one day have it laid unto our Charge, that we did withhold the Truth in unrighteousness. . . . [W]e do believe, it will tend to our rejoicing in the day of the Lord Jesus, that we were made instrumental to bring the Truth into publick view, whereby the World might fare the better for it."

19. John Allin, "Animadversions Upon the Antisynodalia Americana, A Treatise printed in Old England: in the Name of the Dissenting Brethren" (Cambridge: printed by Samuel Green and Marmaduke Johnson for Hezekiah Usher, 1664), preface.

20. Jonathan Mitchel and Elders, "A Defence of the Answer and Argument of the Synod Met at Boston in the Year 1662" (Cambridge: printed by Samuel Green and Marmaduke Johnson for Hezekiah Usher, 1664), preface.

21. *Massachusetts Records* 4, pt. 2: 62. Quoted in Duniway, *The Development of Freedom of the Press in Massachusetts*, 41–42.

22. 13 & 14 Charles II, chapter 33. Cited in Duniway, ibid., 45–46.

23. Thomas à Kempis, *The Imitation of Christ* (Cambridge: printed by Samuel Green, 1667). Evans gives the work's legal history. See Evans, *American Bibliography*, entry #114.

24. William Hubbard, "A Narrative of the Troubles with the Indians" (Boston: printed by John Foster, 1677), prefatory statement by the licensers.

25. Ibid., Hubbard's "Epistle Dedicatory."

26. Samson Bond, "A Publick Tryal of the Quakers in Barmudas" (Boston: printed by Samuel Green, 1682), title page, 50, 75.

27. "A Declaration of the General Court of the Massachusetts Holden at Boston in New-England, October 18, 1659. Concerning the Execution of Two Quakers" (Cambridge: printed by Samuel Green, 1659). Wilfred J. Ritz, comp., *American Judicial Proceedings First Printed Before 1801: An Analytical Bibliography* (Westport, Conn.: Greenwood Press, 1984), cites the broadside, which is no longer extant. See p. 159.

28. Increase Mather, "A Narrative of the Miseries of New-England, by Reason of an Arbitrary Government Erected *there*, Under Sir *Edmond Andros*" (Boston: printed by Richard

Pierce, 1688). This was a reprint; the first edition appeared in London, according to *The An-dros Tracts, Being a Collection of Pamphlets and Official Papers Issued During the Period Between the Overthrow of the Andros Government and the Establishment of the Second Charter of Massachusetts* (New York: Burt Franklin, Research & Source Works Series #131, 1868), 1:5.

29. Commissions to Massachusetts Governors, *Massachusetts Historical Society Proceedings* (June 1893): 273.

30. Increase Mather, "A Narrative of the Miseries of New England," in *Andros Tracts* 2:5.

31. Increase Mather, "Memorial of Grievances Presented by Increase Mather to James II," part of "Memorial of the Dissenters of New England" (1688), in *Andros Tracts* 3:139n.

32. "At the Town-House in Boston: April 18th, 1689" (Boston: printed by Samuel Green, 1689).

33. "Order against seditious publications" (1689), in *Andros Tracts* 3:107.

34. Increase Mather, "The Present State of the New English Affairs" (Boston: printed by Samuel Green, 1689), in *Andros Tracts* 2:16.

35. Increase Mather, "A Vindication of New England" (1690), in *Andros Tracts* 2:21–78. According to Evans, *American Bibliography*, entry #542, "A Vindication" was the duplicate of Evans entry #452. The #452 entry was "printed with Allowance." *Early American Imprints* simply does not repeat the tract at entry #542, instead referring the reader to #452. The *Andros Tracts* version does not include the "printed with Allowance" line. Thus, it may be true that there was no licensing at all on the second version of "A Vindication." However, the two versions appeared only about two years apart, and it is clear that the Puritans of this time frame were tolerating both pro and con pieces relating to church, whether the licensing system was firmly in operation or not. "A Vindication" was not signed, but scholars believe that Mather was its author. See Evans, *American Bibliography*, entry #542.

36. Mather, "A Vindication of New England," 32–33, 43–44.

37. See Chapter 2 of this book.

38. William Bradford, "New England Spirit of Persecution" (Philadelphia, 1693).

39. Ibid.; Thomas, *The History of Printing in America*, quotes much of the pamphlet on 345–54.

40. Henry Noble MacCracken, *Prologue to Independence: The Trials of James Alexander, American, 1715–1756* (New York: James H. Heineman, Inc., 1964), 17, 39–40.

41. James Alexander, quoted in Eugene R. Sheridan, *Lewis Morris, 1671–1746: A Study in Early American Politics* (Syracuse, N.Y.: Syracuse University Press, 1981), 148.

42. Cadwallader Colden to the Earl of Hillsborough, 10 November 1770, in *Collections of The New-York Historical Society for the Year 1877* (Publication Fund Series, 1878), 232.

43. Ibid., 233.

44. Lewis Morris, *Papers of Governor Morris* (Freeport, N.Y.: Books for Libraries Press, 1970), 67.

45. Sheridan, *Lewis Morris, 1671–1746*, 150.

46. Ibid., 151.

47. Ibid., 20.

48. The incident was recalled in both the *New-York Gazette*, 4 November 1734, and the *New-York Weekly Journal*, 11 November 1734.

49. James Alexander to Ferdinand John Paris, 29 May 1733. Summarized in William A. Whitehead, *Analytical Index to the Colonial Documents of New Jersey* (New York: D. Appleton & Co., 1858), 158.

50. James Alexander to Robert Hunter, 8 November 1733, *New Jersey Archives*, V, 360, quoted in Stanley Nider Katz, *Newcastle's New York: Anglo-American Politics, 1732–1753* (Cambridge, Mass.: Belknap Press of Harvard University Press, 1968), 75.

51. Thomas, *The History of Printing in America*, 458, 460, 487.

52. J. A. Leo LeMay and P. M. Zall, eds., *The Autobiography of Benjamin Franklin: A Genetic Text* (Knoxville: University of Tennessee Press, 1981), 21, 25–26. Franklin did not give a date for the encounter, but Thomas said Keimer started his business in 1723 and commented that Franklin helped him get started. See Thomas, *The History of Printing in America*, 362.

53. *Autobiography of Benjamin Franklin*, 26.

54. Ibid.

55. Bradford's obituary in the *New-York Gazette* (New York), 30 May 1752.

56. Thomas cited the rumor that Bradford's new wife, who had several children from an earlier marriage, "was attended with no small injury to [Bradford's] pecuniary interests." *The History of Printing in America*, 460.

57. Thomas's editor noted that in 1710, the thirteen-year-old Zenger was apprenticed to William Bradford. See *The History of Printing in America*, 514 n. 5. The editor cited Zenger's indentures in *The Historical Magazine* 8 (January 1846): 35–36.

58. Thomas held that opinion. *The History of Printing in America*, 487.

59. Cadwallader Colden, *History of Cosby and Clark*, 318–19, in Katz, *Newcastle's New York*, 75.

60. *New-York Weekly Journal*, 17 December 1733.

61. Ibid., 17 December and 24 December 1733.

62. Ibid., 17 December 1733.

63. Ibid., 18 February 1734. Zenger dated the issue 18 February 1733, since February then fell at the end of the year.

64. Ibid.

65. Ibid., 8 April 1734.

66. Ibid., 23 September 1734.

67. Ibid., 30 September 1734.

68. Ibid., 7 October 1734.

69. Ibid., 23 December 1734.

70. Katz, *Newcastle's New York*, gives the legal steps in the case on p. 76.

71. The condemned issues are identified by handwritten notes at the tops of the *Journal's* issues #7 and #47 in the collection of the American Antiquarian Society. The note on #7, which is substantially mirrored in the later note, said, "A vote of the Council of November 2nd 1734 ordered this paper to be burned by the hands of the common hangman near the Pillory." See *New-York Weekly Journal*, 17 December 1733, in the microform edition of the *Journal*, as published by the American Antiquarian Society, Worcester, Mass., in the *Early American Imprints* series.

72. Thomas, *The History of Printing in America*, 488.

73. *New-York Weekly Journal*, 25 November 1734.

74. Ibid., 23 December 1734.

75. Ibid. In this piece, Zenger quoted Bradford's *New-York Gazette*. The quoted material is taken from Zenger's article.

76. *New-York Weekly Journal*, 23 December 1734.

77. Oath of John Peter Zenger to the Court, quoted in Thomas, *The History of Printing in America*, 462.

78. Zenger mentioned speaking to his wife and servants through the cell door. See *New-York Weekly Journal*, 25 November 1734.

79. James Alexander and William Smith, *The Complaint of James Alexander and William Smith to the Committee of the General Assembly of the Colony of New York, etc.* (New York, 1736).

80. James Alexander's *Remarks* on the Zenger trial, quoted in MacCracken, *Prologue to Independence*, 65.

81. James Alexander, *A Brief Narrative of the Case and Tryal of John Peter Zenger* (1736).

82. Colden, *History of Cosby and Clarke*, 339, quoted in Katz, *Newcastle's New York*, 77.

83. Katz, ibid., 77.

4

The Expansion of the Colonial Press, 1735–1765

The new year of 1741 was just a week old, but already it had brought nothing but distress to newspaper publisher Elizabeth Timothy of Charleston, South Carolina.[1] Her son Peter was only a teenager, but at that moment he had just been hauled into court with the world's most famous evangelist.[2]

The trouble had begun when the Reverend George Whitefield arrived in Charleston and got mixed up with Hugh Bryan, a starry-eyed convert to White-field's evangelical brand of Christianity.[3] Peter had been arrested after his mother's newspaper, the *South-Carolina Gazette*, had printed a letter by Bryan that libeled the clergy. At least, South Carolina Chief Justice Benjamin Whitaker deemed it libelous. He also considered it to be "false, malicious, scandalous, and infamous" as well as in contempt of the king. The article said of the clergy that "they themselves break [their] Canons every Day. . . . Oh Shame! Shame! Is this to imitate their Master, who went about doing Good?"[4]

As the supposed publisher of the *Gazette*, fifteen-year-old Peter had been arrested along with Bryan and Whitefield, who had corrected the letter before it was published.[5] Peter Timothy was innocent in the whole matter, and it was his mother's fault that he had been arrested at all. Elizabeth Timothy herself was the real publisher of the *Gazette*, having taken over two years earlier upon her husband Lewis's death. She had printed the offending article. She used Peter's name as publisher, it was true, but that was just to live up to a legal agreement between Peter's father and the *Gazette*'s co-owner, Benjamin Franklin. According to the contract with Franklin, Lewis was to start the paper and leave it to Peter for a career.[6] So now Peter was supposedly the publisher of the paper, when really he was still just a boy. With six children younger than Peter to care for, the baby just now two years old,[7] Elizabeth nearly had her hands too full to worry about George Whitefield and the chief justice as well as Peter and the *Gazette*. Fortunately Peter and his fellow prisoners made bail.[8]

Elizabeth Timothy and her newspaper survived the crisis of January 1741. But the incident serves as a metaphor for the struggle that the fledgling newspaper industry in America faced during the colonial period as it tried to carve out a niche for itself. Elizabeth Timothy was fighting to stay afloat for her family's sake; her children needed their mother to make a living for them. In general, other colonial printers were also struggling to keep their businesses open and put food on the table. There were very few James Franklins and very few *New-England Courants* crusading for particular causes; most printers wanted merely to survive.

The colonial press from 1735–1765 was a colorful product of the men and women who forged ahead with a brand new industry, finding guidance first from their own consciences, then from readers, from each other, and from government. Sometimes they felt pressured by outside parties. Sometimes they took advantage of completely new territory to shape the press as they themselves thought it should be. As pioneers in vastly different geographical, governmental, and economic environments, colonial printers were forced to figure out what worked best in each individual situation. Overall, they did establish the seedlings of the American mass media. Individually, however, they had to fight battles and carve their own niches in their various communities in order to survive. From 1735–1765, the American colonial press searched in haphazard directions for prosperity and success. Each newspaper had its own problems to face.

Like Elizabeth Timothy, most printers never knew what obstacles would raise their ugly heads. Elizabeth had not planned on landing her teenager in court. The article that had caused all the trouble had merely been a contribution from a reader. Most other colonial printers faced equally unexpected situations. The press was so new in America that there was no concrete concept of what should, could, or would work in the press business. The struggle to survive from 1735 to 1765 was a learning process for the American news industry. For many printers, the learning process meant tackling new worlds. Printers took their families and their limited resources to places that hitherto had never seen a printing press. They risked a great deal of money and pride to introduce the art of printing, usually at the behest of colonial governments.

Not that governments had always been enthusiastic about printing. Governor William Berkeley of Virginia had commented in 1671:

I thank God, there are no free schools nor printing [in Virginia], and I hope we shall not have these hundred years; for learning has brought disobedience, and heresy, and sects into the world, and printing has divulged them, and libels against the best government. God keep us from both![9]

By 1730, however, Virginia, like any growing colony, needed a printer to record copies of the law, to print and sell blank legal forms, and to produce or at least distribute cultural amenities such as books. The government decided it would have to take its chances with a press. To that end, Virginia hired William Parks away from the colony of Maryland (although he continued maintaining an office in Annapolis for some time) to do the official government printing. By 1736, Parks had started Virginia's first newspaper.

Parks was a true journalistic trailblazer. He saw fresh opportunities for the press in whole new worlds and took those opportunities before they evaporated. By the time he pioneered journalism in Virginia, he knew what he was doing. He left Annapolis for Williamsburg to start his second print shop and his second newspaper in the American colonies. That did not count his pioneering work in England. He had started the first newspaper in the town of Ludlow in Shropshire in 1719. He had printed the first newspaper in Reading as well, all before he had arrived in Maryland in 1726 at the request of the colony's general assembly. Within a year he had founded the *Maryland Gazette.*[10]

Parks had taken every precaution, based on his English experiences, to ensure that his Maryland newspaper would survive. He had thought through and guessed at the needed elements of a successful American press. "I made it my particular Concern, whilst I was in England," he wrote, "to settle such a correspondence there; by which, upon all Occasions, I [would] be furnished with the freshest intelligence, both from thence, and other Parts of Europe."[11] His first American newspaper, then, cast a distinctly American eye back home to England. Not only was England a great source of news, but it was also the ultimate seat of government for the colonies and the sentimental "home" of many of his readers. He shaped his pioneering newspaper to accommodate the reality of an America that still had its umbilical cord attached to England and had close ties to the rest of Europe.

When Parks was in Maryland, he could not resist the vast lands to the South that had no press as yet. He saw a golden opportunity to expand his business. From Maryland, he sought out jobs in Virginia, even though that colony's governors still balked at inviting a printer to the colony on a permanent basis. Virginia finally broke down and hired him to print the colony's laws in 1730. Six years later, he started the *Virginia Gazette,* his fourth newspaper.[12]

Parks was leaving a trail of newspapers and press offices behind him. He capitalized on the newness of it all. Printing was only a dream in some places; some towns in England and most in America lacked a printing press. When colonies or towns realized the need of a printing press, Parks was prepared. He was ready to offer, as other printers would after him, a way for American leaders to publish laws and proclamations, and a way for the colonial American populace to keep its eye on its English rulers and its European homeland.

Parks's press was a novelty in Virginia and Maryland, but novelty created problems of its own. For one thing, colonial Americans were not entirely used to the concept of their words and deeds being carried in print into other people's households. Parks realized, in fact, that colonials were leery at the thought of it. He decided to introduce colonists to the idea of a widely circulated newspaper by playing up the economic benefits. He wrote to his readers:

All persons who have Occasion to buy or sell Houses, Lands, Goods, or Cattle; or have Servants or Slaves Runaway; or have lost Horses, Cattle, &c. or want to give any Publick Notice; may have it advertis'd in all of these Gazettes printed in one Week, for Three Shillings, and for Two Shillings per week for as many Weeks afterwards as they shall order, by giving or sending their Directions to the Printer hereof.

And, as these Papers will Circulate (as speedily as possible) not only all over This, but also the Neighboring Colonies, and will probably be read by some Thousands of People, it is very likely they may have the desir'd Effect; and it is certainly the cheapest and most effectual Method that can be taken, for Publishing any Thing of this Nature.[13]

If newspaper-deprived Virginians had hitherto seemed unsure about airing their ideas and goods in public, they soon learned that the *Gazette* made an excellent community forum. Parks spearheaded community debate on hot topics. For instance, he printed the petition of Virginia's Quakers to cease seizures of their properties for parish levies. "We . . . are encouraged to hope you will charitably look on our condition, and afford us some relief," the Quakers pleaded.[14] The next week, a reader using the signature "W.W." responded by asking Parks to print a scathing recipe for *"How to Make a Perfect Quaker"*:

First, take a handful of the Herb of Deceit, and a few leaves of Folly, and a little of the Rose of Vain-Glory, with some of the buds of Envy, and a few blossoms of Malice . . . and when they are all simmered and soaked together enough, grate in a little Folly powder and strain it through a cloth of Vanity and suck every morning through a spout of Ignorance, . . . and so you will become a perfect Quaker.[15]

Such controversial topics were accompanied by new dangers and unseen pitfalls. Virginia was still unaccustomed to locally printed debate. Laws and governmental opinions surrounding controversial printing were still amorphous and unsettled. For Virginia's first printer, publishing anything along those lines was a distinct gamble as he tested official and public reaction.

Parks was indeed a gambler. He got hold of a juicy story about a member of the House of Burgesses who had a skeleton in his closet: the burgess had once been a sheep thief. It made good reading in the *Gazette*—but the Burgesses disagreed. They dragged Parks before them for punishment. He produced court records proving the incident was true. Another newspaper moralized about the incident with journalistic pride:

Now, mark the sequel: the prosecutor stood recorded for sheep stealing; a circumstance which he supposed time had fully obliterated, both from the records of the court, and from the minds of the people, and he withdrew, overwhelmed with disgrace, from public life, and never more ventured to obtrude himself into a conspicuous situation or to trouble printers with prosecutions for libels.[16]

It was not to be Parks's last run-in with the unsettled concept of newspaper law. In 1749, the House of Burgesses took him to task for printing a report that "injuriously [reflected] on the Proceedings of the House of Burgesses." Furthermore, the article used abusive and indecent language, in the lawmakers' view. Parks pleaded that the House had ordered him to print the material, and he was accordingly exonerated.[17]

Besides pioneering public discussion, Parks also saw a need to give Virginians their first mass-produced entertainment. When the *Virginia Gazette* began, many Virginians had little if any access to cultural events. The weekly *Virginia Gazette* might be their only entertainment all week. Parks recognized that fact; and, like other colonial editors, he pioneered culture in rather uncultured America by printing literary works in his newspaper.

The *Virginia Gazette* ran lots of verse as a form of entertainment, both amusing and serious. Parks found that love was a popular topic for the *Gazette*'s readers. They delighted in such romance as this:

> In vain, I strove my Love to hide,
> In vain, th' apparent Truth deny'd,
> My Blushes told my Tongue, it ly'd.
> Whether my Breast's involv'd with Cares,
> At her Approach a calm appears,
> Or if my Heart with gloomy Grief
> Is clouded o'er, she brings Relief;
> Her charming Eyes new Joys distil,
> And my fond Soul with Raptures fill.[18]

The *Gazette*'s commentary on love grew bawdy in a series of essays by a writer known only as "Monitor." Monitor, whose subtle humor depended on puns and suggestive topics, was a close imitation of English essayists of the day, giving Virginians a chance to be culturally updated with their counterparts in London.[19] Monitor created six lovelorn females as recurring characters whose antics were intended to entertain the readers. The six sisters, Miss Leer, Miss Sly, Miss Fidget, Amoret, Phillis, and Euphemia, time and time again got themselves into all sorts of suggestive situations. Amoret, for instance, was "forever moist'ning her Lips with her Tongue, that gives them a pouting Ripeness that tempts all the young Fellows in the Town."[20] Similarly, Miss Leer reported about a doctor who was a suitor of a friend of hers. "[H]e's forever feeling of her Pulse; and if he were let alone, I believe o' my Conscience he would trace it from Head to Foot," she commented.[21]

Other Monitor pieces were overtly humorous. A character named Zachary Downright commented that he had been to the opera in London. It was a singularly unpleasant experience. He and his fellow opera-goers were illiterate of the Italian lyrics, and frankly, Downright said, the opera sounded a lot like his mother's and father's arguments.[22]

Parks made it clear that he meant for his Monitor series and similar literary works to entertain the *Gazette*'s readers. Furthermore, he hoped that readers themselves would contribute their own literary works. He noted:

When I first publish'd these Papers, I propos'd to entertain my Customers, now and then occasionally, or when there was a Scarcity of News, with Pieces Instructive or Diverting; in
which I flattered myself with the Assistance of the Gentlemen of this Country, many of whom
want neither Learning, or fine natural Parts, to qualify them for the Task: But I cannot help
taking Notice, that either thro' their too great Modesty, or want of Application in the Service
of the Public, I find myself greatly disappointed in my Expectations of their Assistance.[23]

The lack of help from his readers notwithstanding, Parks had indeed achieved
the first mass circulation of entertainment in Virginia. Taking advantage of his pioneering position in Virginia, as he had done in Annapolis and in Ludlow and
Reading, he was able to introduce a widely circulated newspaper to people who
had not before had a newspaper at their fingertips. His offer of everything from debate to poetry helped define the new field of journalism and helped him carve out
his own niche in colonial Virginia.

It was not always easy to make a living as a colonial printer. Sometimes it took
innovation, creativity, or just plain luck to find a way to make ends meet or to catch
the public eye with something different. Colonial newspapers folded right and left
as their printers tried and failed to find a magic formula for survival. (See Table
4.1.) No one person held the key; even hugely successful Benjamin Franklin was
forced to fold his pioneering German-language American newspaper, the
Philadelphische Zeitung, after just a couple of issues.[24]

Still other printers turned to new types of publications in an attempt to make
their presses profitable. A number tried their hand at news-and-entertainment
magazines. Magazines were untried in the New World as yet, although London
had a few popular ones that were read in the colonies. Their popularity did not escape the notice of Benjamin Franklin, who was always looking for ways to reap financial benefits from his printing press. By 1741, he was plotting to start
America's first magazine. He had definite ideas for the new publication. It would
be based loosely on *Gentleman's Magazine* and *London Magazine*, both highly
popular in England. Franklin's *Pennsylvania Gazette* newspaper was already a success, but he figured he could also find time and energy to turn out a magazine by
hiring John Webbe to edit it for him. As editor, Webbe would receive twenty-five
percent of all the magazine's revenues for the first 2,000 copies that were sold.
After that he would get fifty percent.[25]

Webbe either did not care for Franklin's idea or simply did not care for Franklin.
He wandered over to Franklin's rival printer Andrew Bradford and told him everything about Franklin's plans.[26] Franklin was peeved about the incident.[27] Webbe
admitted that Franklin did speak of hiring him to produce a monthly magazine, but
Webbe commented, "surely his making the proposal neither obliged me to the
writing of one for him to print, nor restrained me from the printing of it at any
other Press without his Leave or Participation."[28] Bradford, long a dull second to
Franklin's successful first, saw a chance to upstage his rival for once. He and
Webbe agreed to produce *The American Magazine*. Webbe was to edit it, and
Bradford to print it.[29]

Table 4.1
Numbers of Newspapers, 1735–1765

Newspapers (9) existing in 1735
　Boston Gazette
　(Boston) *New-England Weekly Journal*
　Boston News-Letter
　(Boston) *Weekly Rehearsal*
　New-York Gazette
　New-York Weekly Journal
　(Philadelphia) *American Weekly Mercury*
　(Philadelphia) *Pennsylvania Gazette*
　(Charleston) *South-Carolina Gazette*

Newspapers (4) established, 1735–1739
　Boston Evening Post
　Boston Post-Boy
　(Williamsburg) *Virginia Gazette* (Parks)
　(Germantown, Pa.) *Hoch-Deutsch Pennsylvanische Ges.*

Newspaper (1) closed, 1735–1739
　(Boston) *Weekly Rehearsal*

Total number of newspapers in existence, 1739: 12

Newspapers (7) established, 1740–1749
　(Annapolis) *Maryland Gazette*
　(Boston) *Independent Advertiser*
　New-York Evening-Post
　New-York Gazette or Weekly Post-Boy
　New-York Weekly Post-Boy
　(Germantown, Pa.) *Pennsylvanische Berichte*
　(Philadelphia) *Pennsylvania Journal*

Newspapers (6) closed, 1740–1749
　(Boston) *New-England Weekly Journal*
　New-York Gazette
　New-York Weekly Post-Boy
　(Germantown, Pa.) *Hoch-Deutsch Pennsylvanische Ges.*
　(Philadelphia) *American Weekly Mercury*
　(Williamsburg) *Virginia Gazette* (Parks)

Total number of newspapers in existence, 1749: 13

Newspapers (16) established, 1750–1759
　(New Haven) *Connecticut Gazette*
　New-London (Conn.) *Summary*
　(Portsmouth) *New-Hampshire Gazette*
　New-York Gazette (Weyman)
　(New York) *Independent Reflector*
　(New York) *Instructor*

Table 4.1   (continued)

(New York) *John Englishman*
New-York Mercury
(New York) *Occasional Reverberator*
(New Bern) *North-Carolina Gazette*
Lancastersche (Pa.) *Zeitung*
(Philadelphia) *Hoch-Teutsche und E. Zeitung*
Philadelphische (Pa.) *Zeitung*
Newport (R.I.) *Mercury*
(Charleston) *South-Carolina Weekly Gazette*
(Williamsburg) *Virginia Gazette* (Hunter)

Newspapers (10) closed, 1750–1759
New-York Evening-Post
(New York) *Independent Reflector*
(New York) *Instructor*
(New York) *John Englishman*
(New York) *Occasional Reverberator*
New-York Weekly Journal
(New Bern) *North-Carolina Gazette*
Lancastersche (Pa.) *Zeitung*
(Philadelphia) *Hoch-Teutsche und E. Zeitung*
Philadelphische (Pa.) *Zeitung*

Total number of newspapers in existence, 1759: 19

Newspapers (13) established, 1760–1765
(Hartford) *Connecticut Courant*
(New London) *Connecticut Gazette*
(Savannah) *Georgia Gazette*
Portsmouth (N.H.) *Mercury*
(Woodbridge, N.J.) *Constitutional Courant*
(New York) *American Chronicle*
New-York Pacquet
(Wilmington) *North-Carolina Gazette*
Germantowner (Pa.) *Zeitung*
(Philadelphia) *Wochentliche Philadelphische Staats.*
Providence (R.I.) *Gazette*
(Charleston) *South-Carolina and American General Gazette*
(Charleston) *South-Carolina Gazette and Country Journal*

Newspapers (6) closed, 1760–1765
New-London (Conn.) *Summary*
(Woodbridge, N.J.) *Constitutional Courant*
(New York) *American Chronicle*
New-York Pacquet

Table 4.1 (continued)

(Germantown, Pa.) *Pennsylvanische Berichte*
(Charleston) *South-Carolina Weekly Gazette*

Total number of newspapers in existence, 1765: 26

Source: The information in this table is derived from Edward Connery Lathem, comp., *Chronological Tables of American Newspapers, 1690–1820* (Barre, Mass.: American Antiquarian Society & Barre Publishers, 1972).

A duel commenced. Bradford announced in his *American Weekly Mercury* that the new magazine would come out in March of 1741.[30] Franklin taunted him by announcing that his own *General Magazine* would be issued in January of 1741.[31] A jealous Bradford sped up his plans, but was not fast enough to catch Franklin by January. Fortunately for Bradford, Franklin was also in too much of a hurry to complete his rush job. Consequently both Franklin and Bradford announced that their respective magazines would be available the second week of February, 1741.[32] Bradford's *American Magazine* actually appeared February 13, three days before Franklin's *General Magazine* came out. Both deceptively dated the new news magazines as "January, 1741."[33]

In the first magazine story ever published in America, Bradford offered an interesting comment on the press of the day. His essay reflected the fact that the press was far-flung and even nonexistent in some places, and the article confirmed the reality that printers frequently had to please various powerful parties or risk losing their patronage. Bradford wrote:

As several Colonies have no Printing-Press; and in others where there is but one, and even in those Places where there are more, it is complained (whether with Justice or no we do not undertake to determine) that the printers are often under the Influence of Parties, and cannot, without much Difficulty, be prevailed upon to publish any Thing against the Side of Question they are of themselves: This MAGAZINE, therefore, is *Offered* as a Remedy against those several Inconveniencies. Here any Person, in whatever Colony residing, will find a ready Admittance to a fair and publick Hearing at all Times. In the Disputes, that may be thus transmitted to us for Publication, we shall *inviolably* observe an exact Neutrality, and *carefully* avoid mingling, with the Arguments on either Side, any Reflections or Remarks of our own.

But while we are zealously endeavoring to *promote* the *Liberty*, we shall as carefully *avoid* contributing to the *Licentiousness* of the *Press*.[34]

Franklin was not as specific in his intentions for the *General Magazine.* He offered only a cryptic note that he intended to publish the magazine monthly and that:

No Care shall be wanted, or Expence spared, to procure the best Materials for the Work, and make it as entertaining and useful as possible. The Character will generally be small, for the sake of comprising much in little Room, but it shall be good, and fairly printed.[35]

Franklin's monthly, like Bradford's, had a goal of reaching readers in all colonies. In his first issue, Franklin printed letters of a general nature that undoubtedly would speak to residents in any locale. He offered, for example, a rather dire cure for lovesickness:

> With close Attack, I lately woo'd a Maid,
> Whose Pride repuls'd whate'er I did or said.
> To heal my Love-sick Mind, I swallow down
> A harsh, tho' sure Prescription of my own:
> Which was, *to pull my Darling all to Pieces,*
> And ne'er leave off, till Success crown'd my Wishes.[36]

Turning to religion as a topic, the *General Magazine* plunged forward with a lengthy debate on the nature of God and salvation. "Is Man in his present Circumstances such a Creature, as he came out of the Hand of God his Creator? Or is he deprav'd and ruin'd by some universal Degeneracy of his Nature?" one piece queried. The next article demanded, "If GOD does cast Infants into Hell for the Sin of others, and yet did not condemn Devils, but for their own Sin; where is his Love to Mankind?" A third contribution warned that zealous Christians "do not, sure, sufficiently consider, that Holiness is the Design of Christianity," and it added that men ought to be truly like Christ, not just worshipful of Him.[37]

With the advent of Franklin's and Bradford's magazines, a new journalistic industry was born. Other magazines followed their lead. Franklin's and Bradford's magazines both died young, but eventually another Bradford, William III, decided to try his hand at magazine publishing. Given his poor success in the news business up to that time, he was taking a distinct gamble by getting into the magazine business. Of course, he had family connections with magazines; his uncle Andrew, founder of *The American Magazine*, had raised him. After Andrew's wife Dorcas died, though, Andrew married Cornelia—and that was when William's troubles began.

Cornelia did not like her new nephew. She "imbibed a settled prejudice" against William for refusing to marry the woman of her choice.[38] The results were not pretty. Cornelia took over her husband's *American Weekly Mercury* upon his death, and William opened a rival cross-town newspaper, the *Pennsylvania Journal.* He had to look to relatives in England to finance the venture.[39] With other newspapers in Philadelphia, including his aunt's, his paper's survival was by no means guaranteed. Desperate to make a success of his career, William explored other facets of the news business. In 1754 he helped open the London Coffee House in Philadelphia. Coffeehouses were excellent places for men to gather and catch up on the latest news. All taverns such as the Coffee House kept newspapers from around the colonies.[40]

The London Coffee House did not improve his overall financial lot any,[41] so William tried yet another way to parlay his knowledge of news into a moneymaker. He went back to his uncle's original idea of a magazine, opening *The American Magazine and Monthly Chronicle* in 1757. William may have borrowed the name of his magazine from his uncle's original, but this time he tried a fresh angle. His uncle had wanted his magazine to be a political chronicle; William, on the other hand, wanted to produce a magazine with a more patriotic, military emphasis. The title page featured a woodcut of some Frenchmen and Indians, Britain's enemies in the ongoing war. Bradford stated in the initial issue that the French and Indian War had created an immediate need for a magazine to report the progress of Britain against the enemy.[42] War articles were prominent, covering such topics as "The History of War in North America," "Of the Uses and Abuses of Militias," and "English Militia Law." There was also an essay about the Pennsylvania militia[43] and a story about the modes of transportation used by the enemy Indians.[44] The articles discussed the British army and offered suggestions for improving Americans' role in defending the colonies. Perhaps the war reports interested George Washington, who was a subscriber.[45]

Bradford may have seen war news as an important topic, but he was not ignorant of what his readers wanted. He included a variety of other articles, and he also printed entertainment in the form of wry commentary. One of his most entertaining features was the essayist known as the "Prattler." The Prattler himself was supposed to be something of a laughable character. "He does nothing but saunter about the taverns, strolls along the wharfs and drinks tea with the ladies," a description went in the initial Prattler column, "yet . . . how can they keep company with him?"[46] The Prattler lived up to his roguish persona by making fun of colonial life. He especially made fun of women and marriage. For example, he included a poem by a man:

'Tis an old maxim—give woman way
And all shall prosper—if the men obey!
From Adam's time, our sex have had their will,
And 'tis but fit that we should have it still.[47]

The Prattler heard lots of complaints from his female readers. Claiming he had been "tried" before a council of ladies, he wrote that the councilwomen were annoyed about "many infamous *Lampoons* against their *Dignity*, with a view to bring them into *Contempt*, and destroy the very *fundamentals* of those innocent and friendly meetings or clubs, which they hold periodically." He defended himself:

It is a scandalous thing for any woman to govern her husband. The females by their matrimonial vow, are solemnly sworn to obey. A man ruled by a woman is the most contemptible animal in the world, and the woman who rules him the most impudent, and yet the young women in certain places hold nocturnal councils in order to devise the best methods of ruling men.[48]

The Prattler was quite similar, in some respects, to William Parks's Monitor in the *Virginia Gazette*, and also to certain features in the London magazines *Review* and *Spectator*, which circulated in the colonies.

That kind of wry commentary was highly popular—but for Bradford and other magazine publishers, it apparently was not popular enough. As innovative an idea as magazines were for America, they did not catch on quickly. They tended to read like the colonial weekly press. Perhaps for that reason, the monthlies never gained the popularity that their publishers had hoped for. The original *American Magazine,* for example, lasted only three issues; Franklin's *General Magazine* lasted only half a year. Most of America's first magazines did not last long.[49] Magazine journalists were forced to rise and fall on trial and error as they pioneered new techniques. Journalistic innovators from 1735–1765 were definitely taking a chance.

The newspaper press, however, had been a great leap forward in American communication. For the first time, Americans could scrutinize the goings-on of the world and of their home colonies on a regular basis. Everyone could know, via the newspaper, what was happening in the House or Assembly, in the next colony, or in the king's palace overseas. At last the American colonies had a mass communication system. Someone who was inspired enough or clever enough or wily enough could turn that young mass medium into a huge advantage.

That person was the Reverend George Whitefield, who began the Great Awakening, the first transcolonial American news event. Opinions on Whitefield and his massive religious revival varied wildly. To various people, he was an inspired messenger of God, a clever speaker, or a wily deceiver. For his part, he seemed to be sincere about saving souls.

The newspaper industry in America essentially became the unwitting publicity agent for the Great Awakening, helping spread knowledge of Whitefield and his fellow evangelists. Newspapers from New England to South Carolina discussed Whitefield and similar revivalists who followed him, creating a public mood of overwhelming curiosity and interest. Printers published Whitefield's journals for sale to the public, causing more interest and yet more curiosity.

Whitefield sparked a sensational religious fervor that swept the colonies. It was as if colonial Americans, so long concerned with mere survival, by the 1740s were desperate for the excitement, entertainment, and spiritual regeneration associated with Whitefield and other itinerant preachers. And Whitefield *was* exciting. He was spiritual and good and yet somehow wicked, too, for he was snubbed by much of the established church. Spiritual leaders often denied him the right to preach in churches, so he preached in the fields. He brought congregations to tears. He saved thousands of souls.[50] Sometimes the revival fervor went to extremes. "[O]n a sudden all the people were in an uproar, and so unaccountably surprised," Whitefield described one preaching service, "that some threw themselves out of the windows, others threw themselves out of the gallery, and others trampled upon one another; so that five were actually killed, and others dangerously wounded."[51]

Such a controversial and exciting character came alive in the nation's press. Before Whitefield even arrived in America, the American press was building his image. The *Virginia Gazette* spoke glowingly of Whitefield's English sermons, saying they were "deservedly approved of." The newspaper noted that Whitefield had a large London following.[52]

Whitefield's journeys through America were covered dramatically by news reports. Teenager Peter Timothy went to court with Whitefield over the printing of a religious article in the *South-Carolina Gazette.* Cornelia Bradford scoffed in her *American Weekly Mercury* that Whitefield had been turned out of the conventional church and was "attended by Numbers of Women and Silly People."[53] Furthermore, Cornelia fumed, Whitefield "occasioned Varience between Husband and Wife, Friends and Relations."[54]

The *New-England Weekly Journal* of Boston had a more favorable reaction. "Among the Hearers [of Whitefield], the Person who gives this Account, was one," the reporter admitted. "I fear Curiosity was the Motive that led me and many others into that Assembly. I had read two or three of Mr. *Whitefield's* Sermons and part of his Journal, and from thence had obtained a settled Opinion, that he was a Good Man." The reporter was swept away by Whitefield. "I went to hear him in the Evening at the *Presbyterian Church*, where he Expounded to above 2000 People within and without Doors," the writer marvelled. "I never in my Life saw so attentive an Audience: Mr. *Whitefield* spake as one having Authority: All he said was *Demonstration, Life* and *Power!*"[55]

Whitefield had a deep effect on many of his listeners, and newspapers leaped on that angle of the story. Benjamin Franklin's *Pennsylvania Gazette* reported:

Since Mr. Whitefield's preaching here, the Dancing School, Assembly and Concert Room have been shut up, as inconsistent with the Doctrine of the Gospel: And though the Gentlemen concern'd caus'd the Door to be broke open again, we are inform'd that no Company came the last Assembly Night.[56]

Newspaper publishers really did not know what to think of Whitefield. The *Pennsylvania Gazette* praised him as a true follower of Jesus Christ,[57] then later accused Whitefield of faking attendance figures at his sermons.[58] On another occasion, the *Gazette* cheered Whitefield, calling him a genuine, generous man. "What a pity," the newspaper moaned, "that such a Godlike Man's Constitution is almost worn out by Apostolick Labours!"[59] Different editors had different reactions to Whitefield and other evangelists. Controversy over what the press should say about the revival and the accompanying feverish religious "enthusiasm" sparked out-and-out press battles in Boston. As one Bostonian put it, the city had "of late . . . been the Seat of Paper War" about the evangelists.[60]

Many Bostonians were pleased with the Great Awakening, including the proprietors of *Christian History,* the nation's earliest religious magazine.[61] On the opposite end of the spectrum was the *Boston Evening Post*, published by Thomas Fleet. Fleet immediately felt antagonistic toward the evangelists. He complained that people who did not wish to go to revivals should not be "stigmatiz'd as *atheists*, Profligates, or very irreligious Persons, as they lately have been by many," especially since these people generally just wanted to hear an ordinary preacher in an ordinary church.[62] Fleet published an article calling Whitefield a quack.[63]

Fleet certainly made a daring attempt to spread his own opinion through his press. His stand, however, was not popular. After some time, he was nearly forced to become a nominal supporter of the evangelical movement for money's sake. He wrote:

The Publisher of this Paper having (as he thinks) been very much neglected of late, by those whom he has endeavoured to serve, and oblig'd to publish many whole Sheets, &c. entirely at his own Expence; This is to inform all whom it may concern, that he has, upon mature Consideration of the Premises, almost come to a Resolution to change Sides.[64]

When Fleet came under fire from Bostonians, including other printers, he felt obliged to state his commitment to free speech:

I have never been of any *Company*, Clan or Party, either in Church or State, but wherever I have had a Right to speak or act, have always done it with openness and freedom, according to my own Judgment, and not that of *others*, which may be one Reason why I have had so few hearty friends at this Time. . . . I have indeed always express'd myself in a free, open and undisguised Manner, as became an *honest* Man, tho' perhaps not as a *prudent* one, as the World now goes.[65]

Interestingly, however, Fleet fell back on an argument that many colonial printers would take up in times of trouble. He was, he insisted, only a printer who printed what people wanted printed, not what he wanted printed. "[A]s I have often declared," he wrote, "so do I again declare, that I am of no Party, but act purely as a *Printer*." He also commented that he printed anything he thought he could make a profit on, no matter what his opinion of it was.[66]

One Presbyterian minister did not buy Fleet's self-defensive explanation about being a printer and got involved in a war of insults against Fleet. Exasperated, Fleet retorted:

I have for a long time observed, that Men who baul out loudest for shutting up the Press, or having it open only for their own Party, are of tyrannical Principles, and Enemies to Liberty both in Church and State, and would be glad to keep the People in the most abject Slavery.[67]

Fleet even called the well-known clergyman and Whitefield supporter Jonathan Edwards "*Censurer General of all Europe*" for finding fault with newspaper accounts of religion—but, Fleet noted, Edwards had never once blamed the press for what was printed. The authors of articles were to blame.[68]

When confronted with controversy over the Great Awakening, Fleet had first given his own opinion and later had claimed that his opinion had nothing to do with what was printed in his paper. His wavering stance represented a common dilemma for colonial printers. Since they did not have an editorial page to resort to, their personal opinions commonly found their way into the news. On the other hand, some printers insisted that they wanted to print public contributions for the public good and could not be expected to handle public controversies. At times when journalists did comment on controversies, readers reminded them harshly that it was a printer's place to print, not to offer personal commentary.[69]

Colonial newspaper editors who held that point of view proved themselves to be more printers than editors. They claimed little editorial control. Rather, they saw themselves as public agents out to make a living. Under fire from his readers, Thomas Fleet came to see journalism in that light. In the pioneer world of the colonial press, the editor's position was still unsure.

For the pioneers of the American printing industry, there were other difficulties besides threats of censure and failures of innovation. There was also the relationship with the readers that had to be established and maintained. The results were often bittersweet. Readers had to be there to make a newspaper worthwhile—but they also seemed bent on making printers' lives miserable with their ceaseless demands and expectations.

At times printers had to deal with outright hostility from the public, as New York printer Hugh Gaine could attest. Gaine had to pioneer a form of public relations in order to please his all-important readers. Without a long history of newspaper practices behind him, he had to sort the whole situation out on his own. As Gaine realized all too clearly, sometimes the balance between printer and reader was more agreeable to the reader than to the printer.

Some of Gaine's readers were determined to force him to bend the *New-York Mercury* to their will. Their battle forced him to grapple with clashing ideas about press freedom, a concept as yet undefined by a constitution or by tradition. The controversy involved the magazine *Independent Reflector*. It was published specifically to argue about attempts to give King's College a secular bent. Gaine refused to print a piece submitted by two feisty readers in support of the *Reflector's* position. Their article was a fictionalized petition against the plans for the college. The readers, William Smith, Jr., and John Morin Scott, shot back:

MR. GAINE:

Your Resolution *not to be any Ways concerned in Disputes,* by which we suppose you mean not to print any Thing in matters of Controversy, is a Resolution that will not only be prejudicial to your Interest, and against the very Design and proper Business of the Press; but is in a very great Degree, an Attack upon its Liberty, which Printers above Men should be sollicitious to maintain and encourage. . . . What we desired you to print was on no controverted Point. . . . Your Promise to give any one of us an Opportunity to answer an Attack upon him, in your Paper, seems inconsistent with your Resolution to be unconcerned in Disputes; nor do we accept your promise, as obliging, since you will first print the Attack, but refuse the Answer, unless it should be written (as you direct) *in a mild manner, and consistent with the Interest of your Calling,* the Judgment of which you reserve only to yourself.

We believe you are averse to Printing any Thing in favor of the *Reflector.*[70]

Gaine did not heed the letter, and the two men hastened to let James Parker's rival *New-York Gazette* publish the piece instead. Parker could not resist a stab at Gaine with a scolding published in the *Reflector*:

A PRINTER ought not to publish every Thing that is offered him; but what is conducive of the general Utility, he should not refuse, but be the Author a Christian, Jew, Turk or Infidel. Such Refusal is an immediate Abridgement of the Freedom of the Press. When on the other Hand, he prostitutes his Art by the Publication of any Thing injurious to his Country, it is criminal.[71]

The whole business was exasperating to Gaine, who finally printed Smith and Scott's letters, and then lashed out bitterly:

I received the above Letters upon my refusing to print two Pieces brought me by the above mentioned Gentlemen; one a Reflection not only upon a particular set of Men, but on a whole Nation; the other could have no other Tendency than to display the Author's *Plagiarism,* as the two first Paragraphs are taken from Vol. 4, No. 287, of Mr. *Addison's Spectator*; I think he ought to have given Credit for such a Procedure, before he caused it to be inserted in the *New-York Gazette* of April 16, 1753.[72]

Gaine was boiling by now. He continued with a "doctor's bill" to Smith and Scott, running up their credit for lies.[73] His list included:

For stealing, from the *Independent Whig,* lies	10
. . . Self-Praise when none due	15
For stealing from Mr. *Addison* and others	16
For vilifying the Printer hereof	6
. . . Their Rage for the *Liberty of the Press,* when its Liberty was never invaded, they having Freedom to chuse two others, Ec	10

The conflict pointed up the fact that concepts of the role of the press were as yet unresolved in the American colonies and that a lively debate was being waged. Gaine thought that a writer was free to submit his work to any publication, while the printer was equally as free to turn down anything he found offensive. Smith and Scott, on the other hand, argued that a printer was obliged to print whatever came his way as an agent of popular opinion. Failure to do so, they said, wrenched freedom of the press from the people and put it into the hands of a few dictatorial printers.

Gaine solved the dilemma to his liking more than a year later by publishing some debate on the fate of King's College after the parties involved agreed to pay him for his trouble. Gaine explained his turnabout in attitude this way:

During the weekly Publication of the late Papers under the Title of The Independent Reflector, great Complaints were made by my Refusal to publish any Thing that was offered by that Author or his Friends; and since the Discontinuance of his Labours, the Controversies of that Day, instead of subsiding, have risen still higher, and become vastly more extensive and interesting;—an almost universal Discontent now appears for want of a FREE PRESS; and the Printer of the *Mercury* after many importunate Applications, is determin'd to give both Parties an Opportunity of being heard thro' his Paper: . . . Therefore, from this Time foreward, shall lay himself under no Restraints, provided the authors will indemnify him, and deposit a *Quantum meruit* for his Services. The Printer only desires that excessive Heats and personal Reflections may be avoided on both Sides; and that the publick would be pleased to consider him entirely disinterested in all he prints; and that no Man would think him an Enemy to any particular Sect of Religion more than another.[74]

Gaine apparently did not give in easily, in spite of the offer of pay. William Livingston, who was involved with funding for the series, complained to a friend, "We have at length with great trouble got Mr. Gaine to enter into an agreement with us to allot us the first part of his newspaper for the publication of our thoughts." He begged his friend for aid in the series, adding, "For if we once drop it, it may be difficult to get the printer in the same humour. He is a fickle fellow, and easily intimidated by our opponents."[75]

Thus, Gaine came to terms with a demanding public, forcing compromise on either side. In the absence of a long newspaper tradition in the colonies, he had to play his part by ear. He tried to follow his own conscience in the matter until his conscience was persuaded by his pocketbook. In the process he ran into readers' amorphous concept of the role of the press that clashed with his own. The arguments in the case revolved around freedom of the press, while no one agreed precisely what that meant. To the pioneers in the youthful newspaper industry, press freedom was just one more difficult concept to deal with in figuring out exactly what the press in America should be all about.

Grappling with readers was one thing. Fighting tooth and nail with other printers for survival was, for many pioneer printers, a very different, very scary proposition. Some printers, such as Gaine, had competition. In some thinly populated American colonies, however, where printing presses did not abound, a number of printers worked for years without fear of nearby competition. Many printers had the luxury of government patronage and enjoyed the security of being the only printer for miles around. As the press matured in young America, however, presses and printers grew relatively more common, and printers began to confront a new situation: rivalry. It was a horror to many of them. The security of being the only printer in an area gave way to the panic of suddenly having to outdo another newspaper in a bid to win readers.

Having a rival was not a happy event for Peter Timothy in South Carolina, now grown up and in full control of his *South-Carolina Gazette*. In 1758, an upstart Scottish bookseller, Robert Wells, opened the *South-Carolina Weekly Gazette* to compete with Timothy's more established journal. There had never been competing newspapers in South Carolina before; in fact, there had never been any competing newspapers in the South.[76] Timothy's *Gazette* immediately took on a nervous attitude. Suddenly he found it imperative to have the news first. He even tore apart his already typeset *Gazette* one day to squeeze in news that English troops had secured the Ohio River. Apparently he did so in an attempt to tell *"our Friends, as early as possible"* before the Wells paper could print it. [77]

If Timothy missed a story, he felt obliged to reprint it from Wells—and then became cross if his source were faulty. Anxious to retain his readers' trust, he blamed Wells openly for mistakes:

We ask our Readers Pardon, for having misinformed them in a Point of so much Consequence as the ensuing *ELECTION* of *REPRESENTATIVES*. We acknowledge, that we have been led into this Error by *copying* (which rarely happens) from the "weekly Gazette" without further Inquiry, supposing the Gentleman who publishes that Paper had his Information from good Authority; but we promise to be more cautious for the future.[78]

Charlestonians perceived early on that there was an undercurrent of jealousy between Timothy and Wells. They found out quickly that Timothy would print negative opinion about Wells.[79] A roguish reader who called himself "M. J." decided to have a little fun at Wells's expense. M. J. was at a tavern, reading aloud a piece of work by Wells, when a friend got a wicked idea for a bit of graffiti. The friend picked up some chalk and wrote a quick little ditty about Wells on the table, guffawing at the same time, "Poor silly fellow!" M. J. sent the graffiti to Timothy for publication:

O Robin! (conscious of the thing)
    Let candid *truth* confess,
Of men, and arms, in *fibs* you sing,
    With *voice*, and *pen*, and *press*.[80]

Wells took advantage of the jingle attack to reply that he would never again respond to such ridiculous attacks by his rival's newspaper. He sent a poem to his rival's *Gazette*:

Mr. TIMOTHY,

I *Robin*, armed with front of brass,
    Will ever give assistance;
Determin'd none shall me surpass,
    When Falsehood meets resistance.

You may the simple truth proclaim,
    Aloud with pen and press;
Such silly practice I disclaim,
    'Twould make me pennyless.

To this plain maxim I agree,
    No living man can thrive,
But he that will most readily
    Hold two and two count five.

Yours, &c.
R. W.[81]

Wells's last verse obviously jabbed at Timothy for blowing up M. J.'s poem all out of proportion. Furthermore, he had accused Timothy in the second verse of being foolish to run such tavern drivel as M. J.'s.

By that time, a reader had written to Timothy in defense of Wells, showing that Charleston was indeed divided in opinion about the two rivals. Wells's supporter pointed out that M. J.'s verse was certainly weak, and commented in praise of Wells:

> Through depths of *muck*, who'd passage force,
>   To gloss thy merit?
> Nay nay, that artifice so weak,
> The publick voice will n'er bespeak.
> For, in the *publisher*, we seek,
>   And find, *thy* wit and spirit.[82]

Timothy showed Wells's response and the anonymous poem of support to M. J., who just had to reply, deriding the two pro-Wells efforts:

> WHEN Robin's *sloven* pen his *cause* betrays,
> In *panegyric, parallel*, and *lays*;
> And Mother jingle *scolds*, in frantic ire,
> Surcharg'd with *lead*, and *gall*, and *muck*, and *mire*;
> Who can withhold his *pity*, from the first,
> Or who his *laughter*, at a *dame* so curst.[83]

The series of rather poorly written poetry undoubtedly provided entertainment to the *Gazette*'s readers. It also showed the personalities of the two publishers who each felt they were fighting for their newspaper's survival. This was all new territory for them; they did not know if it was possible for cross-town newspapers to survive in Charleston. Wells's poetic reaction to the rivalry showed that he would never stoop to the "silly practice" of disparaging his rival in the press. Such a practice, Wells said, might make him "pennyless." Wells was not one to waste money when the survival of his press might be at stake. On the other hand, Peter Timothy showed that he had no regrets about deriding his opponent. He seemed to feel that pointing out his rival's weaknesses would ultimately win the readership of Charleston to his own paper, turning them from the *Weekly Gazette* of his rival.

Both Wells and Timothy grumpily settled in to work near each other. A few weeks after the poetry series, Wells put an ad for his auction business in Timothy's paper, hoping to catch readers who did not take his *Weekly Gazette*.[84] Timothy ran the ad. Undoubtedly, he could use the cash paid for the ad, and Wells always paid his bills.[85]

Timothy's and Wells's poetic outburst about one another may not have been typical of colonial printers suddenly faced with rivalry, but their negative reaction to rivalry was. Other colonial newspaper editors who suddenly found themselves in direct competition also had to feel their way, groping for a solution to what seemed to be a personal crisis and a threat to their ability to make a living. Very few news-paper editors from 1735–1765 had the luxury of history on their side. A few had inherited papers and rivalries over the generations, but most had to figure out how to deal with cross-town or cross-province rivals by doing what seemed right.

Perhaps the most difficult thing about colonial printing from 1735–1765 was the chance every publisher took of offending the government. Most printers de-pended on government printing jobs to survive. Most governments counted on printers to issue proclamations and general information about acts of government to the citizens. Such a mutual relationship could, however, come to a screeching and unexpected halt if a printer accidentally crossed the government. From time to time printers were summoned before assemblies to justify their newspaper stories. In other cases, governments unexpectedly imposed restrictions of various types on the press. Laws and governmental practices regarding the press were so untried that no one knew what kind of governmental attack was around the next bend.

Printer James Parker, for example, was horrified to find his very livelihood under attack by governmental edict in 1756. Parker was publisher of the *New-York Gazette: or, the Weekly Post-Boy* when the provincial government there issued a stamp tax on newspapers and legal documents. The act taxed newspapers at a half-pence per copy.[86] The start of the tax marked the start of Parker's one-man battle against the governmental regulation.

A stamp tax had been in effect in England for some time, but it was a new thing for the colony of New York and for American printers. In reaction, Parker pio-neered a protest movement to explain to New York's government exactly why a tax was detrimental to the press and ought to be revoked. His attempt to tell the gov-ernment to leave printers alone did not center on principles or ideals, but rather on simple facts of economics. Principles and ideals of press independence had not been formulated yet—but Parker's economically based protest would blaze a trail that would clear the way for pan-colonial protest of the colonial Stamp Act nine years later.

However, in 1756 Parker was not thinking ahead to an all-colonial tax. He was simply dismayed—and alone. It seemed that Parker's New York rival Hugh Gaine did not seem to mind the tax. Instead, Gaine calmly passed the cost on to his sub-scribers, explaining to them that the government needed the stamp revenue.[87] Soon after, William Weyman started his own paper without fussing about the stamp duty.[88]

Parker, though, was incensed about the tax. He decided to crusade against it. He published an article begging the assembly to find another way to raise revenue, and he insisted that the tax would ruin him as well as discriminate against him.[89] His arguments failed to persuade the assembly; so a few months later he pointed out that Massachusetts's similar act had lapsed and warned that it had had ruinous ef-fects on Massachusetts trade.[90] Half a year later he burst out in frustration again, complaining that the stamp act was freezing his cash flow.[91] Shortly thereafter, he set out his entire argument against the stamp tax by issuing a broadside addressed to "a Gentleman in the City of *New-York*."[92] Parker's literary "gentleman" was all in favor of taxing newspapers, saying that if it were up to him, he would raise the halfpenny-per-issue tax to sixpence per issue. Parker scoffingly noted that he had once considered this gentleman to be "a Friend to Religion, Liberty and Vertue." Now, however, the gentleman needed to be set straight. In so doing, Parker offered a revealing, though biased, look at the difficulties of surviving as a colonial printer.

In spite of hinting that his appeal would be centered on religion, liberty, and virtue, Parker focused on the economics of the issue. He bemoaned the wretchedly difficult life of a colonial printer:

I must beg Leave to observe to you, Sir, that Mr. [William] *Bradford* was a Printer in *New-York* more than 50 years. . . . He was a very sober, diligent man: I served upwards of eight Years with him, and in 1726, carried about the first News-papers that were printed in that City. The Art was in such wretched Disrepute there, that tho' he had Apprentices or Servants constantly, he never had One in all his Time, but what he was obliged to take of the lowest People: Not one of Substance would ever put their Sons to such an Art. . . . Mr. [John Peter] *Zenger* finding himself unable to subsist by other printing-work, began a News-paper about the Year 1733. They however both died poor.[93]

In London, Parker said, printers were not treated so badly as in America, and in fact, he commented, "there a Printer can live without doing a News-paper." Obviously a newspaper, in Parker's eyes, was the thankless part of a printer's job. He added bitterly that in heavily taxed Ireland, there were no taxes on newspapers, "whilst there are more than five times the Number of Printers." In fact, he noted wistfully, Ireland had recently instituted a bounty for printers who would make types and paper. For his part, he mourned, "I had been planning and scheming some Years past, to erect a Paper-Mill in or near *New-York*, and Things were near ripe for Execution, when the Stamp-Act, like to a killing Frost, nipp'd me in the Bud, and blasted all my Hopes."[94]

Parker next turned to the sad state of Boston printing after the Massachusetts Stamp Act. One printer, he said, was forced to move to New Hampshire, while another went out of business. As Parker told the story, the legislature in Boston finally came to its senses and realized the tax would simply ruin printers without any gain for the government. "[T]hey took the Duty off at the End of two Years, and laid an Excise upon Limes, Lemons and Oranges, used in private Families, in lieu of it, as being more a Tax on Luxury than News-papers are." Parker added doleful statistics, claiming that circulation of Boston newspapers had dwindled from 150 copies to a mere ten copies in one area after the Massachusetts Stamp Act was passed.[95]

Parker was fuming by now. "If News-papers are tax'd, because they are a Luxury," he demanded, "why might not all other Branches of Luxury in Tradesmen also? I could mention several; in particular, Silver-smith's Work." He added judiciously that he had nothing against silversmiths, but he did feel that "every Man of Common-sense" would see that silversmiths offered a more luxury-oriented product than did newspaper printers.[96]

Parker's one-man crusade against the legislature may have had an effect. The legislature, meeting in session at the time the broadside was issued, did not renew the tax, commenting that the stamp duty annoyed people and did not produce enough revenue.[97] Parker published a card of thanks in the *Post-Boy*.[98] At last Gaine and Weyman joined the anti-legislature stand and agreed that the stamp duty had been an unwelcome burden.[99]

Gaine's and Weyman's support would undoubtedly have been helpful to Parker earlier. Due to their lack of cooperation, Parker had managed to take on the establishment himself. He had taken a conservative route, emphasizing more his own economic woes than any moral depravity on the part of lawmakers. It was the safest thing to do in an era when little law had been written about the nature of the press's relationship to government. Parker was testing new American waters when he went forth to battle an attack on his livelihood.

The government could certainly strangle a newspaper, and Parker knew it. He needed to survive, so he wrote his rebuttal to the government carefully to avoid treading on official toes. It worked. Parker's anti-tax campaign was well-fought and carefully reasoned, so that his youthful press could find its way in the evolving world of government.

Parker's protest helped build a bridge for the American press as it left its childhood and grew toward a strong, forceful adulthood. In 1765, the government of England issued a Stamp Act on the American colonies. It was like a call to arms for America's journalists. They came together as one and made a stand against the dreaded act. Thus, in 1765, an era ended. The American press of 1735–1765 had matured from a gawky, unsure teenager into a fiery youthful power that saw things from its own perspective.

Until that time, however, colonial America's newspapermen and newspaperwomen had to be individual pioneers into sometimes scary, sometimes exciting, untouched areas. Their pioneering quests for survival ultimately helped give the press a more established, more confident character, a character that would help colonial printers, with a unified voice of protest, wrestle with the Stamp Act of 1765.

NOTES

1. In the early eighteenth century, the city was actually called "Charlestown." Its name changed to "Charleston" during the American Revolution.

2. *South-Carolina Gazette* (Charleston), 15 January 1741. The newspaper commented only that the publisher was arrested, but it did not specify whether that publisher was the nominal one (Peter) or the actual one (Elizabeth). Historian Isaiah Thomas said that Peter was arrested. See Thomas, *The History of Printing in America*, ed. Marcus A. McCorison (1810; reprint [to which page numbers refer], New York: Weathervane Books, 1970), 568. Thomas spent some time in Charleston as a journeyman printer years after the 1741 incident. However, since he most likely knew Peter Timothy personally, his information is probably reliable.

3. George Whitefield, journal entries of 1 and 4 January 1741. *George Whitefield's Journals* (Gainesville, Fla.: Scholars' Facsimiles & Reprints, 1969), 506.

4. *South-Carolina Gazette,* 8 January 1741.

5. Thomas, *The History of Printing in America,* 568. Although Timothy's birthdate is not recorded, it is likely he was born in 1725, based on a legal document dating from his father's arrival in America. The document, a list of men swearing an oath to King George II, said that Louis Timothée arrived in Philadelphia in September of 1731 with six children, ages 6 to 1. If Peter was the oldest, he was born in about 1725. The document is cited in Marion Reynolds King, "One Link in the First Newspaper Chain, *The South Carolina Gazette,*" *Journalism Quarterly* 9 (1932): 259.

6. Articles of Agreement between Louis Timothée and Benjamin Franklin, *The Papers of Benjamin Franklin,* ed. Leonard W. Labaree (New Haven, Conn.: Yale University Press, 1959), 1:339–42. See also Benjamin Franklin's commentary on Elizabeth Timothy's goal of running the print shop so that she was able to buy the shop outright for her son in J. A. Leo Lemay and P. M. Zall, eds., *The Autobiography of Benjamin Franklin: A Genetic Text* (Knoxville: University of Tennessee Press, 1981), 95–96.

7. *South-Carolina Gazette,* 8 February 1739.

8. Thomas, *The History of Printing in America,* 568.

9. William W. Hening, ed., *The Statutes at Large: Being a Collection of All the Laws of Virginia,* II (Richmond, 1809–1823), 517.

10. Roger Yarrington offered a biographical time line of Parks's life in "William Parks," in Perry J. Ashley, ed., *Dictionary of Literary Biography* (Detroit: Gale Research Co., 1985), 43:353.

11. *Maryland Gazette* (Annapolis), 9 June 1730.

12. Yarrington, "William Parks," 355.

13. *Virginia Gazette* (Williamsburg), 8 October 1736.

14. Ibid., 17 November 1738.

15. Ibid., 24 November 1738.

16. Quoted in Thomas, *The History of Printing in America,* 554. Unfortunately, Thomas did not give the name or date of the newspaper from which he quoted the material.

17. Entry for 11 May 1749, *The Journals of the House of Burgesses of Virginia, 1619–1776* (1749), 403–4.

18. *Virginia Gazette,* 5 May 1738.

19. See Robert D. Arner, "The Short, Happy Life of the Virginia 'Monitor,' " *Early American Literature* 7, no. 2 (1972): 130–47, for an analysis of the Monitor's work. The comparison to English essays is made on p. 132.

20. *Virginia Gazette,* 10 September 1736.

21. Ibid., 12 November 1736.

22. Ibid., 5 November 1736.

23. Ibid., 10 August 1739.

24. *The Papers of Benjamin Franklin* 1:230, 233. On these pages, editor Labaree gives a good explanation of what was going on in the German-language newspaper as a preface to German passages by Louis Timothée in the *Philadelphische Zeitung,* 6 May 1732 and 24 June 1732.

25. *American Weekly Mercury* (Philadelphia), 20 November 1740.

26. Ibid.

27. *Pennsylvania Gazette* (Philadelphia), 13 November 1740.

28. *American Weekly Mercury,* 20 November 1740.

29. *American Weekly Mercury,* 6 November, 1740; and Thomas, *The History of Printing in America,* 448.

30. *American Weekly Mercury,* 6 November 1740.

31. *Pennsylvania Gazette,* 13 November 1740.

32. *American Weekly Mercury* and *Pennsylvania Gazette,* 5 February 1741.

33. *American Weekly Mercury* and *Pennsylvania Gazette,* 12 February 1741, and *American Magazine* (Philadelphia), January 1741. The full names of the magazines were *The General Magazine, and Historical Chronicle, for all the British Plantations in America,* and *The American Magazine, or A Monthly View of The Political State of the British Colonies.*

34. *American Magazine,* January 1741.

35. *General Magazine* (Philadelphia), January 1741.

36. Ibid.

37. Ibid.

38. Thomas Bradford's undated memoir of his father, Bradford Papers, Historical Society of Pennsylvania. The memoir is quoted by Patricia Bradley in a paper presented at the 1991 American Journalism Historians Association convention, entitled "No 'Meer Mechanic': William Bradford and the Search for Legitimacy."

39. Bradley, ibid., 11.

40. *South-Carolina Gazette,* 16 December 1756, offered an ad to that effect, for example.

41. Bradley, "No 'Meer Mechanic,' " 21. Bradley cited tax records of 1756 from the City Archives of Philadelphia to prove that the venture did not make much money.

42. *American Magazine and Monthly Chronicle* (Philadelphia), October 1757. The full name of the magazine was *American Magazine, and Monthly Chronicle for the British Colonies.*

43. Ibid., November 1757.

44. Ibid., January 1758.

45. Robert Carden, "American Magazines that Predate the U.S.," *Media History Digest* 1, no. 1 (1980): 41–42. Carden did not give a source for the information on Washington.

46. *American Magazine and Monthly Chronicle,* November 1757.

47. Ibid., July 1758.

48. Ibid.

49. Among America's first eight magazines, the longest-lived was Jeremiah Gridley's Boston publication, *American Magazine and Historical Chronicle,* which lasted three years, from 1743 to 1746. See Carden, "American Magazines that Predate the U.S.," 38.

50. See, for example, *New-England Weekly Journal* (Boston), 4 December 1739; and George Whitefield's journal of 10 May 1740, reprinted in Richard L. Bushman, ed., *The Great Awakening: Documents on the Revival of Religion, 1740–1745* (Chapel Hill: University of North Carolina Press, 1969), 26.

51. George Whitefield's journal of 22 September 1740, in Bushman, ibid., 29.

52. *Virginia Gazette,* 16 December 1737.

53. *American Weekly Mercury,* 29 January 1746.

54. Ibid., 4 February 1746.

55. *New-England Weekly Journal,* 4 December 1739.

56. *Pennsylvania Gazette,* 1 May 1740.

57. Ibid., 13 December 1739.

58. Ibid., 8 May 1740.

59. Ibid., 5 January 1764.

60. *Boston Evening-Post*, 3 June 1745.

61. M. A. Yodelis called the magazine "less a magazine than a laudatory chronicle of the Great Awakening." ("Boston's First Major Newspaper War: A 'Great Awakening' of Freedom," *Journalism Quarterly* 51 [1974]: 208.)

62. *Boston Evening-Post*, 6 October 1740.

63. Ibid., 6 May 1740.

64. Ibid., 12 September 1743.

65. Ibid., 6 October 1740.

66. Ibid., 30 March 1741.

67. Ibid.

68. Ibid.

69. As an example besides Fleet, see printer Thomas Whitmarsh's plea to the public as he started the *South-Carolina Gazette* on 8 January 1732, and then his scolding at the hands of a reader on 29 January 1732.

70. William Smith, Jun., and John Morin Scott to Hugh Gaine, 6 April 1753, in Paul Leicester Ford, ed., *The Journals of Hugh Gaine, Printer* (New York: Dodd, Mead & Co., 1902; reprint, New York: Arno Press and The New York Times, 1970), 11–12 (page numbers refer to reprint edition).

71. *Independent Reflector* (New York), 30 August 1753.

72. *New-York Weekly Mercury*, 3 September 1753.

73. Ibid.

74. Ibid., 18 November 1754.

75. William Livingston to Noah Welles, 7 December 1754, quoted in Ford, *The Journals of Hugh Gaine, Printer*, 18–19.

76. See lists of colonial newspapers and their dates of operation in Sidney Kobre, *The Development of the Colonial Newspaper* (Pittsburgh, Pa.: Colonial Press, 1944), 147–48.

77. *South-Carolina Gazette*, 29 December 1758.

78. Ibid., 21 February 1761.

79. See, for instance, the *South-Carolina Gazette* for 1 August 1761 and 8 August 1761.

80. *South-Carolina Gazette*, apparently 12 September 1761. The front page of the issue, containing the date of publication, is missing. "Robin," of course, was a diminutive of "Robert," Wells's first name.

81. *South-Carolina Gazette*, 3 October 1761.

82. Ibid.

83. Ibid.

84. Ibid., 31 October 1761.

85. It seems unlikely that Timothy would have continued accepting Wells's ads (which he accepted until Wells's departure from South Carolina in 1774) if Wells had not paid. Plus, Wells was well known for being prompt in business matters, according to Lorenzo Sabine, *Biographical Sketches of Loyalists of the American Revolution* (Boston: Little, Brown & Co., 1864), 2:406.

86. *Colonial Laws of New York* (Albany, 1894), 2:110–16, 188–89, 290–91.

87. *New-York Mercury*, 20 December 1756.

88. *Weyman's New-York Gazette* (New York), 16 February 1759 and 7 January 1760.

89. *The New-York Gazette: or, the Weekly Post-Boy* (New York), 4 October 1756.

90. Ibid., 18 April 1757.

91. Ibid., 17 October 1757.

92. "A Letter to a Gentleman in the City of *New-York*: Shewing the Unreasonableness of the present Stamp-Duty upon News-papers, and the great Burthen of that Duty upon the Printers" (2 November 1759), quoted in Beverly McAnear, "James Parker *Versus* New York Province," *New York History* 22 (1941), 322–30.

93. Ibid., 323–24.

94. Ibid., 325–26.

95. Ibid., 326.

96. Ibid., 329.

97. *Journal of the Votes of the General Assembly of New York, 1691–1765* (New York City), 2:572, 604.

98. *Post-Boy*, 7 January 1760.

99. *New-York Mercury*, 7 January 1760, and *Weyman's New-York Gazette*, 7 January 1760.

5

The Stamp Act Crisis, 1765-1766

The war against the French and their Indian allies had been expensive—monstrously expensive. Britain had poured out the treasury to save the American colonies from becoming French outposts. As the House of Commons saw it, anyone would be grateful to be spared such a fate.[1] Americans indeed heaved a sigh of relief that the long war was finally over. What they did not know was that the House of Commons was planning to make them pay. Great Britain, nearly bankrupted by the war, was looking for revenue. As British officials saw it, America owed some payback for the huge expenditure on her behalf. After conquering French North America, the British national debt stood at £130,000,000—so large a sum that the interest on it amounted to one half of Britain's annual national revenue.[2]

With the expensive conquest came another expensive problem: now British arms and money would have to be used to defend the former French provinces of Canada and Louisiana at an annual cost of £400,000.[3] The money would help keep away the French, who might threaten to return if given a chance. What more likely place to raise the necessary cash than those expensive colonies half a world away? It seemed logical. The people there, British lawmakers reasoned, should be grateful for their sure defense under King George III.[4] The crown hoped to raise about £100,000 to defray roughly a third of the costs of frontier defense.[5]

This time, however, for the first time in the short history of America, and perhaps for the first time in the history of the world, an unexpected ingredient was added to the taxation recipe: a completely unified mass media in protest. When the British Parliament voted overwhelmingly to tax paper goods by imposing a Stamp Act in the American colonies, American newspaper editors joined as one to fight the decision. As individuals, they had seen governmental injustice before; as individuals, they had commented on injustices and taken swipes at the wrongdoers. But this time, in 1765, with the advent of the Stamp Act, the individuals of the press came together. Thus, the press became a true mass-media editorial voice. With that metamorphosis of the press, the Stamp Act was doomed.

The press was not the only voice in protest at the time of the Stamp Act. Americans were already grumbling over Britain's land policies, which limited colonial expansion to the west. Also, Americans were beginning to feel the effects of a tightened colonial system which tended to protect British tradesmen at the expense of the American colonies.[6] The added tax burden caused Americans' distress to explode into rage. Colonists expressed their anger about stamps in many forms— symbols, such as Liberty Trees and Liberty Poles; resolutions against the tax; and boycotts against it. Merchants, farmers, radicals, and others lifted their voices against the hated tax. And so did journalists.

Journalists played a critical role in bringing the various strands of protest together, for the press spread the identical negative sentiment toward the stamp tax to all parts of America. Everyone in every town began to realize that the negative feelings were shared among regions, cities, and whole colonies. The fact that printers followed their usual habit of swapping news from the various colonies augmented the Stamp Act protests, for undoubtedly the reprinted news added legitimacy to the argument. Readers realized the Stamp Act protest was an American event, not just isolated disgruntlement in their own community.[7]

Parliament had only a dim inkling in 1765 that the American colonies could ever know each other so well as to learn to agree with each other. After all, hitherto there had never been true editorial agreement in America. Newspapers circulated in all colonies, and pamphlets circulated widely too, but there had never been a unified voice of the colonies.

That voice was born in the Stamp Act press. Colonial journalists, hit in the pocketbook as well as in principles, had to react. The stamp tax's severe threats to printers' well-being assured that printers were ready and willing to communicate anti–Stamp Act sentiment. Furthermore, since printers already had a network of newspaper exchange in place, they were able to discover quickly what their fellow editors were uncovering in the way of Stamp Act protests.

The voice of protest thus spread from newspaper to newspaper, from town to town, from colony to colony. Thanks to the printers' personal stake in the situation, Stamp Act news was exclusively negative. In that manner, every American saw an exclusively negative explanation of the Stamp Act and its ill effects in the press. For the first time, then, Americans were all given the same picture of the same topic.

The only similar editorial phenomenon up to that point had happened during the Great Awakening of the 1740s. The great religious revival had been the first transcolonial controversy reported far and wide by the press. It was common for newspapers in every colony to carry identical news reports on various topics, from wars to acts of Parliament, but the Great Awakening had been the first American event to command widespread opinionated comment in the press. Editors had disagreed as to the importance or impact of the Great Awakening, with the views often splitting along denominational lines.[8] Readers in Philadelphia had gotten a different point of view on the religious movement than had people in Williamsburg. Although editorial commentary on the Great Awakening had been pervasive, it had not been in unison or consistent.

The Stamp Act was the next all-encompassing American controversy, and this time the media presented a consistent, unvarying opinion of the stamp uproar to all colonists. Printers did not plan a unified attack; rather, they expressed their feelings, which happened to be the same. Thus, somewhat by accident, American journalists in the era of the Stamp Act created a true mass-media editorial campaign. The unplanned campaign helped produce remarkable results.

The emergence of mass persuasion in America completely interrupted Britain's plans to levy a stamp tax to cover the costs of the French and Indian War. Parliament had never before levied a tax in the face of an angry mass media. As Britons were fond of pointing out, Americans had readily accepted taxation from Britain in times past.[9] But in times past, America had not had such a unified mass media.

Parliament, however, did not know that as it contemplated taxing the colonies. The rumblings began in 1764. Rumors began to fly that Britain's North American colonies would get a Stamp Act on paper goods, the very kind of stamp tax that already existed in England.[10] The English, however, paid their tax as a matter of routine. The Americans would not prove to be so docile.

The rumors of an American Stamp Act had their origin in the Sugar Act of April 5, 1764. That act was needed, Parliament explained, to defray the costs of protecting and defending America. It taxed all sugar made in any colony; wines (except French wines); imported indigo and cotton; and imported silk, calico, and linen, among other items.[11] Furthermore, British officials warned, America was under consideration for a stamp tax. The colonies could propose a better method of taxation if they wished.[12]

The colony of New York leaped to its own defense against the sugar tax and hinted at Stamp Act arguments yet to come. The General Assembly expressed its "Concern and Surprize" that Parliament planned "to impose Taxes upon the Subjects *here*, by Laws to be passed *there*."[13] The New York lawmakers had made a subtle break with Great Britain. They saw a separation between "here" and "there." Americans were "here," yet they were subject to control from "there." The idea that Americans were distinct and separate from the British people was germinating. It would be reflected in the crisis to come, as colonists began consistently referring to themselves as "Americans" and less so as "Britons."[14] The reference would become a significant symbol of the growing feeling that Americans had an identity of their own, independent of the mother country.

Despite a shift toward the important concept that Americans were separate, the break was far from complete. For now, members of the New York General Assembly begged for their full rights as Englishmen. The lawmakers felt that English citizens had a right to tax themselves through their own elected representatives. The New Yorkers wanted their own local representatives in Parliament, for such representatives, they insisted, were the legal right of all Englishmen. Only that way would those in authority know what was realistic in terms of taxation.[15] Clearly, the notion of "no taxation without representation" was already in place.

The representation question quickly became the principle behind the anti-tax sentiment. Members of Parliament theoretically represented the entire realm, including America, even though no members of Parliament were from America. Americans disagreed with that concept of government, sensing that Englishmen had only a foggy picture of colonial needs and wants. Also, throughout the period of American colonization, settlers from England had bent and stretched the English governmental system to suit the American terrain. Land was vast and plentiful; thus, even humble colonists could aspire to be landholders—and if landholders, then voters, according to English law. In America, then, voting was not the exclusive right of a wealthy, landed class. Ordinary men were accustomed to having their say in government. The vast distances in America created changes in colonial concepts of representation, too, for it was simply impossible for far-flung settlers to travel to provincial capitals for legal services, court, and so on. As a convenience, Americans had long since evolved a system of local governments based in counties or towns. Representatives were elected from local geographical divisions to the central provincial government, and people came to see these representatives as speaking in particular for them, not for the whole realm.[16] Parliament might claim to speak for the entire realm of Britain, but colonists were used to their own spokesmen in matters that concerned them directly. Thus the colonists practiced actual representation, an advantage they did not have in Parliament. The new taxes proposed by a parliament with no colonial representatives grated on the colonists. They begged to speak with their own voice in Parliament.

Virginia lawmakers' response to the Sugar Act illustrated the colonists' argument that British lawmakers could not possibly understand the needs of their American outposts. The House of Burgesses pleaded with a pitiful voice against the Sugar Act:

The Expenses incurred during the last War . . . have involved us in a Debt of near Half a Million; a Debt not likely to decrease under the continued Expense we are at in providing for the Security of the People against the Incursions of our savage Neighbours, at a Time when the low state of our Staple Commodity, the total Want of Specie, and the late Restrictions upon the Trade of the Colonies, render the Circumstances of the People extremely distressful, and which, if Taxes are accumulated upon them by the *British* Parliament, will make them truly deplorable.[17]

The Sugar Act was a nuisance, stirring up ideological passions and planting the idea in Americans' heads that they were not being treated as Englishmen ought to be treated. When all was said and done, however, the American press did not become inflamed over the Sugar Act.

On the other hand, the Stamp Act, which followed on the heels of the Sugar Act, hit printers squarely in the pocketbook. The king and Parliament had not expected that the press would unleash its fury in unison voice, lashing back from the sting of the Stamp Act's unfairness and expense. As Dr. David Ramsay of Charleston, South Carolina, noted wryly some years later:

It was fortunate for the liberties of America, that News-papers were the subject of a heavy stamp duty. Printers, when uninfluenced by government, have generally arranged themselves on the side of liberty, nor are they less remarkable for attention to the profits of their profession. A stamp duty, which openly invaded the first, and threatened a great diminution of the last, provided their united zealous opposition.[18]

There was no disagreement at all among colonial newspaper editors. They all hated the Stamp Act. Momentary compliance with it evaported quickly. Benjamin Franklin at first bought stamps for the printing firm that he and David Hall owned and tried to get two of his friends appointed as stampmasters.[19] When, however, colonials made threats against his home, spread rumors about his motives, and caricatured him in print, he changed his stance. In 1766 he tried to redeem himself by speaking against the act in the English House of Commons.

No American printer stood in favor of the Stamp Act. A few editors printed the other side of the story, but only grudgingly. Every one of the colonial printers emphasized the anti–Stamp Act sentiment that they themselves felt.

Some printers already had experience with a stamp tax. Hugh Gaine no doubt recalled that he had not protested the New York provincial stamp tax of nine years earlier. He had merely passed the cost of stamps on to his subscribers with the comment that the extra money would help the government.[20] His rival, James Parker, had complained insistently about all manner of dire consequences for the taxed press. Printers would go out of business, he threatened, and newspapers would fold.[21] Massachusetts had also had a colonial stamp tax for two years. Newspapers had indeed folded there; their failures gave Parker fuel for his antistamp fire.[22]

The New York and Massachusetts stamp taxes, however, had not engendered universal hatred. After all, the taxes did not apply in all the colonies. People in Virginia did not much care what New Yorkers paid in taxes, and furthermore, New Yorkers following Hugh Gaine's lead would have tended to submit to the tax in the name of needed governmental revenues.

The Stamp Act of 1765 quickly began producing a markedly different reaction. The colonies grumbled with fits of discontent here and there as people realized the Stamp Act might affect their trade, their profit margin, their cash flow. Printer Samuel Hall in Newport, Rhode Island, published the early arguments. He reported late in 1764 that the government of Rhode Island was disturbed about the proposed Stamp Act. "Among other things," he told the readers of his newspaper, "they voted an Address to his Majesty, respecting the Stamp Duties . . . and the Grievances they are already subjected to by the late Act of Parliament." The General Assembly also sent its colonial agent in Britain an essay "on the Rights of the Colonists . . . that he may print it, or make such Use of it as he shall think best."[23]

With that plan, the General Assembly of Rhode Island helped chart the course that the growing Stamp Act protest would take. The Assembly hoped that Rhode

Island's agent could have the anti–Stamp Act document put into print. Printing would be ideal for spreading discontent.

The idea that printing would have an influence on the public's opinion of the Stamp Act was appealing to journalists. The *Georgia Gazette*, quoting the *Pennsylvania Gazette*, bawled at the supporters of the Stamp Act who dared show their heads, "Can they think to escape the *Scourge of tongues*, or that they will not be burlesqued and *pasquinaded* in every *Newspaper*, and lampooned by every *Pamphleteer*?"[24] Taking another tack, Providence's feisty William Goddard was quick to stir up trouble about the proposed Stamp Act. He was closing his *Providence Gazette; And Country Journal* for financial reasons, but he had the nerve to lay part of the blame for his woes on the proposed Stamp Act. He told his readers he would attempt to revive his paper in six months "provided the oppressive and insupportable STAMP-DUTIES, with which the colonies are threatened, should not, with the utter Ruin of the PRESS and PEOPLE, render it altogether impossible."[25]

Parliament passed the Stamp Act on March 22, 1765, to become law in the colonies on November 1 of that year. The British House of Commons at the outset noted that it was "An act . . . towards further defraying the expences of defending, protecting, and securing [America]." The levy varied according to the item taxed, and many vital items were taxed. Court papers were taxed at a rate of three pence per document. Bail bonds cost two shillings. Petitions, bills, and other such papers from the court of chancery or equity cost a shilling and six pence. The list also included retail licenses for selling wine (four pounds), probates of wills (five shillings), deeds (prices varied according to the deed), playing cards (a shilling), dice (ten shillings), newspaper advertisements (two shillings), almanacs, and calendars (four pence apiece). The list did not stop there. Mortgages were to be taxed, as were diplomas, appointments to office, and articles of apprenticeship. The tax list included just about any conceivable item that could be made of paper or skin or vellum or parchment.[26]

Naturally enough, the Stamp Act also included a tax on pamphlets and newspapers. The price varied according to the size of the paper used to print the item, with a tax of a halfpenny on half-sheet papers and pamphlets; a penny for whole sheets; and a shilling per page of anything over a whole sheet size.[27] The Stamp Act hit everyone hard. Newspapers especially took the act bitterly, as it would cost them both for their actual product and for any customers who wished to advertise. The Sugar Act had been annoying, but the Stamp Act was directly linked to an angry public media, a whole profession of printers who were itching to vent their wrath about their increased costs.

In many respects, printers almost *had* to complain right away, even if they meant to comply with the act, for their customers needed to know that printing costs were going up. Customers had to know they would inherit increased costs for newspaper subscriptions and advertisements, blank forms, and almanacs. Printers were leery of losing business over the matter. They wanted customers to know that it was someone else's fault that prices would be increasing after November 1. Printers might have tried to absorb the increase in cost themselves, but none of them wanted to, of course. Probably most could not have afforded to, anyway.

The result was a nervous and angry bunch of printers who perceived that their livelihoods were hanging in the balance. Their newspapers might be taxed out of existence if people could not afford to buy them. Furthermore, the printers' non-news products, such as blank court forms, were victims of the act. It was natural to lash out. Printers' pocketbooks were affected, and that helped them seize quickly on the recent ideological arguments of the Sugar Act.

The freshly remembered Sugar Act was convenient. Having reported on the opposition to the Sugar Act, it was easy for the men and women of the press to see distressing similarities between the two taxes. It was easy for them to bemoan a lack of representatives in Parliament who could *really* understand America. It was also extremely easy to raise a big howl such as had never been heard for the Sugar Act. Printers, unlike the people who had been most directly affected by the Sugar Act, had direct access to newspapers and pamphlets, which could spread the news of discontent and win the public to their side.

Furthermore, American journalists all agreed. They all despised the Stamp Act. They had never been in such agreement before on an issue. As one, the press lifted up a protest that both reflected and helped spark public furor. The American people could not help but follow the battle over the Stamp Act, for it was obsessively reported in countless issues of various gazettes by the very printers who stood to lose their businesses because of the tax.

Printers simply did not let the subject rest. Even while the *Providence Gazette* was out of business, William Goddard and his mother Sarah did manage to put out an "Extraordinary" edition of the *Gazette* on August 24, 1765, for the express purpose of complaining about the now-serious threat of a Stamp Act, to be instituted in a little over two months' time. They flagged their paper with the assumption that their *Gazette* spoke the true views of Rhode Islanders, and furthermore, that the *Gazette* and the people spoke for the Almighty. "*Vox Populi, Vox Dei*," they proclaimed in the flag, adding beneath, "*Where the Spirit of the LORD is, there is LIBERTY*." They attributed the second statement to St. Paul.[28]

The Goddards swore they would start up the *Gazette* regularly again once a new paper mill in the area was finished, and they vowed they would never charge Stamp Act prices for their newspaper. Their *Gazette* proclaimed that Connecticut Stampmaster Jared Ingersoll was a "vile Miscreant," and they printed a letter from "Colonus," who predicted that colonists could soon say adieu to liberty and to "every Privilege which our brave Ancestors, when driven from the Mother country, fought, found, and 'till of late fully enjoyed in America." Colonus observed that across the colonies, people were trying to take lawful measures to stop the advancing Stamp Act in its tracks. "This laudable Zeal hath burnt into a Flame in BOSTON," Colonus reported.[29]

The report on Boston was colorful. Zealous fighters had hanged an effigy of the stampmaster with a handwritten threat attached: "*He that takes this down is an enemy to his Country*." A couplet was also affixed:

What greater Joy can NEW-ENGLAND see,
Than STAMPMEN hanging on a Tree![30]

The Rhode Island newspaper's detailed report from Boston was indicative of things to come as the Stamp Act drew near. Colonial papers had always swapped news with each other. So now, with anti–Stamp Act fervor heating to fever pitch, suddenly residents of any colony who happened to have access to a newspaper knew exactly what everyone in every other colony thought—and printers, so desperately hit by the Stamp Act, were eager to reprint negative reactions to the tax in support of their own negative opinions.

Printers were not hesitant to express their opinions. Benjamin Edes and John Gill, publishers of the *Boston Gazette*, commented in their newspaper, "[W]e hope the [stamped] Papers will never be seen in America." They added a short anti–Stamp Act rhyme, noting that they intended "to recommend it to the notice of every free born son of *AMERICA*."[31]

Edes and Gill were also good businessmen. There was money to be made off of the Stamp Act, and they knew it. Accordingly, they sold copies of the Stamp Act itself to anyone who cared to read it.[32] They also called for feedback from their readers, but they had already had enough feedback to know that their readers were upset about Stamp Act–related panic in Marblehead.[33] It seemed that couples in Marblehead—twenty-two couples altogether—had suddenly made arrangements to marry in order to avoid paying the stamp tax on related legal documents.[34] Also, word had somehow gotten out that a Marblehead businessman was not averse to the Stamp Act, and that rumor had so besmirched his name that he had to publish an ad pleading that:

[the] Report is a very great Mistake; for I have determined, and still do determine, that I will not take or use [stamps], unless People in general do it, being under no Necessity for such a Conduct in the course of my Affairs:—And I am fully convinced it is the Opinion of the People in Trade in this Town, to conduct themselves in the Same Manner, notwithstanding what has been said to the contrary.[35]

Edes and Gill were well aware that few people in the colonies were happy about the Stamp Act. As other colonial printers did, Edes and Gill made sure their readers knew that most of America was upset about the tax. They published the actions of the Maryland House of Delegates in condemning the Stamp Act,[36] and they printed a lament written in Philadelphia: "[F]arewell, farewell liberty!—AMERICA AMERICA doomed by a premature sentence to slavery!"[37]

Far away in Georgia, settlers on the colonial frontier found out that more established areas of America were angrily protesting the oppressive Stamp Act. The *Georgia Gazette*'s publisher, James Johnston, reported to his Southern readers that New Jersey lawyers had resolved to lose business rather than use stamps. Johnston threw in his two cents' worth in italics: "*A noble resolution, worthy of universal imitation!*"[38]

Johnston was facing a terrible setback if the Stamp Act went into effect. His *Gazette* was new; his readers undoubtedly were not as accustomed to a newspaper as they could have been and thus might easily give it up in the event of increased Stamp Act prices. Johnston knew that the Stamp Act could prove his financial ruin if he had to absorb the extra cost or if he passed the tax to the public and drove down subscriptions and advertising sales. He accordingly announced his intention to shut down the *Gazette*.[39] A week later he changed his mind and announced, "[W]e shall continue printing the same as long as we are allowed to make use of unstampt paper."[40]

Georgians may have been strangers in a remote wilderness, but they had an idea, thanks to the *Gazette*, of what was going on in their own colony and elsewhere. Johnston had a sharp eye for the entertainingly dramatic, and he included Stamp Act news of that variety in his newspaper. For example, he reported a Philadelphian's lament on the Stamp Act, which ended abruptly with the wail, "—but I cannot proceed—tears of vexation and Sorrow stop my pen.—O! my country, my country!"[41] He also printed a clever obituary from the *American Chronicle* of Boston:

The 7th of February 1765, died of a cruel Stamp on her vitals, lady N—th A—an Liberty. She was descended from the ancient and honourable family of the BULLS. . . .

She was of a good and amiable disposition, and always conducted herself in the most dutiful manner. . . . Unhappily for her, her mother, some years since, conceived an irreconcilable jealousy against her, on account of a foreign gentleman who called himself Commerce.[42]

The article next introduced the French king, styled "Lewis Baboon," who tried to lay claim to lands given to America by Bull. A long and expensive quarrel followed, and the Bulls won America for all time. Mama Bull, though, got jealous over Commerce, who by now was paying a great deal of attention to daughter America. Mrs. Bull "accordingly issued out orders that her servants should take her and stamp her in so barbarous a manner that she should not survive the wounds. . . . Thus died the most amiable of women, the best wife, the most dutiful child, the tenderest mother."[43]

Johnston was not the only one to print such fanciful personifications of the Stamp Act. Daniel and Robert Fowle, who ran the *New-Hampshire Gazette, and Historical Chronicle,* clipped and reprinted "A Remarkable DREAM" from the *Boston Evening Post*. In this dream, various paper items, soon to be wronged by the Stamp Act, gathered 'round and pleaded their case. The plaintiffs included such characters as the Bond, Papers of the Court, Summons and Writ, Probate Papers, the Diploma, Licence Paper, Almanack, and, of course, the Newspaper. Newspaper addressed the others:

Oh hard indeed must my fate be,
If from the D—l's foot I mayn't be free,
To hear the D—l's Tail's enough for me.

Who of you all has shown a readier mind,
At once to please . . . all mankind?
I travel far and near, the world I range
And carry with me all that's new and strange.
Advices of importance I convey,
As well as merry tales, to please the gay.
Must I be burden'd by the cruel St—p,
Which will my spead, & progress greatly cramp?

The piece concluded, "He sigh'd and said no more." The Fowles had to explain to their readers that a Devil's Tail was a vulgar name for part of a printing press.[44]

On the day the Stamp Act went into effect, the Fowles also quoted with a certain amount of wry glee the obituary that the publisher of the *Maryland Gazette* had written for his paper, which was dying from the Stamp Act. It read, "The Maryland Gazette, which has been in a declining State for Some Time past, expir'd on Thursday the 10th ult. in uncertain Hopes of a Resurrection to Life again. Aged 1066 weeks."[45]

The *New-Hampshire Gazette*, while not quite expiring as had the *Maryland Gazette*, at least had a dirge to sing for the untimely death of liberty. The Fowles published as their lead article that day, "The LAMENTATION Of the NEW-HAMPSHIRE GAZETTE, in particular, and the PRESS in general, On a *Suspicion* of losing their LIBERTY." The lament filled part of page one and most of page two. The dirge mourned that the *Gazette* "*must Die*, or submit to that which is worse than Death, be *Stamp'd*, and lose my Freedom—Will all the good Deeds I have done signify nothing? If the whole Kingdom of England would save my Life, I am unable to live *under* this Burden; therefore I must *Die!*—O unhappy that I am—."[46]

The publishers outlined the *Gazette* dramatically in mourning lines and proclaimed above the flag, "This is the day before the never-to-be forgotten STAMP ACT was to take place in *America*." They added in an article that they had written themselves, "We are now arrived at the Eve of that remarkable Day, which is appointed to be as fatal to almost all that is dear to us, as the Ides of *March* were, to the Life of *Caesar*. . . . A Day on which our Slavery is to commence."[47]

In spite of all the Fowles' drama and dirges, their efforts were eclipsed by the *Pennsylvania Gazette; and Weekly Advertiser*, whose publisher, William Bradford, used his imagination and a flair for graphics to make a striking statement about the effects of stamps on his newspaper. He made up the front page of October 31, 1765, to look like a big tombstone. It featured a skull and crossbones and digging tools in a tombstone-shaped outline. Bradford included a mourning chant in Gothic type: "The TIMES are Dreadful, Dismal Doleful Dolorous, and DOLLAR-LESS." On the front page the printer also offered his readers a fanciful illustration of a stamp—a skull and crossbones with "O! the fatal Stamp" written below it. Under the flag, he told his readers eloquently that the *Gazette* was dying as of October 31, 1765. "EXPIRING:" he wrote, "In Hopes of a Resurrection to LIFE again." He blamed the suspension of his paper both on the economic "Burthen" and on the need for him to "deliberate, whether any Methods can be found to elude the chains forged for us, and escape the insupportable Slavery."[48]

All around the provinces, newspapers were stirring up anti–Stamp Act sentiment, adding fuel to a fire that was threatening to rage out of control. Editors showed their wrath by making sure everyone relived the most dramatic Stamp Act protests by reading them in colorful detail in the newspaper. It did not matter if a colonist lived in North Carolina. He still knew exactly what hotheaded protesters were doing in New Hampshire, and vice versa.

Editors selected their ammunition carefully. Joseph Royle, proprietor of the *Virginia Gazette*, put out a "SUPPLEMENT Extraordinary" the week before the Stamp Act's inauguration to present a thorough and well-reasoned argument from Boston against the sale of stamped paper. The article quoted a speaker who warned, "[T]his province seems to me to be upon the brink of a precipice, and . . . it depends upon you to prevent us falling." The speaker was in Massachusetts, but as far as Royle was concerned, he was speaking of Virginia as well. The dangers inherent in the Stamp Act in Boston were just as frightening in Virginia. According to the *Gazette*'s report, after the Stamp Act went into effect, "trade and navigation shall cease, by the shutting up the ports of this province for want of legal clearances." It predicted dire hardships for tradesmen and their families.[49]

Other protests were not so eloquently put, but they were protests just the same. From North Carolina, Royle learned that "the Gentleman appointed Distributor of Stamps for that province had resigned his office, on finding how disagreeable it was to the people, who in general have shown as great a dislike to that law as the inhabitants of any of the other colonies have done." Twice in that issue, Royle printed hopeful speculation that the Stamp Act would be repealed quickly in London.[50]

Such exchanges of information from colony to colony or from London to the colonies were electrifying, unifying. A Boston lawmaker made a speech to the General Assembly and referred to a letter from the *Virginia Gazette*, which he used for inspiration. He complained, "[A]nd what is the worst of all evils, . . . his Majesty's American subjects are not to be governed, according to the known stated rules of the constitution, as those in Britain are." The *Massachusetts Gazette* carried the speech—and the *Virginia Gazette*'s sentiments—to its readers. The New England newspaper in the same issue quoted the *Maryland Gazette*'s protest of the Stamp Act.[51] The *Massachusetts Gazette* also reported the Virginia House of Burgesses' protests against the act. In addition, it printed a juicy tale of a mob that harassed the Pennsylvania stamp distributor into agreeing not to distribute the stamps.[52] Likewise, the *Connecticut Courant* gave close attention to colorful stamp protests in the colony—but also kept its readers apprised of such transcolonial Stamp Act news as the forced resignation of two successive stamp distributors in North Carolina[53] and protests in Virginia.[54]

Other papers followed the pattern of telling all the news available from other colonies regarding the Stamp Act. Georgians learned through the *Georgia Gazette* that Stampmaster George Saxby in neighboring South Carolina had resigned. The dreaded stamp paper intended for Georgia, the *Gazette* announced, was already in Charleston, South Carolina, under the care of a Mr. Angus.[55] Two Londoners reported to the *Gazette* that they expected the Stamp Act to be repealed soon.[56] In similar fashion, the *New-Hampshire Gazette* filled its pages with protests from such faraway places as Philadelphia.[57]

Everywhere around the colonies, the newspapers copied one another. Readers in every colony not only knew what was going on locally about the stamp tax, but what was going on hundreds of miles away in other colonies or across the ocean. Newspaper subscribers everywhere learned about the Stamp Act Congress, which met in New York from October 7 to 24 that year. Delegates to the congress made a humble petition to the king for a repeal of the tax and of other legislation restricting American commerce.[58]

By spreading news of Stamp Act protests, printers began to validate local, negative opinions toward the Stamp Act, to support those opinions and boost them as correct and right or at least as popular. Sentiment caught fire like dry wood. Soon the flame of feeling against the Stamp Act appeared to be overwhelming.

Despite the firestorm of American sentiment and despite the plea of the stamp congress, the Stamp Act went into effect on November 1. Printers who were daring enough to remain in business kept up the protests. Thomas Green kept printing the *Connecticut Courant*, even in the absence of stamped paper. When the stamps finally arrived, he commented:

The Stamped Papers are now in the Harbour, and the Day is near at Hand, when this infamous Act is designed to take Place; but it is hoped that every Lover of his Country will spurn, with the highest Indignation, the base Thought of ever purchasing a single one; and despise, execrate and detest the wretch who shall presume to countenance the Use of them, in any way whatever.

Green added that the Stamp Act would "transmit to a numerous Posterity, the horrid chains of absolute Servitude."[59] Green did not give up. As time wore on, he became vicious in his personal protests against the Stamp Act. When the Stamp Act was a good two months old, he reported that "A Letter from Barbados says, they are determined to seize all Vessels coming without Stamp-Paper," and he added himself, *"May they be without Provisions till the Stamp-Act is repealed."* He followed his attack with a letter from a gentleman in Barbados who obviously agreed with him. The gentleman explained that Barbados would be ruined by the stamp laws, for the tax was to be paid in specie, "and we have such a Scarcity of Cash, that . . . our Trade must inevitably perish."[60]

Green clearly perceived the press as the vehicle by which the Stamp Act would be undone. As the new year rolled around, he reported with pride how "The True Sons of Liberty" had used a Boston newspaper as an agent in communicating the people's displeasure to the stamp officer. The newspaper demanded a public resignation at a designated place and time, and it won. It forced the stamp officer to admit that he detested the Stamp Act and would never do his duties.[61]

The press's reaction to the Stamp Act was consistent. Publishers either refused to print with stamps or suspended publication until the storm blew over. Those who still published feared the actual taxes as well as censure. Richard and Samuel Draper, publishers of the *Massachusetts Gazette*, kept producing their weekly newspaper after the Stamp Act went into effect. However, they pulled a trick that was sure to cover them in the event of legal questions. Their October 31, 1765, issue was numbered 3239, but their November 7 issue, a week after the Stamp Act took effect, was numbered zero. They issued papers under the number zero through May 15, 1766. Their May 22, 1766, issue picked up standard numbering again at 3268 and announced just below the flag, "*Friday last arrived here the Brigantine* Harrison . . . *who brought the important Accounts of the* REPEAL *of the* AMERICAN STAMP-ACT."[62] The Drapers offered no reason for the zero numbering, but their implication was that a paper numbered zero was never *really* published and therefore did not meet the legal definition of being a publication—and if something were not published, it could not be published on stamped paper. It was a transparent trick based on a technicality, but there is no record that authorities ever questioned it.

The Drapers' symbolic use of the zero was a counterbalance for their dramatically innovative protest of the Stamp Act. The Drapers had actually heralded the coming of the Stamp Act with a headline, a feature never seen in colonial newspapers. In a special edition, they set the date of the enactment of the act in Gothic type as a headline over a column of news about Stamp Act protests. The Drapers selected a quote from Pope's *Homer* to complement the story: "Oh fatal! FROM *and* AFTER! Jove *fix'd it certain, that whatever Day Makes Man a Slave, takes half his Worth away.*"[63]

While the Drapers created a headline in protest, Jonas Green used his devilish sense of humor. Green, the witty publisher of the *Maryland Gazette*, had suspended the *Gazette* for the duration of the Stamp Act. Occasionally, however, he wanted to publish. So he came out with an issue entitled *The Apparition of The Maryland Gazette, which is not Dead but Sleepeth.* The "apparition," which could not possibly be the *real Maryland Gazette* for the purposes of legalities, did not need to be published on stamped paper as flesh-and-blood newspapers did. Accordingly, the apparition featured a death's-head substituting for a stamp.[64]

Meanwhile, the Stamp Act was compounding preexistent business woes for some printers. South Carolina's two rival printers fretted so over what to do in response to increased Stamp Act prices that they wound up opening the door so that a third printer could start his own newspaper.

The Stamp Act was tricky business for Peter Timothy, editor and printer of Charleston's *South-Carolina Gazette*, and Robert Wells, who held the same position across town at the *South-Carolina and American General Gazette*. Timothy especially had a hard time accepting the fact that his longstanding *Gazette* at last had a cross-town rival,[65] and Wells was concerned about his profit margin.[66] They both worried about the fact that the expense of stamped papers might drive away business, or worse, send business to the other paper. Their readers, meanwhile, were anxious to know exactly what would become of the *Gazettes* after the Stamp Act went into effect.[67]

The Stamp Act was a crisis for Wells and Timothy—so much of a crisis, in fact, that they called an uneasy truce in their ongoing rivalry in order to deal with the situation. They announced jointly in an advertisement:

THE *Subscribers* to the GAZETTES need not be informed that the STAMP-ACT must necessarily occasion an advance in the price; they may be assured, however, that the *addition* will be as moderate as possible, and, that such as do not intimate their intention of discontinuing will be supplied, in the usual manner, after the act takes place.

Every ADVERTISEMENT is subject to a duty of *Two Shillings* sterling, each time it is inserted, which the printers are to pay weekly, it will, therefore, be *absolutely necessary*, that READY MONEY be sent with all advertisements.[68]

Obviously, the two *Gazettes* intended to remain in business, in spite of the Stamp Act. Timothy and Wells apparently were attempting to present a united front in the face of a great threat to their livelihoods.

The men had no deep loyalty to each other, though, and hence no real concern about keeping their bargain. They began to waver in their resolve. The day before the Stamp Act was to go into effect, Wells mentioned offhandedly that he did not know "how long the approaching *Vacation* may continue," but that he would use the time off to collect his bills. It certainly sounded as though he intended to close the *General Gazette*, although he did allow for the possibility of continuing publication by mentioning the price of the newspaper if the Stamp Act really were enforced.[69]

Meanwhile, Timothy got scared. On October 31 he ruled his *Gazette* in mourning lines and pointed out that he would do all kinds of "PRINTING-WORK that does not require STAMPS, *which are not to be had.*" He had, however, made up his mind about the *Gazette*. He had informally polled his readers on the possibility of publishing with stamps, and they had insisted that they would not buy the *Gazette* if he published it. He decided to suspend the newspaper. He complained bitterly that it would be "impossible to continue it without great loss to the printer," since his subscribers "*almost to a man*" had promised not to buy stamped newspapers.[70] The next day, the *South-Carolina Gazette* was out of business, a victim of the Stamp Act.

Wells, perhaps encouraged by the chance to publish Charleston's only newspaper while Timothy's paper was temporarily closed down, decided not to go on vacation after all, and he continued publishing the *General Gazette* as scheduled.[71]

The whole mess gave Charlestonian Charles Crouch an opportunity. He at one time had been Timothy's apprentice, but a dishonest one. He had run away from his apprenticeship and had gotten money to finance his flight by pretending to collect his master's bills.[72] Finally Timothy had fired him for drinking, gambling, and keeping scandalous company.[73] With Timothy's paper gone, Crouch and his friends saw a chance to capitalize on the newspaper situation in Charleston. Some residents of the city approached Crouch about starting a paper to be published without stamps.[74] Crouch would risk legal trouble by publishing so deliberately without stamps—but then again, he was a gambler and decided to take the chance.

Crouch got the new newspaper underway in short order. On December 17, 1765, he issued the *South-Carolina Gazette; and Country Journal*.[75] Defiantly, over the flag he proclaimed, "No *STAMPED PAPER* to be had."[76] Below the flag, he reprinted the rallying cry from the *New-York Gazette:* "The united Voice of all His Majesty's *free* and *loyal* Subjects in AMERICA,——*LIBERTY* and *PROPERTY*, and NO *STAMPS*."[77]

Crouch filled his paper with angry denunciations of the Stamp Act. He led off with the South Carolina Commons House of Assembly's polite but firm resolutions against the act. The polite tone ended quickly, however, as Crouch rounded up tales of Stamp Act protests from across America. There were effigies hanged and burned in New York, along with an illegal parade through the streets (made with a stolen carriage). In Rhode Island there was a mock funeral for liberty. The Massachusetts Assembly issued resolves against the act.[78]

In succeeding issues, Crouch continued to play up the Stamp Act theme. He reported, for instance, a prediction that soon business would be "as usual" in the colonies, without stamps. Another article warned that "*once the tree of liberty is sapped of its moisture, though it be but in one part of its root, it is manifestly in danger of gradually withering away.*"[79] He quoted a New York writer under the pseudonym "Freeman," who was fanatical about opposing the Stamp Act. Freeman urged, "[L]et us oppose them with all our might, even though death should be the consequence—we should die gloriously in our duty in the best of causes."[80] Crouch also quoted a London writer, who observed that "the bomb has burst in North-America."[81] Crouch rode the Stamp Act into a successful career. The one-time disgrace to Peter Timothy's shop parlayed his anti–Stamp Act newspaper into a successful South Carolina journal that lasted until his untimely death in 1775.[82]

Crouch kept fighting the Stamp Act for as long as it lasted. So did other printers. With their livelihoods threatened, they turned out to be a stubborn lot. As far as they were concerned, time would not heal their wounds; only repeal would. John Holt, for one, produced a "Supplement Extraordinary" of his *New-York Journal, or General Advertiser,* to protest the Stamp Act long after it took effect. The *Journal* was brutal. Holt led with a letter from a correspondent who recalled a piece in the *New-York Thursday's Gazette or Weekly Post-Boy* (predecessor to the *Journal*), which had been published months earlier. The correspondent snarled that the article in question was "a detestable Piece signed *Americanus*, in favour of the Stamp-Act." At the time of the original publication, Holt had derided "Americanus" with the statement that "The Author of the following Piece is unknown to the Printer; *it cannot be supposed*, that he is an AMERICAN, or a FRIEND TO LIBERTY."[83] Now, months later, the article's writer recalled that everyone who had read Americanus's piece at the time was absolutely positive that Americanus was a native of Britain using a rather unfortunate pen name. No one, the writer fumed, had "believed that a Native of *America* could be so lost to all Regard for the *Freedom* and *Honour* of the Country, as to endeavor to destroy that sacred Right of taxing ourselves."[84]

However, the *Journal*'s correspondent was now announcing in October 1766 that the writer *was* an American after all, one Joseph Galloway of Philadelphia. Worse yet, this "Affector of American Slavery," as the *Journal* article called him, had been reelected to the Pennsylvania assembly to represent Philadelphia. Furthermore, Galloway was voted Speaker of the House. A shocked correspondent wailed in the *Journal*, "What a blow is this to American Freedom! to see the People of Pennsylvania, hitherto distinguished for their Love of Liberty, bestowing their Favour on a Man who has so daringly attacked their dearest Rights."[85]

Holt reprinted Americanus's original letter in favor of the Stamp Act, including the letter's vicious indictment of the press. Americanus had stated, "[I]t is to be hoped that those indecent reflections which have already been too often repeated in our public papers, will be no longer continued." Not only was the press at fault in Americanus's eyes, but the American people were stupid sheep, following the press. The newspapers, Galloway had written, "only tend to create in the minds of the weak and ignorant, a spirit of disloyalty against the crown, and hatred against the people of England; and to excite the resentment of our superiors against the Americans."[86]

Holt did not take such a slur against the press lightly. He printed a feisty letter lauding the battle against the Stamp Act. "I can't help adding an Observation," the author wrote, "that the Freedom of the Press has already had the salutary Effect of correcting the haughty Spirits of some of our great Men."[87]

Like Holt, Alexander Purdie of the *Virginia Gazette* was still printing angry articles about the Stamp Act months after it passed. He reported that in nearby North Carolina, the king's stamp officers had shown blatant disregard for the needs of local citizens. The local people, in their turn, had gathered together a raft and flammables to go set the stamp-bearing ship, the stamps, and the ship's captain all on fire in the port of Wilmington. The captain had been intimidated enough to leave Wilmington hastily.[88]

Anti–Stamp Act news from other colonies continued to flow from Purdie's press: lawyers in New Jersey were debating how to balance the need for business with the need for protest; Marylanders were strongly opposed to stamps; a Boston writer predicted a quick repeal of the act; New England lawyers were expected to refuse to use stamped legal forms.[89] So much anti–Stamp Act news came in from other colonies, in fact, that Purdie was obliged to announce in a later issue:

[There are] other letters from Gentlemen in London to their correspondents here, to which something is said, more or less, relating to the Stamp Act; but as the sentiments, and indeed the very words, are in general the same with some of those published under the Boston and New York heads, it is thought needless to trouble our readers with a repetition. Let it therefore suffice to inform them that these letters seem to be wrote by men of moderation and good understanding, who are sincere friends to the colonies, and who heartily despise the contrivers and promoters of so base an attempt against the liberties and privileges of a loyal and free people.[90]

Purdie's remarks showed his unabashed hatred of the Stamp Act, as well as his honest admission that news of the Stamp Act was so abundant that details were not really necessary all the time. Obviously, the American press was saturated with Stamp Act protests. As Purdie said in avoiding summarization of a Boston protest, "these transactions being well known here, it is needless to publish them." There was no way anyone could have missed the news, and even Purdie, who wanted to see the tax die quickly, felt that there was enough anti–Stamp Act news out there to justify not printing it on some days.[91]

Purdie was, however, horrified by the realization that American grievances, or rather the reasons for them, had not been properly publicized in England. Fortunately, friends of America had "nobly exerted themselves" in London to help set the record straight and to bring public pressure to bear on Parliament.[92]

The attempt to exert pressure on Parliament took forms other than the newspaper, of course. Songs and sermons derided the act, as did other printed matter such as broadsides and pamphlets. The Stamp Act made excellent material for pamphleteers. One of the most popular Stamp Act pamphlets was written by Daniel Dulany, a conservative Maryland lawyer, who questioned Parliament's sincerity in representing America. *"When a Law, in it's [sic] Execution, is found to be repugnant to the Genius of Liberty, or productive of Hardships or Inconvenience,"* Dulany wrote, "[constituents] *may . . . instruct their Deputies to exert themselves in procuring a Repeal of it."*[93] As a legal expert, Dulany lent an air of authority to the colonial discussion of British law. His arguments were not based on idealistic principles, but, in the colonists' eyes, on legal fact. He explained:

The Right of Exemption from all Taxes *without their Consent*, the Colonies claim as *British* Subjects. They derive this Right from the Common Law, which their Charters have declared and confirmed, and they conceive that when stripped of this Right, whether by Prerogative or by any other Power, they are at the same Time deprived of every Privilege distinguishing Free-Men from Slaves.[94]

Dulany, like so many Stamp Act writers, tried to temper American anger with a calm assurance to Englishmen that America was not seeking anything as outlandish as independence from Britain. Americans wanted to continue being British. Colonists, Dulany noted, "acknowledge themselves to be subordinate to the Mother-Country," and he added that the mother country had a legal right to maintain that subordination.[95] Emphasizing his belief that everything the colonists wanted was perfectly legal, Dulany continued, "We claim an Exemption from all *Parliamentary* Impositions, that we may enjoy those Securities of our Rights and Properties, which we are entitled to by the Constitution."[96]

A writer calling himself a "Plain Yeoman" echoed Dulany's sentiments regarding representation in Parliament. The Yeoman argued that the British notion that Parliament represented all Britons, including American colonists, was a falsehood. It was simply a fact, he pointed out, that the representatives were not American and thus could not in fact represent America.[97] Essentially, the Yeoman accused Britain of imposing taxation without representation. Dulany had expressed much the same idea.

Reasoned arguments in the press such as the Yeoman's and Dulany's gave way to an outpouring of reports on hotheaded acts by the Sons of Liberty. The *Connecticut Courant* reported that "a large Assembly of the respectable Populace" gathered late in 1765 and declared "That every Form of Government rightfully founded, originates from the Consent of the People." The stamp tax, they stated emphatically, had not been imposed by their consent, and hence the tax violated their rights as Englishmen.[98] Echoing the desire for the right of representation, New York Sons of Liberty took a firm stand. They resolved "That we will go to the last Extremity, and venture our Lives and Fortunes, effectually to prevent the said Stamp-Act from ever taking Place in this City and Province." Such a stand was within their rights as Englishmen, they insisted.[99] In New Jersey, a newswriter said, the Sons of Liberty called the Stamp Act an illegal attempt to take away the rights of the people.[100] Virginians condemned the Stamp Act as "oppressive and unconstitutional" and "pregnant with ruin." The press of Pennsylvania picked up the Virginia and New Jersey protests.[101] North Carolina resolves against the tax found their way into the *Maryland Gazette*.[102] The newspaper press continued to draw the circle of protest ever tighter, rallying the colonists against the hated stamps.

Here and there, of course, there were a few pro-British writers who made their way into the American press. The *Maryland Gazette* quoted a writer calling himself "Pacificus," who described Virginians as emaciated, pale, and morally bankrupt. "These yellow Shadows of Men are by no Means fit for a Conflict with our Troops," Pacificus commented, anticipating a military clash over the stamp tax. He quickly decided, though, that there would be no such clash, for he continued, "Nor will ever such romantic Adventures of Chivalry enter into [Virginians'] trembling hearts." Furthermore, he said, New Englanders were mere "pumkins" and "the Joke of America," and no one could really take their complaints seriously. Pacificus went on to describe the protesting colonists with a colorful proverb: *"[E]mpty Barrels make most Noise when touched even with a Tap of our Knuckle."*[103]

Another writer did not necessarily disagree with American sentiment, but he did warn Americans that they had gotten far too caught up in the anti stamp fever and had not considered the consequences of what they wanted. Writing for the *Pennsylvania Journal,* "F. L." recalled that he had read many political articles in American publications that asked for colonial representation in the British Parliament. F. L. suggested:

[Colonial representation] will involve [colonies] in a very burdensome expence. . . . We have few gentlemen in the colonies, who have fortunes sufficient to enable them, and fewer still I fear who have public spirit enough to be willing to reside at the court of Great Britain at their own expence. To send them there without handsome appointments for their support, would be throwing them into the very jaws of temptation; it would be to make it in some sort necessary for many of them at least to betray their trust. . . .

[T]his scheme, if adopted, would not only be grievously expensive to the colonies, but can do them no service. For we may take it for granted that Great Britain will never offer us such a number of representatives in the house, as would give us any considerable weight or influence there.[104]

F. L.'s argument did not impress Americans. They continued fighting the hated stamps with symbol, pen, and boycott.

Parliament finally yielded to a variety of anti–Stamp Act pressures on March 18, 1766. By now British merchants, smarting from boycotts, clamored for repeal. Making the excuse that "*the continuance of the said act would be attended with many inconveniences*" and might hurt commercial interests of the kingdom, Parliament issued a repeal to take effect on May 1.[105]

Parliament, however, was not going to take defeat lightly. On the same day that it passed the repeal, it also passed a Declaratory Act "*for . . . better securing the dependency of his Majesty's dominions in* America *upon the crown and parliament of* Great Britain." Parliament was not happy with American behavior. The Declaratory Act accused several houses of representatives in America of violating the law outright by claiming "*to themselves, or to the general assemblies of the same, the sole and exclusive right of imposing duties and taxes upon his Majesty's subjects in the said colonies and plantations.*" Such illegalities, Parliament huffed, were inconsistent with the colonies' dependence on the crown. Thus, lords, commons, and king agreed to remind the Americans that they "have been, are, and of right ought to be, subordinate unto, and dependent upon the imperial crown and parliament of *Great Britain.*" Furthermore, they stressed, the king and *only* the king, through his Parliament, had the power and authority to make laws to bind America. The lawmakers slapped the recalcitrant Americans with a reminder that they were, after all, "subjects of the crown of *Great Britain*, in all cases whatsoever." Finally, the British lawmakers ordered:

That all resolutions, votes, orders, and proceedings, in any of the said colonies or plantations, whereby the power and authority of the parliament of Great Britain, to make laws and statutes as aforesaid, is denied, or drawn into question, are, and are hereby declared to be, utterly null and void to all intents and purposes whatsoever.[106]

The fight was over—for now. The bitter feelings of the wounded Parliament, accused by Americans of being so stupid and distant, would easily be renewed when Americans again grew restive for their rights and headed toward revolution.

In 1766, though, America had won a victory over the hated Stamp Act, at least in part through the unison efforts of the mass media. For the first time in America, it was as though everyone, everywhere, at the same time, had a chance to see a controversial issue through the eyes of his or her neighbor, as reported in the press. And for the first time, every newspaper printer in America agreed wholeheartedly with the others. Printers unanimously protested the hardship and unfairness of the Stamp Act. They did not waver in their condemnation. They saw the Stamp Act as pure evil and expressed it that way. If any pro–Stamp Act sentiment dared lift its ugly head, the press squashed it flatly and without the slightest doubt that the anti-stamp stance was the correct one.

The Stamp Act died as the American mass media came of age. The long period of gestation of the colonial press was over. At last it had reached a youthful, robust maturity. Members of the press realized that they had a larger ability to influence the public than they had ever had before.

American journalists were thereby prepared to fight effectively and insistently for the causes they believed in. They had perfected the technique of intercolonial news-swapping to capitalize on public sentiment. In so doing, the press had shed its jumbled, disjointed past and was ready to play a significant part as America approached the rebellion against the mother country.

NOTES

1. The Sugar Act, 5 April 1764, commented that revenue was needed to defray the costs which Great Britain had incurred in defending, protecting, and securing America. The Sugar Act is reprinted in Edmund S. Morgan, ed., *Prologue to Revolution: Sources and Documents on the Stamp Act Crisis, 1764–1766* (New York: W. W. Norton, 1959), 4.

2. C. E. Carrington, *The British Overseas: Exploits of a Nation of Shopkeepers* (Cambridge, England: Cambridge University Press, 1950), 105.

3. Ibid.

4. The Sugar Act, in Morgan, *Prologue to Revolution*, 4.

5. Curtis P. Nettels, *The Roots of American Civilization: A History of American Colonial Life* (New York: F. S. Crofts, 1939), 612–13.

6. Ibid., 610–12, 614–15.

7. Many historians have studied the Stamp Act, often considering it the genesis of the American Revolution. Athough Stamp Act historiography has often recognized the press as an important ingredient in the stamp crisis, historians have rarely considered the Stamp Act press as an editorial phenomenon. In general, journalism historians have studied the Stamp Act press with an eye toward explaining the motivation of journalists in 1765.

Clyde Duniway wrote about patriotic motivations for printers in *Development of Freedom of the Press in Massachusetts* (New York: Longmans, Green, & Co., 1906). Such a romantic concept of a nobly patriotic press eventually metamorphosed into the historiographical idea that Stamp Act journalists were propagandists. Such an interpretation was offered by Philip Davidson in *Propaganda and the American Revolution* (Chapel Hill: University of North Carolina Press, 1941). Davidson felt that Stamp Act–era editors took the lead in calling for American liberty, and to that purpose, they issued propaganda.

Another set of historians concurred with the propaganda concept, but they did not see propaganda as springing from editors' patriotic sense of duty. Instead, they felt that external factors played a role in the decision to propagandize. Verner Crane, in *Benjamin Franklin's Letters to the Press, 1758–1775* (Chapel Hill: University of North Carolina Press, 1950), felt that Franklin touted the American cause in the press in an attempt to save his own political career. Edmund and Helen Morgan, in *The Stamp Act Crisis* (Chapel Hill: University of North Carolina Press, 1958), concluded that various groups, external to the press, bullied journalists into printing propaganda.

Other historians felt that economics played a role in the press's reaction to the stamp tax. Arthur Schlesinger said printers were dazed and indecisive when the tax was announced. In *Prelude to Independence: The Newspaper War on Britain, 1764–1776* (New York: Alfred A. Knopf, 1958), he suggested printers feared economic boycott by their readers. Schlesinger saw a public opinion role for the press, but he described printers as being buffeted by economic needs.

A later historian, Stephen Botein, offered a purely economic interpretation in his essay, "Printers and the American Revolution," in Bernard Bailyn and John B. Hench, eds., *The Press and the American Revolution* (Worcester, Mass.: American Antiquarian Society, 1980). Botein felt that Stamp Act journalists needed to make a living. They used that fact as a guideline in making decisions, and clever printers capitalized on the situation by tying their livelihood to overwhelming popular opinion against the Stamp Act.

Rather than analyzing the motivations of printers, as most historical works on the Stamp Act press have done, this chapter details the press as an editorial movement which helped unite the colonies in a way that Britain never imagined.

8. See, for example, a laudatory article on evangelist George Whitefield in the *New-England Weekly Journal* (Boston), 4 December 1739, and a negative article on Whitefield in the *Boston Gazette*, 20 April 1741. Such conflicting examples abounded during the Great Awakening.

9. Thomas Whately, for instance, made this point. See Whately, *The Regulations lately Made concerning the Colonies and the Taxes Imposed upon them, Considered* (pamphlet; London, 1765), reprinted in Morgan, *Prologue to Revolution*, 19.

10. Ibid., 18.

11. The Sugar Act, in Morgan, *Prologue to Revolution*, 4–8.

12. Whately, in Morgan, ibid., 18, and the *Connecticut Courant*, 16 September 1765.

13. New York General Assembly, Petition to the House of Commons, 18 October 1764, reprinted in Morgan, ibid., 8–11.

14. The term "Americans" will be used in this chapter to refer to the residents of Britain's North American colonies, although in actuality Americans were British subjects throughout the Stamp Act crisis.

15. New York General Assembly, Petition to the House of Commons, 18 October 1764, reprinted in Morgan, *Prologue to Revolution*, 8–11.

16. Bernard Bailyn discussed the evolution of the American concept of political representation in *The Origins of American Politics* (New York: Random House, 1967). See in particular pp. 75–88.

17. Virginia House of Burgesses, Petition to the King, 18 December 1764, reprinted in Morgan, *Prologue to Revolution*, 15.

18. David Ramsay, *History of the American Revolution* (Philadelphia, 1789), 1:61–62.

19. Benjamin Franklin, *The Writings of Benjamin Franklin* (New York: Macmillan, 1905–1907), 4:390, 412.

20. *New-York Mercury*, 20 December 1756.

21. See James Parker's broadside of 2 November 1759, entitled *A Letter to a Gentleman of the City of New-York: Shewing the Unreasonableness of the present Stamp-Duty upon News-papers, and the great Burthen of that Duty upon the Printers*. It is reprinted in Beverly McAnear, "James Parker *Versus* New York Province," *New York History* 22 (1941): 322–30.

22. Ibid.

23. *Newport* (Rhode Island) *Mercury*, 26 December 1764.

24. *Georgia Gazette* (Savannah), 7 November 1765. The *Pennsylvania Journal* article quoted came from the 5 September 1765 issue.

25. *Providence* (Rhode Island) *Gazette; And Country Journal*, 11 May 1765.

26. The Stamp Act, reprinted in Morgan, *Prologue to Revolution*, 35–43.

27. Ibid., 40–41.

28. *Providence Gazette; And Country Journal*, 24 August 1765. The Latin phrase said roughly, "Voice of the People, Voice of God."

29. Ibid.

30. Ibid.

31. *Boston Gazette*, 21 October 1765.

32. Ibid., 14 October 1765.

33. Ibid., 21 October 1765.

34. Ibid., 14 October 1765.

35. Ibid., 21 October 1765.

36. Ibid.

37. Ibid., 14 October 1765.

38. *Georgia Gazette*, 14 November 1765.

39. Ibid.

40. Ibid., 21 November 1765.

41. Ibid., 14 November 1765.

42. Ibid., 31 October 1765.

43. Ibid.

44. *New-Hampshire Gazette, and Historical Chronicle* (Portsmouth), 25 October 1765.

45. Ibid., 31 October 1765.

46. Ibid.

47. Ibid. The text appeared to be written by the printers, as it had no signature and no dateline from another city.

48. *Pennsylvania Gazette*, 31 October 1765.

49. *Virginia Gazette* (Williamsburg), 25 October 1765.

50. Ibid.

51. *Massachusetts Gazette*, 31 October 1765.

52. Ibid., 24 October 1765.

53. *Connecticut Courant*, 30 December 1765.

54. Ibid., 28 October 1765.

55. *Georgia Gazette*, 7 November 1765.

56. Ibid., 14 November 1765.

57. *New-Hampshire Gazette*, 25 October 1765.

58. *Proceedings of the Congress at New York* (Annapolis, 1766), pp. 15–19, reprinted in Morgan, *Prologue to Revolution*, pp. 62–65.

59. *Connecticut Courant*, 28 October 1765. The unsigned piece was apparently written by Green himself.

60. Ibid., 30 December 1765.

61. Ibid., 6 January 1766.

62. *Massachusetts Gazette*, 24 October 1765 through 22 May 1766.

63. Ibid., 31 October 1765.

64. Isaiah Thomas, *The History of Printing in America,* ed. Marcus A. McCorison (1810; reprint, New York: Weathervane Books, 1970), 542.

65. See, for example, the *South-Carolina Gazette* (Charleston), 21 February 1761, 12 September 1761 (the dated cover page of this issue is missing, but the paper appears to be the issue of 12 September), and 3 October 1761. Wells's newspaper, identified previously as the *South-Carolina Weekly Gazette*, had changed its name to *South-Carolina and American General Gazette* (Charleston).

66. See, for instance, a piece by Wells in the *South-Carolina Gazette* of 3 October 1761 in which he indicated he intended to avoid becoming penniless in the rivalry with Timothy.

67. *South-Carolina Gazette* and *South-Carolina and American General Gazette*, both of 31 October 1765.

68. *South-Carolina Gazette*, 19 October 1765. Wells's paper most likely carried the ad, too, but his paper of this time frame is not extant.

69. *South-Carolina and American General Gazette*, 31 October 1765.

70. *South-Carolina Gazette,* 31 October 1765.

71. The numbering of the issues of Wells's paper shows that he continued to publish throughout the life of the Stamp Act. None of his papers survives from this period, however.

72. *South-Carolina Gazette*, 5 and 26 February 1753.

73. Peter Timothy to Benjamin Franklin, 14 June 1754, in Leonard Labaree, ed., *The Papers of Benjamin Franklin* (New Haven, Conn.: Yale University Press, 1959), 5:343.

74. Peter Timothy to Benjamin Franklin, 3 September 1768, *The Papers of Benjamin Franklin,* 15:201.

75. The first issue was actually named *South-Carolina Gazetteer; and Country Journal* (Charleston). The *"Gazetteer"* was amended to *"Gazette"* shortly thereafter.

76. Ibid. In the original, the line above the flag was bracketed.

77. Ibid.

78. Ibid.

79. Ibid., 7 January 1766.

80. Ibid., 14 January 1766.

81. Ibid., 4 February 1766.

82. Ibid., 25 August 1775. That issue stated that Crouch had left for Philadelphia aboard a ship. The ship never reached port, according to Thomas, *The History of Printing in America*, 571. Thomas had at one time been a journeyman printer in Charleston and likely knew Crouch personally, so his information is probably reliable.

83. *New-York Journal, or General Advertiser*, 30 October 1766.

84. Ibid.

85. Ibid.

86. Ibid.

87. Ibid., 27 November 1766.

88. *Virginia Gazette*, 7 March 1766.

89. Ibid.

90. Ibid., 14 March 1766.

91. Ibid.

92. Ibid.

93. Daniel Dulany, *Considerations on the Propriety of Imposing Taxes in the British Colonies for the purpose of raising a Revenue by Act of Parliament* (pamphlet; Annapolis, Md., 1765, 2d edition), reprinted in Morgan, *Prologue to Revolution*, 77.

94. Morgan, ibid., 83.

95. Ibid., 84.

96. Ibid., 83–84.

97. *Providence* (Rhode Island) *Gazette*, 11 May 1765.

98. *Connecticut Courant* (Hartford), 30 December 1765.

99. *New-York Mercury* (New York), 13 January 1766.

100. *Pennsylvania Journal* (Philadelphia), 6 March 1766.

101. Ibid., 6 March and 17 April 1766.

102. *Maryland Gazette* (Annapolis), 10 April 1766.

103. Ibid., 20 March 1766.

104. *Pennsylvania Journal*, 13 March 1766.

105. The Act Repealing the Stamp Act, 18 March 1766, reprinted in Morgan, *Prologue to Revolution*, 155.

106. The Declaratory Act, 18 March 1766, reprinted in Morgan, ibid., 155–56.

6

The Uneasy Years, 1766–1775

The Stamp Act crisis was over. The unified American press had seen its dream of repeal come true, and printers sat back happily to survey their success. William Rind gloated to the readers of his *Virginia Gazette*, "[A] *well conducted* NEWS:PAPER *would, at any Time, be important, but most especially at a Crisis, which makes a quick Circulation of Intelligence particularly interesting to all the* AMERICAN COLONIES."[1] Rind breathed a self-congratulatory sigh of relief. He expected that life would go on now. The grievances with the mother country were settled, and everything would return to normal. What he did not realize was that the differences with the mother country had just begun.

As the press tried to deal with the crises of the next decade, freedom of the press would emerge as a major issue. The coming years would see a deep division among journalists as they struggled to define what a free press was. The discussion of press freedom began in lamblike fashion, with eager-to-please innocence. John Mein and John Fleeming promised freedom of expression to all parties when they opened the *Boston Chronicle* in 1767. They vowed to avoid attachment to factions that had so lately caused such strife in the colonies during the Stamp Act. The *Chronicle*, they said, aimed to be impartial and to discuss both sides of political questions so as to "throw some light on the complexion of the times." They offered as the newspaper's credo: "[B]e independent—your interest is intimately connected with this noble virtue—if you depart from this—you must sink from the esteem of the public."[2]

In reality, the declaration of neutrality indicated that a divisive undercurrent was rumbling below the surface. Mein's and Fleeming's statement of the need to be impartial emphasized that the old wounds of the stamp crisis were not healed. The press may have been unified against the Stamp Act, but Britain still needed tax money. Many Americans still felt loyal to their king, whereas others were afraid of continued British oppression. Indeed, Fleeming and Mein recognized that life was *not* going to be normal. The post-Stamp Act peace was already drawing to a quick close, for in an attempt to refill the dwindling treasury and to punish the colonies for their anti–Stamp Act behavior, the mother country had adopted the Townshend Acts.

Through the Townshend Acts, the Stamp Act came back to haunt—but in a bigger way. The Acts, passed in June and July of 1767, set duties for the importation of glass, lead, paint, tea, and paper into America.[3] The duty on imported paper hit printers hard, and the other duties stabbed at various other professions. The tea tax hurt just about everyone. The new taxes sprang from American arguments formulated during the stamp crisis. Colonists had accepted the legality of indirect taxes, such as taxes on imports, while decrying direct taxation without representation. Britain thus began taxing certain imports, including paper. The money raised by these Townshend taxes was to be spent in the colonies.

Having so recently suffered through the stamp crisis, journalists tried to repeat their successful protest. The *Boston Gazette* quoted the radically libertarian "Cato's Letters" against oppression: "Freedom of Speech is the great Bulwark of Liberty; they prosper and die together: *And it is the Terror of Traytors and Oppressors, and a Barrier against them.*"[4] The *Gazette*'s protests clearly stemmed from the fact that Britain, through the paper tax, was once again threatening the press. Samuel Hall felt the same way. He opened the *Essex Gazette* in Salem, Massachusetts, with the sworn purpose of trying to instill "a due sense of the Rights and Liberties of our Country."[5]

Such newspaper talk frustrated Massachusetts Governor Francis Bernard, who in July of 1768 wrote to his superiors in England that the Sons of Liberty suppressed any news that was not favorable to themselves.[6] It seemed to Bernard and his fellow British officials that ever since the beginning of the Stamp Act, radical Patriots such as the Sons of Liberty had taken over the printed word, to the exclusion of all other opinions. Their suspicions seemed correct when the continent's first formal news distribution system began out of Boston.

By fall of 1768, Boston was suffering from both the Townshend Acts and the arrival of British troops, who had been sent there to quell anti-Townshend unrest. Boston journalists had learned a great deal from the Stamp Act. They recognized that a unified press had spread the anti–Stamp Act word to every corner of the colonies, and they hoped that the same type of news reports could help the city out of its current predicament. Printers in other towns sympathized with Boston's plight.[7] With the British now entrenched in Boston, an ingenious local thinker had an idea to make *sure* such news circulation would happen again. He started his plan by sending the publishers of the *Boston Evening Post* a request:

Mssrs FLEETS

Though you have already published an account of the arrival of the fleet and army at Boston, yet a great number of your customers would be glad to find the following Journal of Occurrences *published in your useful and impartial paper, so that they may see in one comprehensive view, the extraordinary transactions of the present day.*[8]

To that the publishers replied, "In compliance with the above request we shall devote a part of our paper for some time to that purpose."[9] Thus, the "Journal of Occurrences" began its scathing daily indictment of the British occupying Boston.

The "Journal" was a daring innovation in journalism. It did not appear only in the *Post*. Its writers sent it to newspapers throughout the colonies. With that, the first deliberate news distribution service in America began. Colonial editors had always clipped news from one another before, but never had there been a news exchange campaign waged in such a calculated manner.

Despite the partisans' claims that the "Journal's" news accounts were impartial, they were nothing of the sort. Between September of 1768 and the summer of 1769, daily reports on the sufferings of Boston found their way quickly to other newspapers across America and even to England. Readers discovered from the "Journal" that the British troops were brutes. After 11 P.M. one night, two sergeants from the Twenty-ninth Regiment got into a quarrel with some townspeople. Town watchmen hurried to break up the argument, and the sergeants responded by drawing their bayonets. Then the sergeants were so vulgar as to tell the watchmen to expect to be sent to hell at the whim of the bayonet. The watchmen, though, held firm and forced the soldiers to back down.[10] Such reports appeared alternately by the impartial-sounding names "Journal of Occurrences" and "Journal of the Times."

The service offered both news items and editorial comment. Its news, spicy and one-sided, hit two major themes. Over and over the "Journal" complained of the evils of military rule in Boston. Also, it offered frequent explanations of how military occupation of the city violated English law.[11] Readers everywhere got such juicy tidbits as the extreme unpopularity of James Murray, a newly appointed justice of the peace for Suffolk County. Bostonians growled with certainty that Murray's sole purpose in office was to force the residents to quarter and billet British soldiers.[12] The "Journal of Occurrences" offered a bitter editorial comment on the matter:

In pursuance of this ministerial plan of policy, we now behold a standing army and swarms of crown officers, placemen, pensioners and expectants, co-operating in order to subdue Americans to the yoke. Our hopes are that the people of Britain do now, or will soon fully perceive that they cannot have our monies in the way of a revenue, and trade both; that what the merchants and manufacturers receive, serves to increase the wealth and oppulence of the naition [sic], while the other only tends to destroy trade and increase ministerial dependence.[13]

The "Journal" came out faithfully. Readers who drank in the reports learned that the wicked troops were depressing Bostonians and wrecking their lives. Early in 1769, for example, colonists read about the scarcity of money in Boston, which the "Journal's" editor blamed on the destruction of trade by the British. Plus, he accused, English revenue officers took the crown-imposed duties that Bostonians paid out and reinvested them in local trade, thus creating monopolies on trade. Since the army arrived, the editor complained, stocks had fallen six percent in value, "and advices intimate, that they were like to be still further affected by the measures pursuing."[14]

The "Journal" did not concern itself solely with Boston, although clearly that city was the central subject of the news service. Since the "Journal" circulated across the colonies, news from everywhere was important if it supported the complaints of the Bostonians. In March of 1769, the "Journal" reported that eleven ladies in Newport, Rhode Island, agreed to gather at each lady's home "in order to excite emulation in serving their country, promoting temperance and industry." At these gatherings, the ladies planned to spin linen into yarn, so that America would not be so dependent on British imports and could instead produce its own clothing. "The above-said ladies," the "Journal" reported, "spun between 6 o'clock in the morning, and 6 o'clock in the evening, 37 skeins and 15 threads, which upon average make three skeins five knots and five threads." The writer said the spinning wheels sounded like Patriotic music.[15] The "Journal" was proud to report the next day that the Newport ladies indeed had been imitated when some eighteen ladies in Jamestown, near Newport, held another spinning match. Two Newport ladies were on hand to help them out. One of the Patriotic Jamestown ladies was just eleven years old. The reporter commented that if gentlemen were as sincere as the ladies were in promoting frugality and industry, America would soon be free from the burden of dependence on Britain "and lay the foundation of American liberty on a basis not to be shaken by any power on earth!"[16]

On June 21, 1769, the "Journal" reported that the much-longed-for order to remove the English troops from Boston had arrived. However, a few stubborn British commanders requested that the soldiers remain in town. The editor of the "Journal" hinted that the commanders had too comfortable a life in Massachusetts, where they had country estates. Naturally, they did not want to leave. The commanders, however, were claiming to their superiors that they were anxious to stay "for the protection of their persons and properties from the rage and violence of the inhabitants."[17]

By the time the "Journal of Occurrences" ceased functioning on August 1, 1769, readers had been told over and over again that the British could not be trusted to be humane. The Englishmen had designs on subjugating the continent by any means possible; they used tax money illegally to monopolize trade; they would not listen to reason; they threatened civilians; they even used vulgar language. The "Journal" spun daily accusations against the British, who seemed to have no redeeming qualities whatsoever. Furthermore, the "Journal" news service showed how everyday Americans were doing their part to free America from the oppressive yoke of Britain. As such news circulated across the colonies, many readers became more accustomed to the idea that the British presence was unwholesome and unwanted. A whole different group of readers, however, began to feel disturbed that the English troops, who were following the solemn orders of the sovereign, were under attack by one-sided press coverage.

Crown-appointed Governor Bernard of Massachusetts saw the press that way. He was so peeved at abuse directed against him in the public prints that he tried to sue printing partners Benjamin Edes and John Gill for seditious libel. Bernard demanded that they identify certain anonymous antigovernment writers who had published with the Edes and Gill press. The lawsuit fell through, but the war between the governor and the press was on.[18] Patriot[19] printers got hold of Bernard's confidential letters about Massachusetts to his superiors. Edes and Gill published them as pamphlets at the request of the local governor's council. Ultimately, the council successfully demanded Bernard's recall.[20] When the governor left for England, the *Boston Gazette* jeered him as "a Scourge to this Province, a Curse to North-America, and a Plague to the whole Empire."[21] Rind's *Virginia Gazette* exclaimed, *"May he never more cross the atlantic, but meet the regard justly due to him, in his native country."*[22]

The press had other methods of damning the British. The *Pennsylvania Chronicle* leaped into the Townshend Acts fray with the "Letters from a Pennsylvania Farmer," which espoused the American Whigs' view of English oppressions. The twelve letters ran in the *Chronicle* from December 1767 to March 1768. The anonymous "Farmer," actually Philadelphia lawyer John Dickinson, invoked the Stamp Act in an attempt to return Americans to their unified opposition to the British. In all of England's dealings with the colonies, he argued, only the Stamp Act and the new Townshend Acts had attempted to raise revenue. Previous acts had been part of mutual trade regulation. The Farmer grumbled that the new tax was calculated *"to raise money upon us,* WITHOUT OUR CONSENT." He could not countenance that, for it amounted to taxation without representation. He exhorted, "HERE then, my dear countrymen, ROUSE yourselves, and behold the ruin hanging over your heads."[23]

The Farmer warned that under the recent acts of Parliament, judges could act arbitrarily, and the colonists had little opportunity of redress. British policy, for instance, welcomed Americans to come to London to discuss grievances, but the Farmer scoffed that the invitation was ridiculous. "We may make a voyage of three thousand miles to complain," he said, "and after the trouble and hazard we have undergone, we may be told, that the collection of the revenue, and maintenance of the prerogative, must not be discouraged."[24]

The Farmer concluded his letter series with an assurance that Americans could successfully battle Britain once again. He asked his readers:

Is there not the strongest probability, that if the universal sense of these colonies is immediately expressed by RESOLVES of the assemblies, in support of their rights, by INSTRUCTIONS to their agents on the subject, and by PETITIONS to the crown and parliament for redress, these measures will have the same success now, that they had in the time of the *Stamp-Act*[?][25]

Other newspapers took up the *Chronicle's* rallying cry by reprinting the Farmer. Sarah Goddard printed the letters in her *Providence Gazette*, along with other anti-

Townshend articles.[26] She was so excited about the series and so upset over the renewed British taxes that she advised her son William, one of the proprietors of the *Pennsylvania Chronicle*, not to print any more anti-Farmer articles offered to him. She begged:

It is no small concern to me, and all who wish you well, to see so many abusive pieces in the Chronicle against the Farmer, who deserves so well of his country. Do not, I beseech you, sully all the honour you have acquired by uniting with enemies of your country, against the best men in it.[27]

As far as Sarah Goddard was concerned, the American cause needed protection, not a balance of opinions from both sides. Pro-British writers threatened American liberties with every stroke of the pen. Mrs. Goddard and many printers like her felt it was their duty to avoid printing opposition British articles. Her concept of a free press did not extend to opening her press—or her son's—to writers supporting Britain's right or need to impose the Townshend taxes.

Perhaps the Farmer goaded Americans into action. Soon angry colonists in many places had formed "The Association" in an attempt to thwart the Townshend Acts with a nonimportation movement. The Associators coaxed or intimidated merchants into signing a document that forbade them from importing most English goods. They hoped their economic blockade would force Britain to her knees on the Townshend matter.[28]

South Carolinians in Charleston eagerly took up the call for nonimportation. True, necessities of life did not fall under the boycott; merchants could still import drugs, planting tools, and already-printed books and pamphlets.[29] But Patriots would have no other British goods in the colony if they could help it. Citizens formed a group known as the General Committee to pressure businessmen into taking part in the boycott. The Committee complained bitterly that Americans were being deprived of their rights and were "made subject to the arbitrary and oppressive proceedings of the civil law, justly abhorred and rejected by our ancestors, the free-men of England." Signers of the Association's pact in South Carolina agreed not to import any British goods until their freedom was restored. They also took the dramatic step of promising that the importation of African slaves would cease on January 1, 1770. They also vowed to forego mourning gloves and scarves traditionally worn at funerals, since those items had to be imported.[30] The three newspaper printers in town agreed to have copies of the Association's nonimportation resolution on hand in their offices for angry Charlestonians to sign.[31]

Not all South Carolinians were so easily persuaded. British sympathizers, perhaps having learned their lesson from the Stamp Act, grew bold and vocal. William Henry Drayton lashed out against the subscribers to the resolutions. He considered himself a loyal and law-abiding citizen; but the Association signers, he said, were "VIOLATING THE CIVIL LIBERTIES OF FREEMEN, and thereby shaking the CONSTITUTION of their COUNTRY to the very foundations." Innocent merchants, he complained, would suffer loss of their livelihood in the boycott.[32]

Peter Timothy printed Drayton's inflammatory piece in his *South-Carolina Gazette*, but only after explaining himself to his readers. He was not in sympathy with Drayton, not in the least. "But," Timothy said, speaking of himself, "he has kept his Press *open* to *all Parties* these thirty Years, without permitting his private interest (which has often suffered) to come in Competition with that of the Public." He said emphatically that the survival of the British constitution depended on free access to the press. Besides, his two rivals in town had refused to print the piece.[33] Timothy's stand in favor of a press open to all parties proved to be successful, for his *Gazette* became a forum for political discussion. He was one of few Patriot printers to renounce his personal opinions openly in favor of a balanced press.

Finally, though, Timothy was forced to give up his notions of balance in order to take a side in the nonimportation controversy. As the colonies struggled with Britain, there seemed to be no way for printers to remain neutral. Late in 1769, Charlestonian Benjamin Matthewes placed an innocent-looking advertisement in the *South-Carolina and American General Gazette*, which was printed by Timothy's Charleston rival, Robert Wells. Matthewes had recently imported various goods from London, Bristol, and Philadelphia. They were available for sale to the public.[34] The next spring, the General Committee checked up on Matthewes and discovered that he had signed the nonimportation agreement. He was in violation.[35]

Matthewes was just trying to get started in the world. His mother, Ann, had gone into the business to help him. She pleaded earnestly that the shipload of imported goods had arrived in Charleston unexpectedly due to some kind of mix-up. Ann had been seriously ill when Benjamin had placed his ill-advised advertisement. He had only wanted to make some money, she pleaded. His mother insisted she would have stopped him from attempting to sell the merchandise, had she known in time. In spite of all her begging, Ann Matthewes knew her son's business was in deep trouble. She tried to explain the situation to the unyielding Committee. She even offered to give the Committee her son's goods.[36]

The Committee, however, would not relent. On May 31, 1770, it announced in Timothy's *South-Carolina Gazette* that the Matthewes team had shamefully breached their contract, "*prefering* their own little *private Advantage* to the general Good of AMERICA." The committee urged everyone to show contempt for the Mattheweses.[37]

The newspaper industry's former Stamp Act–based resolve against the British was starting to bend and strain. Robert Wells of the *General Gazette* in Charleston had been running generic warnings from the Committee from the very start, but he could not countenance the deliberate naming of merchants' names. He did not print the Committee's condemnation of the Mattheweses. Seeing that Wells was wavering, Ann Matthewes rushed to him with a plea of self-defense. She saw the whole affair as Timothy's fault, but she hoped Wells's readers had some compassion. She begged them to "Suspend their Judgement until they have had a full and impartial Statement of her particular situation." Angrily, she said that the Committee was far too harsh. "[N]othing short of the total ruin of me and my Family would suffice," she accused.[38]

Wells was not the only printer who was beginning to doubt the rightness of the Association. John Mein of the *Boston Chronicle* thought the Association was ineffective and should be terminated at once. The only purpose of the Association, as far as he could tell, was to hurt honest businessmen and consequently destroy American trade. His newspaper alleged that 190 Boston importers had already violated the agreement.[39] That report infuriated Boston Patriots, who accused Mein of padding the list of so-called violators with people such as clergy, non-Bostonians, and private citizens who happened to own just one restricted article for private use. In addition, Patriots said, Mein had made a dramatic accusation about Bostonians having restricted goods, but many goods he mentioned were not actually banned under the Association agreement.[40]

Mein was not to be thwarted. He supported his claims by printing manifests of ships that had entered Boston Harbor since January 1, 1769. Three were owned by John Hancock, a leader of the merchants group that had called for nonimportation, and his ships were importing such forbidden items as nails, hemp, cloth, cheese, and blankets.[41] Thus, Mein accused Hancock of setting up the Association for his own good. Hancock denied the charges.[42] Mein enjoyed needling Hancock. He called him a *"Milch-Cow . . .* surrounded with a croud of people, some of whom are stroaking his ears, others tickling his nose with straws, while the rest are employed in riffling his pockets."[43] Hancock's denial of the charges did not intimidate the stubborn Mein, who doggedly kept on printing the manifests. That, however, was too much for radical Patriots. On October 28, 1769, a mob assaulted Mein and his partner, John Fleeming. Frantic for his own safety, Mein fled to a British man-of-war in Boston Harbor and shortly thereafter left town.[44]

Fleeming stayed in Boston and continued to print both the *Chronicle* and the manifests. Hancock tried to silence the *Chronicle* by attaching the Fleeming press in order to collect Mein's debts.[45] The litigation was not needed, however, when Fleeming, too, fled before a mob that threatened his life. He later returned to his job in Boston with the understanding that he had been appointed printer to the Board of Customs. However, the appointment fell through; he was needed only as the official stationer. That was not enough, "as all his other business had been long totally ruined, by the entrigue and outrages of the faction," he sighed. Defeated, he returned to England.[46]

With all the controversy over nonimportation, newspaper printers were confused about what side they should take. It had been easy during the Stamp Act crisis; every journalist in America had agreed that the British stamp tax was wrong. This time, though, the feeling was not so uniform. The public was not of one mind on inflammatory activities such as those of the Association, and unanimity of the press had likewise deteriorated. Printers were unsure what they should do in order to please their readers. Mein and Fleeming wanted to please businessmen, but that angered the Patriot faction. Timothy tried to present both sides but finally decided he had to go along with the General Committee. Robert Wells went along with the Patriots of the Committee and then sided with the anti-Associators.

Other printers were just as torn. William Rind, for one, tried to take neither side. He wrote hopefully that his *Virginia Gazette* was "Open to ALL PARTIES but Influenced by NONE."[47] Other newspapers spoke favorably of England in a backhanded sort of way by pointing out that at least it was more desirable to be Englishmen and to enjoy English liberties than it would be to be part of some lesser nation. Reporting on a Scottish controversy, for instance, the *North-Carolina Gazette* noted that in polite company, men were offering this toast: "*May the light of Liberty never be put out by a* Scotch *Extinguisher!* "[48] Similarly, John Pinkney's *Virginia Gazette* warned that sly Scotsmen were a danger to cultured Englishmen:

Irish impudence is of the downright, genuine, and unadulterated sort. [But] a *Scotchman*, when he first is admitted into a house, is so humble that he will sit upon the lowest step of the staircase. By degrees he gets into the kitchen, and from thence, by the most submissive behaviour, is advanced to the parlour. If he gets into the diningroom, as ten to one but he will, the master of the house must take care of himself; for in all probability he will turn him out of doors, and, by the assistance of his *countrymen*, keep possession forever.[49]

Printers wavered about what to say regarding the deteriorating state of Anglo-American relations. The American press's confused attitude toward English citizenship was alternately favorable and unfavorable.

Then a nightmare came true. On March 5, 1770, British soldiers shot and killed five Boston citizens. Bostonians had provoked the attack by taunting and threatening the soldiers. The incident, however, sparked deep anger in many editors' hearts. All at once, the press described the English as the very representatives of Satan. Newspaper reports on the "Boston Massacre" spread quickly through the colonies, painting the scene in its bloodiest colors and omitting details from the British soldiers' point of view. As the *Georgia Gazette* described it, a mulatto man named Crispus Attucks died "instantly, two balls entering his breast, one of them in special goring the right lobe of his lungs, and a great part of the liver most horridly." The other four victims died in equally vivid detail. The report fumed that the soldiers "displayed a degree of cruelty unknown to British troops." Furthermore, the wicked Englishmen tried to "fire upon or push with their bayonets the persons who undertook to remove the slain and wounded."[50]

The gruesome story of the "Boston Massacre" did not have a real chance to sink in, however. The British soldiers were perhaps tacitly excused by the good news that followed the Massacre. Parliament had repealed all of the Townshend import duties—except the tax on tea. Many colonists were relieved. The repeals outweighed the horror in Boston. No matter how wicked the English soldiers looked in the press, the Boston Massacre failed to put an end to American support for compliance with British regulations. It was almost as though post–Stamp Act Americans were tired of fighting. They wanted harmony with the mother country. They wanted everything to be normal.

"Philanthrop," for example, writing in the *Boston Evening Post*, tried to persuade Americans that any remaining negative attitudes toward the mother country were unfounded. Reasoning that "Man is a social animal," Philanthrop contended that man by nature needs companionship. In fact, he said, man finds safety in numbers and therefore has an instinctive desire to seek "the more valuable blessings and benefits of *society*." Philanthrop launched into a long chain of logic. Because humans know they are sociable, he said, they have a duty to society to "promote the general good." Any American ought to realize that "the public good and his own are so intimately connected and interwoven together" that anything inconsistent with the public good is by nature incompatible with humanity. Thus, Philanthrop concluded, a citizen should hold the public peace as the foremost goal in his life. That meant that every man should keep the laws and remind everyone around him to keep the laws. Certainly, Philanthrop warned, such noble behavior involved "a rational submission to those in *authority*." In fact, no matter what corruption he saw in government, a good person would not try to agitate the public, for that would destroy "that *essential subordination* upon which the well being and happiness of the whole *absolutely depends*." Philanthrop warned that "Arraigning, accusing, and condemning those in the most important stations [would] weaken the pillars of the state."[51]

But the desire for harmony with England, as expressed by Philanthrop and others, did not last. The turmoil and disagreement over Americans' relationship to England bubbled up once more. Journalists were just as caught up as others were in the debate over obedience to British authority. In New York, authorities tried to arrest printer James Parker for producing a broadside by "A Son of Liberty" addressed to "THE BETRAYED INHABITANTS OF THE CITY AND COLONY OF NEW YORK." The colony's General Assembly considered the piece to be seditious. A frightened Parker fingered the author, Alexander McDougall, who went to jail for it.[52] Parker's squeamishness had thus violated the longtime newspaper industry practice of allowing writers their anonymity. Realizing what he had done, Parker tried to make amends by opening his *New-York Gazette or Weekly Post-Boy* to the Whigs. "Attempts to prevent the *Liberty of the Press* in this Province, will be in Vain, while there is a free Press on the Continent," the *Post-Boy* warned, for "all Causes gain Ground by Persecution. . . . [T]rue Englishmen will never yield."[53]

Parker's rival Hugh Gaine of the *New-York Gazette* backed the Assembly in the McDougall case. Gaine ran twelve articles entitled "The Dougliad," which satirically derided McDougall as "Our Hero." In spite of his efforts to make McDougall look like a buffoon, Gaine did offer to let him respond to any criticism printed in the *Gazette*.[54]

McDougall was indicted in court on April 27, 1770, and by then, Parker had taken up his maligned writer's cause. However, after protesting that the indictment would "abridge the Liberty of the Press, suppress the Spirit and Freedom of Enquiry, or damp the Ardour of the People," Parker died on June 2.[55] As a result, there was no witness against McDougall. The Assembly jailed McDougall anyway for not confessing, and he stayed there nearly three months before being freed.[56]

Clearly, the struggle to define the proper Anglo-American relationship also involved a struggle to define press freedom. Parker obeyed British orders about the broadside and then regretted breaking traditional press practices, doing a 180-degree about-face to defy authority. Should the press protect antigovernment pro-testers? Should it protect the government? Parker had had a difficult time deciding, echoing the experience of other printers such as Wells and Timothy.

Some printers and writers were more sure about their role. Isaiah Thomas of the *Massachusetts Spy* considered press freedom a necessity, even though freedom of the press could mean tearing down innocent people. The *Spy* commented:

What are usually called libels, undoubtedly keep great men in awe, and are some check upon their behaviour. . . . It is certainly of less consequence to mankind, that an innocent man should be now and then aspersed, than that all men should be enslaved. . . . The best way to prevent libels, is not to deserve them. . . . Guilty men alone fear them, whose actions will not bear examination, and therefore must not be examined.[57]

Likewise, a *Boston Gazette* correspondent said that candidates for the Assembly should be rejected if they "are enemies to FREEDOM with the PEN," especially if they "long for constituted *inspectors of the press.*"[58] Samuel Adams, the feisty Pa-triot, wrote against "Court Scribblers," saying government-backed writers in-tended only to drug the public with their hypnotic opinions. "They are daily administering the opiate with multiplied arts and delusions," he said, "and I am sorry to observe, that the gilded pill is so alluring to some who call themselves the *friends of Liberty.*"[59]

The squabble over the rightful place of the press was bound to lead to the taking of sides. Wells, Mein, and Fleeming had all recently sided with British authority as a support to business. Others chose to fight authority. Printer Isaiah Thomas took his own advice about feeling free to criticize and lashed out against King George on September 10, 1772. As a result, Massachusetts's new governor, Thomas Hutchinson, threatened legal action against the *Spy's* publisher. The printer replied in disgust, *"We may next expect padlocks on our lips, fetters on our legs, and only our hands left at liberty to slave for our* worse than Egyptian task masters, or—or—FIGHT OUR WAY TO CONSTITUTIONAL FREEDOM!"[60] Meanwhile, Samuel Adams hotheadedly used the press to call for assemblies and associations to form in every town in order to recover American rights.[61]

While the debate went on, an uneasy peace settled over much of America. Anglo-American relations seemed to be calming down. Perhaps the argument with Britain was over. The American press took advantage of the lull to expand. The *Royal Amer-ican Magazine,* for example, put together the colonies' first advice-to-the-lovelorn column. Readers such as "John Jealous" wrote in. He complained that his wife was intimately involved with another man.[62] In another case, a young girl styling herself "Nancy Dilemma" complained that she was "a poor unhappy girl" who loved a poor man. A rich man whom she detested was courting her with her parents' blessing. In fact, her parents insisted she marry the wealthy suitor. "Polly Resolute" replied to Nancy by advising her to "conceive parents authority can extend no farther than what may contribute to the happiness of the child: . . . *marry the man you love!*"[63]

Printers tried other innovations as well. *New-York Gazette* publisher Hugh Gaine and some friends devoted their time and money to building a paper mill so that New York did not have to import its own paper.[64] Gaine begged his readers to save white linen rags so that the Long Island mill could make paper in sufficient quantity. He noted that New Yorkers went through many hundreds of reams of paper each year.[65] Similarly, William Goddard took advantage of the peace to start a new Maryland newspaper, the *Maryland Journal; and the Baltimore Advertiser*. He promised to report everyday information of utmost importance, such as the prices of current goods and the arrivals and departures of ships. He also planned to cover news events such as accidents and deaths. To smooth over the recent argument and friction between the Americans and the English, he promised, "the Freedom of the Press shall be maintained."[66]

Despite such efforts, the attempted return to the everyday business of journalism was tense. Even with American-British relations at a fairly level point, isolated flareups occurred. A mob in Providence, Rhode Island, burned a British customs ship, the *Gaspée*, in 1772. The press discussed the affair well into 1773. Much of the news involved rumors of severe British retaliation, which turned out to be false;[67] but not being the wiser, a Virginian suggested that the House of Burgesses take some sort of action to demand Americans' constitutional rights. The Burgesses replied by voting a resolution to call for Committees of Correspondence in every colony to authenticate rumors of British misbehavior.[68] Other colonies responded, with the Massachusetts House of Representatives congratulating Virginia for its wisdom.[69] The *Gaspée* affair and the subsequent rumors proved that, no matter how smooth relations between Britain and America seemed to be in general, trouble was still in the air. Editors knew it. They could not help but pick up on the anxious atmosphere that pervaded the brief period of tense harmony between the mother country and the colonies. It was as though newspaper publishers in America were waiting for a storm to break.

A new publication in New York, *Rivington's New-York Gazetteer*, echoed the troubled tone by begging for a free press. Proprietor James Rivington informed the public that his newspaper would avoid "acrimonious Censures on any Society or Class of Men," for the publication was to be "as generally useful and amusing as possible." Rivington's prospectus sounded innocent enough, but in a backhanded way, he was emphasizing the sharp differences that were still simmering between the factions in New York. "When so many Persons of a vast Variety of Views and Inclinations are to be satisfied," he wrote, "it must often happen, that what is highly agreeable to some, will be equally disagreeable to others."[70] Rivington obviously observed bitter disagreement among his potential readers. The battle lines were becoming ever clearer. Loyalists were sticking close to the crown, whereas Patriots wanted a radical change of some sort.

The press continued taking sides, too. Rivington took swipes at his rival journalists for aligning with either faction and denying the other side its say. Under pressure from Patriots to avoid printing Loyalist material, Rivington announced that "TRUE SONS OF LIBERTY" would print *only* impartial newspapers.[71] He

likewise quoted a London writer who accused Americans of thwarting press freedom by preventing printers from "daring to publish on both sides."[72] Taking a dig
at hotheaded Patriots, Rivington complained that a printer who tried to be impartial was doomed. But no matter what pressure he himself got, Rivington promised
that his press would publish anything submitted, "whether of the Whig or Tory
flavour."[73]

Rivington's jibes in favor of printing some Loyalist material were not lost on Patriot
printers. John Holt of the *New-York Journal* replied tartly to Rivington that he was not
trying to thwart freedom of the press. Instead, Holt felt it was his duty to inform the
people that they were about to lose their rights. He snapped at Rivington, "In short, I
have endeavoured to propagate such political Principles . . . as I shall always freely
risk my Life to defend."[74] As the smoldering war between Loyal and Whig printers
heated up, the words between Rivington and Holt got hotter and angrier. Holt published a reader's poem about Rivington. It described Rivington as being:

> Without one grain of *honest* sense,
> One virtuous view, or *just* pretence
> To patriotic flame;
> Without a patriotic heart or mind.[75]

The standoff between loyal Americans and discontented Americans was reaching a dangerous level. Some newspaper readers, including the anti-Rivington poet,
could not even stand to see the other side's views printed. The other side, as they
saw it, offered nothing but lies and more lies. Readers wanted to see truth, and
truth meant one side of the story only. Their concept of press freedom and press
access meant the right to print only "correct" opinions.

The storm that had been brewing for so many months materialized in 1773 upon
King George III's attempt to bolster the sagging East India Company's credit and
prosperity.[76] Parliament agreed to the king's request for aid to the company by accepting a plan for East India's businessmen to export tea duty-free to America. The
plan promised that the British would do what they could to thwart Dutch trade in
tea, thus giving the East India Company a monopoly on tea in America.[77]

Many Americans were horrified at the newest restrictions on the tea trade,
which indicated to them once again that Britain wanted nothing better than to use
America to prop up the sagging British economy. The press jumped on the Parliamentary tea act. During the next several months, correspondents saw to it that tea
acquired a terrible reputation. One "expert" wrote that English tea harbored flea-
like insects, making the favorite British drink unsafe for human consumption.[78] A
Pennsylvania author claimed that tea-drinking had made the English race "puny,
weak, and disordered, to such a degree, that were it to prevail a Century more, we
should be reduced to meager Pigmies." American plants, on the other hand, could
be boiled into excellent teas that were very healthy.[79]

Other protests bristled with threats of evil British plans for the colonies. "A Mechanic," writing for the *Pennsylvania Gazette*, predicted that Great Britain, which

practiced "TYRANNY, PLUNDER, OPPRESSION and BLOODSHED," sought only to "become your Masters" through the tea act.[80] The Mechanic's theme of slavery echoed over and over again in newspapers. Another writer warned Americans that all the great companies of Britain would try to get special privileges like those of the East India Company, and "If so, have we a single chance of being any Thing but *Hewers of Wood and Drawers of Waters* to them?"[81] The *Massachusetts Spy* demanded, "Shall the island BRITAIN enslave this great continent of AMERICA which is more than ninety-nine times bigger, and is capable of supporting hundreds of millions of people? Be astonished all mankind, at their superlative folly!"[82]

Of course, some Americans rejoiced that the Parliamentary tea plan had reduced the price of tea. One writer chastised the colonists for fussing over tea when England had been so generous about giving up the stamp duties of the past decade.[83] Another pointed out that it was Parliament's duty to regulate the British Empire.[84] If Americans had to help facilitate that regulation, so be it.

Lots of hatred and some support brewed all over the colonies, but the discussion remained only a heated argument until December of 1773. By then, some radical Bostonians had had enough of the whole tea question. Newspaper publishers Benjamin Edes and John Gill went beyond printing. They helped recruit guards to keep tea ships from unloading their hated cargo. Edes himself acted as a guard. Finally, a group of angry Bostonians met at Edes's house on December 16, 1773, and then slipped away under cover of night to his *Boston Gazette* office. There they dressed as Indians. Other knots of men here and there joined them in the scheme as they hurried to the city wharf, boarded several ships, and threw £15,000 worth of East India Company tea overboard into Boston Harbor. The tea protests thus turned from print and speech into melodrama.[85]

Parliament was not happy. The savages who had wrecked such valuable cargo had to be punished. Accordingly, on June 1, 1774, Parliament instituted the Boston Port Act, which closed the port to commerce until Bostonians repaid the East India Company. In quick succession, Parliament passed three more acts. One completely reworked Massachusetts government, giving the crown's officers more power and snatching authority from the local citizenry. Another act gave the royal governor more power to quarter troops. Also, Parliament ruled, any soldiers who committed murder while putting down disorder could be tried outside of Massachusetts, even in England.[86] The Acts quickly won the nickname "The Intolerable Acts."

Whereas Boston's savage "Indians" had been a little slapstick and perhaps too destructive, suddenly Boston seemed like a martyr city. Journalists from across the colonies protested the Intolerable Acts. Editors from the South bawled with anger. The *North-Carolina Gazette* adopted a motto to show its feelings: "SEMPER PRO LIBERTATE, ET BONO PUBLICO."[87] The *South-Carolina Gazette* went even further: Peter Timothy ruled the newspaper in mourning borders and dredged up the hated Stamp Act. In fact, he said, the whole sorry stamp business "portended less evil to this Continent than the present gathering storm." He urged some sort of protest.[88] A disgusted Georgia writer commented in that colony's *Gazette* that if Parliament put a tax on tea, "why not on my breath, why not on my daylight and smoak, why not on everything?"[89]

The *Virginia Gazette*s also leaped into action. One of the gazettes published the opinion that the Coercive Acts, as they were also called, were "pregnant with great Evils."[90] Virginia readers obtained false reports that the repressive measures against Massachusetts were spreading their way, but with even greater force. One *Virginia Gazette* writer reported the rumor that the crown planned to stop all postal service, change all colonial governors, send 300 tax collectors to the colonies, take away juries, and back up all the measures with a fearsome fleet.[91] Many Virginians were certain that once Boston submitted to British authority, the British would turn their greedy eyes to the rest of America.[92]

Many Americans felt united—by fear. After years of indecision over loyalty or disobedience to the crown, individuals began to assume that what the crown could do in one colony, it could do in any colony. It was no surprise, then, that the call to assemble a Continental Congress in Philadelphia met with a strong response from all regions. The Congress declared the Intolerable Acts and the new British government in Massachusetts unconstitutional, and it urged Americans to "acquaint themselves with the Art of War as soon as possible." The Congress likewise wanted Americans to cease any trading whatsoever with Great Britain.[93] The *South-Carolina Gazette* imbibed the spirit of the Congress and announced, "THE AMERICANS ARE INVINCIBLE."[94]

The Patriot press reinforced the disgruntled Americans' cause with a graphic flair. John Holt printed the most famous of colonial editorial cartoons, a cut-up snake begging the American colonies to "UNITE OR DIE." Each of the ten pieces of the snake was labeled as a section of America. The snake appeared in the flag of the *New-York Journal* from June 23 to December 8, 1774.[95] Holt revised the snake cartoon on December 15. This time it featured a united and coiled snake, its tail in its mouth to form a double ring. The snake encircled a pillar firmly standing on the Magna Carta, probably the best-known written guarantee of the British subject's rights. A liberty cap topped the pillar, and six arms and hands, representing the colonies, held up the pillar. On its body, the snake proclaimed, "UNITED NOW FREE AND ALIVE FIRM ON THIS BASIS LIBERTY SHALL STAND AND THUS SUPPORTED EVER BLESS OUR LAND TILL TIME BECOMES ETERNITY."[96]

The snake theme was popular. Isaiah Thomas adopted a version of it for his *Massachusetts Spy*, amending it to include a dragon that represented Great Britain. The dragon, of course, was attacking the snake, but the snake had stings for its own defense. The cartoon begged the colonies to "JOIN OR DIE!"[97] William and Thomas Bradford of the *Pennsylvania Journal* copied the original Holt snake cartoon into their newspaper on July 27, 1774.

The snake did not go unnoticed. *Rivington's New-York Gazetteer* could not resist a poem written "*On the* SNAKE, *depicted at the Head of some American* NEWS PAPERS.*" The Loyalist poet pointed out wryly:

> YE Sons of Sedition, how comes it to pass,
> That America's typ'd by a SNAKE—in the grass?
> Don't you think 'tis a scandalous, saucy reflection,
> That merits the soundest, severest Correction,
> NEW-ENGLAND's the Head too;—NEW ENGLAND's abused;
> For the *Head of the serpent* we know *should be* Bruised.[98]

A Patriot reader of the *Pennsylvania Journal* had seen the lines in Rivington's paper and just had to reply. He completely twisted the Loyalist's verse back on itself:

> THAT New England's abus'd, and by the sons of sedition,
> Is granted without either prayer or petition.
> And that " 'tis a scandalous, saucy reflection,
> That merits the soundest, severest correction,"
> Is as readily granted. "How comes it to pass?"
> Because she is pester'd with snakes in the grass,
> Who by lying and cringing, and such like pretensions,
> Get places once honoured, disgraced with pensions.
> And you, Mr. Pensioner, instead of repentance,
> (If I don't mistake you) have wrote your own sentence;
> For by such Snakes as this, New-England's abused,
> And the head of these serpents, "you know, should be bruised."[99]

The fact that both sides in the snake controversy paraphrased the Bible indicated that they both thought their viewpoint was just, correct, and holy.[100]

Alarmed Loyalists saw such items as the snake cartoon as further indications that the Patriot press was one-sided and dangerous to the security of the realm. They did their best to persuade the restless colonists to settle down to the peace of British rule. Two of Rivington's Loyal readers, John Grou and John Peters, lamented for the lost souls of the misguided Whigs. "O poor *degenerate* children!" they wailed. "Such destroyers of liberty itself are a disgrace to their mother, if she is the goddess of liberty. For doth not liberty herself allow every man to enjoy his own sentiments?"[101] Their call was an eloquent one for liberty of expression and freedom of thought for anyone, even for Loyalists.

Another Loyalist calling himself "A Philadelphian" tried another line of reasoning. "It is impossible to review the advantages we derive from our connection with Great Britain without wishing it to be perpetual," he said. "We are formed by her laws and religion: we are clothed by her manufacturers and protected by her fleets and armies. Her kings are the umpires of our disputes, and the center of our union." The Philadelphian was overcome with pride. "In a word, the Island of Britain is the fortress in which we are sheltered from the machinations of all the powers of Europe," he reasoned jubilantly.[102]

Certainly, another writer assured, Americans' childish feelings of rebellion were just a phase that most peoples passed through at some point in their history. The writer knew where such adolescent behavior would lead. Normally, he insisted, a bunch of unthinking, lamblike people followed a few oddballs, who manipulated everyone into doing stupid things. These oddballs "begin by reminding the people of the elevated rank they hold in the universe, as men; that all men by nature are equal; that kings are but the ministers of the people." Such attitudes as that, the writer warned, sacrificed true liberty to licentiousness, which in turn would lead to civil war.[103] The anonymous Loyalist writer, instead of allowing for expression on both sides, clearly longed for a silencing of radical Americans who would lead their fellow colonists astray. Such radical expression, he thought, was entirely dangerous.

By this time, Americans were walking a taut rope between mere complaint and bloody rebellion. Rapidly now, they teetered from the thin line between the two sides and fell one way or the other. Isaiah Thomas, for one, had opened his *Massachusetts Spy* with an intent to be impartial. Emotions were running so high, however, that he could not maintain that stand. Hard-line Tories turned against him and cancelled their subscriptions. In turn, he transformed the *Spy* into a one-sided newspaper in favor of the Patriot cause.[104] Andrew Steuart of the *North-Carolina Gazette* moaned, "What Part is [a printer] now to act? . . . Continue to keep his Press open and free and be in Danger of Corporal Punishment, or block it up, and run the risque [*sic*] of having his Brains knocked out? Sad Alternative."[105]

While some Patriots did their best to attempt impartiality, most of the writers who cried out for an impartial press were Loyalists. As Rivington had pointed out, Patriot factions attempted to pressure newspapers into compliance with their point of view. A Patriot Convention of Committees, for example, announced that several New York and Boston printers were publishing too many articles from the Loyalist faction. The Committee suggested that Americans no longer take the offending newspapers.[106] The rebellious Americans saw a one-sided press as crucial to their cause. There could be no argument. They had complete faith in the influence of the press, and they wanted to channel that influence correctly.

Retorting with ideas that would someday sound deeply American, one Loyalist complained in a Boston newspaper: "The ears of a genuine son of liberty are ever open to all doctrines; it is his glory to hear them, examine them, to adopt them if they are true, to confute them if they are false."[107] Loyalist reader "Plain Heart" likewise begged American malcontents to "Wake up my friends, act like men, like free men, like reasonable creatures. . . . See and judge for yourselves."[108] He felt sincerely that "Truth delights in free enquiry."[109] "Bellisarius" published an opinion that

These inconsiderate people [Patriots] have made themselves idols, vz. Liberty Trees, Newspapers, and Congresses, which by blindly worshipping, have so engrossed their minds, that they neglect their honest professions and spend all of their time [in] taverns where they talk politicks, get drunk, damn King, Ministers, and Taxes and vow they will follow any measures proposed to them by these demagogues, however repugnant to religion, reason, and common sense.[110]

In the same spirit, a writer in the *Boston Weekly News-Letter* warned Americans against being deceived by radicals, either in person or in printed form. He said of people who fell into the trap of radicalism:

[T]heir reason is lulled into a perfectly stupid lethargy, and then mere sounds govern their judgments. The words king, parliament, ministers, governors, mandamus councillors, revenue, tea &c. carry the idea of slavery with them, while with as little color or reason the words congress, charter, patriots, delegates, charter councillors, independence, coffee, &c. carry with them all the powers of necremancy to conjure down the spirit of tyranny.[111]

Loyalist writers accused Patriots of being licentious and of falling prey to "the popular frenzy."[112] Others pleaded with protesting Americans to realize that freedom most likely would come gradually through Britain and her constitution. However, separated from Britain, America might see "rivers of blood" spilled before a government could be formed and any rights given.[113]

In remote Georgia, printer James Johnston tried to maintain balanced coverage of the news in his paper.[114] Blinded by their own passionate viewpoints, however, subscribers could not see his balance. A group of Patriot readers accused Johnston of excluding news of the American radicals in Boston.[115] A Loyalist, meanwhile, said the Patriot faction had misused its right to print in the *Gazette* by publishing false information.[116] At least one friend of Johnston, Georgia Chief Justice Anthony Stokes, realized how far the printer had gone to print both sides, no matter what his personal feelings were. "I am persuaded that you have inserted some Things that were contrary to your Principles," Stokes wrote. "Had you refused so to do, those People would probably have done all they could do to ruin you."[117]

Stokes's point was insightful. The brief periods of peace between Britain and America had eroded badly. The press's unanimity from the Stamp Act had disappeared. No one agreed anymore on the proper relationship between Britain and America. A confrontation was almost certain.

By 1775, on the eve of the first shots of the American Revolution, the American people had forced themselves to take sides. Whereas Americans had shown a nearly unanimous dislike of the Stamp Act a decade earlier, over the next ten years Britain had succeeded in breaking the unanimity by repeatedly enforcing restrictions on the unruly colonists. With British restrictions coming so hard and so fast, it was too difficult to continue a unified fight. Law-and-order colonists seeking the benefits of the British Empire agreed that Britain needed them—their obedience, their loyalty, their tax revenues. Philosophers seeking an independent sense of self-rule came to believe that America no longer needed Britain. The press, reflecting such a splintered public opinion, also splintered.

The divided American press between 1766 and 1775 went further than merely reflecting the raw emotions expressed among the people. Instead of just reciting the quarrel, the press's battle to define a relationship with the mother country evolved into a battle over press philosophy. Patriot groups tried in vain to redirect the press back into its valuable Stamp Act unanimity by pressuring printers against giving the Loyalists' side of the story. Loyal journalists countered by turning the concept of a free, impartial press into a rallying cry.

Loyalists were no farsighted journalistic geniuses, of course. They did not gaze into a crystal ball and foresee a balanced, impartial press as an ideal. In fact, when the war loomed into reality, Loyalist printers would shout their one-sided viewpoints in their newspapers loudly and angrily, just as Patriots would.

During the uneasy decade before the start of the war, Loyalists' views were just as strongly held as those of the Patriots. Loyalist printers begged for an impartial, two-sided press out of self-defense, not out of some higher concept of journalistic principles. They simply perceived that their opinions and livelihoods were in danger if Patriots succeeded in forcing a showdown with the mother country. That perception would come true during the Revolution.

The press philosophies presented by both Loyalists and Patriots would inevitably clash. In the short run, the forthright Patriot philosophy to advocate one side of the story would win out. As American forces and British troops opened fire at Lexington and Concord, the entire press in America, both Loyal and Patriot, would choose the philosophy of the Patriots: one-sided, biased, persuasive news coverage. The practice would serve well during the war.

NOTES

1. *Virginia Gazette* (William Rind, Williamsburg), 16 May 1766. There were many papers named *Virginia Gazette*, some of them operating simultaneously. Thus, newspapers by that name will be identified with their proprietor's name in parentheses.

2. *Boston Chronicle*, 21 December 1767. Fleeming's name is sometimes incorrectly recorded as "Fleming."

3. Carolyn H. Knight, *The American Colonial Press and the Townshend Crisis, 1766–1770: A Study in Political Imagery* (Lewiston, N.Y.: Edwin Mellen Press, 1990), 77.

4. *Boston Gazette*, 9 November 1767.

5. *Essex Gazette* (Salem, Mass.), 2 August 1768.

6. Francis Bernard to Lord Hillsborough, 18–19 July 1768, in Francis Bernard and others, *Letters to the Ministry* (Boston, 1769), 44–46. Quoted in Arthur M. Schlesinger, *Prelude to Independence: The Newspaper War on Britain, 1764–1776* (New York: Alfred A. Knopf, 1958), 93.

7. See, for example, the account in the *New-York Journal*, 13 October 1768, of the British troops' arrival in Boston.

8. *Boston Evening Post*, 12 December 1768.

9. Ibid.

10. "Journal of Occurrences" for 22 June 1769. Quoted in Oliver Morton Dickerson, comp., *Boston Under Military Rule, 1768–1769 as Revealed in A Journal of the Times* (Boston: Chapman & Grimes, 1936), viii. The writer(s) of the "Journal" was anonymous.

11. Dickerson, ibid., xi.

12. "Journal of Occurrences" for 27 October 1768. Quoted in Dickerson, ibid., 12.

13. "Journal of Occurrences" for 28 October 1768, ibid., 13.

14. "Journal of Occurrences" for 13 January 1769, ibid., 49.

15. "Journal of Occurrences" for 30 March 1769, ibid., 85.

16. "Journal of Occurrences" for 31 March 1769, ibid., 85–86.

17. "Journal of Occurrences" for 21 June 1769, ibid., 111. The writer apparently mentioned the country estates to show that British soldiers could move freely to them without being harmed by the public, but the description did seem to be a veiled accusation about why the British *really* did not want to leave Massachusetts.

18. Josiah Quincy, Jr., *Reports of Cases Argued and Adjudged in the Superior Court of Judicature of the Province of Massachusetts Bay between 1761 and 1772*, ed. S. M. Quincy (Boston, 1865) 263–70; and Francis Bernard to John Pownall, Richard Jackson, and Lord Shelburne, 12 and 14 March 1768, *Bernard Papers* 6:102, 103, 278–80. Quoted in Schlesinger, *Prelude to Independence*, 97.

19. In general, the terms "Patriot" and "Whig" can be used interchangeably when referring to the newspapers that supported colonial rights. In the early years of the growing opposition to British rule, however, the term "Whig" was used most often by contemporaries, while "Patriot" gained increased popularity as passions heated up near the beginning of the Revolution.

20. *Boston Gazette* and *Boston Evening Post*, 3 April 1769, and Francis Bernard to John Pownall, 12 April 1769, *Bernard Papers* 8:280–82.

21. *Boston Gazette*, 7 August 1769.

22. *Virginia Gazette* (William Rind), 24 August 1769.

23. The letters appeared in newspapers but also were reprinted as pamphlets. See "Letters from a Farmer in Pennsylvania, to the Inhabitants of the British Colonies," (Philadelphia: printed by David Hall and William Sellers, 1748), reprinted in G. Jack Gravlee and James R. Irvine, eds., *Pamphlets and the American Revolution* (Delmar, N.Y.: Scholars' Facsimiles & Reprints, 1976), 7–9 and 11–12. Each pamphlet in the collection is individually numbered; so page numbers given refer to "Letters from a Farmer."

24. *Pennsylvania Chronicle*, 25 January 1768.

25. "Letters from a Farmer in Pennsylvania," in Gravlee and Irvine, *Pamphlets and the American Revolution*, 71.

26. *Providence Gazette*, starting 19 December 1767. For examples of anti-Townshend articles, see the *Gazettes* of 5, 12, and 26 December 1767.

27. Sarah Goddard to William Goddard, early 1768, in William Goddard, *The Partnership: or the History of the Rise and Progress of the Pennsylvania Chronicle, &c.* (Philadelphia: William Goddard, 1770). Quoted in Susan Henry, "Sarah Goddard, Gentlewoman Printer," *Journalism Quarterly* 57 (1980): 28.

28. William Henry Drayton, ed., *The Letters of Freeman, Etc.*, ed. Robert M. Weir (London: 1771; reprint, Columbia: University of South Carolina Press, 1977), 10–11 (page references are to reprint edition).

29. Ibid.

30. Ibid.

31. Ibid., 11.

32. *South-Carolina Gazette*, 14 December 1769.

33. Ibid.

34. *South-Carolina and American General Gazette* (Charleston), 4 December 1769.

35. *South-Carolina Gazette*, 31 May 1770.

36. *South-Carolina and American General Gazette*, 31 May 1770.

37. *South-Carolina Gazette*, 31 May 1770.

38. *South-Carolina and American General Gazette*, 15 June 1770.

39. *Boston Chronicle*, 1 June 1769. Mein's partner, John Fleeming, may have had just as much to do with the denunciations of the Association as Mein. However, Fleeming himself seemed to indicate Mein was responsible early in the controversy. See "Memorial of John Fleeming . . . to Lord North," 12 November 1773, quoted in O. M. Dickerson, "British Control of Newspapers on the Eve of the Revolution," *New England Quarterly* 24 (1951): 464.

40. *Boston Gazette*, 12 June and 13 July 1769.

41. *Boston Chronicle*, 25 September 1769, shows some of Hancock's imports.

42. *Boston Gazette*, 28 August, 18 September, 9 and 23 October 1769.

43. *Boston Chronicle*, 26 October 1769. Hancock was named in the satire by a pseudonym; however, a corresponding list of actual names matched Hancock to the "milch cow" description.

44. "Memorial of John Fleeming to Lord North," quoted in Dickerson, "British Control of Newspapers," 464.

45. L. Kinvin Wroth and Hiller B. Zobel, eds., *Legal Papers of John Adams* (Cambridge, Mass.: Belknap Press of Harvard University Press, 1965), 1:200.

46. "Memorial of John Fleeming to Lord North," in Dickerson, "British Control of Newspapers," 465.

47. *Virginia Gazette* (William Rind), 14 April 1768.

48. *North-Carolina Gazette* (New Bern), 24 June 1768.

49. *Virginia Gazette* (John Pinkney, Williamsburg), 20 October 1774.

50. *Georgia Gazette* (Savannah), 11 April 1770.

51. *Boston Evening-Post*, 14 January 1771.

52. E. B. O'Callaghan, comp., *Documentary History of the State of New York* (Albany, 1849–51), 3:528–36.

53. *New-York Gazette or Weekly Post-Boy*, 19 March 1770.

54. *New-York Gazette and Weekly Mercury*, 9 April 1770.

55. *New-York Gazette or Weekly Post-Boy*, 7 May 1770.

56. See O'Callaghan, *Documentary History*, 2:536, and Isaiah Thomas, *The History of Printing in America*, ed. Marcus A. McCorison (1810; reprint, New York: Weathervane Books, 1970), 262–63 (page references are to reprint edition). Thomas was a newspaper editor during this period.

57. *Massachusetts Spy*, 19 April 1771. The passage was stolen from one of "Cato's Letters."

58. *Boston Gazette*, 6 May 1771.

59. Ibid., 14 October 1771.

60. *Massachusetts Spy*, 8 October 1772.

61. *Boston Gazette*, 5 October 1772.

62. *Royal American Magazine* (Boston), May 1774.

63. Ibid., April 1774.

64. *New York Gazette*, 13 December 1773.

65. Ibid., 28 March 1774.

66. *Maryland Journal; and the Baltimore Advertiser* (Baltimore), 20 August 1773.

67. Willard C. Frank, Jr., determined that much information about the *Gaspée* affair in the *Virginia Gazette*s was mistaken. See "Error, Distortion and Bias in the *Virginia Gazettes*, 1773–74," *Journalism Quarterly* 49 (1972): 730.

68. *Virginia Gazette* (William Rind), 18 March 1773.

69. Frank, "Error, Distortion and Bias," 731; and *Virginia Gazette* (William Rind), 1 July 1773.

70. *Rivington's New-York Gazetteer* (New York), 22 April 1773.
71. Ibid., 14 July 1774.
72. Ibid., 11 August 1774.
73. Ibid., 8 December 1774.
74. *New-York Journal*, 18 August 1774.
75. Ibid., 15 September 1774.
76. *Virginia Gazette* (William Rind), 4 March 1773.
77. *Virginia Gazette* (Alexander Purdie and John Dixon, Williamsburg), 2 September 1773.
78. *Virginia Gazette* (William Rind), 16 December 1773.
79. Quoted from the *Pennsylvania Journal* in the *Virginia Gazette* (Purdie and Dixon), 13 January 1774.
80. *Pennsylvania Gazette*, 8 December 1773.
81. *Pennsylvania Chronicle*, 15 November 1773.
82. *Massachusetts Spy*, 11 November 1773.
83. *Virginia Gazette* (Purdie and Dixon), 25 November 1773.
84. Ibid., 2 December 1773.
85. Schlesinger, *Prelude to Independence*, 178–80.
86. *Boston Gazette*, 16 May, 6 June, and 15 August 1774.
87. *North-Carolina Gazette* (New Bern), 2 September 1774. Roughly, the Latin proclaimed that the *Gazette* was "always for liberty, and the public good."
88. *South-Carolina Gazette*, 13 June 1774.
89. *Georgia Gazette*, 27 July 1774.
90. *Virginia Gazette* (Purdie and Dixon), 11 August 1774.
91. *Virginia Gazette* (Clementina Rind, Williamsburg), 30 June 1774.
92. *Virginia Gazette* (Purdie and Dixon), 9 June 1774.
93. *Virginia Gazettes* (both of Pinkney and of Purdie and Dixon), 6 October 1774.
94. *South-Carolina Gazette*, quoted in *Virginia Gazette* (Pinkney), 15 December 1774.
95. The snake symbol is most commonly known today as the "Join or Die" cartoon. Its initial appearance was in 1754, according to Albert Matthews, "The Snake Devices, 1754–1776, and the Constitutional Courant, 1765," *Colonial Society of Massachusetts* (December 1907): 409–10.
96. Thomas offered the interpretation of the symbols in *The History of Printing in America*, 504.
97. Ibid., 252. The cartoon appeared in the *Spy* starting on 7 July 1774.
98. *Rivington's New-York Gazetteer*, 25 August 1774.
99. *Pennsylvania Journal*, 31 August 1774.
100. Genesis 3:14–15.
101. *Rivington's New-York Gazetteer*, 2 September 1774.
102. *Pennsylvania Gazette* (Philadelphia), 18 May 1774.
103. *Boston Post-Boy Advertiser*, 26 December 1774.
104. Thomas, *History of Printing*, 164.
105. Quoted in Robert M. Weir, "The Role of the Newspaper Press in the Southern Colonies on the Eve of the Revolution: An Interpretation," in Bernard Bailyn and John B. Hench, eds., *The Press & the American Revolution* (Worcester, Mass.: American Antiquarian Society, 1980), 103. Weir gives the source of the quote as Charles C. Crittenden, "North Carolina Newspapers before 1790," *James Sprunt Studies in History and Political Science* 20, no. 1 (1928): 37.

106. *New-York Gazette and Weekly Mercury*, 20 February 1775.

107. *Rivington's New-York Gazetteer*, 15 December 1774.

108. *Boston Weekly News-Letter*, 2 March 1775.

109. Ibid., 16 February 1775.

110. *Rivington's New-York Gazetteer*, 6 April 1775.

111. *Boston Weekly News-Letter*, 16 February 1775.

112. Ibid., 12 January 1775.

113. *Rivington's New-York Gazetteer*, 16 February 1775.

114. James Johnston to Anthony Stokes, 15 December 1775, in Allen D. Candler, ed., *The Colonial Records of the State of Georgia* (Atlanta: Franklin Printing & Publishing Co., 1906), 38, pt. 2: 47. Also, *Georgia Gazette*, 5 October 1774.

115. *Georgia Gazette*, 26 October 1774.

116. Ibid., 7 December 1774.

117. Anthony Stokes to James Johnston, 16 December 1775, in Candler, *Colonial Records*, 38, pt. 2: 48.

7

The Revolutionary Press, 1775–1783

War at last was at hand. On April 19, 1775, American and British soldiers exchanged shots at Lexington and Concord in Massachusetts. The colonists were in open rebellion against Great Britain. The military clash, so long anticipated in the wrenching war of words of the past decade, created deeper hatred than ever before between the factions that operated the American press. From the moment the first shot was fired, all attempts at impartiality and balance in the press ceased. Patriot newspapers viciously attacked the Loyalist cause. Loyalist newspaper editors launched all-out attempts to discredit the American effort for independence.

For many people, including an angry mob of Patriotic readers from Connecticut, newspaper accounts of the war were serious business. The Connecticut mob was tired of editor James Rivington spewing his Loyalist version of events in his New York and Connecticut *Gazette*. On a chilly November day in 1775, they formed a self-appointed vigilante group, banded together for a showdown with Rivington, and rode into New York City. Bullying their way into Rivington's house, they robbed him of his printer's type and stole some of his other property for good measure. To their glee, Rivington fled to England. He complained that the mob had singled him out "in open Defiance of all Law, and in direct Violation of the sacred Rights of Humanity."[1]

The incident symbolized the Revolutionary press. Over the next eight years, America and Britain would fight bitterly on the military battlefield. The press and its readers would fight just as bitterly on the paper battlefield of newspapers and pamphlets. Neutrality and press access were no longer practiced. This was, after all, the battle for people's hearts and souls and loyalties. Each faction accordingly did its best to exclude any good reports from the other side.

Just months after the war started, a ne'er-do-well who had lately come from England fired an early round in the press's war for readers' support. His eloquence stung many unsure colonists into making a stand for the Patriot cause. The English author, Thomas Paine, issued the pamphlet called *Common Sense* on January 10, 1776. It was the hottest reading in America, selling 500,000 copies practically overnight, and Paine was publishing a third edition by mid-February.[2]

Paine's pamphlet reasoned with Americans who were caught in the confusion over loyalties and disloyalties. In straightforward language, *Common Sense* argued that many Americans had simply gotten into the habit of not questioning Britain's behavior, and that unthinking attitude in turned lulled people into assuming that British rule must be right. Paine declared, however, that "the good People of this Country, . . . have an undoubted Privilege to enquire into the Pretensions of both [king and Parliament], and equally to reject the Usurpation of either." Not only was such inquiry a right, but it would serve as a beacon to all mankind, as Paine saw it. "The Cause of America is in a great Measure the Cause of all Mankind," he said. "Many Circumstances hath, and will arise, which are not local, but universal, and through which the Principles of all lovers of Mankind are affected."[3]

Paine called for American independence. The only reason Americans were hesitant to declare their independence, he insisted, was that they had no plan for government, and so he offered one. Colonies would be divided into districts to elect at least thirty delegates per colony to Congress, and a president would be chosen from the delegates to Congress. Twenty-six congressmen and five representatives of the people at large would frame an American version of the Magna Carta, "Always remembering, that our strength and happiness, is Continental, not Provincial." This Magna Carta, Paine said, should guarantee freedom and the right to own property, and especially secure the freedom of religion.[4]

Paine well understood what leery Americans would worry about. "But where says some is the King of America?" *Common Sense* asked. "I'll tell you Friend, he reigns above, and doth not make havoc of mankind like the Royal Brute of Great Britain." Paine contended that the word of God was sovereign, as represented in the laws—and "in America THE LAW IS KING."[5] He warned the timid of heart:

A government of our own is our natural right: and when a man seriously reflects on the precariousness of human affairs, he will become convinced, that it is infinitely wiser and safer, to form a constitution of our own, while we have it in our power, than to trust such an interesting event to time and chance. . . . Ye that oppose independence now, ye know not what ye do: ye are opening a door to eternal tyranny, by keeping vacant the seat of government.[6]

Paine appealed for Americans to help all of humanity by setting a dramatic new example. The entire Old World, he said, was overrun with oppression. Freedom was unknown in both Asia and Africa, and Europe looked on liberty as a stranger. In America, he said, with the people's help, freedom would find a home at last.[7]

Common Sense's popularity helped solidify American thought on the issues of freedom and separation from the mother country. "I find Common Sense is working a powerful change in the minds of men," George Washington wrote. Charles Lee commented after reading the pamphlet, "I own myself convinced by the arguments of the necessity of separation." Major Joseph Hawley rejoiced that "I have read Common Sense and . . . every sentiment has sunk into my well prepared heart."[8]

On July 4, 1776, Paine's dreams of independence came true—in theory, at least. The Continental Congress, meeting in Philadelphia, declared America free from Great Britain.

Benjamin Towne was the first editor to publish the Declaration of Independence.[9] He printed it in full, without comment, on page one of his *Pennsylvania Evening Post* on July 6. Although the Declaration had the distinction of winning a front-page spot in the newspaper, Towne treated it as more symbol than substance. The war was not over by any means. In his next issue, Towne wrote one sentence in honor of the public reading of the Declaration: "Yesterday, at twelve o'clock, INDEPENDANCY [*sic*] was declared at the State-House of this city, in the presence of many thousand spectators, who testified their approbation of it by repeated acclamations of joy."[10] That was all. Independence seemed more wishful thinking than actual fact. The war continued, but the story of the Declaration and copies of the document circulated via the press.

As a symbol, the Declaration captured the hearts of readers across the colonies. Towne reported a few days later that a large crowd in Easton, Pennsylvania, gave three loud huzzahs upon receiving news of the Declaration, and they cried as one, "MAY GOD LONG PRESERVE and UNITE the FREE and INDEPENDANT [*sic*] STATES of AMERICA."[11] New York's *Weekly Journal* added similar exultations on July 11 by announcing the Declaration of Independence with a headline of type two-thirds of an inch tall. In an era without headlines, such a statement was dramatic. The Continental Army shouted huzzahs at the news of the Declaration, and when New Yorkers received word of independence, they toppled a statue of King George III—"the just defeat of an ungrateful tyrant!" a correspondent cheered in a published report.[12]

But the struggle with Britain still raged. Towne's newspaper continued to be filled with reports from the battlefield.[13] A writer for Towne's *Post* accurately described the situation as an ongoing struggle for liberty.[14] American independence was not yet an established fact.

The writer of *Common Sense* himself joined the American Continental Army and, at the end of the year, had the disheartening adventure of having to retreat across New Jersey away from the British. Thomas Paine was well aware that many men in the army, feeling beaten and hopeless, were forming new doubts about the ultimate success of the American cause and were even beginning to question the necessity of it. "The rebels," one British officer reported contemptuously, had "fled like scared rabbits."[15] As Christmas approached, the morale of both soldiers and civilians alike seemed at its lowest point. The triumphant British army had moved into comfortable winter quarters at Trenton, New Jersey, apparently unconcerned about the American troops across the Delaware River. It was an emergency, a crisis of faith, and Paine knew it. Something had to be done to rally the colonists.

During the army's retreat, Paine may have begun writing the first essay of what he called *The Crisis*. Legend has it that he composed the piece on the head of a drum at a fire in the camp of General George Washington's army, with the cold and ragged soldiers gathered around.[16] If there is any truth to the legend, it could be that only the beginning and the end of the essay were completed at that time. On the advice of several officers, he then left the army at Trenton and went to Philadelphia in order to produce a publication that might stir colonists.

He found fear spreading and the civilians berating Washington's retreat as disgraceful. Paine said the situation drove him to write "in what I may call a passion of patriotism,"[17] producing the first essay in the *Crisis* series. It appeared first on the front page of the *Pennsylvania Journal* on December 19. It was then reprinted as a pamphlet and soon by printers throughout the colonies. It began with the now-famous lines:

These are the times that try men's souls. The summer soldier and the sunshine patriot will, in this crisis, shrink from the service of their country; but he that stands it now deserves the love and thanks of man and woman. Tyranny, like hell, is not easily conquered; yet we have this consolation with us, that the harder the conflict, the more glorious the triumph. What we obtain too cheap, we esteem too lightly: it is dearness only that gives every thing its value.[18]

Once again, Paine's simple, poetic cadence touched something deep in American souls. The Continental Army required its soldiers to read the *Crisis*. Many soldiers ceased to doubt and took up their guns with new resolution.[19] On Christmas night (or early in the morning of December 26) Washington led his troops back across the Delaware River through a violent snowstorm, at Trenton attacked the Hessian mercenaries whom the British had hired, and captured or killed almost a thousand of them. Although the victory was due in part to the fact that the Hessians had been drinking heavily all night, Paine's essay was credited with giving heart to the colonial troops. It also encouraged colonists to volunteer for the army, for, as one of Paine's comrades in the military said, the essay's opening lines "were in the mouths of every one going to join."[20]

The publication of the *Crisis*, like the publication of *Common Sense*, was an electrical spark in the war of persuasion. Paine's stirring works illustrated the basic fact of the matter: the press of the American Revolution existed principally to persuade.

Newspaper correspondents, editors, and publishers faced the phenomenal task of reporting the long, widely flung war in an era when the best communications technology depended on sailing ships and horseback to move news around. News reports were also strictly limited by the fact that editors who were bent on persuasion had to find correspondents who would write the news in its best, most convincing light. In spite of such challenges, war reporting succeeded in achieving editorial goals of thorough but one-sided and persuasive news coverage.

For all papers, the war added difficulties to a news gathering system that was not sophisticated, to say the least. Neither newspapers nor British or Patriot leaders provided for anything approaching organized coverage of the Revolution. Newspapers relied for their information on the chance arrival of private letters, official messages, and other newspapers. Each paper printed some local information which was picked up by others, but even that information was paltry; and reports of major events sometimes consisted of no more than a paragraph. While such a system during peacetime functioned reasonably well for colonial purposes, it was by later standards crude at best, and war added difficulties. News was tardy. The postal service, which had developed barely beyond its infancy, was hampered by the interference of military campaigns, poor financing, and bad roads that stayed in disrepair. English newspapers, which had been a prime source of news before the war, were received irregularly. As a result, news of major events was delayed sometimes a month or more; Americans were ill-supplied with information; and rumors and false news abounded.

One of the Patriot press's biggest problems was shortage of supplies, especially newsprint. As a reaction to the Stamp Act and the Townshend Acts, colonists had agreed not to import certain items from Britain, giving Americans the impetus to begin manufacturing presses and type. Paper mills also multiplied in number; but even though some mills existed in the colonies at the time of the Revolution, shortages in the paper supply caused the press much trouble. Paper prices went up sharply, mainly because of the scarcity of rags needed in paper making. The threat that the shortage might mean a cessation or at least a substantial diminution of newspaper publishing worried Patriot leaders.[21] Newspapers carried pleas for saving rags, and Patriot organizations urged people to save rags. Maryland and the Carolinas offered money to entrepreneurs willing to start their own mills.[22] George Washington begged for secret importation of paper from Europe to supply the army with paper for orders and written messages. American mills, he said, were scrambling to produce enough cartridge paper for the army and printing paper for Patriotic presses.[23]

Some printers, of course, saw the British cause as the correct one. Two years after that fateful day in 1775 when he was run out of town, James Rivington returned from exile in time to report the key battles of Brandywine, Germantown, and Saratoga. When he came back in 1777, the British occupied New York, and Loyalist Rivington could make a triumphant return to his press there. His fellow pro-British editor Hugh Gaine reported the gala scene:

On Thursday Evening last the house of Locsley and Elms, King's Head Tavern, was elegantly illuminated, to testify to the Joy *the true Sons of Freedom* had on the arrival of Mr. Rivington from England. This Gentleman, with unparallel'd Fortitude, having nobly disdain'd to offer to the World any inflammatory Pieces, which might be productive of introducing Anarchy, instead of Constitutional Authority, into this once happy Country, felt, in the severest Degree, the Rage of popular Delusion.—*Liberty* he always firmly adher'd to, Licentiousness from his Soul he ever detested.—A person in Honour to free press, extempor[aril]y pronounced this:

> RIVINGTON is arriv'ed—let ev'ry Man
> This injur'd Person's Worth confess;

His loyal Heart abhor'd the Rebel's Plan,
And boldly dar'd them with his *Press*.[24]

As Rivington reopened his New York print shop, the American army's progress was at a standstill, but Britain could not seem to deal a decisive blow to her rebellious colonies. France was interested in entering the war against its perennial arch-enemy England, but France needed a dramatic American win to spur any further diplomatic discussion about aid to the rebellious colonists. The crucial months of September and October 1777 provided a metaphor for American heartbreak and triumph as the fledgling nation sought a major victory. The struggle was emphasized in the biased, persuasive press. The press coverage of the war in the fall of 1777 was typical of news reporting throughout the American Revolution.

The American Continental Army under General George Washington had a hard autumn in 1777. It lost key battles at Brandywine and Germantown outside of Philadelphia on September 11 and October 4, respectively. As a result, the British entered the American capital of Philadelphia with little trouble.

The horror of the situation was painfully obvious to the Patriots. Before the Battle of Brandywine, Washington had told his men that the British were preparing to "put the contest on the event of a single battle: If they are overthrown, they are utterly undone, the war is at an end." He had begged his army to "behave like men" in order to bring the war to an immediate conclusion.[25] Washington had considered the battle critical because other nations were watching America intently, considering intervention on America's behalf. Washington had warned his men, "The eyes of all America, and of Europe, are turned upon us."[26]

Despite such inspiration, the Americans lost at both Brandywine and Germantown. The consecutive defeats created a golden opportunity for Loyalist newspaper correspondents[27] and editors to spread anti-Patriot sentiment. As far as Rivington was concerned, he could not have picked a more auspicious time to return to his press in New York. The bleakness of the American cause was much to his editorial advantage. Reporting on the Battle of Brandywine, his newspaper scoffed, "most of the [American] militia returned to their respective habitations with a resolution no longer to take part in the present unnatural rebellion." British General Sir William Howe was closing in on the rebel capital at Philadelphia, and the rebel Congress had fled to nearby Bethlehem. Congress, though, could not last long, according to Rivington's *Gazette*; part of Howe's army had marched to within a few miles of the American legislative body.[28]

A week later, Rivington gloated to his readers, "Since my last, we have got a confirmation of the TOTAL ROUTE [*sic*] and DISPERSION of the REBEL ARMY."[29] The American attack on Germantown was "the most daring folly" and "a desperate attempt" by America to salvage something for its downhearted troops. The Americans, though, could put up only a "feeble" battle, as Rivington's correspondent described it.[30]

Rivington could not conceal his quest for revenge throughout the jubilant British campaign. He reported that the cowardly rebels, seeing the "aweful force" of the Royal army, utterly panicked and fled. Howe's troops, Rivington said, chased the Americans for many miles, killing 3,000 of them. "This event has greatly dispirited the enemy," the *Gazette* reported.[31] On the other hand, His Majesty's troops were the epitome of good conduct, according to Rivington's news sources. At Brandywine, British soldiers ignored American fire and charged the rebels, who "took to their heels." As a result of such Patriot panic, the British were ultimately able to enter Philadelphia with great pomp. The *Gazette* proudly described the British troops marching into the American capital:

The fine appearance of the soldiery, the strictness of their discipline, the politeness of the officers, and the orderly behaviour of the whole body, immediately dispelled every apprehension of the inhabitants, kindled joy in the countenances of the well affected, and gave the most convincing refutation of the scandalous falsehoods which evil and designing men had long been spreading to terrify the peaceable and innocent. A perfect tranquility has since prevailed in the city.[32]

Rivington's report was obviously taking a stab at Patriot publications for spreading "scandalous falsehoods." He wanted his readers to know that any contrary war coverage by Patriot editors was patently untrue.

Indeed, Patriot editors and newswriters saw the action in and around Philadelphia from an entirely different angle. They made no attempt to hide their biases or to reconcile their news coverage with different reports by the Loyalist press. Like Rivington, they acted as though the other faction's coverage oozed lies at every sentence.

Two of those Patriot editors were Rivington's New Haven rivals, Thomas and Samuel Green of the *Connecticut Journal*. Just as Rivington was earnestly trying to convert readers to the war gospel as told by the British, the Green brothers were trying to polish the tarnished image of the defeated Americans. The *Journal* was far more gentle in its story of the losing Americans than Rivington's *Gazette* had been. The *Journal* blamed the loss at Brandywine on a bit of bad intelligence— Howe had attacked at a different spot than the Americans had been led to believe. The correspondent, who was on the battlefield, excused the American loss: "I am confident as I am of my own existence that if the attack had been made where it was expected, Mr. Howe and his army would certainly have been entirely routed."[33]

Instead of being as gentlemanly as Loyalist news items claimed, the General Howe described by the *Connecticut Journal* was cruel and sinister. He paid local citizens to pilfer livestock, for instance, thereby starving the Americans. The poor American troops, by the time of the battle, "[had] had no food for the whole day, and little or no sleep for 48 hours." In contrast to the evil Howe, Washington encouraged his men "with such benignity and affability as almost seem'd to be more than human."[34]

To persuade its readers that all was not lost, the *Journal* took an opportunity to jab at the British cause. "The face of the English papers seems to appear favourable to America," the *Journal* reported. "The people in England are very uneasy, and seem to doubt the Howes being able to subdue the REBELS this campaign." The newspaper also quoted a Customs House official in England who desperately hoped for reconciliation between Britain and America so that England could resume its American trade and, more importantly, avert a domestic rebellion. American readers inferred that restless Englishmen were ready to take to the streets and demand an end to the war. After all, the newspaper said, England was suffering a shortage of cash due to the American war.[35]

While optimism was rising, however, the disheartening news of Germantown came to the *Journal* for the next week's issue. The Greens buried it on page three, taking up the first two pages of the issue with a glorification of Americans involved in a skirmish against British General John Burgoyne in New York. The *Journal*'s report on Germantown emphasized first how the Americans thought they had won the day—until they discovered that the British were up to some dirty tricks. As the soldier writing the piece told it, "[E]very house in town soon became a garrison for British troops, who got their light field pieces into the chambers." After that, the British took advantage of a persistent fog to fire repeatedly into stubble and hay, creating fire and thick smoke. The confused Americans could no longer distinguish enemy fire from their own, and had to retreat. The writer assured readers that the American army was *not* giving up; in fact, even pacifist Quakers now wanted to take up arms for the Patriot cause.[36]

Subsequent reports from Germantown in the *Journal* hinted that the able Americans had suffered only from ill fortune. One article said that the British had not pursued the fleeing Americans; thus, the Americans could have held their ground. "Alas!" the writer mourned, "Never was an attack better managed until retreat."[37] Readers of the Greens' *Journal* could only assume that a horrible run of luck had led to the defeat of the American army, and that British troops were otherwise ripe for the plucking.

Philadelphia newspapers, of course, were a good deal closer to the action at Brandywine and Germantown, but their editors suffered the difficulty of trying to please the British now occupying the city. As long as Philadelphia had been home to the Continental Congress, *Pennsylvania Evening Post* publisher Benjamin Towne had been a Patriot. When the victorious British arrived, though, Towne closed the *Evening Post* and reopened it as a Loyalist mouthpiece. Describing the parade of British conquerors into Philadelphia, he said, "[N]umbers who had been obliged to hide themselves from the former tyranny, and to avoid being forced into measures against their conscience, have appeared to share the general satisfaction, and to welcome the dawn of returning liberty."[38]

Towne made sure the losing Americans looked as cowardly as his new British masters perceived them to be. He reported with a derisive note:

After all the preparations made by Mr. Washington's army to dispute the passage of the Schuylkill [River], and the boasts thrown out of their only wanting an opportunity to meet his majesty's troops, they deserted all their works at the Swedish ford without firing a gun, and returned precipitately to the hills, where they continued, not venturing to make the least opposition to the royal army during their March to Germantown, nor since, till Saturday morning last, when their main body, supposed to be about twelve thousand, but which they magnified by their own accounts to near double the number . . . made an attack before day on the outlines of the royal army in the north end of Germantown.[39]

Towne's article gloated that a mere 2,500 British troops had routed the Americans and had chased them nine miles. Another party of Americans had tried to attack, "but scampered off" when a few British mounted soldiers showed up.[40]

The revised *Evening Post*'s mission was to convert the misled people from the false Patriot point of view. The paper snarled about the Patriot press's "glaring falsehoods, evidently designed to deceive those at a distance." According to the *Post*, Congress and Governor William Livingston of New Jersey were scheming to report that the Americans had won victories at Brandywine and Germantown. The newspaper said Livingston planned to have the falsehoods published in the Trenton *Gazette*. To prove its claim, the article quoted a letter to Livingston, which said that Brandywine looked like a defeat, but "you may be assured [it] is the most unlucky affair that general Howe has ever encountered on this continent."[41]

Towne was not the only Philadelphia printer to opt for a change in outlook after the British takeover. James Humphreys, Jr., proprietor of the *Pennsylvania Ledger*, had been a Patriot. He shut down the *Ledger* for a year, but shortly after the British victory, he revived it with the king's arms in its flag.[42] It was impossible for Patriot printers to stay in business in British-occupied Philadelphia, as John Dunlap found out. He was forced to evacuate his press from Philadelphia and to issue his *Pennsylvania Packet or General Advertiser* from Lancaster. The move necessitated a nearly three-month-long shutdown. Dunlap retained his Patriot outlook.[43]

Dunlap, however, had not been in business during the Brandywine and Germantown defeats. The Loyalists had their Philadelphia press, but the Patriots were denied their say. George Washington was discouraged by the ill treatment of his army in the Philadelphia press. In a letter to his brother, he said in a disheartened tone, "To recite at this time, the circumstances of the Ingagement of Brandywine, which have been bandied about in all the Newspapers would be totally unnecessary."[44]

As news coverage of Brandywine and Germantown showed, the press saw itself as part of the battle. Loyalist newspapers tried to play up British glories, clearly hoping to persuade readers that the British could not and should not be beaten. For their part, Patriot printers squeezed their information hard to wring good news and optimism out of the defeats. The Patriot press was begging readers to keep the faith for the next time. As it turned out, the next time would be the turning point of the war.

On the New York frontier, Britain's General John Burgoyne was having trouble with the American press. The Patriot *Connecticut Journal* seemed to smirk when it published Burgoyne's pique over the newspapers that lampooned him as his army prepared to meet the Americans under General Horatio Gates. Gates had written a letter to Burgoyne, accusing him of paying Indians to scalp Americans, and threatening to have the information printed "in every Gazette" to persuade people the story was true.[45] Gates hoped the gazettes would turn the public against the British. Burgoyne was afraid he was right. The British leader huffed in reply:

I disdain to justify myself against the rhapsodies of fiction and calumny, which, from the first of this conflict, it has been an unvaried American policy to propagate, but which no longer impress upon the world. . . .

You seem to threaten me with European publications, which affect me as little as any other threats you could make; but in regard to American publications, whether your charge against me, which I acquit you of believing, was penned *from* a Gazette, or *for* a Gazette, I desire, and demand of you as a man of honour, that should it appear in print at all, this answer may follow it.[46]

It was not the first time the American press had irked Burgoyne. He had once complained, "The Press, that distinguished Appendage of public Liberty, and when fairly and impartially employed its best Support, has been invariably prostituted to the most contrary Purposes [during this Revolution]."[47]

As he battled with Gates in the newspapers, Burgoyne's military situation was growing desperate. He had expected Howe's army to join his, not to go on to Philadelphia.[48] By mid-October he was badly outnumbered by American forces. The *Connecticut Journal* told its readers that the American army was hammering away at Burgoyne little by little. The general, in fact, was ordering retreat. "He hath left his camp, heavy baggage, three hundred odd sick, with surgeons, nurses, &c. retreating," a writer explained in the *Journal*. "We are in pursuit, and expect to catch them. . . . How will they pass the 5000 men at Batten Kill and Saratoga, when pushed by Gen. Gates[?]" Another article assured readers that the British soldiers would soon fall into American hands.[49]

Meanwhile, according to the Patriot press, allies of the British were turning vicious. The *Journal* published a report that Indians and Tories had robbed two houses and murdered, scalped, and stripped four men. "O earth, cover thou not such innocent blood!" the article wailed. The *Journal* added that Burgoyne was destroying everything in front of him as he retreated, including an American general's gracious home.[50]

Surrounded, desperate, and out of supplies, Burgoyne's troops formally capitulated at Saratoga on October 17, 1777. News of the dramatic surrender trickled in slowly, finding its way to a squeezed-in spot on page three in the *Connecticut Journal* on October 22. The Green brothers apologized to their readers for having only scanty information, but they could announce that the Americans had surrounded Burgoyne's forces, who had surrendered to Gates. The Greens reported that "we had public rejoicings, on account of the good news."[51]

The few details gradually became a torrent of American patriotism in the Greens' *Journal*. The newspaper published Gates's hasty letter containing the Articles of Convention which Burgoyne had signed. Gates could scarcely add further details because he was rushing to stop a spur of the British army under General

John Vaughn from a town-burning rampage. Another article by the Greens themselves commented on the burning of Kingston, New York, which ruined all but one
house. "Britain, how art thou fallen! Ages to come will not be able to wipe away
the guilt, the horrid guilt, of these and such like deeds, lately perpetrated by thee!"
the Greens accused.[52]

A correspondent sent in a report from the surrender site at Saratoga. "It was a
glorious sight to see the haughty Britons march out and surrender their arms to an
army, which, but a little before, they despised and called poltroons," the writer
said. In the same issue, the *Journal* reported that American soldiers had stopped
the British from burning Poughkeepsie.[53]

With excitement in the air after the win at Saratoga, Patriots realized that they
had an excellent chance to capitalize on the good news. A government official
named Elijah Hubbard put an advertisement in the Greens' *Journal* to make an appeal for aid to "*Ragged, Barefooted Soldiers.*" He begged Connecticut towns
which had not sent their quota of clothing (as determined by the governor and
council) to do so before the weather got cold.[54] The Greens published an address
by Washington, promising pardons for deserters who now returned to the American army.[55] The publicity about Saratoga also provided an opportunity to reinforce
disgust in readers' minds about the enemy. The British made use of a large number of Hessian troops, which the Greens ridiculed in a letter from a London writer:

The Hessians are the dirtiest troops in the universe, from their nastiness, added to the Scotch
filth, the British soldiers in America have contracted the most noxious disorders.

The following is the fate of Old England:—An unnatural war, an unnatural season, and
an unnatural ministry; commerce failing, taxes rising, and the people repining; our engage-
ments with foreign powers violated, our remonstrances derided, and our ambassadors despised. An excellent situation for the first maritime nation in the world.[56]

While the Greens at last had the right to tout a victory, Loyalist editor Rivington
was in a dilemma. Eight days after the surrender at Saratoga, he grumbled to the
readers of his *New-York Loyal Gazette* that reports which had come in relative to
Burgoyne were "too ridiculous to justify a repetition" and would not be printed in
his paper. Without specifying what the news was, he accused the rebels of making
up the information. In fact, he said, the Patriot faction had "fabricated the story
with a view to inlist [*sic*] men; and, to give an air of truth to it, at Elizabeth Town
they caused guns to be fired, bonfires to be made, and every other demonstration
of joy and triumph." Lending a negative air to the supposedly phony festivities, he
added that the rebels dealt out "rum to the rabble, without measure."[57]

As time wore on, Rivington grew desperate to refute rumors of a huge American victory. He insisted to his readers that he had no "properly authenticated" reports from Burgoyne's army. He refused to print the tales that were floating around
New York until absolutely approved by Burgoyne himself. He begged his readers
to forgive him for avoiding gossip. Meanwhile, he did report on the burning of
Kingston, but he wrote the incident off as part of "the damage done the rebels." In

fact, Rivington blamed the rebels for the action, saying the Americans had provoked it.[58] The story of the incident at least made the British army sound active, rather than defeated.

Perhaps in an attempt to counter rumors about a surrender, Rivington set out a plan for how to deal with the rebels upon their defeat. "When the rebels submit, and are brought to due repentence," he suggested in the *Gazette*, "our general plan should be, to grant them every indulgence which the just commercial interest of Britain will allow of, and their power to annoy us permit."[59]

The situation was clearly beginning to deteriorate. Stories of British defeat did not seem to be dying down. Rivington frantically exhorted his readers "to support that righteous form of government under which you possess true liberty." He warned New Yorkers that the time might come when they would have to serve their mother country in some fashion. A Loyalist military troop was being formed, and men should join it, Rivington said. "Shall we tamely submit to that abject slavery which they are preparing for us, without one manly effort to prevent it?" the *Gazette* demanded. "Honour and virtue forbid!"[60]

More than two weeks after the surrender, Rivington's subscribers finally got to read the Articles of Convention between Burgoyne and Gates. Rivington hid the article on page three, however, after a rehash of the victories at Brandywine and Germantown.[61] Those battles had been news weeks earlier, but Rivington felt they merited reprinting. Clearly, he was trying to minimize the importance of Saratoga. To that end, in his next issue he again recounted the Germantown defeat. He also ran an address by the governor of New Jersey, bemoaning a lack of salt and cash, as well as poor obedience to military law. After yet another account of the loss at Germantown, the *Gazette* reported with an unmistakable note of satisfaction that "great jealousies and divisions had arisen in both the civil and military branches of the rebel states," with a number of people determined to remove Washington as commander.[62]

Rivington finally published the word "defeat" in connection with Saratoga a month and five days after the surrender. He clipped the articles circulating in various Patriot papers, including one writer's thanks to God for delivering "the Thirteen United American States" in their time of need. Softening the news, Rivington added an article that British soldiers had prevented American troops from burning Poughkeepsie.[63] Of course, the Greens had earlier blamed British troops for trying to burn Poughkeepsie.

Returning once more to the Germantown news to lessen the sting of Saratoga, Rivington printed a letter from an officer written to "*your universally-approved paper.*" The letter blasted George Washington's description of the Battle of Germantown as "perhaps, the most extravagant piece of Jesuitical [*sic*] quackery that has been exhibited during the present rebellion." The officer said Washington's assessment of the battle was blatantly untrue. Calling Washington a "military quack," he contended that the American general had minimized a British victory. Whereas Washington had blamed the loss on the fogginess of the day, the British officer could only sneer. "To the rebels this [fog] was a misfortune of a very *par-*

ticular nature," he jeered, "to the royal army it could be *none*; their optics not being *quite* so much obscured as those of the sons of sedition and rebellion."[64]

Far off in Pennsylvania, Washington heard of Burgoyne's "glorious, and fortunate surrender"[65] and announced to his men, "Let every face brighten, and every heart expand with grateful Joy." He ordered chaplains to present short sermons on the event, and he commanded that thirteen cannons and a *feu-de-joy* be fired after the sermons.[66] The importance of the win was not lost on Washington. He wrote to one of his generals that because of Saratoga, American liberty would likely be embraced wholeheartedly.[67] The implication was that foreign nations would recognize America's independence.

Meanwhile, the Loyalist press of Philadelphia was as unenthusiastic as Rivington was in dispensing the news of Saratoga. Perhaps editors in Philadelphia saw the British occupation of the capital as far more important an event than a battle in New York. In any case, the *Pennsylvania Evening Post* reported Burgoyne's loss on November 8, a week before Rivington used the word "defeat" in New York. It printed Burgoyne's own low-key explanation of the loss; he had assured Howe in a letter that "No exertions have been left untried." Burgoyne stated simply that his army was outnumbered, and he never got any reinforcements. The *Evening Post* followed the letter with the Articles of Convention.[68] Similarly, the *Pennsylvania Ledger* printed Burgoyne's explanation of the surrender and the terms of capitulation, alongside news of a much earlier victory for Burgoyne at Ticonderoga.[69]

The exiled American Congress, still meeting near Philadelphia, was hungry for whatever intelligence the press could furnish. South Carolinian John Laurens, a soldier in Washington's army outside of Philadelphia, eagerly scanned the city's journals for news that Congress would find important. His father, Henry Laurens, was the president of Congress and therefore the political leader of the young United States. John Laurens got hold of the *Pennsylvania Ledger* issue that detailed Burgoyne's surrender. He dutifully copied Burgoyne's explanation of the capitulation for his father to read. He also quoted some telling advertisements from the *Ledger*: the British army wanted to hire local men to cut wood for the winter, and the army would pay wages to wagon drivers in the area. The army would hire wagons by the day, but if local citizens hid their wagons, soldiers would confiscate them.[70] To the elder Laurens, the Loyalist press was a valuable indicator of the British army's condition.

John Laurens freely criticized the Loyalist press of Philadelphia. For one thing, he felt that the papers gave poor coverage of the wounding of a Hessian general. He also asked his father to read a "Harangue" by Howe printed in one of the newspapers. The younger Laurens warned his father that Howe would use the printed piece to "delude [men] into the loyal Corps."[71] Young Laurens was quite convinced of the power of news in the battle for Americans' loyalties.

Henry Laurens discovered that printed news of the American victory was highly popular with Pennsylvanians, who seemed unable to get their hands on enough journals. Laurens wrote to his son that "the avidity of the people for intelligence brought not only Members of Congress but scores of out of door applicants, to beg a reading [of a newspaper]—for bare rehearsal will not satisfy." Laurens added a big hint: "[H]ence you will learn that the Printed Papers as often as you can obtain them will be very acceptable."[72]

Laurens may have been eager for the news from Philadelphia, but he did scoff at the Loyalist printers in the area. They belonged, he said, to Sir William Howe.[73] As a balance, he read pamphlets and newspapers from a Patriot printer in South Carolina.[74]

Laurens and his fellow American leaders appreciated the value of good news. Congress promoted James Wilkinson, the soldier who had brought the news of Saratoga to them, to the post of brigadier general. Of course, not everyone thought that spreading news was such an important job. The officers in the Continental army were none too happy about Wilkinson's good fortune. John Laurens reported to his father that officers were grumbling that a man should be "so extraordinarily advanced for riding Post with good News." The men would rather he were rewarded with a good horse for his swiftness, not an increase in rank. In fact, Laurens expected some colonels to resign over the incident.[75]

In British-controlled Philadelphia with its Loyalist press, timely, truthful, and detailed reports on Saratoga were rare. The news that was available could influence every move Congress and the United States made. It was worth a brigadier generalship, as far as the young nation's leaders were concerned. After all, America had pinned its hopes for European recognition on a big victory. Congress therefore sent news of Saratoga, both by messenger and in newspaper form, to its diplomats in France.

Benjamin Franklin, alerted that an American messenger was on the way, paced outside his hotel at Passy, near Paris. Rumors had already filtered into France about a terrible series of American defeats that had resulted in the fall of Philadelphia. That rumor, if true, would certainly not increase America's chances for diplomatic recognition in Paris. When messenger Jonathan Loring Austin rode up, Franklin did not even let him get off his horse before he begged, "Sir, *is* Philadelphia taken?"[76]

"Yes Sir," Austin replied. Franklin clasped his hands together in a gesture of resignation and turned to go into his hotel. Austin hailed him back. "But sir, I have greater news than that. GENERAL BURGOYNE *and his whole army are prisoners of war!*" Years afterward Austin recalled, "The effect was electrical."[77]

Austin had brought additional messages to Franklin and his fellow American commissioners in Paris, Silas Deane and Arthur Lee. The Massachusetts Council had sent a letter informing the diplomats of Burgoyne's defeat. The Council included newspapers detailing the movements of Burgoyne's troops prior to the surrender.[78] Likewise, the Massachusetts Board of War had written to the commissioners in French, to make it easier to disseminate the news to the French governmental officials whom American leaders earnestly wanted to impress. The Board said that Burgoyne had been "made overconfident by earlier successes." It enclosed newspapers to furnish the details of the surrender.[79]

An interested Patriot, William Bingham, also sent some gazettes to the American commissioners for their information. He congratulated the diplomats on Burgoyne's defeat and speculated what the effect of such important news might be on Europe. "I hope at least the Court of France may be influenced by it, to take a more decisive Part in our Favor," he said.[80] Similarly, Thomas Cushing, Sr., of Boston sent some newspapers to the commissioners and begged for information from Europe. "What will the Courts of Europe say upon this great Event?" he asked. "Will France and Spain any longer Hesitate Whether or not they shall Consider us deserving and having a place among the Acknowledged Nations of the World?" He sincerely hoped the courts of Europe would now find America worthy of their military protection.[81]

Franklin and his colleagues hoped for the same. The commissioners informed the French Foreign Minister, the Comte de Vergennes, of Burgoyne's surrender and promised to send further details "as soon as we can collect them from the Papers."[82] In turn, the American commissioners made use of the European press to spread the word throughout the continent. The Duc de la Rochefoucauld collaborated with Franklin to translate parts of American news articles about Burgoyne's defeat for publication in a French newspaper.[83] An official in The Hague informed the commissioners that he had found out about the American victory in a French journal that had clipped a *Boston Gazette* article.[84] An anonymous supporter wrote to Franklin from Brussels, saying the news of Saratoga "made a sensation here in Brussels and throughout these provinces. All rejoice who know of the yoke that your mother country, or rather the servants of despotism, are trying to impose on you."[85]

The European news campaign was a smashing success. The commissioners were able to write home that the news of Saratoga "apparently occasion'd as much general Joy in France, as if it had been a Victory of their own Troops over their own Enemies." In the post-Saratoga euphoria, France acknowledged American independence and agreed to support the new nation in its fight for freedom.[86] As Franklin's fellow American diplomat Arthur Lee recalled:

[Conrad Gérard, secretary to Vergennes] said as there now appeared no doubt of the ability and resolution of the states to maintain their independency, he could assure them it was wished they would reassume their former proposition of an alliance, or any new one they might have, and that it could not be done too soon.[87]

Franklin was thrilled to report the ultimate formulation of two treaties with France, one involving commerce and one involving mutual defense. The Treaty of Amity and Commerce and the Treaty of Alliance "are at length happily compleated, and were finally signed . . . on the 6th Instant," Franklin announced in February 1778.[88]

Back in America, the Patriot press jubilantly printed news of the treaties and of the *feu-de-joy* that accompanied the announcement of the alliance with France. After the *feu-de-joy* guns were fired, officers paraded thirteen abreast (for the thirteen United States), arms interlinked to signify a perfect union. "The appearance was pretty enough," the article reported.[89]

The Loyalist press also printed the news of the treaties, citing Burgoyne's defeat as the driving factor behind them. Editor Humphreys of the *Pennsylvania Ledger* hoped against hope that the news of the French alliance was just another piece of rebel propaganda. He told his readers:

Of this extraordinary publication we doubt not but our readers will think as we do—that we have good reason to suspect it is, what many former publications from the same quarter have been, a seasonable *piece of* misrepresentation. *There is an art, well known by these adepts, of mixing truth and falsehood, or of conveying falsehood in the vehicle of truth.*[90]

Humphreys added, "Surely we have reason to distrust the restless and enterprising spirit of France, and of those other commercial powers who are said to favour the project of American independency!"[91]

As far as Humphreys was concerned, the battle for the public's heart and soul still went on. Treaty or no treaty, the press simply would not, and could not, forget its duty to romanticize one side and degrade the other. Humphreys's fellow editors agreed. The war still had a long way to go, and although the entrance of France after Saratoga would be a turning point, the news remained partisan and persuasive.

Of course, persuasive news reports from one side deeply angered the other side. Thus, the ongoing attempt to persuade got a number of journalists into trouble as the war tipped first toward one side and then to the other. Editors could scarcely take chances on declaring any battles decisive or all-important. After being the first to print the Declaration of Independence, Towne of Philadelphia had converted to the British side and then back to the Patriot side as the two sides battled for the American capital.[92] By the time Lord Cornwallis surrendered his British troops to Washington at Yorktown in October 1781, Towne could only report the battle as a thrilling but still undecisive event. He had changed sides often enough himself to realize that the war might change directions at any moment. He did, however, stop the presses of his *Post* to announce the rumor that Cornwallis's large army had surrendered. He made it the lead story.[93] In early November he was able to print the official story of the surrender. Towne recognized the surrender as a "great, important and happy event." The French, who had become indispensible to the American cause, figured prominently in the victory at Yorktown and were accordingly praised in the press.[94]

In spite of the fact that Yorktown would later be seen as the beginning of the end of the Revolution, the press was quite well aware that the war was still going on. The *Post* continued to carry war news from New York and Pennsylvania, and it added a warning not to celebrate the Yorktown victory so heartily as to forget to continue the struggle.[95] War reports still rolled in. Yorktown had not ended the fight for independence.

The war kept a grip on South Carolina longer than anywhere else on the continent, and as a result, both of the longstanding newspapers in Charleston shut down as conquering armies sent their proprietors into exile. The South Carolina press's experience was fairly typical. All over America, newspapers opened and closed at the whims of war. Many closed due to lack of paper, but many closed—or opened—as conquering governments tried to promote their viewpoints and to silence the voice of the losing faction. Although not telling the whole story, the figures on newspaper mortality reveal something of the effect of the Revolution. At the beginning of the war, thirty-eight newspapers were publishing in the colonies. Between 1775 and 1783, seventy-five new papers were started. During those same years, seventy-six newspapers folded.[96] Such a high death rate during a period of eight years illustrates the hazards war posed for publishing.

The war certainly proved hazardous for South Carolina publishers. The British captured Charleston in May 1780, and the capture caused a flurry of activity among local printers.[97] John Wells, for example, Patriot proprietor of the *South-Carolina and American General Gazette*, suddenly decided to follow his father's wishes and become a Loyalist. Robert Wells, John's father and the founder of the *General Gazette* many decades earlier,[98] had admitted his Loyalist leanings in print by siding against nonimportation in 1770.[99] He had fled to England at the outbreak of the American Revolution.[100] After his father left, John Wells had taken over the press, and he had become a Patriot.[101] John Wells, after all, was a savvy businessman. As long as the British failed to take Charleston, the Patriot faction remained securely in power. When the British succeeded in capturing the city, however, Wells promptly became pro-British again.[102]

His cross-town rival Peter Timothy, publisher of the *Gazette of the State of South-Carolina* since 1746,[103] had not been so savvy. He, too, had taken sides in the nonimportation movement so many years ago, siding with the Patriot faction. Timothy had kept a steady course after that. He became known as an ardent Patriot, both in press and in other matters. He served as Clerk of the General Assembly, and he had even been elected to the Assembly as a delegate. In an unprecedented move, the House of Assembly voted to let him keep his clerk job while also serving as a delegate.[104] Peter Timothy was just too valuable to the Patriot cause to justify a reduction in duties.

After such commitment to Patriot activities, Timothy really had no other choice when the British conquerors marched into Charleston. Rather than shifting with the prevailing political winds, he shut down his *Gazette of South-Carolina*.[105] Not surprisingly, the British warned Timothy and a small group of other influential Patriots to cease their anti-British activities. The conquering army put the radical leaders on parole in Charleston, allowing them to move about freely so long as they did not interfere with British business.[106]

Months of such tense freedom passed peacefully. Then, on a hot, thick August morning in 1780, Timothy and his wife Ann were startled from their bed by an irritating pounding on their door. An armed band of British soldiers ordered Timothy out of the house. He was under arrest, they snarled. The soldiers left a guard behind to keep an eye on Mrs. Timothy and the children.[107] Little Benjamin Franklin Timothy, age nine, was the oldest able-bodied male now at home.[108] Peter Timothy felt it was typical inhuman British behavior to post a guard at so defenseless a household.[109] Later Timothy found out the soldiers had searched his private papers.[110]

The British soldiers marched Timothy and twenty-eight other radical prisoners to the city's Exchange, where they were kept in the dingy, cold cellar.[111] From there they marched to the ship *Sandwich* in the harbor to await further instructions.[112] None of the captives knew why they were there, but they soon found out. The British general Lord Cornwallis felt that Timothy, along with other Patriots, might be involved in a conspiracy to burn Charleston and massacre Loyalists.[113] He decided to thwart any such activity by exiling all of them to St. Augustine in Florida.[114]

St. Augustine—the very words struck dread into the hearts of the Charleston captives. The city was teeming with Loyalists, and it was an extremely dangerous sea journey away.[115] The captives protested bitterly, but to no avail. Friends and relatives streamed to the wharf "to take a melancholy leave of us," one captive wrote. "[A]nd a grievous sight it was indeed to see Husbands parting with their distressed Wives, Fathers bidding Farewell to their beloved children, and Friend separating from Friend, perhaps many, never to meet again." A great many were in tears.[116]

Despite the dangerous sea trip, the leading Patriots of Charleston arrived safely. In St. Augustine, Timothy and his fellow prisoners were forced to rent their own lodgings for a huge sum. Some of the men had to write home for money.[117] As if that were not humiliating enough, a local resident kept sending them pumpkins as an insult.[118] British soldiers were also exasperating. As prisoner Josiah Smith described it:

But to crown all, a truly ridiculous company, consisting mostly of Officers, headed by their Veteran Commandant, all of them seemingly much heated by liquor and attended by their Regimental Music &c Paraded the Street . . . between 7 & 8 O'Clock, who in passing by our habitation, Insulted us with the tune Yankey Doodle &c the which tune has also been often Struck up by the relief Guards in their marching to & from the Castle, doubtless by way of Insult, and in derision to our Company of Suffering Americans.[119]

The Charleston prisoners were rarely allowed to see a newspaper, and they were made to believe that America was decisively losing the war. The commandant in St. Augustine threatened to hang six of them to retaliate for American atrocities elsewhere.[120] It came as something of a shock, then, when Timothy and his fellow captives were told that they were to be exchanged for British prisoners and freed. However, they read in a newspaper that their wives and children and any other dependents had also been banished to Philadelphia.[121]

Timothy and the others had to buy passage aboard a ship to Philadelphia at their own expense, as did their families. Somehow, they all scraped the money together.[122] The Timothy family stayed in exile in Philadelphia for over a year until the defeated British left Charleston. Timothy decided not to revive the *Gazette*, but instead to start over again in Antigua.[123] Unfortunately, he never made it. His ship sank in a storm off the coast of Delaware.[124]

Meanwhile, John Wells and his brother William Charles had stayed in Charleston to publish a deeply Loyal version of the *General Gazette*, now renamed *Royal Gazette*. As the war drew to a close, though, they faced the same prospects that Timothy had faced when the British had taken over Charleston. With the vanquished British leaving, the Loyal Wells printers were no longer welcome to stay in Charleston. They, like so many other Loyalists, were forced to flee to St. Augustine.[125]

Although St. Augustine was a little more palatable to the Wells brothers than it had been to Peter Timothy, John Wells decided not to go straight to Florida, but instead to go home and reconcile with his father in England.[126] William Charles Wells disassembled the family's press and took it and a pressman to St. Augustine. He intended to start East Florida's first newspaper.[127] But William Charles was horrified to learn after he had gotten all the way to St. Augustine that the pressman had no clue how to put together a printing press. *That*, the pressman informed him at this late date, was the job of a press joiner.[128]

It was supremely frustrating. Wells searched among the books he had rescued from Charleston and discovered his brother's old *Printer's Grammar*, which contained a crude drawing of a press. Wells studied the picture for days, trying to match it up to the dismantled press. After wrestling with the bits and pieces, he got the thing together, with the help of a Negro carpenter.[129]

The *East-Florida Gazette* was soon in business. The weekly spoke of how hard life was for the evacuated Loyalists. Florida was but a stop for some; many Loyalists expected to wind up in miserably cold Canada or in the West Indies.[130] The *Gazette* begged Loyalists not to move away "without endeavouring to make some terms for themselves. . . . While they are together they may command some kind of respect and attention, and work upon the fears, if not upon the justice, of the nation."[131]

Wells simply could not give up his Loyalist stance, which in turn made it difficult for his readers to discern how they might make terms with the new United States. Wells's new *Gazette* lambasted American leaders as arbitrary and oppressive. America, Wells sneered, "cannot but bemoan her folly mostly proceeding from her own choice."[132]

After a fruitless return to Charleston to collect his father's debts, a visit that caused a great deal of bitterness in the highly Patriotic Charleston press,[133] William Charles Wells went back to St. Augustine and then to England. His brother John returned from London to run the *East-Florida Gazette*.[134]

As it had been for Peter Timothy, though, St. Augustine turned out to be a temporary stop for John Wells. On September 3, 1783, Britain ceded Florida to Spain, and by 1784, Wells and his fellow Loyalists were forced to evacuate once again.[135] Disappointed, John Wells moved his press to Nassau, where he opened the *Bahama Gazette*. Although he was not happy there, he never moved again.[136]

As the South Carolinians' experience showed, the attempts by the press to persuade and to be on the winning side cost men their livelihoods. Although the coincidental exiles of Charleston's rivals to St. Augustine were not identically repeated everywhere, the Timothy-Wells experience was typical in other respects. Both presses took sides in the Revolution, as was standard. Both fought the battle for their readers' hearts and minds, much as Rivington and the Greens had done in the North. Neither Timothy nor Wells had been impartial. Both had become so strongly allied with one party or the other that, in the end, when their faction was defeated, they had no choice but to leave town.

Partiality, then, had its price. Although Paine had been wildly successful with his partisan pamphlets, newspapermen such as Timothy and Wells literally lost their homes and businesses for siding so vehemently with either side. Timothy even lost his life in connection with his stubborn stand for the Patriots.

A few partial publishers were a little more fortunate. After an agonizing fight to remain neutral, Georgia printer James Johnston could no longer hide his true feelings. He was forced by his conscience to side with the British in the Revolution. Thus, he turned his *Georgia Gazette* into the Loyalist *Royal Georgia Gazette*. As the war drew to a close in Georgia, however, Johnston was in trouble. He closed the *Royal Georgia Gazette* after the June 6, 1782, issue, and disappeared for awhile. The new executive council of the state of Georgia passed a law banning 117 known Loyalists, including the printer, from the state. If he returned to Georgia, Johnston faced jail and deportation to Britain. Soon his property was confiscated and sold, but Johnston managed to leave the printing materials, which technically belonged to the state, in the hands of his wife.[137]

But Georgia needed a printer, and Johnston was willing to resume the job under the new government. After all, there were few qualified printers in Georgia. In 1782, Georgia passed an Amercement Act, which allowed him to return to the state. Governor John Martin himself saw to it that Johnston regained his old house (Martin ordered government officials to find a new home for the man who had bought the property),[138] and Johnston returned to his old job.[139] Perhaps Johnston's dogged attempts to be impartial for so long softened the attitude of the victors who rehired him.

Soon he reopened his newspaper under a new name, celebrating Georgia's new status: *Gazette of the State of Georgia*. Early in 1783, Johnston printed an address of welcome to American war hero Nathanael Greene, commander of the Southern Department of the American army. The *Gazette* touted Greene's divinely blessed success, which resulted in the "total expulsion of the enemy from the Southern States."[140] It was a marked change from the Loyalist attitude of Johnston's newspaper a few months earlier.

A peace treaty was under negotiation in Paris, and in April 1783, Johnston finally got word that Parliament had declared America independent. Like all American newspapers, the *Gazette* was jubilant. At last, the long, long war was over. The *Gazette* exulted in the "great and joyful news of PEACE."[141]

As soon as Americans read the news of peace, they organized grand celebrations. Newspapers spread the jubilee to all parts of the continent by describing the glorious joy in the various cities. Johnston told of revelers in Augusta, Georgia, who held "a very elegant and sumptuous entertainment" for more than 300 ladies and gentlemen. The large crowd feasted together on a luscious banquet and enjoyed hearing a cannon fired thirteen times, once for each of the new states. Artillery was fired after toasts in honor of "The Free, Sovereign, and Independent States of America," the *Gazette* reported. The newspaper also recorded the revelry in Savannah, including a public dinner at the courthouse. The governor of the state attended. The festivities included toasts to American ladies and the firing of artillery, as well as "the huzzah of the populace." As darkness fell, Savannah "was illuminated, and the evening spent with every demonstration of joy."[142]

Completing the final transformation to the American point of view, Johnston adopted the tactics which so many Patriot newspapers had used throughout the war: he began to needle the British. He printed a number of derisive articles against the losers. In "A Eulogy to the Memory of the Late King," a poet bade farewell to the monarchy in America: "Peace to thy royal shade, illustrious King! Sleep sweetly on beneath thy blazon'd tomb."[143]

Johnston was a rare printer who managed to prosper after landing on the wrong side of the Treaty of Paris. Having taken sides, he understood what the peace treaty meant: he had to stand for the new United States once and for all. There would be no more Loyalist rhetoric in his pages.

In spite of his good fortune, Johnston's decision to take sides was typical. All printers were forced to take a stand, and many suffered for their choice. The nature of printing and publishing during the Revolution was partisan as the two sides battled to win readers' hearts.

It could be argued that, in the end, it mattered little if newspaper readers were or were not won over to a particular side; the only people who really counted were the armies or the European diplomats who waited patiently to intervene on America's behalf. Perhaps it made no difference what kind of press the people back home saw, whether it be Loyalist or Patriot.

American and British leaders, however, did not disdain the influence of the press. They put great stock in the persuasive reports in the newspapers. Clearly, both Loyalist and Patriot factions saw the printed word as the spark behind any great upsurge of public feeling. Journalists, political leaders, and generals sincerely believed that printed efforts at winning the public heart were necessary—even vital—to their cause. They expected their press to behave accordingly. News reports in the Revolution, therefore, were certainly never meant to contain mere factual coverage or to describe battles and events objectively. Instead, coverage of news was a deliberate, highly valued attempt to paint the two sides in their most persuasive colors.

Journalists, for their part, perceived that they could not—and indeed, would not—avoid taking sides. Following the prevailing public opinion on what the press should be, they held fast to the side they felt was right. In many cases, the resolute stubbornness of printers forced them to go out of business.

The American Revolutionary press simply did not deal in impartiality. It dealt in persuasion to the utmost degree, even if it meant the loss of livelihood, home, and life itself.

NOTES

1. *Rivington's New-York Gazette* (New York), 11 October 1777. The full name of the newspaper was *Rivington's New-York Gazette: or the Connecticut, Hudson's River, New-Jersey, and Quebec Weekly Advertiser*. On 18 October 1777, Rivington changed the title to *Rivington's New-York Loyal Gazette*. The incident with the Connecticut mob happened in late November 1775 and was detailed in Rivington's 11 October 1777 newspaper after he returned from exile.

2. Mary Margaret Roberts, "Introduction: Paine's *Common Sense*," in G. Jack Gravlee and James R. Irvine, eds., *Pamphlets and the American Revolution: Rhetoric, Politics, Literature, and the Popular Press* (Delmar, N.Y.: Scholars' Facsimiles & Reprints, 1976), i. Each pamphlet reprinted in the book is separately numbered; all numbers given refer to the facsimile of *Common Sense*.

3. Thomas Paine, *Common Sense*, printed in facsimile in Gravlee and Irvine, ibid. The quotation is from Paine's unnumbered introduction.

4. Ibid., 53–56. The quoted material is from page 56.

5. Ibid., 57.

6. Ibid., 58–59.

7. Ibid., 60.

8. Quoted in Henry Steele Commager and Richard B. Morris, eds., *The Spirit of 'Seventy-Six: The Story of the American Revolution as Told by Participants* (New York: Harper & Row, 1958), 283.

9. According to historian Frank Luther Mott, Towne was the first to print the great document. See Mott, *American Journalism: A History of Newspapers in the United States Through 250 Years, 1690 to 1940* (New York: Macmillan, 1941), 88.

10. *Pennsylvania Evening Post* (Philadelphia), 9 July 1776.

11. Ibid., 11 July 1776.

12. Ibid., 13 July 1776.

13. Ibid., 11 July 1776.

14. Ibid., 13 July 1776.

15. Quoted in Frank Moore, *Diary of the American Revolution: From Newspapers and Original Documents* (New York: Scribner, 1860), 1:350.

16. The origins of *The Crisis* are discussed in Howard Fast, *The Selected Work of Tom Paine & Citizen Tom Paine* (New York: Modern Library, 1945), 45.

17. Paine to Henry Laurens, 14 January 1779, *The Complete Writings of Thomas Paine*, 2 vols. (New York: Citadel Press, 1945), 2:1164.

18. Thomas Paine, *Pennsylvania Journal* (Philadelphia), 19 December 1776.

19. Commager and Morris, *The Spirit of 'Seventy-Six*, synopsize the soldiers' reactions on p. 505.

20. Charles Biddle, quoted in Alfred Owen Aldridge, *Man of Reason: The Life of Thomas Paine* (Philadelphia: J. B. Lippincott Co., 1959), 49.

21. Isaiah Thomas, *The History of Printing in America*, ed. Marcus A. McCorison (1810; reprint, New York: Weathervane Books, 1970), 135–36.

22. Arthur M. Schlesinger, *Prelude to Independence: The Newspaper War on Britain, 1764–1776* (New York: Alfred A. Knopf, 1958), 307–8.

23. George Washington to the Board of War, 27 February 1778, in John C. Fitzpatrick, ed., *The Writings of George Washington from the Original Manuscript Sources, 1745–1799* (Washington, D.C.: U.S. Government Printing Office, 1933), 10:520–21.

24. *New-York Gazette; and Weekly Mercury*, 29 September 1777.

25. George Washington's General Orders, 5 September 1777, in Fitzpatrick, ed., *The Writings of George Washington*, 9:181–82.

26. Ibid., 182.

27. A great many newspaper articles in the Revolutionary era were literally letters written by people on the scene. This chapter refers to those writers as "correspondents."

28. *Rivington's New-York Gazette*, 11 October 1777.

29. Ibid., 18 October 1777.

30. Ibid., 8 November 1777.

31. Ibid., 11 October 1777.

32. Ibid., 8 November 1777.

33. *Connecticut Journal* (New Haven), 8 October 1777.

34. Ibid.

35. Ibid. The comment about the Howes referred to William Howe and his brother Richard, who was Britain's naval commander in America.

36. Ibid., 15 October 1777.

37. Ibid., 22 October 1777.

38. *Pennsylvania Evening Post*, 11 October 1777.

39. Ibid.

40. Ibid.

41. Ibid., 16 October 1777.

42. The full name of the paper was *Pennsylvania Ledger: or the Virginia, Maryland, Pennsylvania, and New-Jersey Weekly Advertiser*. It was suspended after the 30 November 1776 issue, and reopened on 10 October 1777 as the *Pennsylvania Ledger: or the Weekly Advertiser*. That issue featured the revised flag. The paper, under both names, was published in Philadelphia.

43. Dunlap's newspaper was issued in Philadelphia through 9 September 1777 as *Dunlap's Pennsylvania Packet or General Advertiser* and reappeared in Lancaster on 29 November 1777 as *Pennsylvania Packet or General Advertiser*.

44. George Washington to Samuel Washington, 27 October 1777, in Fitzpatrick, *The Writings of George Washington*, 9:450.

45. The accusation was spelled out plainly in the *New-York Gazette*, 6 October 1777.

46. *Connecticut Journal*, 15 October 1777.

47. Ibid., 21 June 1775. The full name of the newspaper at that time was the *Connecticut Journal, and the New-Haven Post-Boy*. The article was supposedly by General Thomas Gage, but scholar George Billias says the piece was written by Burgoyne rather than Gage. See "John Burgoyne: Ambitious General" in George Athan Billias, ed., *George Washington's Opponents: British Generals in the American Revolution* (New York: William Morrow & Co., 1969), 158.

48. Scholars agree that Burgoyne and Howe somehow suffered a major misunderstanding about reinforcing the New York army. See, for instance, Maldwyn A. Jones, "Sir William Howe: Conventional Strategist," in Billias, *George Washington's Opponents*, 40, and Hoffman Nickerson, *The Turning Point of the Revolution, or Burgoyne in America* (Boston: Houghton Mifflin Co., 1928), 95–98.

49. *Connecticut Journal*, 15 October 1777.

50. Ibid., 22 October 1777.

51. Ibid. Technically Burgoyne did not surrender, but instead signed Articles of Convention. However, the event so closely resembled a surrender that the press denominated it as such.

52. Ibid., 29 October 1777.

53. Ibid., 5 November 1777. *Poltroon* is a synonym for *coward.*

54. Ibid., 12 November 1777.

55. Ibid., 19 November 1777.

56. Ibid.

57. *Rivington's New-York Loyal Gazette,* 25 October 1777.

58. Ibid., 1 November 1777.

59. Ibid.

60. Ibid., 8 November 1777.

61. Ibid.

62. Ibid., 15 November 1777.

63. Ibid., 22 November 1777.

64. Ibid.

65. George Washington to Samuel Washington, 27 October 1777, in Fitzpatrick, *The Writings of George Washington,* 9:450.

66. George Washington's General Orders, 18 October 1777, ibid., 390–91. A *feu-de-joy* was a ceremonial firing of guns.

67. George Washington to Brigadier General James Potter, 18 October 1777, ibid., 391.

68. *Pennsylvania Evening Post,* 8 November 1777.

69. *Pennsylvania Ledger,* 5 November 1777.

70. John Laurens to Henry Laurens, 5 November 1777, in David R. Chesnutt, ed., *The Papers of Henry Laurens* (Columbia: University of South Carolina Press, 1990), 12:25–28.

71. Ibid., 29.

72. Henry Laurens to John Laurens, 12 November 1777, ibid., 47.

73. Henry Laurens to the Marquis de LaFayette, 6 December 1777, ibid., 134.

74. John Wells, Jr., to Henry Laurens, 28 November 1777, ibid., 108.

75. John Laurens to Henry Laurens, 26 November 1777, ibid., 91.

76. "Memoir of Jonathan Loring Austin," *Boston Monthly Magazine* II (1826), 59, quoted as an editorial explanation in William B. Willcox, ed., *The Papers of Benjamin Franklin* (New Haven, Conn.: Yale University Press, 1986), 25:234–35. Willcox says the magazine cited an interview with Austin as a source for the memoir.

77. Ibid., 234.

78. The Massachusetts Council to the American Commissioners, 24 October 1777, ibid., 98.

79. Massachusetts Board of War to Benjamin Franklin and the American Commissioners, 24 October 1777, translated from the French by Archives du Ministère des affaires étrangères, ibid., 99.

80. William Bingham to the American Commissioners, 28 November 1777, ibid., 201.

81. Thomas Cushing, Sr., to Benjamin Franklin, 30 October 1777, ibid., 126–27.

82. American Commissioners to the Comte de Vergennes, 4 December 1777, ibid., 236.

83. Louis-Alexandre, Duc de la Roche-Guyon and de la Rochefoucauld, to Benjamin Franklin, 18 December 1777, ibid., 310–11. The exact date in December is a guess by the editors of the *Papers.*

84. Charles-Guillaume-Frédéric Dumas to Benjamin Franklin and the Commissioners, 16 December 1777, ibid., 293.

85. Anonymous letter to Benjamin Franklin, December 1777, ibid., 381–82.

86. The American Commissioners to the Committee for Foreign Affairs, 18 December 1777, ibid., 305.

87. Journal of Arthur Lee, 6 December 1777, in Commager and Morris, *The Spirit of 'Seventy-Six*, 680.

88. Benjamin Franklin to the Massachusetts Board of War, 17 February 1778, in *The Papers of Benjamin Franklin*, 25:684.

89. *Pennsylvania Packet*, 13 May 1778.

90. *Pennsylvania Ledger*, 9 May 1778. Humphreys put the opinion in brackets, which have been removed here.

91. Ibid.

92. Mott, *American Journalism*, 88.

93. *The Pennsylvania Evening Post, and Public Advertiser* (Philadelphia), 22 October 1781. The *Post*'s name had been expanded from *The Pennsylvania Evening Post*, as it was called at the time of the Declaration of Independence.

94. Ibid., 3 November 1781.

95. Ibid., 17 November 1781.

96. Computed from Edward Connery Lathem, comp., *Chronological Tables of American Newspapers, 1690–1820* (Barre, Mass.: American Antiquarian Society and Barre Publishers, 1972), 9–22.

97. *South-Carolina and American General Gazette* (Charleston), 6 September 1780.

98. The newspaper was founded in November of 1758 as *The South-Carolina Weekly Gazette* (Charleston). The first issue of the newspaper does not survive, but the issue numbered 12 existed until it was lost in 1924. Subtraction from #12, dated 7 February 1759, puts the startup date of the *Weekly Gazette* at about 22 November 1758. The source of this information is the American Antiquarian Society, *South Carolina Miscellaneous Titles, 1758–1820*, checklist number 1873 (New York: Readex Microprint Corp., 1983) microprint.

99. See Chapter 6 of this book.

100. Robert Wells is difficult to track, for his name continued to appear in connection with the publishing firm until 1782, long after he was in England. However, an ad for an overseer who needed to apply to Robert Wells appeared in the *General Gazette* of 9 June 1775. After that no ads bore his name except in connection with the publishing business. He apparently had gone home to England shortly after June 9. John Laurens spoke to Wells in London in the fall of 1775. See Henry Laurens to John Laurens, 26 September 1775, in "Letters from Hon. Henry Laurens to his Son John, 1773–1776," *The South Carolina Historical and Genealogical Magazine* 5 (April 1904): 75.

101. The change was obvious in the *General Gazette* of 2 August 1776.

102. See *South-Carolina and American General Gazette*, 19 July 1780.

103. Timothy had been the nominal publisher of the newspaper, originally named *South-Carolina Gazette*, since his father's death in 1739. However, he was a child at the time, and the newspaper was actually edited by his mother, Elizabeth. She announced that she had taken over the paper on 4 January 1739, and she continued publishing it in her son's name. Since she always used Peter's name as publisher, the date at which she turned over the press to him is guesswork. Peter apparently turned twenty-one in 1746, and thus he probably took over the press that year. His age was calculated from a reference to the fact that Peter's father Lewis had six children, ages six to one, in 1731. Peter was apparently the oldest child. See Marion Reynolds King, "One Link in the First Newspaper Chain, *The South Carolina*

Gazette," Journalism Quarterly 9 (1932): 259. King gave his source as *Pennsylvania Archives* (second series), 17:29, 31–32.

104. William Tennent, "Historic remarks on the session of Assembly begun to be holden Tuesday, September 17th, 1776," in Newton B. Jones, ed., "Writings of the Reverend William Tennent, 1740–1777," *South Carolina Historical Magazine* 61 (October 1960): 189.

105. The last issue of the *Gazette of the State of South-Carolina* was published on 9 July 1780.

106. David Ramsay, *The History of South-Carolina from its First Settlement in 1670 to The Year 1808* (Charleston: David Longworth, 1809), 1:462. Ramsay was one of the parolees.

107. The description of Peter Timothy's capture and subsequent imprisonment is a composite of descriptions by two of his fellow prisoners, David Ramsay and Josiah Smith. See Ramsay, *History of South-Carolina* , 370–72, and Josiah Smith, "Josiah Smith's Diary, 1780–81," *South Carolina Historical and Genealogical Magazine* 33 (January 1932): 2–4. Since Smith's diary is divided among several volumes of the magazine, subsequent citations will be listed as "'Josiah Smith's Diary,' volume number (date): page(s)."

108. Benjamin Franklin Timothy's only older brother was an invalid. See Hennig Cohen, *The South-Carolina Gazette, 1732–1775* (Columbia: University of South Carolina Press, 1953), 246. The fact that Benjamin and his brother were the only surviving male children is obvious by Peter Timothy's will. *Record of Wills, 1783–1786*, Book XX, Charleston County (South Carolina) Probate Court.

109. Peter Timothy's will, made in April of 1780, characterized the British, then attacking Charleston, as "an Enemy who do not promise to exercise all that Humanity which distinguishes a generous Foe." Quoted in Cohen, *The South-Carolina Gazette*, 246.

110. Ramsay, *History of South-Carolina*, 1:371.

111. Ibid., 444.

112. "Josiah Smith's Diary," 33 (January 1932): 3.

113. Ramsay, *History of South-Carolina*, 371.

114. "Josiah Smith's Diary," 33 (January 1932): 5.

115. Johann Schoepf described the ocean off St. Augustine as being extraordinarily dangerous due to a difficult bar to cross. Johann David Schoepf, *Travels in the Confederation [1783–1784]* (Germany, 1788; reprint and translation, New York: Burt Franklin, 1968), 2:227. (Page numbers refer to reprint edition.)

116. "Josiah Smith's Diary," 33 (January 1932): 6.

117. Ibid., 11–12, 19–20, 25.

118. Ibid., 20.

119. Ibid.

120. Ramsay, *History of South-Carolina*, 372–73.

121. "Josiah Smith's Diary," 33 (July 1932): 199.

122. "Josiah Smith's Diary," 33 (October 1932): 289.

123. Isaiah Thomas, *The History of Printing in America*, ed. Marcus A. McCorison (1810; reprint, New York: Weathervane Books, 1970), 569.

124. Ibid.

125. *Royal Gazette* (Charleston, S.C.), 7 August 1782.

126. Historians argue over when John Wells went home to Britain. William Charles Wells said in *Two Essays: One Upon Single Vision With Two Eyes, the Other on Dew* (London: A. Constable & Co., 1818), that he sent John home to reconcile with his father. *Two*

Essays is cited in Christopher Gould, "Robert Wells, Colonial Charleston Printer," *South Carolina Historical Magazine* 79 (January 1978): 33. John was obviously in England at some point, for William Charles commented that John arrived in East Florida from England in 1784. See William Charles Wells, *Extract Memoir*, quoted in Louisa Susannah Wells [Louisa Susannah Aikman], *The Journal of a Voyage from Charlestown to London* (New York: New York Historical Society, 1906; reprint, New York: New York Times & Arno Press, 1968), 99. (Page numbers refer to reprint edition). Also, Gould (citing *American Loyalist Transcripts*, 56:75) said John Wells claimed that he never left South Carolina during the war. To make all these claims by the brothers fit, it would appear that John left Charleston after the war, went home to reconcile with his father, and then returned to run the *East-Florida Gazette* (St. Augustine) in 1784.

127. "Obituary: Memoir of William Charles Wells, M.D.," *Gentleman's Magazine* 122 (November 1817): 468.

128. Ibid.

129. Ibid.

130. *East-Florida Gazette*, quoted in *South-Carolina Weekly Gazette* (Charleston), 12 July 1783. This was the second newspaper to be called *South-Carolina Weekly Gazette*.

131. Ibid., 28 June 1783.

132. Ibid., 17 July 1783.

133. See, for example, *South-Carolina Weekly Gazette*, 12 August 1783.

134. "Obituary: Memoir of William Charles Wells, M.D.," 468, and William Charles Wells, *Extract Memoir*, 99.

135. Douglas C. McMurtrie, "The Beginnings of Printing in Florida," *Florida Historical Quarterly* 23 (October 1944): 65, 68. The last known *East-Florida Gazette* was issued in March of 1784; probably John Wells evacuated shortly thereafter.

136. Thomas, *History of Printing in America*, 610.

137. Allen D. Candler, ed., *The Revolutionary Records of the State of Georgia* (Atlanta: Franklin-Turner Co., 1906) I: 373–97, 446; III: 125.

138. "Official Letters of Governor John Martin, 1782–1783," *The Georgia Historical Quarterly* 1, no. 4 (December 1913): 332.

139. Candler, *Revolutionary Records*, III: 221, 232.

140. *Gazette of the State of Georgia* (Savannah), 30 January 1783.

141. Ibid., 10 April 1783.

142. Ibid., 1 and 9 May 1783.

143. Ibid., 12 June 1783.

8

Reflections on the
Early American Press

The early American press was more complex than it might seem at first glance. Not only was it more complex, but the thinking of early Americans about the role and operation of the press was quite sophisticated, even when compared with that of later generations. Printers and colonists dealt with a number of touchy questions involving the press, and their discussions exhibited mature thought on a medium that was in its infancy. Historians have been prone to explain the early press as virtually one-dimensional. According to the standard historical view, early newspapers were either the origin of modern American journalism or the automatic result of huge, impersonal forces such as economics that were at work in the milieu of the time.[1]

In explaining the early press of the nation, however, the answers are neither simple nor obvious. Historians have wrestled with a variety of questions: Why did newspapers first appear? What was the essential nature of the early American press? What factors accounted for that character? What purpose did newspaper operators see for themselves? What role did ideas about the practice of journalism play in the colonial press? What role did the press play in influencing public opinion? To these questions there are no easy responses. Despite the difficulties involved, however, let us attempt briefly to address some of the key questions.

Probably the first question asked about the colonial press is why newspapers first appeared. The fact that Boston was the home not only of America's first newspaper (*Publick Occurrences*) but also its second, third, and fifth (the *News-Letter*, the *Gazette*, and the *New-England Courant*) makes that city's newspapers an alluring point of inquiry. Most historians' explanations of the founding of those papers take viewpoints emphasizing either professional journalism concerns or environmental forces. The professional view normally explains the early newspapers as attempts by their founders to challenge authority in order to help liberate society from control by government or religious powers. In that context, *Publick Oc-currences* and the *Courant* are presented as bold journalistic challenges to government and church officials by Benjamin Harris and James Franklin, respectively. The *News-Letter*'s John Campbell, on the other hand, is explained as a timid mouthpiece of the government of Massachusetts who failed to exercise that vigorous independence required of true journalists.

The cultural view has been prone to argue that the newspapers appeared as the result of sweeping forces that came together near the end of the seventeenth century. Those forces included such factors as the growth of the colonial economy, an increase in the population of colonial towns, and spreading literacy.[2] When these forces converged in colonial America in the late 1600s, the reasoning goes, the appearance of newspapers was inevitable.

Even though both the professional and the cultural explanations are attractive, there are inherent difficulties in both of them. One is struck, for example, by the lack of evidence from primary sources to support them. The professional characterization of Harris and Franklin, for example, typically draws on selective quotations from their newspapers that are read as if they support the characterization. Beyond those quotations, historical treatments have failed to examine what type of person either Harris or Franklin truly was or to scrutinize the content of their papers to determine its real meaning. When Harris and Franklin are examined closely, it becomes evident that they were not journalists challenging authority for the sake of liberation of the people. Instead, each was attempting to achieve a goal that coincided with the interests of a particular religious group. In Harris's case, the goal was that of the automony of the Puritan commonwealth in Massachusetts. With Franklin, it was to aid in the ascendancy of Anglicanism.

Similarly, the cultural explanation starts to fall apart once it is examined closely. The mode of cultural reasoning tends to paint general background details of the growth of the economy, population, and literacy and to draw the conclusion that by 1690 conditions were ripe for the establishment of newspapers. Then, almost naturally, newspapers began to appear. As with the professional explanation, however, the clear relationship of that background to the newspapers themselves is never demonstrated through direct evidence. It is not shown, for example, that Benjamin Harris had economics, population, or an adequate readership in mind when he decided to start *Publick Occurrences*. Even if it were unreasonable to expect the historian to produce such evidence, one must wonder why—if conditions were so favorable for newspapers in 1690—it was another fourteen years before another newspaper appeared in Boston (the *News-Letter* in 1704) and another fifteen years before the third (the *Gazette* in 1719). Similarly, why did newspapers not appear in other towns when they had reached the state that had existed in Boston in 1690?

The best explanation at this point is that the first newspapers appeared because of particular individuals in particular situations. The Puritan religious and philosophical background in Massachusetts had created an environment in which discussion of ideas was encouraged, and the Puritans had developed a society comparatively free of control from British authority. Royal attempts to achieve authority created a situation in which it was possible for contesting views—Puritan and royal—to be expressed. Supporters of the British crown had the power of the government to protect them, while the Puritans had established enough autonomy to be able to confront the crown. Thus, the environment had, as the cultural argument would go, made it possible for a newspaper to be started—although the environmental factors were obviously different from those that have been explained by the cultural view. It was not, however, until a particular situation had developed—the chaos following the overthrow of the Andros government in 1689—and a particular individual, Benjamin Harris, had entered the scene that a newspaper appeared. The same combination—a particular individual in a particular situation—was also true of the other newspapers started in Boston during the next half century or so. John Campbell, the postmaster, believed it was part of his official duties to publish a *News-Letter*. William Brooker, Campbell's successor as postmaster, began the *Gazette* after Campbell refused to relinquish the *News-Letter*, because Brooker believed that a newspaper was by right the province of the postmaster. Similarly, the *New-England Courant* began publication because of the founders' personal antipathy to Cotton Mather and because of John Checkley's ardent religous beliefs. The situation was not, as journalism historians have been prone to argue, one of general public discontent with the authority of the Puritan clergy; rather, it was one in which particular individuals had personal and religious reasons for starting a newspaper to promote their views. Personal reasons played similarly key roles in the founding of Boston's other early newspapers. Outside Boston, newspapers appear to have been started mainly—although there were exceptions—because printers realized that they provided one means of bringing in income to their printing operations. For the historian looking for grand generalizations about the establishment of early American newspapers, the fact that printers diversified into newspapers to supplement their incomes does not fit the concept of broad environmental forces that cultural historians have preferred, and it appears to have no relevance at all to the professional journalism explanation. It may, indeed, be directly contrary to it.

Regardless of the reason for the appearance of newspapers, a more important question about the early American press relates to its character. The question is, quite simply, What was the essential nature of early American newspapers? Once that question is answered, there remains a second, related question: What factors accounted for that character?

The key concern of historians of the colonial press has properly centered on the question of how the press can best be understood. The most frequent proposals to answer the question have been these: The press was the projection of the personality and character of the individuals who ran the newspapers; Newspapers comprised an institution whose development and character were the result of the general forces in colonial society; or, The colonial press was the origin of American journalism. The most provocative question about the Revolutionary press, on the other hand, has been the nature of the motivation and ideology of printers. Were they dedicated to the ideals of liberty and democracy, as the nineteenth-century and later Consensus historians believed? Or did printers betray their true reactionary motives by their failure to advocate liberal social reform, as Progressive critics argued?

If individuals were, as the nineteenth-century Romantic historians believed, the key factors in colonial newspaper history, what was the character of those individuals? Did the Romantic historians paint an unrealistically favorable picture of newspaper operators? Did they place too much importance on the role of the individual, as the Cultural historians claimed, overlooking the influence of forces in the environment? Or did the Cultural historians themselves, by emphasizing outside forces, inaccurately downplay the role of the individual? As a counterexplanation, were the early printers really journalists, as those historians with a professional journalism view argued? Thus, can early newspapers best be understood in terms of the origins of journalism?

The answer to the question of what the press's character was is not easy to answer. The reason is that the character of the press was not as one-dimensional or uniform as historians have been prone to suggest. Thus, one cannot routinely answer that the press was journalistic, that it was profit-oriented, that it was opposed to the government or religious establishment, or that it conveniently fit any other mold. The early press was multifaceted, and what was true of one newspaper was not necessarily true of another.

One thing we can say is that newspapers gained much from America's transatlantic connections. Originally, American printers relied completely on England for the mechanics of their trade, obtaining all of their equipment and supplies from England. In other ways, however, the connections between America and the mother country were just as pervasive. They included such matters as the colonists'—especially the planters' and merchants'—desire to be informed about affairs in England, the fact that England and the colonies were bound together in colonial wars until 1763, the colonists' acceptance of the English lead in using the press to expand the political community, the common concerns about freedom of the press, and the colonial adoption of certain journalistic forms such as the essay inspired by Addison and Steele's *Spectator* series. It is no exaggeration to say that the early American newspaper was in some degree a transplanted English newspaper.

Part of the problem, however, in ferreting out the character of the early press is that much of the historical effort has been aimed at providing a monolithic explanation. Romantic historians of the nineteenth century explained early printers as patriotic figures of high integrity who had contributed to the progress of America. Developmental historians could see early printers only as journalists, and they wished to explain the character of newspapers in terms of later standards of professional journalism. Progressive historians, on the other hand, reduced all of early printing history to an ideological conflict between conservatives and liberals. Cultural historians believed, however, that all of those explanations were irrelevant, and they replaced them with the assumption that environmental forces could explain everything. All four approaches have their shortcomings, but of the four, the cultural explanation is probably the most subtle and sophisticated. Even with it, however, there are immediate, fundamental questions that occur. For example, in attempting to demonstrate that cultural forces influenced the press, what evidence is necessary? Is it adequate to produce, as Cultural historians have tended to do, evidence of general trends in society, or must the historian demonstrate a direct relationship between such forces and individual newspapers?

One can begin discerning the character of the early press by turning away from monolithic explanations and looking at concrete factors. Some insight can be gained from the lively and sophisticated debate waged by Americans of the time about what the proper role of the press should be. The debate did not deal in superficialities or crude arguments. It exhibited, instead, reasoning that was as informed as much debate today. One of the fundamental assumptions of early Americans was that the press should be closely involved with the concerns of society, rather than being at a professional distance, as it is today. Thus the early press often was integrally involved with public activities. From the beginning of settlement in the New World, American colonists had believed that the printing press was of critical importance. That view was evident in the thinking of the Puritans of Massachusetts, who believed that the individual was the authority in spiritual matters and must, therefore, have the freedom and means to inquire into religious doctrine. They therefore recognized the indispensable nature of the press in making reading material available and in providing a mechanism by which individuals could present their beliefs to others. There were certain bounds beyond which the press was not to go—printing blasphemous material, for example—but even the limitations on the press were signs of the critical importance ascribed to it. The press was also important in political affairs throughout the formative period in American history. It served as a prime instrument used by the key players in the successive debates over the relationship of colonial representatives to proprietary and crown officials, the nature of the political and economic association between the colonies and the mother country, and the independence movement in the colonies. In most other areas of life the press seemed to play a part, from theological debate, to economic policies, to cultural manners, to daily business transactions.

One of the loudest and longest-running debates was over what the stance of the press should be in public controversies. The question was whether it should be neutral or partisan. The answer was implicitly contradictory. As a general principle, the press was to be impartial. However, early Americans also generally agreed that it should be on the side of "right." Thus, Puritans, for example, believed that the press should be open to anyone wishing to express his theological views as long as those views did not go to extremes. In political issues, participants accepted the fact that the printing of opposing views could not be punished by law, but they believed that printers should be responsible enough not to publish dangerous sentiments. As the passions of the Revolutionary period grew more intense, however, the grudging acceptance of neutrality disappeared; and Patriots argued that if printers failed to be partisan, then they were not to be tolerated.

Printers likewise found themselves divided over printing principles. The concept of neutrality had originated with the perception of the printing press simply as a mechanical device, with the printer merely a businessman who operated the machine and who was hired to reproduce material for members of the public. This tradition that had developed in the 1600s in the printing business was transferred to the printing of newspapers in the 1700s. Thus, there developed the general concept that newspapers should publish material from a variety of points of view without regard to how the printer personally felt.

Despite that concept, however, most newspaper publishers had their personal biases on a variety of subjects, and the columns of their newspapers reflected their opinions. Typically, on a controversial issue, three-quarters of a newspaper's stories might be slanted toward the publisher's bias. Yet opponents of the newspaper's slant generally argued in such situations that the proper role of newspapers was to present material that fairly represented the variety of viewpoints. The typical response of editors was to state that they were not personally biased, and that they were merely printing what the public brought to them. If only one side brought them information, then they could print only one side. That explanation too often conveniently overlooked the fact that a reader's complaint was not over the newspaper's printing of opposing arguments but rather over the newspaper's propensity for publishing material on one side only. The editors' explanation was probably transparent to most informed readers; yet editors commonly used it as a defense.

Perhaps ironically, the more biased an editor was, the more often he seemed to present the defense. The reason was that frequent bias called forth frequent criticism, thus resulting in the need for frequent defense. That cycle can be seen in the case of Thomas Fleet of Boston. There was perhaps no publisher who stated this defense more frequently and ardently than he. An Anglican, Fleet engaged vociferously in the church arguments with the Puritan clergy, and he likewise took pointed stands on political issues. Yet when criticized for the apparent bias in his newspaper, the *Weekly Rehearsal*, he responded that he "declares himself of no Party, and invites all Gentlemen of Leisure and Capacity, inclined on either Side, to write any thing of a political Nature, that tends to enlighten and serve the Publick, to communicate their Productions [to the *Rehearsal*], provided they are not overlong, and [are] confined within Modesty and Good Manners."[3] Similarly, in 1741, when criticized for publishing mostly critical material about the evangelist George Whitefield and specifically a sermon by John Wesley condemning some of Whitefield's theology and methods, Fleet contended that he printed Wesley's piece "not because I liked it, but because several Gentlemen of Learning and good Sense . . . desired to have it printed, and I had a prospect of getting a Penny by it."[4]

Fleet's partisanship was a forerunner of attitudes that were to develop later. Whereas publishers had been expected to be neutral during the early colonial period, with the onset of the events that eventually led to the American Revolution, printers were expected to be partisan—intensely partisan. Such expectations demonstrated a truism about the public's view of the press throughout American history, from colonial times to the present. In calm times, we expect the press to be

evenhanded and balanced in its treatment of issues. When issues heat into controversy, however, the participants in the debate are apt to want the press to take their
side, and they are quick to criticize it for bias if it does not.

On other details of printing, similar variety was present in the thinking in early
America. In that most tantalizing of areas, freedom of the press, one searches early
pamphlets and newspapers in vain for a monolithic view and a simple explanation.
Colonial Americans' views were not broadly libertarian, but neither were they
generally intolerant. Puritans, for example, contrary to what most journalism historians have assumed, did not have as their sole purpose in life the suppression of
opposing views. Early American thinking was prone to a mixture of broad appre-
ciation for the importance of freedom of expression and the conception that there
were reasonable limits beyond which expression should not go. Within the context
of the times and in comparison to the thinking of other societies, one would have
to conclude that the importance Americans placed on freedom of expression was
quite expansive. Some of that outlook came directly out of the traditions of western and especially English-speaking Europe. English ideas were transported to the
American colonies in radical form by the dissidents in the Anglican Church—the
Puritans—and by separatist groups such as the Anabaptists. In developing American thinking on freedom of the press, the Puritans played the most important role.
Press freedom grew early as a result of the general philosophical and religious
ideas that they held.

With time, however, as the spiritual views of life were diluted with practical, political, and material ones, developments in press freedom resulted primarily from
politics and factionalism. Whereas the Puritan view of freedom had a higher motive of religious idealism, much of the later argument for press freedom grew out
of self-interest. Advances in press freedom were made as factions involved in controversies argued for their right to print their sides. In a situation in which neither
side could prevent the other from also printing, the self-serving arguments tended
to open thinking about the right to publish.[5]

Of course, in determining the character of the early American press, the character of the individuals who operated the newspapers was essential. In attempting to
draw a comprehensible picture of publishers, one needs to resist the temptation of
one-dimensional explanations. Despite the complexity of printing and printers,
however, there are certain generalizations that can be made.

The first is that most publishers ran their newspapers as offshoots of their print
shops. Outside of the early Boston editors, there were few who went into printing
with the primary purpose of publishing a newspaper. Most were involved in other
occupations and decided that newspapers were a convenient sideline. Whether the
publishers were postmasters, booksellers, or printers, newspapers were not their
original concerns. The largest number of publishers had started as printers, and
they decided to begin newspapers simply as another product of their printing establishment.

The fact that so many publishers had been trained as printers affected their approach to newspapering. That training brought a concern for typographical qual-

ity to the newspapers they produced, resulting in a general mechanical consistency in early American newspapers. Few publishers tried daringly new experiments, in part the result of their training in mechanical rules and standards. The practice in the job-printing business, as noted earlier, of doing any work that a customer brought in carried over, in modified form, into newspaper publishing. The result was the general principle that newspapers should publish material from a variety of points of view. Most publishers thought of their newspapers as part of their printing business and therefore were particularly concerned about their papers' financial stability, although few of them grew wealthy.

Indeed, most newspaper operators were satisfied, in modern parlance, just to make a living. However, it should be emphasized that any historical view that they were motivated solely by financial concerns is too narrow. Such an interpretation arises more from historians' own perspectives than from the facts of the printers' lives. The Progressive historians' warm attachment to liberal ideology, for example, raises questions about the balance of their perspective. In arguing their case that printers were motivated by financial self-interest and narrow social views, they have never made a convincing presentation. Printers were from a broad range of backgrounds and differed widely in their views. Even the super-Patriot Peter Timothy, for example, in 1772 asked Benjamin Franklin to arrange a job for him as a British royal employee.[6] On the other hand, Tory printers such as James Rivington argued forcefully for their side despite the clear danger that expressing royalist sympathies posed for the economic welfare of their newspapers. Similarly, one must ask whether the Economic historians' emphasis on a single cause provides an overly simplistic explanation of motivations and purposes that were complex. There is comparatively little evidence that printers took the stands that they did or published specific material solely for financial reasons. Most were motivated by a variety of factors, including not only income but also political sentiments, religious beliefs, concern for their communities, and a myriad of other interests.

There is every reason to assume that religious faith, for example, worked a stronger influence than profit motive did. Although journalism historians have been prone to argue that the colonial press was struggling to free itself from a stifling religious control, there actually was a close relationship between religion and the press. The strength that publishers' faith had in the operation of their newspapers can be seen especially clearly in the early Boston press and during the Great Awakening of the 1740s. Outside of the conspicuous example of Benjamin Franklin, hardly any publisher produced a newspaper in which his or her Christian faith did not play a part.

Also not to be overlooked in generalizing about early publishers is that some believed that they had a duty to produce a newspaper. Whether believing that they needed to provide a vehicle of news or a forum for ideas, many began their newspapers out of the honest belief that they had to provide a service for their communities. Some postmasters, such as John Campbell of Boston, believed that their positions required that they assemble a collection of news for local inhabitants.

Others believed that for religious or political purposes they needed to make possible a means for the presentation of beliefs. As time passed, others came to believe generally that it was simply necessary that a town have a newspaper in order to keep residents informed about what was going on in their community and in the world at large.

Whether one can call their motives journalistic, in the modern sense, is uncertain. Journalism historians, however, have frequently proposed that ideas about the practice of journalism played the key role in the early press. The most common assumption has, indeed, been that the best way to explain the press is in journalistic terms—that is, to look at the early press in light of modern journalism practices and standards. Since most early publishers did not think of themselves as journalists in the modern sense, however, one must wonder how appropriate it is to describe them mainly in such terms. How reasonable is it to read back into history, as journalism historians have been prone to do, the principles of "proper" journalism as practiced in the historians' own time? In examining the journalistic practices of the early press, it seems best to recognize that newspapers were doing certain things that later came to be standard practices in journalism, but that the publishers were not doing them because they intuitively recognized that those were the things that true journalists were supposed to do. They reported news, for example, but they did not think of themselves as reporters. They published opinions, but they did not consider themselves editorial writers. What they did think of themselves as doing was providing information and ideas that they thought would be worthwhile for their readers.

In trying to achieve that purpose, most publishers adopted a variety of standard principles and practices. In their concept of news and other content, for example, there was little variation from one paper to the next. Most emphasized foreign, especially European and English, news. Intercolonial news was next in importance, and yet almost every newspaper published some local news. Along with news, essays and literary material dealing with religion, public affairs, commercial activities, and cultural subjects occupied the columns. There was also uniformity in methods of news gathering. Newspapers relied mainly on other newspapers, both foreign and domestic, for their news. They got other news items from government documents and proceedings, the contents of private letters from correspondents in other locales, and occasionally from conversations with local residents or travelers passing through town. It goes without saying that there was no systematic procedure, in the modern sense, of news gathering by a reporting staff. There is no reason to assume, however, that readers expected anything different. They were not looking for the thoroughness of coverage that one expects today, and readers in the eighteenth century seemed perfectly content with the eighteenth-century approach to news. The newspaper concept of timeliness also seemed perfectly adapted to the times. Most publishers were intent on publishing the most recent news available—and if it happened to be about events six months old, that was all right. News kept up with the speed of transportation. Ships carrying English news took months to make the transatlantic crossing, and news traveled from one colony to another in a matter of several days or a few weeks. The fact that news was not published for some time after an event occurred did not upset readers. Within the concepts of colonial time and travel, publishers were concerned that they publish the freshest information available. They were, in the context of their own age, almost as conscious of timeliness as today's television journalists who transmit their reports by satellite.

A final question that has enticed historians is that of the press's influence on the American Revolution. Was the press important in affecting public opinion, or was it ineffectual? In attempting to answer that question, one must ask several other questions dealing specifically with historical research into the topic of media persuasiveness. What evidence is necessary to argue the case of media influence? In the absence of "scientific" evidence required by today's social and behavioral theorists among communication researchers, can the historian justifiably make claims about press influence on the Revolution? On the other hand, if we begin with the general assumption that mass communication has some type of influence, is it any more valid for researchers to make claims that the press was *not* influential than to presume that it was?

In attempting to answer the question of press influence on the Revolution, most historians agree that printers were of critical importance.[7] However, among historians who have made studies focused specifically on the question of influence, the verdict has been split. Many scholars have argued that the most important factor in bringing about the Revolution was public opinion and that the newspaper was the primary agent in changing public opinion. That conclusion can be found in such studies as John C. Miller's 1936 biography *Sam Adams, Pioneer Propagandist*; Philip Davidson's detailed 1941 work, *Propaganda in the American Revolution, 1763–1783*; Arthur M. Schlesinger's *Prelude to Independence* (1958); a series of articles by R. A. Brown on various northeastern newspapers; and a score of other articles and books on various printers and newspapers.[8]

Hardly any historian challenged the influence thesis until the 1950s, when research into the effects of mass communication in modern America started casting doubts about the media's persuasiveness. In light of such research, a number of historians started to question the assumption that the press of the past had exercised a strong, persuasive influence. Relying on communication theory, some historians of the Revolutionary press began with the assumption that colonists' predisposition and events of the real world had a greater impact on shaping public opinion than the press had.[9]

As persuasiveness theory in communication research has, over the past decade, begun once again to swing toward the view that the mass media do exercise influence, historians are not as predisposed to assume that influence probably did not exist and that empirical proof must be presented. A reasonable approach for the historian today seems to be to consider a number of factors in addressing the issue. Historians may begin by recognizing that people living in the eighteenth century believed that the press was influential. Although their understanding of persuasiveness theory was not sophisticated by modern social science standards, Americans of the eighteenth century were close to the situation and might have had insight that escapes the historian. A second major consideration is that the press-persuasion relationship may have been different in the 1700s than it is today because the media state was different. Whereas today's audiences are bombarded by messages from the media, colonial America had, for all practical purposes, only five mass media (all printed): pamphlets, broadsides, magazines, books, and newspapers. In such an environment, in which the competition of messages was not as great as it is today, it would not be surprising if each medium occupied a comparatively more important role. Furthermore, people living in the eighteenth century had a different outlook than we do today. They tended to be less skeptical about media content. Content was so different as to allow such an attitude. Opinions were part of the news, and readers were expected to have the intelligence to accept or reject statements as printed. Furthermore, printers made no attempt to present dispassionate, "objective" reports; thus, there was less reason for readers to suspect news as mere pretension. In constructing their attitudes they also relied more on logic and the opinions of others than on empiricism. Today everyone is his own expert, and we are dubious about everything we are told. That attitude is not conducive to media persuasiveness.

At the same time, historians must recognize that early Americans who made claims about press influence provided hardly any concrete evidence. While broadly stating the case for the role of the press in affecting opinion, they invariably cast their claims in terms of people other than themselves. Although many declared that the press had momentous results, hardly any eighteenth-century writer can be found who left a record that he himself had been influenced by the press. However, given the general assumption that the information and knowledge that we acquire influence us, it is not a long jump to assume that the information and knowledge that colonists acquired through the press—despite the absence of concrete statements from them—did indeed influence them.

Whatever the effect was that the press had, one thing is certain. That is, Americans of the eighteenth century had a strong belief in the importance of the role the press played in the affairs of society. They used it as a means to keep them informed of the world about them and to express their own most fundamental beliefs. They still held to the idea that had pervaded Western civilization since Johann Gutenberg began to print with movable type in the 1400s, a belief in the power of the printed word. As they built their small, scattered towns of the 1600s into an independent nation in the last part of the 1700s, they used the press throughout the process. From Benjamin Harris's *Publick Occurrences* to the newspapers published by the most ardent Patriot printers of the American Revolution, journalism had been intimately involved with the affairs of America.

NOTES

1. See the bibliographical essay that serves as the Appendix to this book for a discussion of the explanations that historians have applied to the early American press.

2. For the most lucid presentations of this view, see Sidney Kobre, *The Development of the Colonial Newspaper* (Pittsburgh, Pa.: Colonial Press, 1944); and Charles E. Clark, "The Newspapers of Provincial America," *Proceedings of the American Antiquarian Society* 100 (1990): 367–89.

3. Boston *Weekly Rehearsal*, 2 April 1733. See Boston *Evening Post*, 10 November 1740, for a similar statement that Fleet wished "to be look'd upon only as a Printer, and not as a Party."

4. Boston *Evening Post*, 27 March 1741.

5. The limitations placed on printing during the Revolutionary period serve as evidence that self-interest frequently was at the heart of the arguments over press freedom and demonstrate what could occur when power was heavily weighted to one side.

6. Peter Timothy to Benjamin Franklin, 24 August 1772, *The Papers of Benjamin Franklin*, Leonard Labaree, ed. (New Haven, Conn.: Yale University Press, 1954), 19:284.

7. For the earliest historical statement of this view, see David Ramsay, *History of the American Revolution*, 2 vols. (Philadelphia, 1789), 2:319.

8. John C. Miller, *Sam Adams, Pioneer Propagandist* (Boston: Little, Brown, 1936); Philip Davidson, *Propaganda in the American Revolution, 1763–1783* (Chapel Hill: University of North Carolina Press, 1941); Arthur M. Schlesinger, *Prelude to Independence: The Newspaper War on Great Britain, 1764–1776* (New York: Alfred A. Knopf, 1958); R. A. Brown, "New Hampshire Editors Win the War: A Study in Revolutionary Propaganda," *New England Quarterly* 12 (1939): 35–51; "The Newport Gazette, Tory Newssheet," *Rhode Island History* 13 (1954): 97–108, and 14 (1955): 11–20; and "The Pennsylvania Ledger: The Tory News Sheet," *Pennsylvania History* 9 (1942): 161–75.

9. This argument is presented most cogently by Carl Berger, *Broadsides and Bayonets: The Propaganda War of the American Revolution* (Philadelphia: University of Pennsylvania Press, 1961). Berger believed that propagandists' schemes were less meaningful in affecting opinions and beliefs than were events such as military victories. For a fuller discussion of the historical debate about press influence on the Revolution, see the bibliographical essay at the end of this book.

Bibliographical Essay

As a subject for study, America's early press has held considerable interest for historians. Its special attraction is that the colonial period provided the beginnings of American journalism. It was during the colonial period that the country had its first newspapers and its earliest attempts at various journalistic practices. Historians have directed most of their work at the large contexts of the nature of the press and the role newspapers played in American colonial life and in the development of American journalism. The questions they have tried to answer have dealt for the most part with the influence of the press in the early life of America, the influence colonial society had on the press, and the origins of journalistic practices.

In studying the colonial press, historians have been influenced greatly by their own times and the conditions of journalism and society at the time of their writing. In general, historians of the nineteenth century, writing during an era in which pride in American progress and achievements was popular, took a nationalistic approach and explained the press as influential or important in the early development of the nation. Most later historians generally attempted to explain the press either in terms of professional journalistic practices or in terms of the press's interaction with society. Developmental historians, whose studies of the colonial press proliferated after 1930 and were written at a time during which journalism was gaining sophistication as a profession, attempted to explain the colonial press as the origin of later practices in journalism. Their work was often concerned with chronicling early developments, and their historical view incorporated directly the journalistic standards of their own time. Cultural historians held a broader view of journalism history. Rather than focusing narrowly on the press as a professional institution, they examined the press within the broader context of its society. Their underlying theme was that the characteristics of the press were the result of social influences, although the press at the same time played an important role in colonial society.

Despite such differences in outlook, historians tended to agree about the nature and importance of the colonial press. Journalism, they believed, was in its crude beginnings, but its rawness and inexperience were not serious faults because they were the natural characteristics at such an early stage. On the other hand, historians thought of the infant newspapers as influential and significant factors in both the national life and the day-to-day affairs of their own localities. Thus, with few exceptions historians concluded that the colonial press performed in a way that merits little criticism.

The role the press played in the events of the Revolutionary period, and the effect the period had on the press, likewise have intrigued historians. Were printers the advocates of revolutionary thought, or were they traditional in attitudes and moderate in actions? Did they influence a move in American public opinion toward acceptance of independence, or did they have little effect on American thinking and on the conduct of the Revolution itself?

The thread that ties together most historical works on the Revolutionary press is the examination of how the press performed under the circumstances that the Revolution imposed. Developmental historians—those interested in detailing the progress made toward the modern profession of journalism—studied the press of the Revolutionary period with less regard for the relationship between the war and newspapers than for evolutions and changes in journalistic practices. These historians were attracted particularly to such details as the content of newspapers, procedures of news coverage, and economic aspects of running a printing shop. They thought of Revolutionary printers more as early practitioners of journalistic ideals than as partisans in political conflict. This view gained strength beginning in the 1930s as journalism developed stronger and stronger characteristics as a profession and as journalism educators began to write about history.

Most historians, however, were more interested in the press as it related specifically to the independence movement and the Revolution. Among such historians there were sharply divergent views. In general, two broad topics provided the sources of disagreement. One was the political attitudes that printers held; the other was the amount of influence printers exercised in the initiation and the outcome of the Revolution. In analyzing Revolutionary printers' attitudes, most historians argued that printers truly were ideological revolutionaries in their views on liberty and political democracy. A more recent group of historians, however, was not nearly so favorable in its evaluation of the printers' attitudes. These historians, who had viewed the growth of journalism as a business in the twentieth century and who believed that economics could explain the primary motivation of people's actions, concluded that printers had taken particular stands on Revolutionary issues because such stands would benefit their printing businesses.

On the question of the influence writers and printers had on the Revolution, historians split into two clearly opposing schools. The traditional and predominant school accepted with little doubt the conclusion that the press had exercised pervasive impact in both bringing about the Revolution and effecting the American victory. The other school—which gained adherents beginning in the 1950s, when research into persuasive theory of mass communication began to question the media's influence on public opinion—challenged the traditional acceptance of the effectiveness of the Revolutionary press. It argued instead that real events were more important than propaganda and writers' arguments in molding public opinion.

Most nineteenth-century works on the early press were biographical treatments of prominent printers and writers. Usually written from a Nationalist or Romantic approach, they often considered their subjects as important patriotic figures who contributed to the progress of America and her institutions. Usually from respectable, conservative families from the Northeast, historians especially favored journalists who were from that region and who were patriotic but not disrespectful toward established values and traditions.

Romantic historians also found considerable interest in the printing trade of the colonial period and in the nature of the contents of newspapers. Like later historians, they believed that printing was a major aspect of colonial life and public affairs and recognized the essential nature of the relationship between printing and newspaper publishing. Much of their work, however, consisted of little more than cataloging contents and compiling bibliography.

The ideological interpretation of Revolutionary printers as revolutionary in their attitudes has been an enduring one, beginning with the works of the Nationalist and Romantic historians. It was propounded in the first history of American newspapers, Isaiah Thomas's *History of Printing in America* (1810), and has its advocates even today. Yet the underlying concepts of historians who argued that the printers were radical differed considerably, and historians who came to the same conclusion about printers' ideology disagreed on their motivations. Reflecting their nationalistic outlook, historians of the nineteenth century took pride in America's dedication to liberty and pictured Patriot printers and writers as staunch advocates of democracy while portraying Great Britain in the role of tyrant.

Although Developmental historians, who provided the largest number of studies of early American journalism, often considered the press important to the Revolutionary movment, they were more concerned with the press as the genesis of journalism in America. They viewed the history of journalism as the story of its progress from a crude beginning to its advanced nature during the time of their own studies. It was in colonial journalism that they searched for and often believed they found the origin of many later aspects of the American press. Thus, in general, Developmental historians explained colonial journalism primarily as the beginning of the progress that was to be seen in journalism in the eras that followed. Many of their studies therefore were concerned with documenting journalistic firsts and the origins of press practices. Such topics, for example, as English influences on American journalism, pamphlets as predecessors of newspapers, America's first newspaper, its first newspaper chain, its first Sunday paper, its oldest continuously published newspaper, early episodes in the development of freedom of the press, and the origin of advertising abounded in Developmental studies.

Developmental historians generally agreed that colonial journalists were libertarians who opposed the control that civil and religious authorities had in colonial thought and society. Thus, they considered one of the primary aspects of colonial press history to have been journalists' struggle for liberty and equality against authorities, whom historians usually viewed negatively as oppressors of civil liberty and free thinking. Some Developmental historians reasoned that one of the earliest major victories of colonial journalism was in freeing itself from the influence of religious authorities. They argued that the press, in a struggle against the theocracy that controlled colonial society, won its freedom from interference by religious authorities in a gradual process as a by-product of the larger issue of freedom of expression. Various historians pictured the colonial journalists in such roles as heroes of freedom of the press who had the temerity to oppose authority, guardians of the liberties of the public, and opponents of racism. The picture of colonial journalists that emerged from Developmental historians generally was one of stalwart fighters for the rights of the press and the welfare of the public.

Developmental historians argued, however, that printers were not essentially partisan or political. Concerned with the development of journalistic practices including objectivity and impartiality, these historians generally viewed with favor printers' attempts to avoid taking sides in the Revolutionary dispute. They were especially concerned about the challenge the partisan political conditions of the Revolutionary period presented to the journalistic ideals of nonpartisanship, impartiality, press independence, and freedom of expression. The predominant view of the Developmental school of interpretation was that those print-

ers who became partisan did so only after they found that impartiality was difficult in practice. "The very nature of the printer's business," wrote Charles Thomas in 1932, "made neutrality in a civil struggle impossible for him. The ordinary inhabitant, even though he
favored one side and had no desire to be neutral, could remain in a city and conduct his
business regardless of the fortunes of war if he was willing to remain quiet; but the editor of
a newspaper could not remain quiet. The few who tried to remain neutral soon discovered
such a course to be impossible."[1]

While believing that the press should be impartial toward sides in political conflict, however, many Developmental historians were convinced that the press itself should be in conflict with authority. Thus, whereas nondevelopmental historians had considered the press to
be an arm of the Revolutionary movement because of partisan motives, these Developmental historians argued that the press should oppose authority, no matter what the nature of that
authority, because the primary purpose of the press is to guard against power-seeking officials. The history of American journalism, they believed, was a struggle of the press against
such individuals, and the Revolutionary press provided the genesis of journalists' recognition that their proper role was an antigovernment one. During the colonial period the press
may have been a tool of government, because officials feared to set it free; but in the period
just preceding the Revolution, wrote two Developmental historians, printers demonstrated
that the press "could be used as a powerful instrument of revolt, and thereby realized the
worst fears of tyrants and dictators." Revolutionary printers thus laid a foundation for
American journalism, whose practitioners have been feared "by those who crave absolute
power and authority . . . [for] a printing press in the hands of a man who is bound in its use
only by the voice of his own conscience is a threat to total government."[2]

A similar conclusion about printers' ideology emerged from the later Progressive historians, but these historians took issue with the positive view of mainstream ideals that Developmental and nineteenth-century historians had propounded. Instead, they argued that
the American Revolution was as much a revolt against the control America's wealthy class
had on the country as against English authority. Progressive historians, most of whom believed that conservatives were motivated primarily by economic self-interest, reasoned that
those Revolutionary printers served best who had advocated the cause of the common man
against the economic and political domination by the elite.

Likewise, Progressive historians condemned Revolutionary printers who failed to support social justice and class equality. They believed printers' business interests frequently
provided the motivation for their social attitudes. Influenced by concerns over American
racial attitudes and the civil rights of America's Black citizens in modern society, these historians focused their attention on racial views in early America. In studying the Revolutionary press, they concluded that later prejudice had its origin in colonial times and that
even those printers who supported Patriot liberty in the Revolution had little concern for the
welfare of African Americans. In general, they concluded that Revolutionary printers were
a prejudiced group with repressive views.

The Progressive historians' views on the motivations of Revolutionary printers closely
resembled those held by a group of recent historians who began to give more attention to the
economic motivations of printers. Many of these Economic historians, however, concluded
that printers' attitudes had little to do with political or social ideology but were determined
solely by their business interests. Although resembling Progressive historians in their emphasis on economic causes in history, these historians—unlike the Progressives—placed little emphasis on class conflict. They were writing at a time when twentieth-century news
media had come to be run to a large extent by corporations and publishers who devoted

more attention to business operations than to journalistic aspects of the media. Economic historians argued that the same such interest in newspapers as business properties could be found among publishers in all eras of American history. Thus, these historians reasoned, in determining Revolutionary printers' attitudes, financial factors were of prime importance. In general, they concluded that one of two situations normally existed: that printers would have preferred to be neutral and objective but wound up supporting those groups that provided the income for them, or that printers set out to make money and cared little about what stands they had to take or journalistic practices they had to use to make their operations profitable.

Such emphasis on economic motivations and class and social differences and was criticized sharply by Consensus historians. Reacting against the Progressive explanation of the Revolutionary press as an agent in a conflict between groups over the social and economic structures, these historians argued that even though Americans may have disagreed on isolated issues, their differences took place within a broader realm of agreement on underlying principles. The Revolution and the press's role in it, Consensus historians argued, were primarily democratic rather than economic or social.

The foremost advocate of this interpretation was Bernard Bailyn. He expounded the argument first in his 1965 work *Pamphlets of the American Revolution, 1750–1776* and then elaborated it in *The Ideological Origins of the American Revolution*, the 1967 winner of both the Pulitzer Prize and the Bancroft Prize for history. Pamphlets were perhaps the most important forum for the expression of opinion during the Revolutionary period, according to Bailyn. They revealed that "the American Revolution was above all else an ideological, constitutional, political struggle . . . [and] that intellectual developments in the decade before Independence led to a radical idealization and conceptualization" of American attitudes. The ideas of England's "Commonwealthmen" such as John Trenchard and Thomas Gordon, who had advocated radicalism on behalf of religious dissenters, social radicals, and politicians opposing the government, were transmitted directly to the colonists. American leaders feared that a sinister conspiracy had developed in England to deprive citizens of the British empire of their long-established liberties. It was this fear that lay at the base of the views expressed in the pamphlets. The ideas in the pamphlets then became the determinants in the history of the period by causing colonists to change their beliefs and attitudes. These ideas challenged traditional authority and argued that "a better world than had ever been known could be built where authority was distrusted and held in constant scrutiny; where the status of men flowed from their achievements and from their personal qualities, not from distinctions ascribed to them at birth; and where the use of power over the lives of men was jealously guarded and severely restricted."[3]

Cultural historians shared little of other historians' concern for ideology. Instead, they were especially interested in the interrelationship between journalism and colonial society. Their works normally dealt with the nature and cultural role of the press, and they found that journalism usually mirrored society and that social, political, cultural, and political factors greatly influenced journalism. At the same time, they considered the press the primary medium through which society voiced its opinions and an important factor in influencing public views—a focus of colonial opinion and a forum of discussion. Although colonial papers served as media for the expression of opinion, Cultural historians considered them important also for their function of providing news to their readers.

As to the question of the early press's influence on the issues and conditions of its time, Cultural historians split into two camps. Most assumed that the press was important to the life of colonial society, but a handful questioned whether the press was really an integral factor in the vitality of America or of individual communities. Those who believed the press was influential argued that it derived its force from the fact that it reflected the values and ideals of society. Those who questioned its influence contended that even though newspapers were convenient and useful, they were not essential or vital to community affairs.

Despite such diverse interpretations, the historical view of printers as advocates of revolution and liberty dominated, and a number of historians proceeded to an analysis of a related subject. The question they attempted to answer was this: Assuming that printers and writers favored independence, what influence did they have on bringing about the American Revolution and on its execution?

Most historians agreed with the assessment of David Ramsay in his 1789 work, *History of the American Revolution*. He asserted that writers had been indispensable. "[T]he pen and the press," he wrote, "had merit equal to that of the sword."[4] Ramsay accepted without question the view that typified his era: that the press was of enormous importance in molding public opinion. Such a belief has underlain most historical studies of the role of the press in the Revolution. With that belief as a starting point, most historians' works were attempts primarily to document how the press exercised its potential for persuasion.

The first historian to provide an extensive documentation of the influence thesis was Arthur M. Schlesinger. In a number of articles and finally a book-length study, he argued that the most important factor in bringing about the Revolution was public opinion and that the newspaper was the primary agent in changing public opinion. In a 1935 article, "The Colonial Newspapers and the Stamp Act," Schlesinger stated his thesis in a preliminary form. When American colonists "began to feel the tightening grip of imperial control after 1767," he said, "they naturally resorted to the printing press to disseminate their views and consolidate a favorable public support."[5] In this and several articles on newspapers in various towns, Schlesinger concluded that the papers were an important medium for propaganda and played a significant role in transforming the public's attitudes. This interpretation then was expounded most completely in Schlesinger's 1958 book, *Prelude to Independence: The Newspaper War on Great Britain, 1764–1776*. The book was intended as a study of the role of the press in bringing about the "real American revolution": the "radical change in the principles, opinions sentiments, and affections of the people" that preceded the Revolution.[6] It detailed the press's part in the reaction to each of the successive events that eventually culminated in the war for independence. Unlike most colonists, who saw events from the limited perspective of their own colony, printer-editors often had moved around among several colonies, Schlesinger wrote, and thus were more continental in their outlook. They therefore held the view that what affected one colony affected all, and they advocated unity among the colonies. The repeal of the Stamp Act, whose passage was unwise because it struck so directly at printers, was a tremendous victory for the press and encouraged printers to more intense opposition to British authority. In many events afterward, such as the Tea Act of 1773 and the public uproar against it, it was the press, according to Schlesinger, that played a leading role. Eventually, the press's agitation resulted in the colonists declaring war. Although Schlesinger pointed out that a number of factors other than newspapers had helped instigate the war, he argued that the independence movement could hardly have succeeded "without an ever alert and dedicated press."[7] Within a decade after Schlesinger's first article appeared, a number of other historians authored works varying in subject matter but arriving at the same conclusion.

Such studies confronted few dissenters while it was generally accepted that the mass media exercised influence on public opinion. Beginning in the 1950s, however, as researchers began to doubt media persuasiveness, a number of historians started to exhibit a more dubious attitude toward contentions that the press of the past had exercised a strong, persuasive influence on American society. Borrowing on recent communication theory, several historians of the Revolutionary press began to examine it without being predisposed to conclude that it had influenced colonists' attitudes toward independence. Generally, these historians reasoned that colonists' predisposition and events of the real world had a greater impact on shaping public opinion than the press had.

This reinterpretation of press influence was presented most cogently in Carl Berger's *Broadsides and Bayonets: The Propaganda War of the American Revolution* (1961). A study of both American and British propaganda efforts in various media during the war years of the Revolution, the book argued that propagandists' schemes were less meaningful in affecting opinions and beliefs than were events such as military victories. Words were less important than facts. By 1777 at the latest, Berger argued, most minds were made up, and there was little that propaganda efforts could do to change them. British and American supporters and officials made a number of attempts to convert, persuade, or intimidate people who seemed vulnerable, but most of their propaganda was futile. Both sides failed in their efforts aimed at achieving such goals as subverting the Hessian allies of Britain, winning support of American Indians, and fomenting a slave insurrection in the American South. Because hard facts and people's beliefs about what was really occurring held more weight than what propagandists told people to believe, Hessians remained loyal to their military agreements with Britain, Indians stayed neutral or took sides as they were impelled by solid economic or political motives, and Britain's provocation of slave insurrection merely embittered and fortified slaveholders. The greatest impact on public opinion, according to Berger, came not from the work of propagandists, such as Benjamin Franklin's diplomacy in Europe, but from the news of the war, such as the American victory at Saratoga. As a rule, Berger concluded, neither persuasive appeal, nor threats, nor tricks could compare in influence with military victories or political and economic facts.

NOTES

1. Charles Thomas, "The Publication of Newspapers during the American Revolution," *Journalism Quarterly* 9 (1932): 358.

2. Kenneth Stewart and John Tebbel, "The Editors of Revolt," in *Makers of Modern Journalism* (New York: Prentice-Hall, 1952), 3–23.

3. Bernard Bailyn, ed., introduction to *Pamphlets of the American Revolution, 1750–1776* (Cambridge, Mass.: Belknap Press of Harvard University Press, 1965).

4. David Ramsay, *History of the American Revolution*, 2 vols. (Philadelphia, 1789), 2:319.

5. Arthur M. Schlesinger, "The Colonial Newspapers and the Stamp Act," *New England Quarterly* 8 (1935): 63–83.

6. Arthur M. Schlesinger, *Prelude to Independence: The Newspaper War on Great Britain, 1764–1776* (New York: Alfred A. Knopf, 1958), 40.

7. Ibid., 285.

Sources

UNPUBLISHED PAPERS AND DOCUMENTS

Andrew Bradford papers, Historical Society of Pennsylvania, Philadelphia.
Thomas Bradford papers, Historical Society of Pennsylvania, Philadelphia.
William Bradford papers, Duke University Library, Durham, N.C.
William Bradford papers, State Library of Massachusetts, Boston.
John Campbell papers, Yale University, New Haven, Conn.
Benjamin Franklin papers, American Philosophical Society Library, Philadelphia.
Benjamin Franklin papers, Historical Society of Pennsylvania, Philadelphia.
Benjamin Franklin papers, Library of Congress, Washington, D.C.
Benjamin Franklin papers, Princeton University Library, Princeton, N.J.
Benjamin Franklin papers, University of Pennsylvania Library, Philadelphia.
Benjamin Franklin papers, Yale University, New Haven, Conn.
Hugh Gaine papers, Library of Congress, Washington, D.C.
William Goddard papers, Library of Congress, Washington, D.C.
William Goddard papers, New York Public Library, New York.
David Hall papers, New York Public Library, New York.
Thomas Hancock papers, American Antiquarian Society, Worcester, Mass.
Thomas Hancock papers, Boston Public Library, Boston.
James Parker papers, Rutgers University Library, Newark, N.J.
James Rivington papers, Library of Congress, Washington, D.C.
Alexander Robertson papers, New York State Library, Albany.
James Robertson papers, New York State Library, Albany.
John Rogers papers, American Antiquarian Society, Worcester, Mass.
John Rogers papers, University of North Carolina Library, Chapel Hill.
William Sellers papers, Franklin Institute, Philadelphia.
Isaiah Thomas papers, American Antiquarian Society, Worcester, Mass.
John Trumbull papers, Library of Congress, Washington, D.C.

Thomas Wharton papers, Historical Society of Pennsylvania, Philadelphia.

Record of Wills, 1783–1786, Book XX, Charleston County (South Carolina) Probate Court.

PUBLISHED PAPERS, DIARIES, AND DOCUMENTS

Alexander, James. *A Brief Narrative of the Case and Tryal of John Peter Zenger.* 1736.

Andros Tracts, The: Being a Collection of Pamphlets and Official Papers. . . . Boston: Prince Society, 1868–1874.

Bridenbaugh, Carl, ed. *The Pynchon Papers.* 2 vols. Boston: Colonial Society of Massachusetts, 1982.

Buranelli, Vincent, ed. *The Trial of Peter Zenger.* New York: New York University Press, 1957.

Bushman, Richard L., ed. *The Great Awakening: Documents on the Revival of Religion, 1740–1745.* Chapel Hill: University of North Carolina Press, 1969.

Campbell, John. *Diary of John Campbell.* Massachusetts Historical Society Proceedings, 1st ser., 9 (1866–67): 485ff.

Candler, Allen D., ed. *The Revolutionary Records of the State of Georgia.* Atlanta: Franklin-Turner Co., 1906.

Chesnutt, David R., ed. *The Papers of Henry Laurens.* Columbia: University of South Carolina Press, 1990.

Commager, Henry Steele, and Richard B. Morris, eds. *The Spirit of 'Seventy-Six: The Story of the American Revolution as Told by Participants.* New York: Harper & Row, 1958.

Commissions to Massachusetts Governors. Massachusetts Historical Society Proceedings, 1st ser. (June 1893): 273–87.

Compleat Collection of State Trials, A. 4 vols. London: 1719.

Complete Writings of Thomas Paine, The. 2 vols. New York: Citadel Press, 1945.

Crane, Verner W. *Franklin's Letters to the Press, 1758–1775.* Chapel Hill: University of North Carolina Press, 1950.

Drayton, William Henry, ed. *The Letters of Freeman, Etc.* London, 1771. Reprint, ed. Robert M. Weir, Columbia: University of South Carolina Press, 1977.

Dunton, John. *The Life and Errors of John Dunton.* New York: Garland Publishing, 1974. Reprint of the 1705 edition printed for S. Malthus, London.

Fast, Howard, ed. *The Selected Works of Thomas Paine Set in the Framework of His Life.* New York: Duell, Sloan, Pearce, 1945.

Fitzpatrick, John C., ed. *The Writings of George Washington from the Original Manuscript Sources, 1745–1799.* Washington, D.C.: U.S. Government Printing Office, 1933.

Foote, Henry Wilder. *Annals of King's Chapel.* 2 vols. Boston: Little, Brown & Co., 1896.

Ford, Paul L., ed. *The Journals of Hugh Gaine.* 2 vols. New York, 1902.

Ford, Worthington C. *Letters from James Parker to Benjamin Franklin,* Proceedings of the Massachusetts Historical Society, 2d ser., 16 (May 1902): 186–232.

Franklin, Benjamin. *The Autobiography.* New York: Modern Library, 1944.

Franklin, Benjamin. *The Writings of Benjamin Franklin.* New York: Macmillan, 1905–1907.

George Whitefield's Journals. Gainesville, Fla.: Scholars' Facsimiles & Reprints, 1969.

Hart, W. H. *Index Expurgatorius Anglicanus.* London, 1872.

Heimert, Alan, and Andrew Delbanco, eds. *The Puritans in America.* Cambridge, Mass.: Harvard University Press, 1985.

Hening, William W., ed. *The Statutes at Large: Being a Collection of All the Laws of Virginia,* II. Richmond, 1809–1823.

Hutchinson, Thomas. (1711–1780). *The History of the Colony and Province of Massachusetts-Bay.* 2 vols. Cambridge, Mass.: Harvard University Press, 1936.

Jones, Newton B., ed. "Writings of the Reverend William Tennent, 1740–1777." *South Carolina Historical Magazine* 61 (October 1960): 189–203.

Labaree, Leonard W., ed. *The Papers of Benjamin Franklin.* New Haven, Conn.: Yale University Press, 1959.

————, ed. *Royal Instructions to British Colonial Governors 1670–1776.* 2 vols. New York: D. Appleton-Century, 1935.

Levy, Leonard W. *Freedom of the Press from Zenger to Jefferson.* Indianapolis: Bobbs-Merrill, 1966.

Luttrell, Narcissus. *A Brief Historical Relation of State Affairs,* 6 vols. Oxford: Luttrell Society, 1857.

————. *Narcissus Luttrell's Popish Plot Catalogues.* Oxford: Luttrell Society, 1956.

Mather, Cotton. *Diary of Cotton Mather, 1681–1708.* Boston: Massachusetts Historical Society Collections, ser. 7 vv. 7–8, 1911.

Morgan, Edmund S., ed. *Prologue to Revolution: Sources and Documents on the Stamp Act Crisis, 1764–1766.* New York: W. W. Norton, 1959.

Morris, Lewis. *Papers of Governor Morris.* Freeport, N.Y.: Books for Libraries Press, 1970.

Mott, Frank Luther, and Chester E. Jorgenson. *Benjamin Franklin: A Representative Selection.* New York: American Books, 1936 (rev. 1962).

O'Callaghan, E. B., comp. *Documentary History of the State of New York.* Albany: 1849–1851.

"Official Letters of Governor John Martin, 1782–1783," *The Georgia Historical Quarterly* 1, no. 4 (December 1913): 332–44.

Quincy, Josiah, Jr. *Reports of Cases Argued and Adjudged in the Superior Court of Judicature of the Province of Massachusetts Bay between 1761 and 1772.* Edited by S. M. Quincy. Boston, 1865.

Records of the Colony of Rhode Island and Providence Plantations, in New England. Edited by John Russell Bartlett. Providence, 1856–1865.

Report of the Record Commissioners Containing Boston Births, Baptisms, Marriages, and Deaths, 1630–1699. Boston: Rockwell & Churchill, 1883.

Ritz, Wilfred J., comp. *American Judicial Proceedings First Printed Before 1801: An Analytical Bibliography.* Westport, Conn.: Greenwood Press, 1984.

Sewall, Samuel. *The Diary of Samuel Sewall, 1674–1729.* Edited by M. Halsey Thomas. New York: Farrar, Straus & Giroux, 1973.

Silverman, Kenneth, comp. *Selected Letters of Cotton Mather.* Baton Rouge: Louisiana State University Press, 1971.

Slafter, Edmund P. *John Checkley: or Evolution of Religious Tolerance in Massachusetts Bay.* 2 vols. Boston: Prince Society, 1897.

Smith, Josiah. "Josiah Smith's Diary, 1780–81," *South Carolina Historical and Genealogical Magazine* 33 (January, July, and October 1932).

State of Pennsylvania. *Minutes of the Provincial Council of Pennsylvania.* Philadelphia: Jo. Severns & Co., 1852.

United Kingdom. Public Record Office. *Calendar of State Papers, Domestic Series, of the Reign of Charles II* (1660–1685). Edited by Mary Anne Everett Greene. London: Longman, 1860.

Whitmore, William H. *The Massachusetts Civil List for the Colonial and Provincial Periods, 1630–1774*. Baltimore: Genealogical Publishing Co., 1969; reprint of the 1870 edition.

Willcox, William B., ed. *The Papers of Benjamin Franklin*. New Haven, Conn.: Yale University Press, 1986.

Wroth, L. Kinvin, and Hiller B. Zobel, eds. *Legal Papers of John Adams*. Cambridge, Mass.: Belknap Press of Harvard University Press, 1965.

CONTEMPORANEOUS NEWSPAPERS, PAMPHLETS, AND OTHER PUBLICATIONS

American Antiquarian Society, *Early American Newspapers*. (The original files are housed in the society's archives at Worcester, Mass. In its microfiche form, the collection contains copies of most American newspapers published between 1690 and 1820.)

American Antiquarian Society, *Early American Imprints, 1639–1800*. Edited by Clifford K. Shipton. (The original files are housed in the society's archives at Worcester, Mass. In its microfiche form, the collection contains copies of most pamphlets and broadsides published in America in the seventeenth and eighteenth centuries. An indexed guide to the collection is provided by Charles Evans, *American Bibliography*, Chicago: Blakeley Press, 1903.)

Bailyn, Bernard, ed. *Pamphlets of the American Revolution, 1750–1776*. Cambridge, Mass.: Belknap Press of Harvard University Press, 1965.

Dickerson, Oliver Morton, comp. *Boston Under Military Rule (1768–1769) as Revealed in A Journal of the Times*. Boston: Chapman & Grimes, 1936 (a collection of newspaper items).

Ford, Worthington C. *Franklin's New England Courant*. Massachusetts Historical Society Proceedings, 1st ser., 57 (1924).

Gravlee, G. Jack, and James R. Irvine, eds. *Pamphlets and the American Revolution*. Delmar, N.Y.: Scholars' Facsimiles & Reprints, 1976.

Miller, Perry. *The New England Courant: A Selection of Certain Issues.* . . . Boston: American Academy of Arts and Sciences, 1956.

Moore, Frank. *Diary of the American Revolution: From Newspapers and Original Documents*. New York: Scribner, 1860.

Weeks, Lyman H., and Edwin M. Bacon, eds. *An Historical Digest of the Provincial Press*. Boston: Society for Americana, 1911.

Zall, Paul M. *Comical Spirit of Seventy-Six: The Humor of Francis Hopkinson*. San Marino, Calif: Huntington Library, 1976.

REFERENCE GUIDES

American Antiquarian Society, *South Carolina Miscellaneous Titles, 1758–1820*. New York: Readex Microprint Corp., 1983 (microprint).

Cappon, Lester J., and Stella F. Duff. *Virginia Gazette Index, 1736–1780*. 2 vols. Williamsburg, Va.: Institute of Early American History and Culture, 1950.

Greene, Evarts B., and Virginia D. Harrington. *American Population Before the Federal Census of 1790*. New York: Columbia University Press, 1932.

Lathem, Edward Connery. *Chronological Tables of American Newspapers 1680–1820.* Barre, Mass.: American Antiquarian Society and Barre Publishers, 1972.

Lemay, J. A. Leo. *A Calendar of American Poetry in Colonial Newspapers and Magazines and in the Major English Magazines through 1765.* Worcester, Mass.: American Antiquarian Society, 1972.

McCoy, Ralph E. *Freedom of the Press: An Annotated Bibliography.* Carbondale: Southern Illinois University Press, 1968.

———. *Freedom of the Press: A Bibliocyclopedia, Ten Year Supplement (1967–1977).* Carbondale: Southern Illinois University Press, 1979.

Nelson, William. *Some Account of American Newspapers, Particularly of the 18th Century, and Libraries in Which They Are Found.* New Jersey Archives. Paterson, N.J.: 1894–1897.

Seybolt, Robert Francis. *The Town Officials of Colonial Boston 1634–1775.* Cambridge, Mass.: Harvard University Press, 1939.

Sloan, Wm. David. *American Journalism History: An Annotated Bibliography.* Westport, Conn.: Greenwood Press, 1989.

Whitehead, William A. *Analytical Index to the Colonial Documents of New Jersey.* New York: D. Appleton & Co., 1858.

SELECTED SECONDARY SOURCES

Aldridge, A. Owen. *Thomas Paine's American Ideology.* Newark, Del.: University of Delaware Press, 1984.

Arner, Robert D. "The Short, Happy Life of the Virginia 'Monitor,' " *Early American Literature* 7, no. 2 (1972): 130–47.

Asbury, Raymond. "The Renewal of the Licensing Act in 1693 and its Lapse in 1695," *The Library* 33 (1978): 296–322.

Avery, Donald. "The Colonial Press, 1690–1763," 23–40 in *The Media in America: A History,* ed. Wm. David Sloan, James G. Stovall, and James D. Startt. 2d ed. Scottsdale, Ariz.: Publishing Horizons, 1993.

Bailyn, Bernard, and John B. Hench, eds. *The Press and the American Revolution.* Worcester, Mass.: American Antiquarian Society, 1980.

Benjamin, S.G.W. "A Group of Pre-Revolutionary Editors: Beginnings of Journalism in America," *Magazine of American History* 17: 1 (January 1887): 1–28.

Berger, Carl. *Broadsides and Bayonets: The Propaganda War of the American Revolution.* Philadelphia: University of Pennsylvania Press, 1961.

Berthold, Arthur Benedict. *American Colonial Printing as Determined by Contemporary Cultural Forces 1639–1763.* New York: Burt Franklin, 1934.

Blanchard, Margaret. "Freedom of the Press, 1690–1804," 93–122 in *The Media in America: A History,* ed. Wm. David Sloan, James G. Stovall, and James D. Startt. 2d ed. Scottsdale, Ariz.: Publishing Horizons, 1993.

Bleyer, Willard Grosvenor. "The Beginning of the Franklins' New-England Courant." *Journalism Bulletin [Quarterly]* 4, no. 2 (June 1927): 1–5.

Bloore, Stephen. "Samuel Keimer," *Pennsylvania Magazine of History and Biography* 44 (1920): 255–87.

Bond, Donovan H., and W. Reynolds McLeod, eds. *Colonial Newsletters to Newspapers.* Morgantown: West Virginia University, 1977.

Botein, Stephen. " 'Meer Mechanics' and an Open Press: The Business and Political Strategies of Colonial American Printers," *Perspectives in American History* 9 (1975): 127–225.

Brigham, Clarence S. *A History and Bibliography of American Newspapers, 1690–1820.* Worcester, Mass.: American Antiquarian Society, 1947.

———. *Journals and Journeymen: A Contribution to the History of Early American Newspapers.* Philadelphia: University of Pennsylvania Press, 1950.

Brown, R. A. "New Hampshire Editors Win the War: A Study in Revolutionary Propaganda," *New England Quarterly* 12 (1939): 35–51.

Canfield, Cass. *Sam Adams' Revolution 1765–1776.* New York: Harper & Row, 1976.

Carlson, C. Lennart. "Samuel Keimer: A Study in the Transit of English Culture to Colonial Pennsylvania," *Pennsylvania Magazine of History and Biography* 61 (1937): 357–86.

Cheslau, Irving G. *John Peter Zenger and "The New-York Weekly Journal"; A Historical Study.* New York: Zenger Memorial Fund, 1952.

Clark, Charles E. "Boston and the Nurturing of Newspapers: Dimensions of the Cradle, 1690–1741," *New England Quarterly* 64 (1991): 243–71.

———. "The Newspapers of Provincial America," *Proceedings of the American Antiquarian Society* 100 (1990): 367–89.

Clark, Ronald W. *Benjamin Franklin: A Biography.* New York: Random House, 1983.

Cline, Carolyn Garrett. "The Hell-Fire Club: A Study of the Men Who Founded the New England Courant and the Inoculation Dispute They Fathered." Master's thesis, Indiana University, 1976.

Cohen, Hennig. *The South Carolina Gazette 1732–1775.* Columbia: University of South Carolina Press, 1953.

Cook, Elizabeth Christine. *Literary Influences in Colonial Newspapers 1704–1750.* New York: Columbia University Press, 1912.

Covert, Cathy. "Passion Is Ye Prevailing Motive: The Feud Behind the Zenger Case," *Journalism Quarterly* 50 (1973): 3–10.

Crane, Verner W. "Benjamin Franklin and the Stamp Act," *Colonial Society of Massachusetts Transactions* 32 (1937): 56–77.

———. *Benjamin Franklin, Englishman and American.* Baltimore: Williams & Wilkins, 1936.

Cullen, Maurice R., Jr. "Middle-Class Democracy and the Press in Colonial America," *Journalism Quarterly* 46 (1969): 531–35.

Davidson, Phillip. *Propaganda in the American Revolution, 1763–1783.* Chapel Hill: University of North Carolina Press, 1941.

De Armond, Anna J. *Andrew Bradford: Colonial Journalist.* Newark, Del.: University of Delaware Press, 1949.

Demeter, Richard L. *Primer, Presses and Composing Sticks: Women Printers of the Colonial Period.* Hicksville, N.Y.: Exposition Press, 1979.

Dickerson, O. M. "British Control of American Newspapers on the Eve of the Revolution," *New England Quarterly* 24 (1951): 455–68.

Duniway, Clyde Augustus. *The Development of Freedom of the Press in Massachusetts.* New York: Longmans, Green, 1906.

Eaton, Arthur Wentworth Hamilton. *The Famous Mather Byles: The Noted Boston Tory Preacher, Poet, and Wit, 1707–1788.* Boston: W. A. Butterfield, 1914.

Fäy, Bernard. *Franklin, The Apostle of Modern Times.* Boston: Little, Brown, & Co., 1929.

Foner, Eric. *Tom Paine and Revolutionary America*. New York: Oxford University Press, 1976.

Franklin, Benjamin, V, ed. *Boston Printers, Publishers, and Booksellers, 1640–1800*. Boston: G. K. Hall, 1980.

Frasca, Ralph. "Benjamin Franklin's Printing Network," *American Journalism* 5 (1988): 145–58.

Garcia, Hazel. "Of Punctilios Among the Fair Sex: Colonial American Magazines, 1741–1776," *Journalism History* 3 (1976): 48–52, 63.

Harlan, Robert. "David Hall and the Stamp Act," *The Papers of the Bibliographical Society of America* 61 (1967): 13–37.

Henry, Susan. "Colonial Woman Printer as Prototype: Toward a Model for the Study of Minorities," *Journalism History* 3 (1976): 20–24.

Hildeburn, Charles Swift Riche. *A Century of Printing. The Issue of the Press in Pennsylvania, 1685–1784*. Philadelphia: Matlocks & Harvey, 1885–86.

———. *Sketches of Printing in Colonial New York*. New York: Dodd, Mead, 1895.

Hixson, Richard. *Isaac Collins: A Quaker Printer in 18th Century America*. New Brunswick, N.J.: Rutgers University Press, 1968.

Hoffman, Ronald. "The Press in Mercantile Maryland: A Question of Utility," *Journalism Quarterly* 46 (1969): 536–44.

Hudak, Leona M. *Early American Women Printers and Publishers: 1639–1820*. Metuchen, N.J.: Scarecrow Press, 1978.

Humphrey, Carol Sue. "Producers of the 'Popular Engine': New England's Revolutionary Newspaper Printers," *American Journalism* 4 (1987): 97–117.

———. "The Media and Wartime Morale: The Press and the American Revolution," 65–77 in *The Significance of the Media in American History*, ed. James D. Startt and Wm. David Sloan. Northport, Ala.: Vision Press, 1994.

Huxford, Gary. "The English Libertarian Tradition in the Colonial Newspaper," *Journalism Quarterly* 45 (1968): 677–86.

Isaacs, George A. *The Story of the Newspaper Printing Press*. London: Co-operative Printing Society, 1931.

Jones, Horatio G. *Andrew Bradford: Founder of the Newspaper Press in the Middle States of America*. New York: Arno Press, 1970.

King, Marion Reynolds. "One Link in the First Newspaper Chain, *The South Carolina Gazette*," *Journalism Quarterly* 9 (1932): 257–68.

Knight, Carolyn H. *The American Colonial Press and the Townshend Crisis, 1766–1770: A Study in Political Imagery*. Lewiston, N.Y.: Edwin Mellen Press, 1990.

Kobre, Sidney. *The Development of the Colonial Newspaper*. Pittsburgh, Pa.: Colonial Press, 1944.

Konkle, Burton A. *The Life of Andrew Hamilton, 1676–1741, "The Day-Star of the American Revolution."* Philadelphia: National Publishing Co., 1941.

Konweiser, Harry Myron. *Colonial and Revolutionary Posts: A History of the American Postal Systems*. Richmond, Va.: Dietz Printing Co., 1931.

Leder, Lawrence H. "The Role of Newspapers in Early America 'In Defense of Their Own Liberty,' " *Huntington Library Quarterly* 30 (November 1966): 1–16.

Levy, Leonard W. *Emergence of a Free Press*. New York: Oxford University Press, 1985.

———. *Legacy of Suppression*. Cambridge, Mass: Belknap Press of Harvard University Press, 1960.

Littlefield, George Emery. *Early Boston Booksellers, 1642–1711.* New York: Burt Franklin, 1969; reprint of the 1900 edition.

———. *The Early Massachusetts Press 1678–1711.* New York: Burt Franklin, 1969; reprint of the 1907 edition.

Lorenz, Alfred L. *Hugh Gaine: A Colonial Printer-Editor's Odyssey to Loyalism.* Carbondale: Southern Illinois University Press, 1972.

MacCracken, Henry N. *Prologue to Independence: The Trials of James Alexander, 1715–1756.* New York: James H. Heineman, 1964.

Marble, Annie R. *From 'Prentice to Patron: The Life Story of Isaiah Thomas.* New York: Appleton-Century, 1935.

McMurtrie, Douglas C. *A History of Printing in the United States.* New York: Bowker, 1936.

———. *The Beginnings of Printing in Virginia.* Lexington, Va.: Washington & Lee Press, 1935.

Miller, John C. *Samuel Adams, Pioneer Propagandist.* Boston: Little, Brown, 1936.

Miner, Ward F. *William Goddard, Newspaperman.* Durham, N.C.: Duke University Press, 1962.

Morgan, Edmund Sears, and Helen Morgan. *The Stamp Act Crisis: Prologue to Revolution.* Chapel Hill: University of North Carolina Press, 1953.

Morse, Jarvis Means. *Connecticut Newspapers in the Eighteenth Century.* New Haven, Conn.: Yale University Press, 1935.

Muddiman, J. G. "Benjamin Harris, the First American Journalist," *Notes and Queries* (August 20, 1932): 129–33; (August 27, 1932): 147–50; (September 3, 1932): 166–70; (September 24, 1932): 223; (October 15, 1932): 273–74.

Nelson, Harold L. "Seditious Libel in Colonial America," *American Journal of Legal History* 3 (April 1959): 160–72.

Oswald, John Clyde. *Benjamin Franklin, Printer.* Garden City, N.Y.: Doubleday, Page, 1917.

———. *Printing in the Americas.* New York: Gregg Publishing, 1937.

Paltsits, Victor Hugo. "New Light on 'Publick Occurrences': America's First Newspaper," *American Antiquarian Society* (April 1949): 75–88.

Partington, Wilfred. "The First American Newspaper and the 'New England Primer,' " *The Bookman* (January 1933): 103–4.

Parton, James. *Life and Times of Benjamin Franklin.* New York, 1864.

Pomerantz, S. I. "The Patriot Newspaper and the American Revolution," 305–31 in *The Era of the American Revolution,* ed. R. B. Morris. New York: Columbia University Press, 1939.

Price, Warren C. "Reflections on the Trial of John Peter Zenger," *Journalism Quarterly* 32 (1955): 161–68.

Ramsay, David. *History of the American Revolution.* 2 vols. Philadelphia, 1789.

Rich, Wesley Everett. *The History of the United States Post Office to the Year 1829.* Cambridge, Mass.: Harvard University Press, 1924.

Richardson, Lyon F. *A History of Early American Magazines, 1741–89.* New York: Thomas Nelson & Sons, 1931.

Rutherford, Livingston. *John Peter Zenger, His Press, His Trial, and a Bibliography of Zenger Imprints.* New York: Dodd, Mead, 1904.

Sabine, Lorenzo. *Biographical Sketches of Loyalists of the American Revolution.* 2 vols. Boston: Little, Brown & Co., 1864.

Sappenfield, James. *A Sweet Instruction: Franklin's Journalism as a Literary Apprenticeship*. Carbondale: Southern Illinois University Press, 1973.

Schlesinger, Arthur M. *Prelude to Independence: The Newspaper War on Great Britain, 1764–1776*. New York: Knopf, 1958.

Schuyler, Robert Livingston. *The Liberty of the Press in the American Colonies Before the Revolutionary War*. New York: Thomas Whitaker, 1905.

Shipton, Clifford. *Isaiah Thomas: Printer, Patriot, Philanthropist, 1749–1831*. Rochester, N.Y.: Printing House of Leo Hart, 1948.

————, ed. *Sibley's Harvard Graduates*. Boston: Massachusetts Historical Society, 1937.

Sloan, Wm. David. "American Revolutionary Printers, 1765–1783: Powerful Radicals or Ineffective Conservatives?" 41–57 in *Perspectives on Mass Communication History*. Hillsdale, N.J.: Lawrence Erlbaum Associates, 1991.

————. "The Colonial Press, 1690–1765: Mirror of Society or Origin of Journalism?" 28–40 in *Perspectives on Mass Communication History*.

Sloan, Wm. David, and Thomas A. Schwartz. "Historians and Freedom of the Press, 1690–1801: Libertarian or Limited?" *American Journalism* 5 (1988): 159–78.

Smith, J. Eugene. *One Hundred Years of Hartford's Courant: From Colonial Times through the Civil War*. New Haven, Conn.: Yale University Press, 1949.

Smith, Jeffery A. *Printers and Press Freedom: The Ideology of Early American Journalism*. New York: Oxford University Press, 1988.

Spaulding, E. Wilder. "The *Connecticut Courant*, A Representative Newspaper in the Eighteenth Century," *New England Quarterly* 3 (1930): 443–63.

Steele, Ian K. *The English Atlantic 1675–1740: An Exploration of Communication and Community*. New York: Oxford University Press, 1986.

Tapley, Harriet Silvester. *Salem Imprints, 1768–1825: History of the First Fifty Years of Printing in Salem, Massachusetts*. Salem: Essex Institute, 1928.

Tatham, Campbell. "Benjamin Franklin, Cotton Mather, and the Outward State," *Early American Literature* 6 (Winter 1971–72): 223–33.

Teeter, Dwight L. "King Sears, the Mob and Freedom of the Press in New York, 1765–75," *Journalism Quarterly* 41 (1964): 539–44.

————. "Press Freedom and the Public Printing: Pennsylvania, 1775–83," *Journalism Quarterly* 45 (1968): 445–51.

Thomas, Charles M. "The Publication of Newspapers during the American Revolution," *Journalism Quarterly* 9 (1932): 358–73.

Thomas, Isaiah. *The History of Printing in America*. Albany, N.Y.: Munsell, 1810. Reprint, New York: Weathervane Books, 1970.

Tourtellot, Arthur. *Benjamin Franklin: The Shaping of Genius: The Boston Years*. Garden City, N.Y.: Doubleday & Co., 1977.

Van Doren, Carl. *Benjamin Franklin*. New York: Viking, 1936.

Walett, Francis G. *Massachusetts Newspapers and the Revolutionary Crisis, 1763–1776*. Boston: Massachusetts Bicentennial Commission, 1974.

————. *Patriots, Loyalists, and Printers*. Worcester, Mass.: American Antiquarian Society, 1976.

Wax, Donald. "The Image of the Negro in the *Maryland Gazette*, 1745–1775," *Journalism Quarterly* 46 (Spring 1969): 73–80, 86.

Wells, William V. *The Life and Public Services of Samuel Adams*. Boston: Little, Brown, 1865.

Wheeler, J. Towne. *The Maryland Press, 1777–1790*. Baltimore: Maryland Historical Society, 1938.

Williams, Julie Hedgepeth. "The Media and Personification of Society: The *Gazette* of Colonial South-Carolina," 45–64 in *The Significance of the Media in American History*, ed. James D. Startt and Wm. David Sloan. Northport, Ala.: Vision Press, 1994.

Wilson, C. Edward. "The Boston Inoculation Controversy: A Revisionist Interpretation," *Journalism History* 7: 1 (1980): 16–19, 40.

Wolf, Edwin. *Franklin's Way to Wealth as a Printer*. Philadelphia, 1951.

Wroth, Lawrence C. *History of Printing in Colonial Maryland, 1686–1776*. Baltimore: Typathetac of Baltimore, 1922.

———. *The Colonial Printer*. Rev. ed. Portland, Me.: Southworth-Anthoensen Press, 1938.

———. *William Parks, Printer and Journalist of England and Colonial America*. Richmond, Va.: Appeals Press, 1926.

Yodelis, Mary Ann. "Boston's First Major Newspaper War: A 'Great Awakening' of Freedom," *Journalism Quarterly* 51 (1974): 207–12.

———. "Courts, Counting Houses and Streets: Attempts at Press Control, 1763–1775," *Journalism History* 1 (1974): 11–15.

———. "The Press in Wartime: Portable and Penurious," *Journalism History* 3 (1976): 2–6, 10.

———. "Who Paid the Piper? Publishing Economics in Boston, 1763–1775," *Journalism Monographs* 38 (1975).

Index

About the Authors

WM. DAVID SLOAN is Professor of Journalism at the University of Alabama at Tuscaloosa. He is the author of *The Significance of the Media in American History* (1994) and eleven other books.

JULIE HEDGEPETH WILLIAMS is a doctoral candidate in the Department of Mass Communications at the University of Alabama at Tuscaloosa. She has co-authored *The Great Reporters: An Anthology of Newswriting at Its Best* (1992).

ISBN 0-313-27525-4

90000>

EAN

9 780313 275258

HARDCOVER BAR CODE